11 - 19 PROGRESSION

Pearson Edexcel A level Mathematics

Pure Mathematics

Year 2

Practice Book

Series Editor: Harry Smith

Authors: Jack Barraclough, Laura Connell, Tara Doyle, Su Nicholson

Pearson

Contents

How to use this book

The Pure Mathematics Year 2 Practice Book is designed to be used alongside your Pearson Edexcel AS and A level Mathematics Pure Year 2 textbook. It provides additional practice, including problem-solving and exam-style questions, to help make sure you are ready for your exam.

- The chapters and exercises in this practice book match the chapters and sections in your textbook, so you can easily locate additional practice for any section in the textbook.
- Each chapter finishes with two sets of problem-solving practice questions at three different difficulty levels.
- An Exam question bank at the end of the book provides mixed exam-style questions to help you practise selecting the correct mathematical skills and techniques.

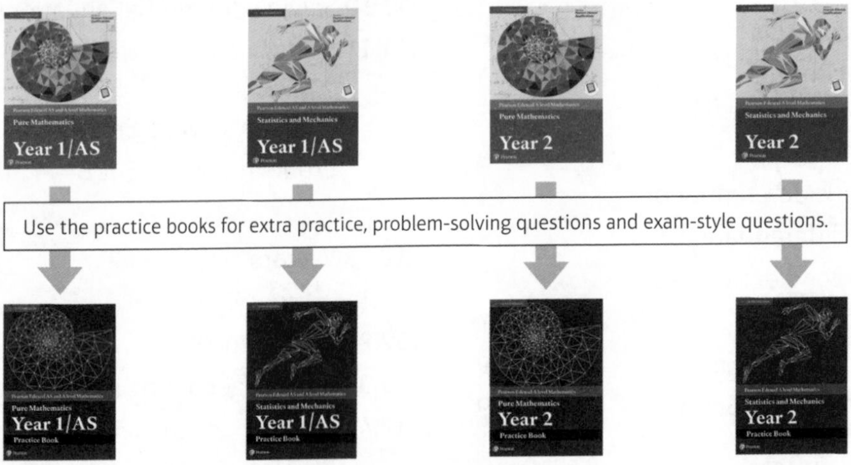

Finding your way around the book

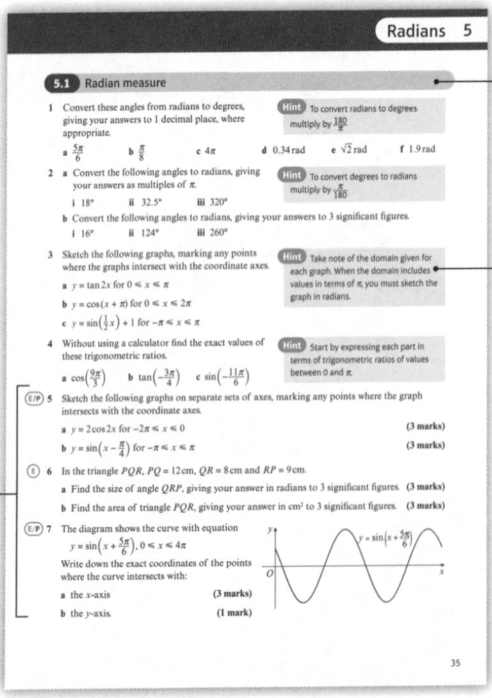
Radians 5

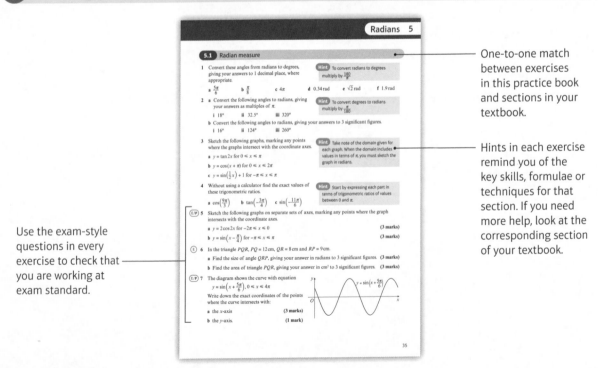

5.1 Radian measure

1 Convert these angles from radians to degrees, giving your answers to 1 decimal place, where appropriate.

Hint To convert radians to degrees multiply by $\frac{180}{\pi}$

a $\frac{5\pi}{6}$ b $\frac{\pi}{8}$ c 4π d 0.34 rad e $\sqrt{2}$ rad f 1.9 rad

2 a Convert the following angles to radians, giving your answers as multiples of π.

Hint To convert degrees to radians multiply by $\frac{\pi}{180}$

i $18°$ ii $32.5°$ iii $320°$

b Convert the following angles to radians, giving your answers to 3 significant figures.

i $16°$ ii $124°$ iii $260°$

3 Sketch the following graphs, marking any points where the graphs intersect with the coordinate axes.

Hint Take note of the domain given for each graph. When the domain includes values in terms of π, you must sketch the graph in radians.

a $y = \tan 2x$ for $0 \leqslant x \leqslant \pi$

b $y = \cos(x + \pi)$ for $0 \leqslant x \leqslant 2\pi$

c $y = \sin\left(\frac{1}{2}x\right) + 1$ for $-\pi \leqslant x \leqslant \pi$

4 Without using a calculator find the exact values of these trigonometric ratios.

Hint Start by expressing each part in terms of trigonometric ratios of values between 0 and π.

a $\cos\left(\frac{9\pi}{3}\right)$ b $\tan\left(-\frac{3\pi}{4}\right)$ c $\sin\left(-\frac{11\pi}{6}\right)$

E/P 5 Sketch the following graphs on separate sets of axes, marking any points where the graph intersects with the coordinate axes.

a $y = 2\cos 2x$ for $-2\pi \leqslant x \leqslant 0$ **(3 marks)**

b $y = \sin\left(x - \frac{\pi}{4}\right)$ for $-\pi \leqslant x \leqslant \pi$ **(3 marks)**

E 6 In the triangle PQR, $PQ = 12$ cm, $QR = 8$ cm and $RP = 9$ cm.

a Find the size of angle QRP, giving your answer in radians to 3 significant figures. **(3 marks)**

b Find the area of triangle PQR, giving your answer in cm^2 to 3 significant figures. **(3 marks)**

E/P 7 The diagram shows the curve with equation

$y = \sin\left(x + \frac{5\pi}{6}\right)$, $0 \leqslant x \leqslant 4\pi$

Write down the exact coordinates of the points where the curve intersects with:

a the x-axis **(3 marks)**

b the y-axis. **(1 mark)**

35

One-to-one match between exercises in this practice book and sections in your textbook.

Hints in each exercise remind you of the key skills, formulae or techniques for that section. If you need more help, look at the corresponding section of your textbook.

Use the exam-style questions in every exercise to check that you are working at exam standard.

Exam-style questions are flagged with (E) and have marks allocated to them.

Problem-solving questions are flagged with (P)

Bronze questions might have more steps to lead you through the technique, or require a more straightforward application of the skills from that chapter.

Silver questions are more challenging, and provide less scaffolding. If you're struggling with the Silver question, try the Bronze question first.

You can find more exam-style questions on this chapter in the Exam question bank.

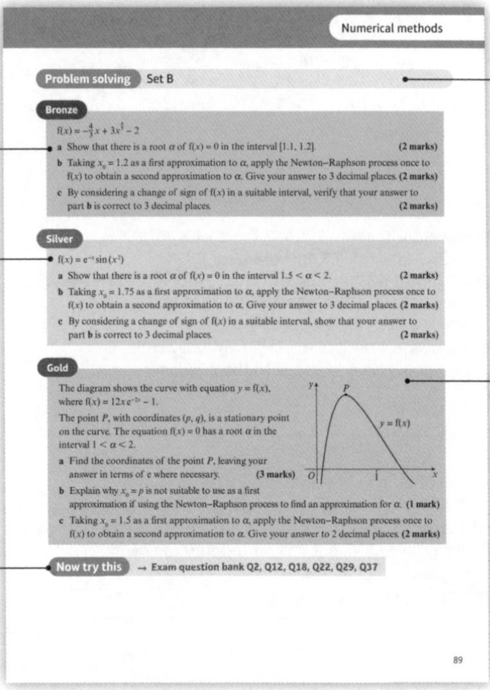

Numerical methods

Problem solving Set B

Bronze

$f(x) = -\frac{4}{3}x + 3x^{\frac{1}{3}} - 2$

a Show that there is a root α of $f(x) = 0$ in the interval [1.1, 1.2]. **(2 marks)**

b Taking $x_0 = 1.2$ as a first approximation to α, apply the Newton–Raphson process once to $f(x)$ to obtain a second approximation to α. Give your answer to 3 decimal places. **(2 marks)**

c By considering a change of sign of $f(x)$ in a suitable interval, verify that your answer to part **b** is correct to 3 decimal places. **(2 marks)**

Silver

$f(x) = e^{-x}\sin(x^2)$

a Show that there is a root α of $f(x) = 0$ in the interval $1.5 < \alpha < 2$. **(2 marks)**

b Taking $x_0 = 1.75$ as a first approximation to α, apply the Newton–Raphson process once to $f(x)$ to obtain a second approximation to α. Give your answer to 3 decimal places. **(2 marks)**

c By considering a change of sign of $f(x)$ in a suitable interval, show that your answer to part **b** is correct to 3 decimal places. **(2 marks)**

Gold

The diagram shows the curve with equation $y = f(x)$, where $f(x) = 12xe^{-2x} - 1$.

The point P, with coordinates (p, q), is a stationary point on the curve. The equation $f(x) = 0$ has a root α in the interval $1 < \alpha < 2$.

a Find the coordinates of the point P, leaving your answer in terms of e where necessary. **(3 marks)**

b Explain why $x_0 = p$ is not suitable to use as a first approximation if using the Newton–Raphson process to find an approximation for α. **(1 mark)**

c Taking $x_0 = 1.5$ as a first approximation to α, apply the Newton–Raphson process once to $f(x)$ to obtain a second approximation to α. Give your answer to 2 decimal places. **(2 marks)**

Now try this → Exam question bank Q2, Q12, Q18, Q22, Q29, Q37

89

Each chapter ends with two sets of exam-style problem-solving questions which draw on material from throughout the chapter and from earlier chapters.

Gold questions involve tricky problem-solving elements, or might require you to think more creatively. If you can answer the Gold questions then you can be confident that you are ready to tackle the hardest exam questions.

One challenge of the exam is that you aren't usually told which techniques or strategies you need to apply to a particular question. The questions in the Exam question bank are not ordered by topic, so you need to choose the appropriate mathematical skills.

There are a lot more questions in the Exam question bank than there will be on your exam paper. Don't try and tackle them all at once, but make sure you try some of the trickier questions from the end of the question bank.

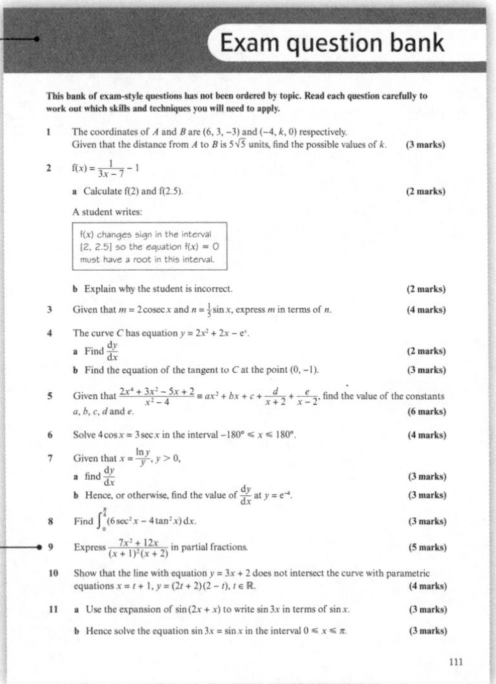

Exam question bank

This bank of exam-style questions has not been ordered by topic. Read each question carefully to work out which skills and techniques you will need to apply.

1 The coordinates of A and B are $(6, 3, -3)$ and $(-4, k, 0)$ respectively. Given that the distance from A to B is $5\sqrt{5}$ units, find the possible values of k. **(3 marks)**

2 $f(x) = \frac{1}{3x - 7} - 1$

a Calculate f(2) and f(2.5). **(2 marks)**

A student writes:

> f(x) changes sign in the interval [2, 2.5] so the equation f(x) = 0 must have a root in this interval.

b Explain why the student is incorrect. **(2 marks)**

3 Given that $m = 2\operatorname{cosec} x$ and $n = \frac{1}{5}\sin x$, express m in terms of n. **(4 marks)**

4 The curve C has equation $y = 2x^2 + 2x - e^x$.

a Find $\frac{dy}{dx}$ **(2 marks)**

b Find the equation of the tangent to C at the point $(0, -1)$. **(3 marks)**

5 Given that $\frac{2x^4 + 3x^2 - 5x + 2}{x^2 - 4} \equiv ax^2 + bx + c + \frac{d}{x+2} + \frac{e}{x-2}$, find the value of the constants a, b, c, d and e. **(6 marks)**

6 Solve $4\cos x = 3\sec x$ in the interval $-180° \leqslant x \leqslant 180°$. **(4 marks)**

7 Given that $x = \frac{\ln y}{y}$, $y > 0$,

a find $\frac{dy}{dx}$ **(3 marks)**

b Hence, or otherwise, find the value of $\frac{dy}{dx}$ at $y = e^{-4}$. **(3 marks)**

8 Find $\int_0^{\frac{\pi}{4}} (6\sec^2 x - 4\tan^2 x)\,dx$. **(3 marks)**

9 Express $\frac{7x^2 + 12x}{(x+1)^2(x+2)}$ in partial fractions. **(5 marks)**

10 Show that the line with equation $y = 3x + 2$ does not intersect the curve with parametric equations $x = t + 1$, $y = (2t + 2)(2 - t)$, $t \in \mathbb{R}$. **(4 marks)**

11 **a** Use the expansion of $\sin(2x + x)$ to write $\sin 3x$ in terms of $\sin x$. **(3 marks)**

b Hence solve the equation $\sin 3x = \sin x$ in the interval $0 \leqslant x \leqslant \pi$. **(3 marks)**

111

Published by Pearson Education Limited, 80 Strand, London, WC2R 0RL.

www.pearsonschoolsandfecolleges.co.uk

Series editor Harry Smith
Edited by Haremi Ltd
Typeset by York Publishing Solutions Pvt. Ltd., INDIA

First published 2019

22 21
10 9 8 7 6 5 4 3 2

British Library Cataloguing in Publication Data
A catalogue record for this book is available from the British Library

ISBN 9781292274676

Printed and bound in Great Britain by Bell and Bain Ltd, Glasgow

Note from the publisher
Pearson has robust editorial processes, including answer and fact checks, to ensure the accuracy of the content in this publication, and every effort is made to ensure this publication is free of errors. We are, however, only human, and occasionally errors do occur. Pearson is not liable for any misunderstandings that arise as a result of errors in this publication, but it is our priority to ensure that the content is accurate. If you spot an error, please do contact us at resourcescorrections@pearson.com so we can make sure it is corrected.

1.1 Proof by contradiction

1 Write down the negation of each statement.

a There are infinitely many prime numbers.

b If n^2 is even, then n must be even.

c If pq is odd, then at least one of p and q is odd.

Hint A statement that asserts the falsehood of another statement is called the **negation** of the statement.

2 Prove by contradiction that there is no greatest even number.

Hint You prove a statement by contradiction by assuming it is **not** true. Then use logical steps to show your assumption leads to something impossible. You can then conclude that your assumption was incorrect, and the original statement was true.

3 Prove by contradiction that if a and b are integers, then $a^2 - 4b - 7 \neq 0$.

Hint Start by assuming that there exist integers a and b such that $a^2 - 4b - 7 = 0$. Rearrange and use the fact that any odd number can be written in the form $2n + 1$, where n is an integer.

4 Prove by contradiction that there is no smallest positive rational number.

Hint A **rational number** can be written in the form $\frac{a}{b}$, where a and b are integers.
An **irrational number** cannot be written in the form $\frac{a}{b}$, where a and b are integers.
The set of rational numbers can be written as $\mathbb{Q}$.

(E/P) 5 Prove by contradiction that if n^3 is odd, then n must be odd. **(3 marks)**

(E/P) 6 Prove by contradiction that there are no non-zero integer solutions to the equation $x^2 - y^2 = 1$. **(4 marks)**

(E/P) 7 Prove that $\sqrt{5}$ is irrational. **(6 marks)**

(E/P) 8 Prove by contradiction that the difference between any rational number and any irrational number is irrational. **(6 marks)**

1.2 Algebraic fractions

1 Simplify:

a $(x - 3) \times \frac{1}{x^2 - 9}$

b $\frac{x^2 - 1}{3} \times \frac{1}{x^2 + 2x + 1}$

c $\frac{x^2 + 5x}{y - 2} \times \frac{y^2 - 2y}{x^2}$

Hint To multiply algebraic fractions, first factorise the numerators and denominators where possible. Then cancel any common factors, and multiply the numerators and multiply the denominators.

2 Simplify:

a $\frac{x}{x+2} \div \frac{x^3}{x^2+x-2}$ b $\frac{9x^2-16}{5x-10} \div \frac{3x-4}{10}$

c $\frac{2x^2+3xy-2y^2}{5xy} \div \frac{x^2+2xy}{10x^2}$

Hint To divide two algebraic fractions, multiply the first fraction by the reciprocal of the second fraction.

3 Express as a single fraction in its simplest form:

a $\frac{5}{x+3} + \frac{2}{x-1}$ b $\frac{4}{2(x-3)} + \frac{5}{3(x+1)}$

c $\frac{2x}{x-5} - \frac{3x}{x+5}$ d $\frac{x+1}{2x-3} - \frac{2x}{x+2}$

Hint To add or subtract two fractions, find a common denominator.

4 Express as a single fraction in its simplest form:

a $\frac{5x}{4x^2-9} + \frac{3}{2x-3}$ b $\frac{2}{x^2+x-12} + \frac{1}{x^2-5x+6}$

c $\frac{5}{4x^2+4x+1} - \frac{3}{4x^2-1}$ d $\frac{x-1}{x^2+3x+2} - \frac{x-2}{x^2-2x-3}$

Hint You may need to factorise the denominators to find the lowest common multiple.

E/P 5 Simplify $\frac{x^2+4x+4}{y^2-6y+9} \div \frac{x^2-4}{y^2-9}$ **(4 marks)**

E/P 6 Simplify $\frac{x^2-2x-15}{2x^2-12} \times \frac{x^3-6x^2}{x^2-5x-24}$ **(4 marks)**

E/P 7 Express $\frac{2x^2-5x}{25x^2-1} + \frac{3x}{5x-1}$ as a fraction in its simplest form. **(4 marks)**

E/P 8 Express $\frac{3x-2}{2x^2-5x-3} - \frac{5}{2x+1}$ as a fraction in its simplest form. **(4 marks)**

E/P 9 $f(x) = x + \frac{5}{x+3} + \frac{40}{x^2-2x-15}, x \in \mathbb{R}, x \neq -3, x \neq 5$

a Show that $f(x) = \frac{x^3-2x^2-10x+15}{(x+3)(x-5)}$ **(4 marks)**

b Hence show that f(x) can be further simplified to give $f(x) = \frac{x^2-5x+5}{x-5}$ **(4 marks)**

1.3 Partial fractions

1 Express in partial fractions:

a $\frac{8x-1}{(x+1)(x-2)}$

b $\frac{2x+13}{(2x-1)(x+3)}$

c $\frac{7-11x}{(3x-1)(2x+1)}$

Hint For part **a**, write $\frac{8x-1}{(x+1)(x-2)} \equiv \frac{A}{x+1} + \frac{B}{x-2}$

Then find A and B by rearranging and substituting suitable values of x.

2 Express in partial fractions:

a $\dfrac{7x-15}{x^2-5x}$ b $\dfrac{3(x+7)}{x^2-9}$

c $\dfrac{9x-1}{2x^2-9x-5}$

Hint Factorise each denominator to work out the denominators for the partial fractions.

3 Express in partial fractions:

a $\dfrac{6x^2-43x+50}{x(x-2)(x-5)}$

b $\dfrac{4x^2+11x+9}{(x-1)(x+2)(x+3)}$

c $\dfrac{5x^2-22x+6}{x(x-3)(2x-1)}$

Hint For part **a**, write

$\dfrac{6x^2-43x+50}{x(x-2)(x-5)} \equiv \dfrac{A}{x}+\dfrac{B}{x-2}+\dfrac{C}{x-5}$

You can also find A, B and C by multiplying across and comparing coefficients. Often a combination of substitution and comparing coefficients is the most efficient way to find the numerators.

4 Given that $\dfrac{1+15x-10x^2}{(x-2)(1-2x)} \equiv A+\dfrac{B}{x-2}+\dfrac{C}{1-2x}$, find the values of the constants A, B and C.

Hint Start by multiplying both sides by $(x-2)(1-2x)$ to remove the fractions.

E/P 5 Given that $\dfrac{4}{(x+1)(3x-2)} \equiv \dfrac{A}{x+1}+\dfrac{B}{3x-2}$, find the values of the constants A and B. **(3 marks)**

E/P 6 Express $\dfrac{5x-3}{(2x+3)(x+2)}$ in partial fractions. **(3 marks)**

E/P 7 Express $\dfrac{3}{9-y^2}$ in partial fractions. **(3 marks)**

E/P 8 Given that $\dfrac{33x-x^2-44}{(x-1)(x+5)(2x-3)} \equiv \dfrac{A}{x-1}+\dfrac{B}{x+5}+\dfrac{C}{2x-3}$, find the values of the constants A, B and C. **(4 marks)**

E/P 9 Given that $\dfrac{2x^2-11}{(x+1)(x-2)} \equiv A+\dfrac{B}{x+1}+\dfrac{C}{x-2}$, find the values of the constants A, B and C. **(4 marks)**

1.4 Repeated factors

1 $f(x)=\dfrac{5x^2-5x+2}{x^2(x-2)}$, $x \neq 0$, $x \neq 2$. Given that $f(x)$ can be expressed in the form $\dfrac{A}{x}+\dfrac{B}{x^2}+\dfrac{C}{x-2}$, find the values of the constants A, B and C.

Hint x is a repeated factor, so you need separate denominators of x and x^2 in the expanded partial fraction.

2 $g(x)=\dfrac{8x^2-x+3}{(x+1)^2(2x-1)}$, $x \neq -1$, $x \neq \frac{1}{2}$

Given that $g(x)$ can be expressed in the form $\dfrac{A}{x+1}+\dfrac{B}{(x+1)^2}+\dfrac{C}{2x-1}$, find the values of the constants A, B and C.

Hint $(x+1)$ is a repeated linear factor, so you need denominators of $(x+1)$ and $(x+1)^2$.

(E/P) 3 $\frac{4x-1}{(2x+1)^2} \equiv \frac{A}{2x+1} + \frac{B}{(2x+1)^2}$. Find the values of the constants A and B. **(3 marks)**

(E/P) 4 Given that $\frac{x^2+7x+32}{(x-2)(x+3)^2} \equiv \frac{A}{x-2} + \frac{B}{x+3} + \frac{C}{(x+3)^2}$, find the values of the constants A, B and C. **(4 marks)**

(E/P) 5 Express $\frac{6x^2-13x+15}{2x^3-3x^2}$ in the form $\frac{A}{x} + \frac{B}{x^2} + \frac{C}{2x-3}$, where A, B and C are constants to be found. **(4 marks)**

(E/P) 6 Express $\frac{x^2-5x+16}{x^3-4x^2+4x}$ as a sum of partial fractions. **(6 marks)**

1.5 Algebraic division

1 Use algebraic division to show that

$$\frac{x^2-5x+7}{x-3} \equiv x-2+\frac{1}{x-3}$$

Hint This is an improper algebraic fraction because the degree of the numerator is greater than or equal to the degree of the denominator. You can divide the numerator by the denominator to obtain a polynomial and a remainder.

2 **a** Find the remainder when x^2-5x+9 is divided by $x+1$.

b Hence, or otherwise, write $\frac{x^2-5x+9}{x+1}$ in the form $Ax+B+\frac{C}{x+1}$, where A, B and C are constants to be found.

Hint For part **b**, you can use the relationship $\mathrm{F}(x) = \mathrm{Q}(x) \times \text{divisor} + \text{remainder}$ to write $\frac{\mathrm{F}(x)}{\text{divisor}} = \mathrm{Q}(x) + \frac{\text{remainder}}{\text{divisor}}$

3 Given that $\frac{x^3-x^2-9}{x+3} \equiv Ax^2+Bx+C+\frac{D}{x+3}$, find the values of the constants A, B, C and D.

Hint You could use algebraic long division, or you could multiply both sides by $(x+3)$ and use substitution and comparing coefficients.

4 Given that

$$x^3-2x^2+5 \equiv (Ax^2+Bx+C)(x-4)+D$$

find the values of the constants A, B, C and D.

Hint You can compare coefficients when the identity is written in this form.

(E/P) 5 $\frac{18x^2+22x-7}{(x+2)(3x-1)} \equiv A+\frac{B}{x+2}+\frac{C}{3x-1}$. Find the values of the constants A, B and C. **(4 marks)**

(E/P) 6 Given that $\frac{2x^3-4x^2+5x-1}{x-3} \equiv Ax^2+Bx+C+\frac{D}{x-3}$, find the values of the constants A, B, C and D. **(4 marks)**

(E/P) 7 Given that $\frac{x^4-3x^2+5}{x^2+2} \equiv Ax^2+B+\frac{C}{x^2+2}$, find the values of the constants A, B and C. **(4 marks)**

(E/P) 8 Given that $\frac{4x^2-5x-3}{(x+1)(2x-1)} \equiv A+\frac{B}{x+1}+\frac{C}{2x-1}$, find the values of the constants A, B and C. **(4 marks)**

E/P **9** $3x^4 - 5x^3 + 6x^2 - 12x + 5 \equiv (Ax^2 + Bx + C)(x^2 + 2) + Dx + E$

Find the values of the constants A, B, C, D and E. **(5 marks)**

Problem solving Set A

Bronze

a Simplify $\dfrac{3x^2 + x - 2}{x^2 - 1}$ **(3 marks)**

b Hence, or otherwise, express $\dfrac{3x^2 + x - 2}{x^2 - 1} - \dfrac{1}{x^2 - x}$ as a single fraction in its simplest form. **(3 marks)**

Silver

Express $\dfrac{2x^2 - 3x}{2x^2 + x - 6} - \dfrac{6}{x^2 + x - 2}$ as a single fraction in its simplest form. **(7 marks)**

Gold

Express $\dfrac{2x^3 + 3x^2 - 5x - 6}{3x^2 + 5x + 2}$ in the form $Ax + B + \dfrac{C}{Dx + E}$ where A, B, C, D and E are constants to be found. **(9 marks)**

Problem solving Set B

Bronze

Express $\dfrac{39x^2 - 49x + 15}{(3x - 2)^2(1 - x)}$ as a sum of partial fractions. **(4 marks)**

Silver

Show that $\dfrac{3x^2 - 2x + 4}{x^2 - x - 6}$ can be written in the form $A + \dfrac{B}{x - 3} + \dfrac{C}{x + 2}$ and find the values of the constants A, B and C. **(5 marks)**

Gold

$$f(x) = \frac{3x^2 + 3}{2x^3 - 5x^2 - 4x + 3}$$

The graph of $y = f(x)$ has a vertical asymptote with equation $x = -1$. Use this information to express $f(x)$ as the sum of three fractions with linear denominators. **(8 marks)**

Now try this → **Exam question bank Q5, Q9, Q49, Q62, Q69, Q75, Q78**

2 Functions and graphs

2.1 The modulus function

1 $f(x) = |x^2 + 5x|$. Write down the value of:

a $f(-3)$ **b** $f(2)$ **c** $f(-1)$

Hint The modulus of a number a is its non-negative numerical value. It is written as $|a|$. In general:

- $|f(x)| = f(x)$ when $f(x) \geqslant 0$
- $|f(x)| = -f(x)$ when $f(x) < 0$.

2 $g(x) = |2 - 3x| + 1$. Write down the value of:

a $g(1)$ **b** $g(10)$ **c** $g(-1)$

3 Sketch each graph and mark the coordinates of any points of intersection with the coordinate axes.

a $y = |x + 1|$ **b** $y = |2x + 1|$

c $y = |3x - 4|$ **d** $y = |3 - 2x|$

e $y = \left|\frac{1}{2}x + 3\right|$ **f** $y = -|3x + 1|$

Hint The graph of $y = |ax + b|$ is the graph of $y = ax + b$ with the section of the graph below the x-axis reflected in the x-axis.

4 **i** For each pair of functions, sketch $y = f(x)$ and $y = g(x)$ on the same set of axes.

ii Hence solve $f(x) = g(x)$.

a $f(x) = |2x - 3|$, $g(x) = 7$

b $f(x) = |2 - 5x|$, $g(x) = 3x + 5$

c $f(x) = |3x + 2|$, $g(x) = \frac{x}{2} + 5$

Hint You can solve $f(x) = g(x)$ algebraically by solving two equations. For example, in part **a**:

$2x - 3 = 7$ (1)

$-(2x - 3) = 7$ (2)

5 Solve the inequality $|4x - 5| > 2x$. Write your answer in set notation.

Hint Solve $|4x - 5| = 2x$, then use sketches of $y = |4x - 5|$ and $y = 2x$ to work out which values of x satisfy the inequality.

← **Year 1, Section 3.4**

(E) 6 **a** Sketch the graph with equation $y = |4x + 3|$, marking the locations of any points where the graph cuts or meets the coordinate axes. **(2 marks)**

b Find the values of x which satisfy $|4x + 3| \leqslant 7$. **(2 marks)**

(E) 7 **a** $f(x) = |5 - 3x|$. Sketch the graph with equation $y = f(x)$, stating the coordinates of any points where the graph cuts or meets the coordinate axes. **(2 marks)**

b Find the values of x for which $f(x) = x$. **(4 marks)**

(E/P) 8 Solve the inequality $|2x - 6| > 5 - x$. **(4 marks)**

(E/P) 9 **a** Sketch the graph with equation $y = -|3 - x|$. **(2 marks)**

b Find the values of x which satisfy $-|3 - x| = -\frac{x + 5}{3}$ **(5 marks)**

2.2 Functions and mappings

1 State whether each mapping from the set of x-values to the set of y-values is one-to-one, many-to-one or one-to-many.

> **Hint** A **mapping** transforms one set of numbers, the **domain**, onto another set of numbers, the **range**.

a $y = 5 - x^2$

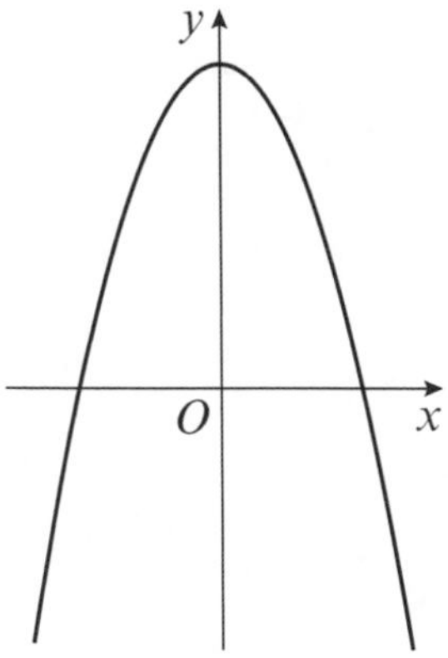

b $y = 10 - 3x$

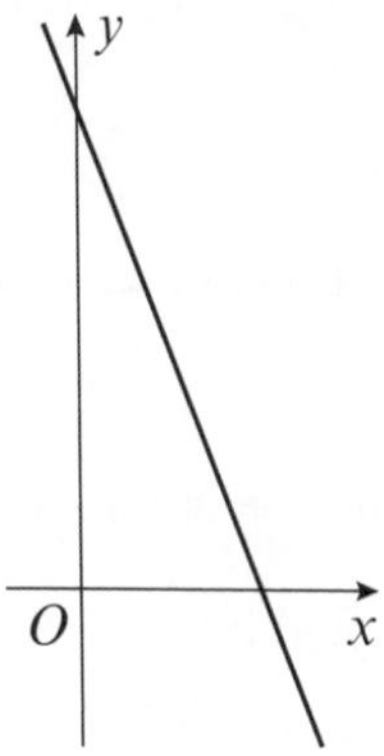

c $y^2 = x + 9$

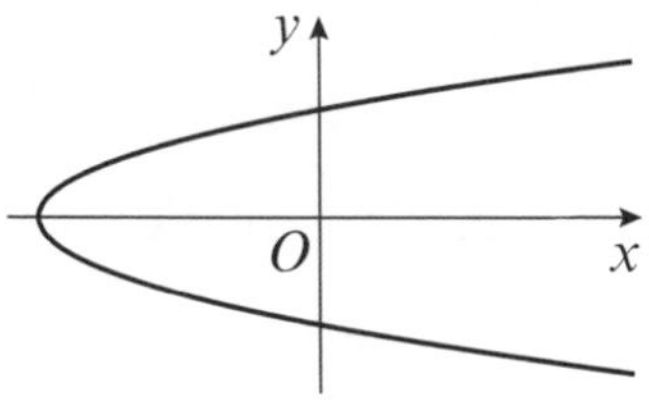

d $y = \sin x$

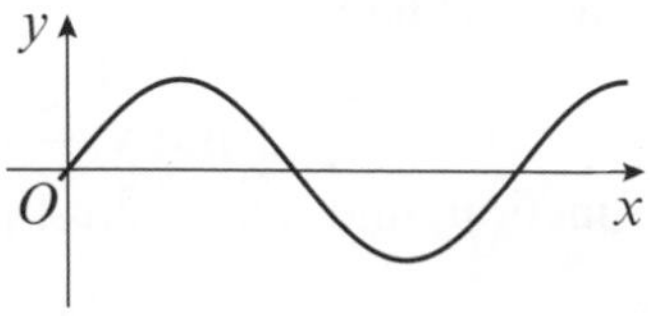

2 State a possible domain which would make each mapping a function and write it using function notation.

a $y = \sqrt{x+2}$ **b** $y = \dfrac{1}{x+1}$ **c** $y = \tan x$

> **Hint** A mapping is a **function** if every element in the domain maps to one distinct element in the range. This means functions are either one-to-one or many-to-one.
>
> It is possible to convert some mappings into functions by restricting the domain.

3 For each function:

i sketch the graph of $y = f(x)$

ii state the range of $f(x)$

iii state whether the function is one-to-one or many-to-one.

a $f(x) = (x + 2)^2, x \in \mathbb{R}, x \geqslant 0$

b $f(x) = 3\sin x, x \in \mathbb{R}, 0 \leqslant x \leqslant 180°$

c $f(x) = 2e^x, x \in \mathbb{R}, x \geqslant 0$

d $f(x) = \sqrt{x-3}, x \in \mathbb{R}, x \geqslant 3$

> **Hint** You should only sketch the graph of the function for values of x in its **domain**.
>
> The **range** will be the set of y-values that are mapped to by the function.

4 The function f(x) is defined by

$$f(x) = \begin{cases} 5 - \frac{1}{2}x, & x \in \mathbb{R}, x < 2 \\ (x-4)^2 + 2, & x \in \mathbb{R}, x \geqslant 2 \end{cases}$$

Hint This is an example of a **piecewise-defined function**. It consists of two parts, one linear for $x < 2$ and one quadratic for $x \geqslant 2$. The function is not continuous as it jumps at $x = 2$ but it is still defined for all real values of x.

a Sketch the graph of $y = f(x)$.

b Explain why f(x) is a function and state the value of f(2).

c State the range of f(x).

d Solve f(x) = 11.

(E) 5 The function f is defined by $f : x \mapsto x^2 - 3x + 4, \quad x \in \mathbb{R}, 0 \leqslant x < 4$.

a Find the range of f(x). **(3 marks)**

b State whether the function is one-to-one or many-to-one. **(1 mark)**

(E/P) 6 The function f(x) is defined by

$$f(x) = \begin{cases} e^x + 5, & x \in \mathbb{R}, x \leqslant 0 \\ x^2 - 8x + 6, & x \in \mathbb{R}, x \geqslant 0 \end{cases}$$

a Sketch the graph of $y = f(x)$. **(4 marks)**

b State the range of f(x). **(1 mark)**

* (E/P) 7 The function g defined by $g(x) = x^2 - 5x + 8$ has domain $x \in \mathbb{R}, x \geqslant a$. Given that g is a one-to-one function, find the smallest possible value of the constant a. **(6 marks)**

(E/P) 8 The function h(x) is defined by

$$h(x) = \begin{cases} 2 + x, & x \in \mathbb{R}, x \leqslant 4 \\ 10x - x^2 - 17, & x \in \mathbb{R}, x > 4 \end{cases}$$

a Sketch the graph of $y = h(x)$. **(4 marks)**

b State the value of h(4). **(1 mark)**

c State the range of h(x). **(1 mark)**

d Find the exact values of x for which h(x) = 5. **(4 marks)**

2.3 Composite functions

1 Given $f(x) = x^3$, $g(x) = x - 2$ and $h(x) = \frac{x}{2}$, find:

a fg(4) **b** gf(2) **c** $g^2(-1)$

d gh(6) **e** fgh(10)

Hint fg(x) means apply g first, then apply f, so fg(x) = f(g(x)).

2 Given the functions $p(x) = 3x - 1$, $q(x) = 4 - x^2$ and $r(x) = \frac{1}{x}$, find expressions for:

a pq(x) **b** qr(x) **c** $p^2(x)$

d rp(x) **e** pqr(x)

Hint In part **a**, $pq(x) = 3(4 - x^2) - 1$. Simplify your answers as much as possible.

3 The functions f and g are defined by $f : x \mapsto |4x - 5|$ and $g : x \mapsto \frac{x-1}{2}$ respectively.

a Find $fg(-5)$. b Solve $fg(x) = 2x$.

Hint For part **b**, sketch $y = fg(x)$ and $y = 2x$ on the same set of axes. The number of points of intersection will be the number of solutions to the equation $fg(x) = 2x$.

E/P 4 $f(x) = e^x$, $x \in \mathbb{R}$ and $g(x) = 2\ln x$, $x \in \mathbb{R}$, $x > 0$.

a Find an expression for $gf(x)$, simplifying your answer. **(2 marks)**

b Show that there is only one real value of x for which $gf(x) = fg(x)$. **(3 marks)**

E/P 5 $f(x) = 4x^2 - 8x$, $x \in \mathbb{R}$ and $g(x) = k - x$, $x \in \mathbb{R}$ where k is a non-zero constant.

a Find the range of $f(x)$. **(3 marks)**

b Find an expression for $gf(x)$ in terms of x and k. **(2 marks)**

c Given that the range of gf is $gf(x) < 6$, find the set of possible values of k. **(2 marks)**

E/P 6 The function f is defined for all real values of x as $f(x) = 8 - (x - 2)^2$.

a State the range of $f(x)$. **(1 mark)**

b Find the value of $ff(-2)$. **(3 marks)**

E/P 7 Given that $f(x) = 2x^2$, $x \in \mathbb{R}$ and $g(x) = \frac{1}{x-1}$, $x \in \mathbb{R}$, $x \neq 1$,

a state the range of $f(x)$ **(1 mark)**

b find an expression for $fg(x)$ **(2 marks)**

c solve the equation $fg(x) = 18$. **(4 marks)**

E/P 8 The functions p and q are defined by $p : x \mapsto 3^x$, $x \in \mathbb{R}$ and $q : x \mapsto x - 2$, $x \in \mathbb{R}$ respectively.

a Find an expression for $pq(x)$. **(2 marks)**

b Find an expression for $qp(x)$. **(2 marks)**

c Solve $pq(x) = qp(x)$, giving your answer in the form $\frac{\ln a}{\ln b}$ **(3 marks)**

2.4 Inverse functions

1 For each function $f(x)$,

i determine the equation of the inverse function $f^{-1}(x)$

ii sketch the graphs of $y = x$, $y = f(x)$ and $y = f^{-1}(x)$ on the same set of axes.

a $f : x \mapsto 2x - 5$, $x \in \mathbb{R}$ b $f : x \mapsto \frac{x-3}{2}$, $x \in \mathbb{R}$

c $f : x \mapsto x^3 - 1$, $x \in \mathbb{R}$ d $f : x \mapsto 1 - 3x$, $x \in \mathbb{R}$

Hint The **inverse** of a function maps the elements in the range of the function back onto the original elements in its domain. The graphs of $y = f(x)$ and $y = f^{-1}(x)$ are reflections in the line $y = x$.

2 For each function g(x),

i determine the equation of the inverse function $g^{-1}(x)$

ii state the domain and range of $g^{-1}(x)$

iii sketch the graphs of $y = g(x)$ and $y = g^{-1}(x)$ on the same set of axes

iv solve the equation $g(x) = g^{-1}(x)$.

Hint The domain of g(x) is the range of $g^{-1}(x)$ and the range of g(x) is the domain of $g^{-1}(x)$.

a $g(x) = 2x - 3, x \in \mathbb{R}, x \geqslant 0$

b $g(x) = \sqrt{x-2}, x \in \mathbb{R}, x > 2$

c $g(x) = \frac{4}{x-3}, x \in \mathbb{R}, x > 3$

d $g(x) = (x-1)^2 - 5, x \in \mathbb{R}, x \geqslant 1$

3 $f(x) = \frac{2}{x}, x \in \mathbb{R}, x \neq 0$

a Show that f is self-inverse.

b Write down an expression for ff(x).

Hint A function f(x) is **self-inverse** if $f(x) = f^{-1}(x)$.

4 The function g is defined by

$g : x \mapsto x^2 - 4x, x \in \mathbb{R}, 0 \leqslant x \leqslant 6$

Explain why the function g does not have an inverse.

Hint Sketch the function to check whether it is one-to-one for the given domain.

(E/P) 5 The function f(x) is defined by $f(x) = \frac{3x-5}{x-3}, x \in \mathbb{R}, x \neq 3$.

a Show that $ff(x) = x$. **(3 marks)**

b Hence write down $f^{-1}(x)$. **(1 mark)**

(E/P) 6 The function f is defined by $f : x \mapsto \ln(3x-1), x \in \mathbb{R}, x > \frac{1}{3}$

a Find $f^{-1}(x)$ and state its domain and range. **(4 marks)**

b Sketch the graphs of $y = f(x)$ and $y = f^{-1}(x)$ on the same set of axes, stating the exact coordinates of the points where the graphs cross the axes. **(4 marks)**

(E/P) 7 The function g(x) is defined by $g(x) = x^2 - 6x + 8, x \in \mathbb{R}, x > 3$.

a Find $g^{-1}(x)$ and state its domain and range. **(6 marks)**

b Find the exact value of the solution to the equation $g(x) = g^{-1}(x)$. **(3 marks)**

(E/P) 8 The function f is defined by $f(x) = \frac{2x+1}{x-3}, x \in \mathbb{R}, x > 3$.

a Find $f^{-1}(x)$ and state its domain and range. **(4 marks)**

b Solve the equation $f^{-1}(x) = 8$. **(2 marks)**

2.5 $y = |f(x)|$ and $y = f(|x|)$

1 For each function f(x), sketch the graphs of $y = f(x)$ and $y = |f(x)|$.

a $f(x) = x^2 - x - 12, x \in \mathbb{R}$

b $f(x) = \cos x, 0 \leqslant x \leqslant 360°$

Hint To sketch the graph of $y = |f(x)|$:

- Sketch the graph of $y = f(x)$.
- Reflect any parts of the graph below the x-axis, (where $f(x) < 0$) in the x-axis.
- Delete the parts of the graph below the x-axis.

2 For each function f(x), sketch the graphs of $y = \mathrm{f}(x)$ and $y = \mathrm{f}(|x|)$.

a $\mathrm{f}(x) = 6 + 5x - x^2, x \in \mathbb{R}$

b $\mathrm{f}(x) = 2\sin x, -360° \leqslant x \leqslant 360°$

Hint To sketch the graph of $y = \mathrm{f}(|x|)$:
- Sketch the graph of $y = \mathrm{f}(x)$ for $x \geqslant 0$.
- Reflect this in the y-axis.

3 The diagram shows a sketch of part of the curve with equation $y = \mathrm{g}(x), x \in \mathbb{R}$.

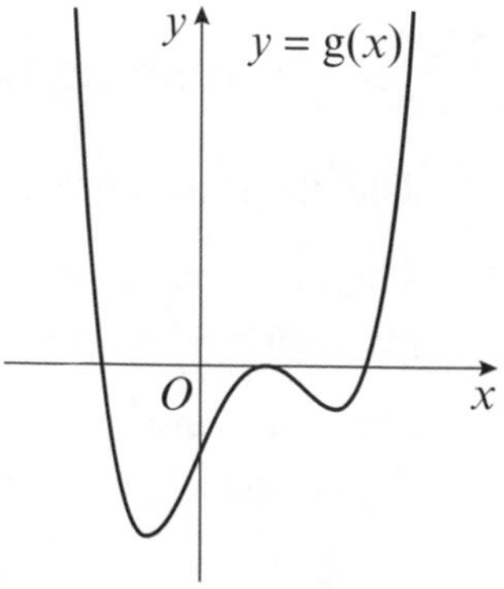

On separate diagrams, sketch the curves with equations:

a $y = |\mathrm{g}(x)|$

b $y = \mathrm{g}(|x|)$

(E) 4 The diagram shows a sketch of the curve with the equation $y = \mathrm{f}(x), x \in \mathbb{R}$.

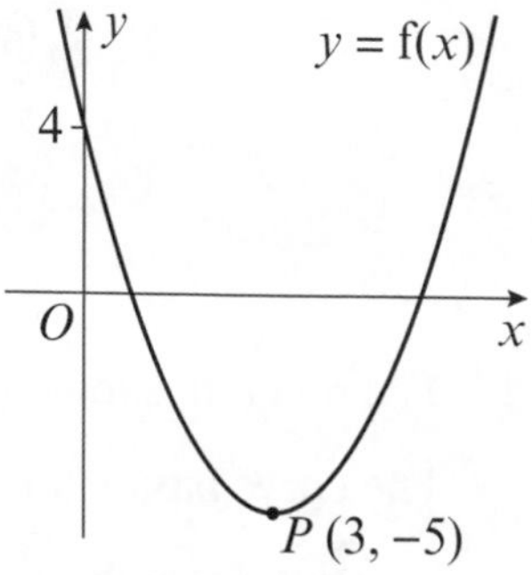

The curve has a turning point at $P(3, -5)$ and also passes through the point $(0, 4)$.

a Write down the coordinates of the point to which P is transformed on the curve with equation $y = |\mathrm{f}(x)|$. **(2 marks)**

b Sketch the curve with equation $y = \mathrm{f}(|x|)$. On your sketch, show the coordinates of all turning points and the coordinates of the point where the curve cuts the y-axis. **(3 marks)**

(E) 5 Sketch the graphs of:

a $y = |\ln x|$ **(2 marks)**

b $y = \ln(|x|)$ **(3 marks)**

In each case, state the coordinates of any points of intersection with the axes.

(E) 6 The diagram shows a sketch of the curve with equation $y = \mathrm{f}(x)$. The curve passes through the points $P(-4, 0)$, $Q(0, -10)$ and $R(3, -15)$.

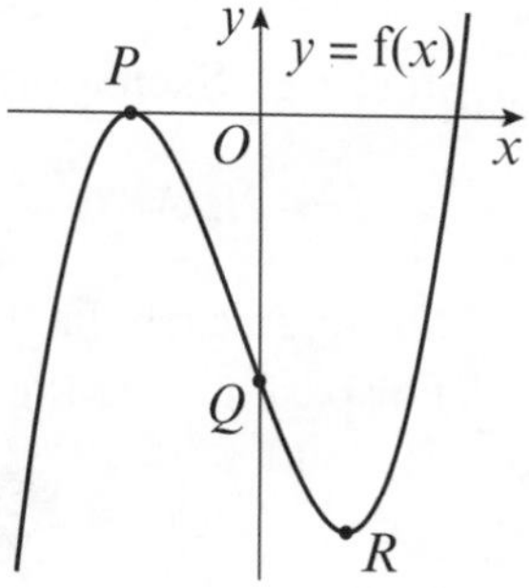

On separate diagrams, sketch the graphs with equations:

a $y = |\mathrm{f}(x)|$ **(3 marks)**

b $y = \mathrm{f}(|x|)$ **(3 marks)**

On each sketch, where possible, show the coordinates of the points corresponding to P, Q and R.

(E/P) 7 The function g is defined by $g : x \mapsto \frac{3}{x-2}$, $x \in \mathbb{R}$, $x \neq 2$.

a Sketch the graph of $y = |g(x)|$. Indicate clearly the equation of the vertical asymptote and the coordinates of the point at which the graph crosses the y-axis. **(3 marks)**

b Find the values of x for which $\left|\frac{3}{x-2}\right| = 4$. **(3 marks)**

2.6 Combining transformations

1 The diagram shows a sketch of the graph of $y = f(x)$.

The curve passes through the origin O, the point $A(2, 8)$ and the point $B(8, -16)$.

Sketch the graph of $y = f(x + 3) + 4$ and find the coordinates of the images of the points A and B.

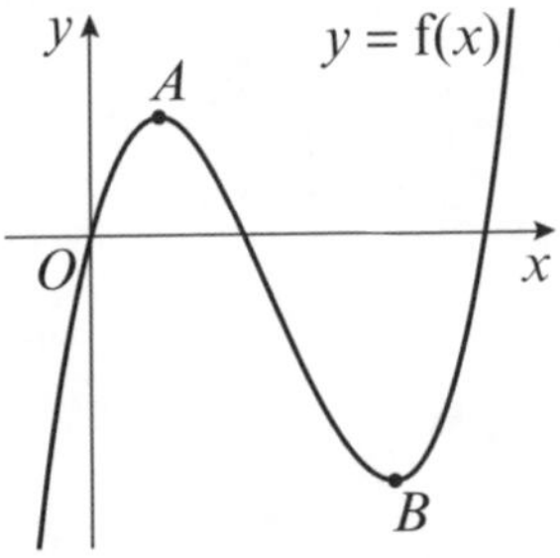

Hint $y = f(x) + a$ is a translation of the graph of $y = f(x)$ by the vector $\begin{pmatrix} 0 \\ a \end{pmatrix}$

$y = f(x + a)$ is a translation of the graph of $y = f(x)$ by the vector $\begin{pmatrix} -a \\ 0 \end{pmatrix}$

← **Year 1, Section 4.5**

2 The diagram shows a sketch of the graph of $y = g(x)$.

The curve passes through the points $A(-2, -7)$, $B(0, -2)$ and $C(2, 4)$.

Sketch the graphs of:

a $y = 3g(x - 1)$ **b** $y = g\left(\frac{x}{2}\right) - 2$

Find the coordinates of the images of the points A, B and C.

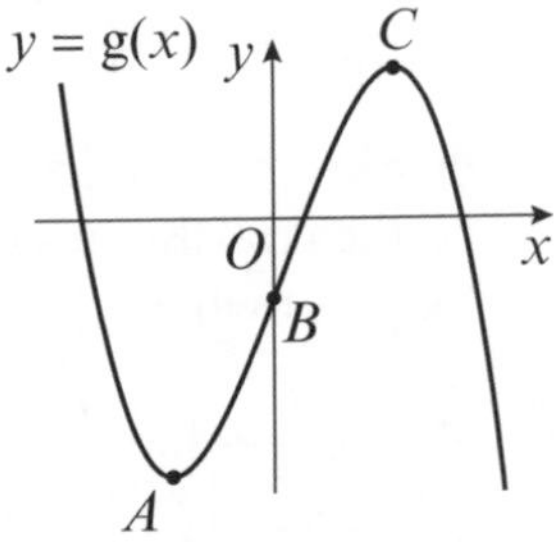

Hint $y = ag(x)$ is a vertical stretch by scale factor a of the graph of $y = g(x)$.

$y = g(ax)$ is a horizontal stretch by scale factor $\frac{1}{a}$ of the graph of $y = g(x)$.

In part **a**, apply the translation first and then the stretch. ← **Year 1, Section 4.6**

3 $f(x) = e^x$. Sketch the graphs with equations:

a $y = -2f(x) - 1$ **b** $y = -f(|x|)$

Show, on each diagram, the point where the graph crosses the y-axis.
For part **a**, state the equation of the asymptote.

Hint The graph of $y = -f(x)$ is a reflection of the graph of $y = f(x)$ in the x-axis.

These graphs can be considered as vertical stretches with scale factor -1.

← **Year 1, Section 4.6**

E/P **4** The diagram shows a sketch of the graph of $y = f(x)$.

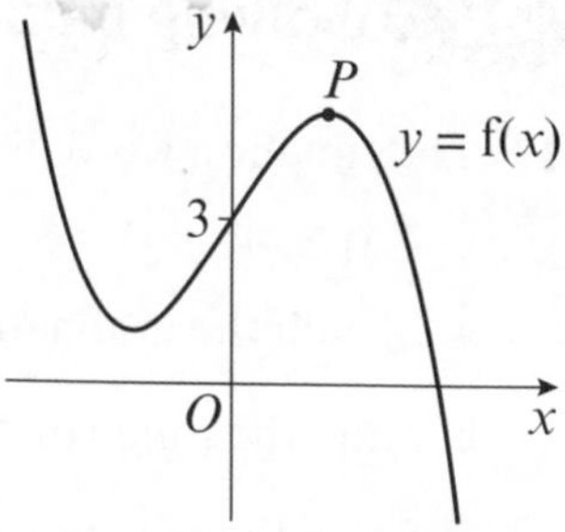

The graph cuts the y-axis at the point (0, 3) and the point $P(1, 5)$ is the local maximum turning point.
On separate sets of axes, sketch the graphs of:

a $y = f(-x) + 1$ **(3 marks)**

b $y = f(x + 2) + 3$ **(3 marks)**

On each sketch, show the coordinates of the point at which your graph intersects the y-axis, if known, and the coordinates of the point to which P is transformed.

E/P **5** The diagram shows the graph of $y = f(x)$.

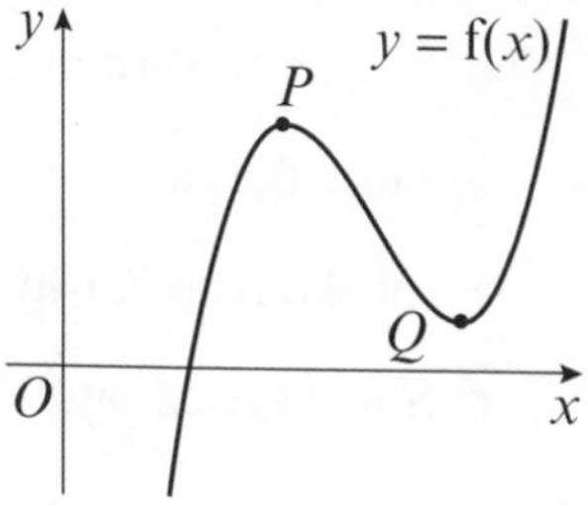

The points $P(3, 5)$ and $Q(5, 1)$ are turning points on the graph.
On separate diagrams, sketch the graphs of:

a $y = -3f(x) + 1$ **(3 marks)**

b $y = f(|x|) - 1$ **(3 marks)**

For each graph, indicate the coordinates of any turning points.

E/P **6** The diagram shows a sketch of the curve with equation $y = f(x)$.

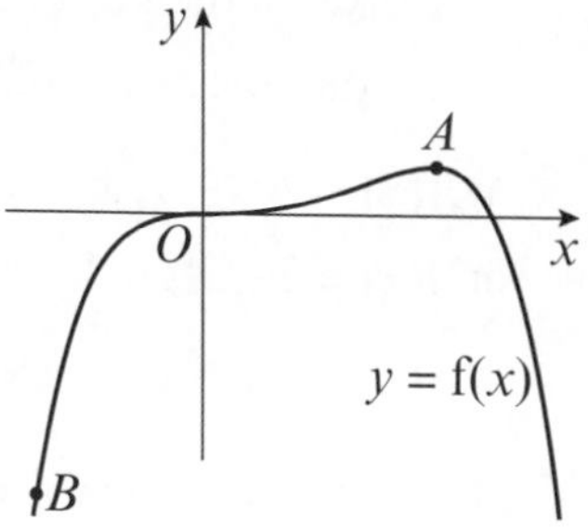

The curve passes through the origin O and the points $A(9, 10)$ and $B(-9, -70)$.

On separate diagrams, sketch the graphs of:

a $y = \dfrac{f(x + 2)}{2}$ **(3 marks)**

b $y = f(2x) - 3$ **(3 marks)**

Indicate on each diagram the coordinates of the points corresponding to A and B.

E/P **7** The function g is defined by $g : x \mapsto (x + 1)^2 - 4, x \in \mathbb{R}$.

a Draw a sketch of the graph of $y = g(x)$, labelling the turning point and the x- and y-intercepts. **(3 marks)**

b Write down the coordinates of the turning points on the graphs with equations:

i $y = 2(|g(x)|) + 2$ **ii** $y = -3g(x + 1)$ **iii** $y = g(2x) + 1$ **(6 marks)**

E/P **8** The diagram shows part of the graph of $y = f(x), x \in \mathbb{R}$.

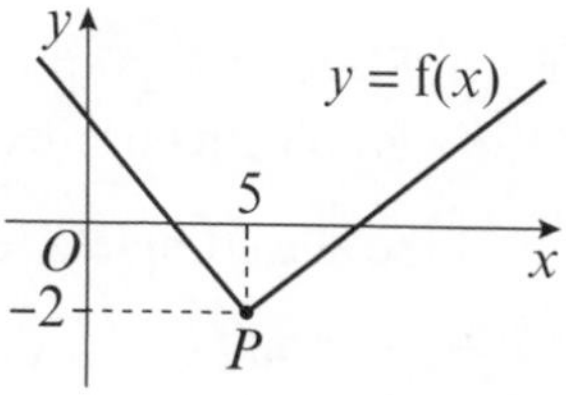

The graph consists of two line segments that meet at the point $P(5, -2)$, as shown in the diagram.
On separate diagrams, sketch the graphs of:

a $y = 2f(x + 5)$ **(3 marks)**

b $y = |f(-x)|$ **(3 marks)**

On each diagram, show the coordinates of the point corresponding to P.

2.7 Solving modulus problems

1 The function f is defined as
$f(x) = 2|x + 1| - 3, x \in \mathbb{R}$

a Sketch the graph of $y = f(x)$.

b State the range of the function.

c Solve the equation $f(x) = x + 4$.

Hint Use transformations to sketch the graph. Start with $y = |x|$, then apply a translation by the vector $\begin{pmatrix} -1 \\ 0 \end{pmatrix}$, then a stretch with scale factor 2 in the y-direction, and then a translation by the vector $\begin{pmatrix} 0 \\ -3 \end{pmatrix}$.

2 The function g is defined as
$g(x) = 9 - 3|x - 2|, x \in \mathbb{R}$

a Sketch the graph of the function.

b State the range of the function.

c Give a reason why $g^{-1}(x)$ does not exist.

d Solve the equation $g(x) \leqslant 3$, giving your answer in set notation.

Hint The part of the function inside the modulus signs must always be greater than or equal to 0.

3 For each function f(x):

i sketch the graph of $y = f(x)$

ii state the range of the function.

a $f(x) = 2|x| - 1, x \in \mathbb{R}$

b $f(x) = 2 - 3|x + 1|, x \in \mathbb{R}$

c $f(x) = 5 + \frac{|x - 2|}{2}, x \in \mathbb{R}$

E/P 4 The diagram shows a sketch of part of the graph $y = f(x)$, where $f(x) = 3|2 - x| + 4, x \geqslant 0$.

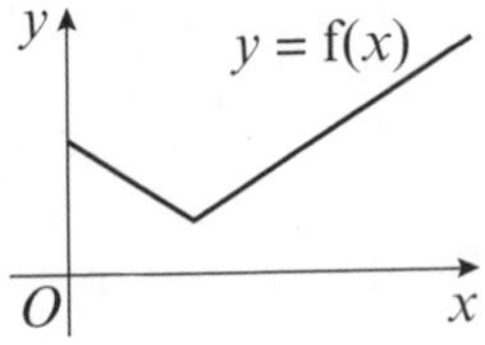

a State the range of f(x). **(1 mark)**

b Solve the equation $f(x) = x + 20$. **(3 marks)**

c Given that the equation $f(x) = k$, where k is a constant, has two distinct roots, state the set of possible values for k. **(2 marks)**

E/P 5 **a** Sketch the graph of $y = |x| - 5$. **(3 marks)**

b Explain why $|x| - 5 \leqslant |x - 5|$ for all real values of x. **(3 marks)**

E/P 6 **a** Sketch the graph with equation $y = |5x - 4|$, stating the coordinates of any points where the graph cuts or meets the axes. **(2 marks)**

Find the complete set of values of x for which:

b $|5x - 4| > 3 - 2x$ **(4 marks)**

c $|5x - 4| > \frac{8}{5} - 2x$ **(2 marks)**

(E/P) **7** Given that p and q are positive constants,

a on separate diagrams, sketch the graphs with equations:

i $y = |3x - p|$ **ii** $y = |3x - p| + q$

Show, on each sketch, the coordinates of any points at which the graph crosses or meets the axes. **(4 marks)**

Given that the equation $|3x - p| + q = 2x + 8$ has solutions $x = 0$ and $x = k$,

b find k in terms of p. **(4 marks)**

Problem solving Set A

Bronze

The functions f and g are defined by $f : x \mapsto 3 - 2x^3, x \in \mathbb{R}$ and $g : x \mapsto \frac{2}{x} - 5, x \in \mathbb{R}, x > 0$.

a Find the inverse function $f^{-1}(x)$. **(2 marks)**

b Show that the composite function gf is given by $gf : x \mapsto \frac{10x^3 - 13}{3 - 2x^3}$ **(4 marks)**

c Solve $gf(x) = 1$. **(3 marks)**

Silver

The function f is defined by $f(x) = e^{2x} + 2, x \in \mathbb{R}$.

a Find $f^{-1}(x)$. State the domain of this inverse function. **(3 marks)**

The function $g(x)$ is defined by $g(x) = \ln(x + 3), x \in \mathbb{R}, x > -3$.

b Find $fg(x)$ and state its range. **(4 marks)**

c Solve $fg(x) = 66$. **(3 marks)**

Gold

The function f is defined by $f : x \mapsto \frac{x - 5}{x^2 + 2x - 3} - \frac{2}{x + 3} + 2, x \in \mathbb{R}, x > 1$.

a Show that $f(x) = \frac{2x - 3}{x - 1}, x > 1$. **(4 marks)**

b Find the range of $f(x)$. **(2 marks)**

c Find $f^{-1}(x)$. State the domain of this inverse function. **(3 marks)**

The function g is defined by $g : x \mapsto 3x^2 - 4, x \in \mathbb{R}$.

d Solve $fg(x) = \frac{1}{5}$ **(3 marks)**

Problem solving Set B

Bronze

The diagram shows a sketch of the graph $y = \mathrm{f}(x)$, where $\mathrm{f}(x) = k - 3|x - 4|$.

The graph cuts the y-axis at $(0, -6)$.

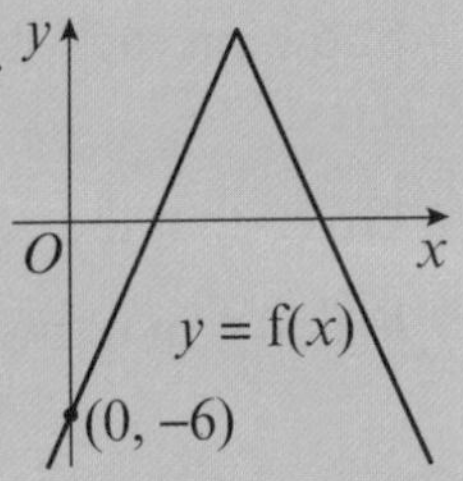

a Find the value of k. **(2 marks)**

b State the range of $\mathrm{f}(x)$. **(1 mark)**

On separate diagrams, sketch the graphs of:

c i $y = |\mathrm{f}(x)|$ **ii** $y = \mathrm{f}(|x|)$ **(4 marks)**

d Solve $\mathrm{f}(x) = \frac{x}{2} + 1$. **(5 marks)**

Silver

The diagram shows a sketch of the graph $y = \mathrm{f}(x)$ where

$\mathrm{f}(x) = 2|x + 3| - 4$

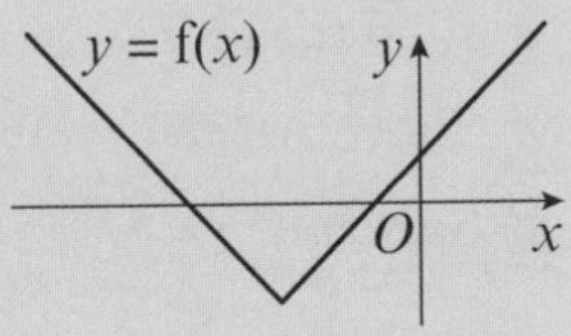

a State the range of $\mathrm{f}(x)$. **(1 mark)**

On separate diagrams, sketch the graphs of:

b i $y = |\mathrm{f}(x)|$ **ii** $y = \mathrm{f}(|x|)$ **(4 marks)**

c Find the set of values of x for which $\mathrm{f}(x) \leqslant 4 - 0.5x$. **(5 marks)**

d Find the set of values of x for which $\mathrm{f}(x) = k$ has:

i 0 solutions **ii** 1 solution **iii** 2 solutions. **(3 marks)**

Gold

$\mathrm{f}(x) = a - |x + b|$, $x \in \mathbb{R}$, where a and b are real constants.

The diagram shows the graph with equation $y = \mathrm{f}(x)$.

The graph cuts the x-axis at the points $(-8, 0)$ and $(4, 0)$.

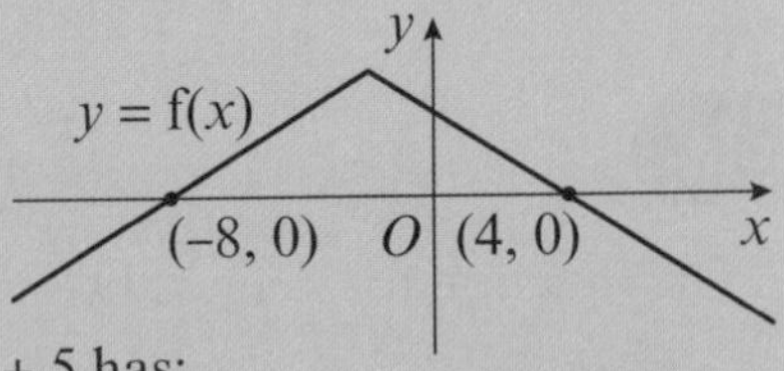

a Find the values of a and b. **(3 marks)**

b Find the set of values of p for which the equation $\mathrm{f}(x) = px + 5$ has:

i 0 solutions **ii** 1 solution **iii** 2 solutions. **(6 marks)**

Now try this → Exam question bank Q26, Q32, Q55, Q63, Q66, Q79, Q82, Q85

3.1 Arithmetic sequences

1 For each arithmetic sequence:

i write down the first 4 terms of the sequence

ii write down the values of a and d.

a $4n + 3$ **b** $7 - 3n$

c $8 + \frac{1}{2}n$ **d** $2n - 5$

> **Hint** In an **arithmetic sequence**, the difference between consecutive terms is constant.
> The formula for the nth term, u_n, of an arithmetic sequence is $u_n = a + (n - 1)d$, where a is the first term of the sequence and d is the common difference.

2 For each arithmetic sequence, find an expression for the nth term and find the 10th term.

a 2, 6, 10, 14, … **b** 5, 3, 1, −1, …

c −2, 1, 4, 7, … **d** $8y, 5y, 2y, -y, \ldots$

3 Calculate the number of terms in each arithmetic sequence.

a 2, 5, 8, …, 95, 98

b 75, 73, 71, …, −3, −5

c −3, 1, 5, …, 109, 113

d $-4k, -2k, 0, \ldots, 98k, 100k$

> **Hint** Find an expression for the nth term, u_n, and set it equal to the final term in the sequence.

4 In an arithmetic sequence, the fourth term is 17 and the 10th term is 47.
Find the first term and the common difference.

> **Hint** Use the general form for the nth term to set up two simultaneous equations in a and d.
> ← **Year 1, Section 3.1**

5 The first term of an arithmetic sequence is 20 and the common difference is $-\frac{1}{2}$

a Find the value of the 25th term.

The rth term of the sequence is 0.

b Find the value of r.

6 The nth term of an arithmetic sequence is $3n - 4$.

a Write down the first three terms of the sequence.

b State the value of the common difference.

E/P **7** An arithmetic sequence has first term a and common difference d.

The fourth term of the sequence is −2 and the ninth term is −22.

a Find the value of a and the value of d. **(3 marks)**

The nth term of the sequence is −54.

b Find the value of n. **(3 marks)**

(E/P) **8** a, b and c are three consecutive terms in an arithmetic sequence.

a Show that $\frac{a+c}{2} = b$. **(3 marks)**

The first three terms of a different arithmetic sequence are 15, p^2 and $-p$, where p is a constant.

b Find the two possible values of p. **(3 marks)**

(E/P) **9** The first three terms of an arithmetic sequence are k, $4k - 3$ and $3k + 10$.

a Find the value of k. **(3 marks)**

b Find the value of the 50th term of this sequence. **(3 marks)**

3.2 Arithmetic series

1 Find the sums of the following arithmetic series:

a $5 + 9 + 13 + 17 + \ldots$ (20 terms)

b $3 + 8 + 13 + 18 + \ldots$ (15 terms)

c $12 + 10 + 8 + 6 + \ldots$ (40 terms)

d $8 + 7.5 + 7 + 6.5 + \ldots$ (25 terms)

Hint $S_n = \frac{n}{2}(2a + (n-1)d)$

2 Find the sums of the following arithmetic series:

a $6 + 9 + 12 + \ldots + 51$

b $52 + 47 + 42 + \ldots + (-103)$

c $-2 + 1 + 4 + \ldots + 175$

d $120 + 112 + 104 + \ldots + 0$

Hint Start by working out the value of n from the given last term.

3 Prove that the sum of the first 60 natural numbers is 1830.

Hint The natural numbers are the positive integers, 1, 2, 3, 4, ...

$S_{60} = 1 + 2 + 3 + \ldots + 59 + 60$

$S_{60} = 60 + 59 + 58 + \ldots + 2 + 1$

Work out $2S_{60}$ and divide the result by 2.

4 Find the least number of terms required for the sum of the arithmetic series $5 + 8 + 11 + 14 + \ldots$ to exceed 1000.

Hint Find the values of a and d for this series, then find the least positive integer n that satisfies $S_n = \frac{n}{2}(2a + (n-1)d) > 1000$

5 The rth term of an arithmetic series is $4r - 5$.

a Write down the first three terms of the series.

b State the value of the common difference.

c Show that $S_n = n(2n - 3)$.

(E/P) **6** **a** Prove that the sum of the first n natural numbers is $\frac{n(n+1)}{2}$

You may not use the formula for the sum of an arithmetic series in your proof. **(3 marks)**

b Hence find the sum of the even integers from 2 to 200. **(2 marks)**

(P) **7** $u_1, u_2, \ldots. u_n$ are the terms of an arithmetic sequence.

a Given $u_4 = 103$ and $u_{12} = 79$, find the value of u_{25}.

The sum of the first n terms of the sequence is 1925.

b Find the value of n.

(E) **8** An arithmetic sequence has first term a and common difference d.

The sum of the first 12 terms of the sequence is 366.

a Show that $12a + 66d = 366$. **(2 marks)**

Given also that the eighth term of the sequence is 38,

b write down a second equation in a and d **(1 mark)**

c find the value of a and the value of d. **(4 marks)**

(E/P) **9** An arithmetic sequence has first term a and common difference d.

The sum of the second term and the sixth term is 14.

a Show that $a + 3d = 7$. **(3 marks)**

The sum of the first 20 terms of the sequence is -120.

b Find the value of a and the value of d. **(4 marks)**

(E/P) **10** The first term of an arithmetic series is a and the common difference is d.

The 15th term of the series is 11 and the 20th term of the series is $\frac{37}{2}$

a Show that that the first term of the series is -10, and write down the second term. **(4 marks)**

The sum of the first n terms of the series is 2055.

b Find the value of n. **(4 marks)**

(E/P) **11** The second, third and fourth terms of an arithmetic sequence are $3k$, $4k + 5$ and $7k$ respectively, where k is a constant. Show that the sum of the first n terms of the sequence is kn^2, where k is a rational number to be found. **(5 marks)**

(E/P) **12** The third, fourth and fifth terms of an arithmetic sequence are $3k$, $4k + 3$ and $6k - 9$ respectively, where k is a constant. Show that the sum of the first n terms of the sequence is a square number. **(5 marks)**

3.3 Geometric sequences

1 For each geometric sequence, find:

i the common ratio

ii the nth term.

a 2, 6, 18, 54, …

b 60, 30, 15, 7.5, …

c 10, −20, 40, −80, …

d 40, 60, 90, 135 …

Hint The formula for the nth term, u_n, of a geometric sequence is $u_n = ar^{n-1}$, where a is the first term and r is the common ratio.

2 a Write down the sequence from question **1** which is alternating.

b Given that p, q and r are three consecutive terms in a geometric sequence, show that $pr = q^2$.

Hint A geometric sequence alternates if the terms are alternately positive and negative.

3 The terms 5, x and $x + 10$ form the first three terms of a geometric sequence.

Given that the terms of the sequence are positive, find:

a the value of x

b the 10th term of the sequence.

Hint $\frac{u_2}{u_1} = \frac{u_3}{u_2}$

4 Find the first term in the geometric progression 4, 12, 36, 108, … that is larger than 1 000 000.

Hint $a = 4$ and $r = 3$, so you need to find the smallest positive integer that satisfies $4 \times 3^{n-1} > 1\,000\,000$

You can solve this inequality by taking logs on both sides. ← Year 1, Section 14.6

(P) 5 The fourth term of a geometric series is 16 and the seventh term of the series is 250.

For this series, find:

a the common ratio

b the first term.

(E/P) 6 The first three terms of a geometric sequence are $k + 4$, $3k$ and $2k^2$, where k is a positive constant.

Find the value of k. **(4 marks)**

(E/P) 7 The third term of a geometric sequence is 108 and the sixth term is 32. Find:

a the 20th term **(3 marks)**

b the first term in the sequence which is less than 1. **(3 marks)**

(E/P) 8 A geometric sequence has first term 150 and common ratio r, where $r > 0$.

The fifth term of the sequence is 50.

a Show that r satisfies $4\ln r + \ln 3 = 0$. **(3 marks)**

b Hence, or otherwise, find the value of r correct to 3 significant figures. **(1 mark)**

E/P **9** The first three terms of a geometric series are $5k$, $4k + 3$ and $6k + 7$, where k is a positive constant. Find:

a the value of k **(6 marks)**

b the first term in the sequence to exceed 10 000. **(3 marks)**

3.4 Geometric series

1 Find the sums of the following geometric series. Give your answers to 3 significant figures if necessary.

a $2 + 6 + 18 + 54 + \ldots$ (10 terms)

b $48 + 24 + 12 + 6 + \ldots$ (12 terms)

c $3 - 6 + 12 - 24 + \ldots$ (8 terms)

d $810 + 540 + 360 + 240 + \ldots.$ (9 terms)

Hint The sum of the first n terms of a geometric series is given by the formula
$S_n = \frac{a(r^n - 1)}{r - 1}, r \neq 1$ (easier to use if $|r| > 1$)
or $S_n = \frac{a(1 - r^n)}{1 - r}, r \neq 1$ (easier to use if $|r| < 1$)

2 Find the sums of the following geometric series. Give your answers to 3 significant figures if necessary.

Hint First find the number of terms, n, using nth term $= ar^{n-1}$.

a $5 + 10 + 20 + \ldots + 640$

b $13\,122 + 4374 + 1458 + \ldots + 2$

c $1024 - 256 + 64 - \ldots - \frac{1}{16}$

d $128 + 192 + 288 + \ldots + 1458$

3 Find the least value of n such that the sum of the first n terms of the geometric series $3 + 6 + 12 + 24 + \ldots.$ exceeds 1 000 000.

Hint Work out the values of a and r from the terms given. Use the formula for the sum to n terms to set up an inequality, and use logs to find the least positive integer that satisfies the inequality.

P **4** The fourth term of a geometric series is 24. The fifth term of the series is 48.

For this series, find:

a the common ratio

b the first term

c the sum of the first 20 terms.

E **5** A geometric series has first term 10 and common ratio $\frac{3}{5}$. Calculate:

a the 10th term of the series to 3 decimal places **(2 marks)**

b the least value of n such that the sum to n terms is greater than 20. **(4 marks)**

E/P **6** A geometric series has first term 20 and common ratio $\frac{4}{5}$

Given that the sum to k terms is greater than 50,

a show that $k > \frac{\ln 0.5}{\ln 0.8}$ **(4 marks)**

b find the smallest possible value of k. **(1 mark)**

(E/P) 7 The first three terms of a geometric series are $2k - 4$, $k + 2$ and $k - 1$, where k is a positive integer.

a Find the value of k. **(6 marks)**

b Hence find the 20th term of the series, correct to 3 significant figures. **(2 marks)**

c Find the sum of the first 20 terms of this series, correct to 3 significant figures. **(3 marks)**

(E/P) 8 The second term of a geometric series is 96. Given that $a + ar + ar^2 = 292.8$, where a is the first term of the series and $r < 1$ is the common ratio, find the sum of the first 10 terms of the series. Give your answer to 3 significant figures. **(9 marks)**

(E/P) 9 A geometric series is such that the sum of the first two terms is equal to the third term.

a Show that the common ratio of the series is independent of the first term. **(2 marks)**

Given further that the common ratio is positive and that the first term of the series is 2,

b find the sum of the first 20 terms of the series, correct to 3 significant figures. **(8 marks)**

3.5 Sum to infinity

1 a Explain why the geometric series $2 + 0.2 + 0.02 + 0.002 + ...$ is convergent.

b Find the sum to infinity of this series.

Hint A geometric series is convergent if $|r| < 1$ (or $-1 < r < 1$).
This means that the sum of the first n terms in the series tends to a limit as n increases.
This limit is called the sum to infinity of the series and can be found using the formula $S_\infty = \frac{a}{1-r}$

2 For each of the following series:

i state, with a reason, whether the series is convergent.

ii If the series is convergent, find the sum to infinity.

a $5 + 2 + 0.8 + 0.32 + \ldots$

b $0.1 + 0.3 + 0.9 + 1.2 + \ldots$

c $81 - 27 + 9 - 3 + \ldots$

d $20 + 18 + 16 + 14 + \ldots$

3 The fifth term of a geometric series is 2.4576 and the seventh term is 1.572864.

a Explain why this series is convergent.

b Find the sum to infinity of the series.

Hint You can use the general form of the nth term of a geometric series to find the values of a and r.

4 A geometric series has first term 8 and sum to infinity 25.

Hint Substitute into $S_\infty = \frac{a}{1-r}$

a Find the common ratio.

A different geometric series has sum to infinity 40 and common ratio $\frac{1}{5}$

b Find the first term.

5 For a geometric series with first term a and common ratio r, $S_4 = 80$ and $S_\infty = 81$.

Hint $S_n = \frac{a(1-r^n)}{1-r}$ and $S_\infty = \frac{a}{1-r}$, so $S_n = S_\infty \times (1 - r^n)$

a Find the possible values of r.

b Given that all the terms in the series are positive, find the value of a.

(E) 6 The first term of a geometric progression is 4 and the sum to infinity is 12.

Find the common ratio. **(3 marks)**

(E) 7 **a** State the condition for an infinite series with common ratio r to be convergent. **(1 mark)**

b Find the sum to infinity of the geometric series $\frac{3}{8} + \frac{3}{16} + \frac{3}{32} + \dots$ **(3 marks)**

(E/P) 8 In a convergent geometric series, the common ratio is r and the first term is 4.

Given that $S_\infty = 20 \times S_4$, find:

a the value of the common ratio, giving your answer to 4 significant figures **(3 marks)**

b the value of the fifth term. **(2 marks)**

(E/P) 9 The first term of a geometric series is 80. The sum to infinity is 120.

a Find the common ratio. **(3 marks)**

b Find, to 2 decimal places, the difference between the fourth and fifth terms. **(2 marks)**

c Calculate the sum of the first 6 terms. **(2 marks)**

(E/P) 10 A geometric series has first term a and common ratio r.

The second term of the series is $\frac{12}{5}$ and the sum to infinity of the series is 10.

a Show that $50r^2 - 50r + 12 = 0$. **(4 marks)**

b Find the two possible values of r. **(2 marks)**

c Find the corresponding two possible values of a. **(2 marks)**

Given that r takes the smaller of its two possible values,

d find the smallest value of n for which S_n exceeds 9.99. **(2 marks)**

3.6 Sigma notation

1 For each series:

i write out every term in the series.

ii Hence find the value of the sum.

Hint The Greek capital letter 'sigma' is used to represent a sum. For example, $\sum_{r=1}^{4}(2r+1) = 3 + 5 + 7 + 9$, which is an arithmetic series with $a = 3$, $d = 2$ and $n = 4$.

a $\sum_{r=1}^{6}(4r-3)$ **b** $\sum_{r=1}^{5}2r^3$

c $\sum_{r=0}^{4}\cos(90r°)$ **d** $\sum_{r=3}^{7}3\left(-\frac{1}{2}\right)^r$

2 An arithmetic sequence has nth term $u_n = 5n - 1$.

a Write down the first term and the common difference of the sequence.

b Hence find $\sum_{r=1}^{12}(5r - 1)$.

3 A geometric sequence has nth term $u_n = 3 \times 2^{n-1}$

a Write down the first term and the common ratio of the sequence.

b Hence find $\sum_{r=1}^{20} 3 \times 2^{r-1}$

Hint $\sum_{r=1}^{n} a \times b^{r-1} = a + ab + ab^2 + ab^3 + \ldots + ab^{n-1}$ is the sum of an n term geometric sequence with first term a and common ratio b.

4 Find:

a $\sum_{r=1}^{10}(3r + 2)$

b $\sum_{r=1}^{20} 3$

c $\sum_{r=1}^{\infty} 5\left(\frac{2}{3}\right)^r$

Hint In part **b** there is no r in the expression following the summation, so 3 is added to itself 20 times.

Part **c** is a geometric series. Find the first term and the common ratio.

5 $\sum_{r=8}^{30}(5 - 2r)$ represents an arithmetic series.

a Explain why

$$\sum_{r=8}^{30}(5 - 2r) = \sum_{r=1}^{30}(5 - 2r) - \sum_{r=1}^{7}(5 - 2r)$$

b Hence find $\sum_{r=8}^{30}(5 - 2r)$.

Hint Use $\sum_{r=1}^{n}(5 - 2r) = \sum_{r=1}^{m}(5 - 2r) + \sum_{r=m+1}^{n}(5 - 2r)$

(E) 6 Find the value of $\sum_{r=10}^{15} 4 \times 3^{r-1}$ **(3 marks)**

(E) 7 Find $\sum_{r=1}^{10} 10 \times 3^r$ **(3 marks)**

(E/P) 8 Given that $\sum_{r=1}^{k}(3r + 6) = 750$,

a show that $(k - 20)(3k + 75) = 0$. **(3 marks)**

b Hence find the value of k. **(1 mark)**

(E/P) 9 Given that $\sum_{r=1}^{k} 4 \times 2^r = 262\,136$,

a show that $k = \frac{\ln 32\,768}{\ln 2}$ **(4 marks)**

b For this value of k, calculate $\sum_{r=k+1}^{20} 4 \times 2^r$. **(3 marks)**

(E/P) 10 The infinite geometric series given by $1 + 4x + 16x^2 + \ldots$ is convergent.

a Write down the range of possible values of x. **(3 marks)**

Given that $\sum_{r=1}^{\infty}(4x)^{r-1} = 5$,

b find the value of x. **(3 marks)**

(E/P) 11 Show that $\sum_{r=1}^{10}(4 + 3r + 2^{r-1}) = 1228$. **(4 marks)**

3.7 Recurrence relations

1 Find the first four terms of the sequences defined by the following recurrence relations:

a $u_{n+1} = 2u_n - 1, u_1 = 3$

b $u_{n+1} = u_n - 4, u_1 = 10$

c $u_{n+1} = \frac{(u_n)^2}{2}, u_1 = 4$

Hint A recurrence relation defines each term in a sequence in terms of the previous term.

2 For each sequence:

i state whether the sequence is increasing, decreasing or periodic

ii if the sequence is periodic, write down its order.

a 3, 7, 11, 15, 19, …

b 1, 0, −1, 0, 1, 0, −1, 0, 1, …

c 11, 8, 5, 2, −1, …

Hint In an **increasing** sequence $u_{n+1} > u_n$ for all $n \in \mathbb{N}$.
In a **decreasing** sequence $u_{n+1} < u_n$ for all $n \in \mathbb{N}$.
In a **periodic** sequence, the terms repeat themselves in a cycle. This means there is an integer k such that $u_{n+k} = u_n$, for all $n \in \mathbb{N}$. The value k is called the order of the sequence.

3 For each sequence:

i write down the first 5 terms of the sequence

ii state whether the sequence is increasing, decreasing or periodic

iii if the sequence is periodic, write down its order.

a $u_n = 3n - 1$ **b** $u_n = 2^{1-n}$ **c** $u_n = \sin(180n - 30°)$

d $u_{n+1} = 2u_n + 1, u_1 = 1$ **e** $u_{n+1} = 4 - u_n, u_1 = 8$ **f** $u_{n+1} = u_n - 4, u_1 = 10$

4 A sequence $a_1, a_2, a_3, \ldots$ is defined by

$a_1 = k$

$a_{n+1} = a_n + (-1)^n$

a Show that $a_2 = a_4$.

Given that $k = 3$,

b find $\sum_{r=1}^{400} a_r$

c write down the value of a_{399}.

Hint $a_2 = k + (-1)^2 = k + 1$
$a_3 = (k + 1) + (-1)^3 = k$, and so on.
The sequence is periodic. You can find the sum of the values in one period and use this to find the sum of the first 400 terms.

E/P **5** A sequence is defined for $n \geqslant 1$ by the recurrence relation $u_{n+1} = pu_n + q, u_1 = 4$ where p and q are constants. Given that $u_2 = 3$ and $u_3 = 1$, find the values of p and q. **(4 marks)**

E/P **6** A sequence is given by $u_1 = 5, u_{n+1} = ku_n - 8$, where k is an integer.

a Show that $u_3 = 5k^2 - 8k - 8$. **(2 marks)**

b Given that $u_3 = 40$, find the value of k. **(3 marks)**

c Hence find the value of u_5. **(2 marks)**

(E/P) **7** A sequence has nth term $u_n = \sin(90n°)$, $n \geqslant 1$.

a Find the order of the sequence. **(1 mark)**

b Find $\sum_{r=1}^{200} u_r$. **(2 marks)**

(E/P) **8** A sequence of numbers $a_1, a_2, a_3, \ldots$ is defined by $a_1 = k$, $a_{n+1} = 5a_n + 4$, $n \in \mathbb{N}$.

a Find a_3 in terms of k. **(2 marks)**

b Show that $\sum_{r=1}^{4} a_r$ is a multiple of 4. **(3 marks)**

(E/P) **9** A sequence of numbers $a_1, a_2, a_3, \ldots$ is defined by $a_1 = 3$, $a_{n+1} = 1 - \frac{1}{a_n - 2}$, $n \in \mathbb{N}$.

a Find $\sum_{r=1}^{50} a_r$. **(3 marks)**

b Hence find $\sum_{r=1}^{50} a_r + \sum_{r=1}^{49} a_r$ **(1 mark)**

3.8 Modelling with series

1 Matt is training to compete in a marathon. He starts with a 6 km run one Sunday.

He then increases his run by 2 km each following Sunday.

> **Hint** Real-life situations can be modelled with series. Any situation where a sequence of values increases or decreases by a constant amount can be modelled as an arithmetic sequence.

a Show that on the fifth Sunday of training he runs 14 km.

b Find an expression, in terms of n, for the length of his run on the nth Sunday.

A marathon is 42 km.

c After how many weeks will Matt be running the length of a full marathon?

Matt trains for a total of 20 weeks.

d How many kilometres will he have run in total in his entire training period?

2 At the end of year 1, the adult population of a town is 28 000.

A model predicts that the adult population will increase by 2.5% each year.

a Show that the predicted adult population at the end of year 2 is 28 700.

> **Hint** Any real-life situation where a sequence of values increases or decreases in the same ratio can be modelled as a geometric sequence.
>
> Numerical answers must be given to an appropriate degree of accuracy.
>
> Answers to questions about modelling situations must be given in the context of the question.

b Write down an expression for the predicted population at the end of year n.

c Find the predicted population at the end of year 10.

d Give one criticism of this model.

(E/P) **3** A girl saves money over a period of 52 weeks. She saves 10p in week 1, 15p in week 2, 20p in week 3 and so on until week 52. Her savings can be modelled as an arithmetic sequence.

a Find the amount she saves in week 52. **(3 marks)**

b Calculate her total savings over the 52-week period. **(3 marks)**

(E/P) **4** Emma wants to take out a £6000 loan. She wants to make 24 monthly repayments on the loan.

She finds these two options.

Option 1: Payments increase by a fixed amount each month. First payment is £120 and final payment is £396.

Option 2: First payment of £110. Payments increase by 7% each month.

Identify the cheapest loan option for Emma and work out the difference in the amount of interest charged. **(8 marks)**

(E/P) **5** A car was purchased for £15 000 on 1st January. On 1st January each following year, the value of the car is 75% of its value on 1st January in the previous year.

a Show that the value of the car exactly 3 years after it was purchased is £6328 to the nearest pound. **(1 mark)**

b Find the number of years it takes after purchase for the value of the car to fall below £1000. **(3 marks)**

(E/P) **6** The cost of home insurance with an insurance company for the first year is £250.

Every year the cost increases by 5%.

a Find the cost of home insurance for the fourth year, giving your answer to the nearest penny. **(2 marks)**

b Find the total cost of home insurance for the first 10 years. **(3 marks)**

The insurance company offers a discount on home insurance to customers who also purchase car insurance.

10% discount in annual payment up to a maximum of £35

c Find the total cost for home insurance for the first 10 years with this discount. Give your answer to the nearest pound. **(4 marks)**

(E/P) **7** A ball is dropped from a height of 2 metres. After each bounce, the ball reaches a height which is $\frac{3}{4}$ of its previous height. The successive heights of the ball can be modelled as a geometric series.

a After how many bounces does the ball first bounce to a height which is less than 10 cm? **(7 marks)**

b How far has the ball travelled in total when it hits the ground for the 10th time? **(4 marks)**

c Give one criticism of this model for large numbers of bounces. **(1 mark)**

Problem solving Set A

Bronze

An arithmetic sequence has 16th term 25, and 25th term 47.5.

a Find the first term of the sequence. **(3 marks)**

The sum of the first n terms of the sequence is 712.5.

b Find the value of n. **(4 marks)**

Silver

An arithmetic series is defined as $p + 2p + 3p + ... + 200$ where p is a constant.

Given that the sum of this series is 1700, find the value of p. **(5 marks)**

Gold

An arithmetic sequence has first three terms $3k + 2$, $5k + 7$ and $7k + 12$, where k is a constant.

Given that the 60th term of the sequence is positive, find the range of possible values for k.

(5 marks)

Problem solving Set B

Bronze

Find $\sum_{r=8}^{\infty} 3 \times \left(\frac{1}{2}\right)^r$, giving your answer as a fraction in simplest form. **(5 marks)**

Silver

Given that $\sum_{r=8}^{k} (2r - 5) = 299$, where k is a positive constant, find the value of k. **(6 marks)**

Gold

Given that $\sum_{r=1}^{16} (3r + 2^r + k) = 131\,550$, where k is a constant, find the value of k. **(6 marks)**

Now try this → Exam question bank Q24, Q27, Q61, Q64, Q68, Q73, Q76, Q80

4.1 Expanding $(1 + x)^n$

1 Find the binomial expansion up to and including the term in x^3 of:

a $\frac{1}{(1+x)^2}$ b $(1+x)^{\frac{1}{2}}$ c $(1+x)^{\frac{4}{3}}$

d $(1+x)^{-\frac{1}{3}}$ e $(1+x)^{-5}$ f $(1+x)^{-\frac{5}{2}}$

Hint $(1+x)^n = 1 + nx + \frac{n(n-1)}{2!}x^2 + \frac{n(n-1)(n-2)}{3!}x^3 + \ldots + \left(\frac{n(n-1)\ldots(n-r+1)}{r!}\right)x^r + \ldots$

This expansion is valid when $|x| < 1$, $n \in \mathbb{R}$.

2 For each expression:

i find the binomial expansion up to and including the term in x^3

ii state the range of values of x for which the expansion is valid.

a $\frac{1}{(1+2x)^3}$ b $\sqrt{1-x}$ c $\left(1+\frac{x}{2}\right)^{\frac{2}{3}}$

d $(1-5x)^{-4}$ e $\frac{1}{\sqrt[3]{1-2x}}$ f $\left(1-\frac{x}{3}\right)^{-2}$

Hint Replace x with (bx) in the binomial expansion formula. Remember that $(bx)^n = b^n x^n$.

The expansion of $(1 + bx)^n$ is valid for $|bx| < 1$, or $|x| < \frac{1}{|b|}$

3 a Find the first four terms, in ascending powers of x, in the binomial expansion of $\sqrt{1-4x}$.

b By substituting $x = 0.01$ in your expansion, find a decimal approximation for $\sqrt{6}$.

c State why the approximation is valid for $x = 0.01$.

Hint When $x = 0.01$, $\sqrt{1-4x} = \sqrt{0.96} = \sqrt{6 \times \frac{16}{100}} = \frac{2}{5}\sqrt{6}$

4 $f(x) = \frac{4+x}{\sqrt{1+3x}}$

Hint Write $f(x)$ as $(4+x)(1+3x)^{-\frac{1}{2}}$

a Find the first three terms, in ascending powers of x, of the binomial expansion of $f(x)$. Give each term in its simplest form.

b State the range of values of x for which the expansion is valid.

(E/P) 5 Given that the binomial expansion of $(1 + kx)^{-5}$, $|kx| < 1$, is $1 - 8x + Ax^2 + \ldots$

a find the value of the constant k **(2 marks)**

b find the value of the constant A, giving your answer as a fraction in its simplest form. **(3 marks)**

(E/P) 6 $f(x) = \frac{1-x}{1+3x}$

a Show that the series expansion of $f(x)$ up to and including the term in x^3 is $1 - 4x + 12x^2 - 36x^3$ **(4 marks)**

b State the range of values of x for which the expansion is valid. **(1 mark)**

E/P 7 $g(x) = \frac{5}{1+4x} - \frac{3}{1-2x}$

a Find the series expansion of $g(x)$ in ascending powers of x, up to and including the term in x^2. Simplify each term. **(6 marks)**

b State the range of values of x for which the expansion of $g(x)$ is valid. **(1 mark)**

c Find the percentage error made in using your expansion in part **a** to estimate the value of $g(0.01)$. Give your answer to 2 significant figures. **(3 marks)**

E/P 8 a Find the binomial expansion of $\sqrt{1-6x}$, $|x| < \frac{1}{6}$, in ascending powers of x up to and including the term in x^3, simplifying each term. **(4 marks)**

b By substituting $x = \frac{1}{300}$, find a decimal approximation for $\sqrt{2}$. Give your answer to 5 decimal places. **(5 marks)**

E/P 9 a Use the binomial expansion to show that $\sqrt{\frac{1-5x}{1+x}} \approx 1 - 3x - \frac{3x^2}{2}$, $|x| < 1$. **(6 marks)**

b Substitute $x = \frac{1}{8}$ into $\sqrt{\frac{1-5x}{1+x}} \approx 1 - 3x - \frac{3x^2}{2}$ to obtain an approximation for $\sqrt{3}$.

Give your answer in the form $\frac{a}{b}$ where a and b are integers. **(3 marks)**

4.2 Expanding $(a + bx)^n$

1 For each expression:

i find the binomial expansion up to and including the term in x^3

ii state the range of values of x for which the expansion is valid.

a $\frac{1}{(2+3x)^2}$ b $\sqrt{4-x}$ c $(8+2x)^{\frac{2}{3}}$

Hint To expand $(a + bx)^n$ where a and b are constants, first take out a factor of a^n.

$(a+bx)^n = \left(a\left(1+\frac{b}{a}x\right)\right)^n = a^n\left(1+\frac{b}{a}x\right)^n$

The expansion of $(a + bx)^n$ is valid for $\left|\frac{b}{a}x\right| < 1$ or $|x| < \left|\frac{a}{b}\right|$.

2 For each expression:

i find the binomial expansion up to and including the term in x^3

ii state the range of values of x for which the expansion is valid.

a $\frac{3}{5-2x}$ b $\frac{1-x}{(2-x)^2}$ c $\sqrt{\frac{4+x}{1-x}}$

Hint $\sqrt{\frac{4+x}{1-x}} = (4+x)^{\frac{1}{2}}(1-x)^{-\frac{1}{2}}$

$= 2\left(1+\frac{x}{4}\right)^{\frac{1}{2}}(1-x)^{-\frac{1}{2}}$

E/P 3 Given $f(x) = (5-3x)^{-3}$,

a find the binomial expansion of $f(x)$, in ascending powers of x, up to and including the term in x^3. Give each coefficient as a simplified fraction. **(5 marks)**

b State the range of values of x for which the expansion is valid. **(1 mark)**

E/P **4** **a** Find the first three terms in the binomial expansion of $\frac{1}{\sqrt{6+2x}}$, $|x| < 3$.
Give each coefficient in simplified surd form. **(5 marks)**

b Hence or otherwise, find the first three terms in ascending powers of x, of the expansion of $\frac{3x-1}{\sqrt{6+2x}}$ **(4 marks)**

E/P **5** The first three terms in the binomial expansion of $\frac{1}{\sqrt{a+bx}}$ are $\frac{1}{3} - \frac{2x}{27} + \frac{2x^2}{81}$

a Find the values of the constants a and b. **(6 marks)**

b State the range of values of x for which the expansion is valid. **(1 mark)**

c Find the coefficient of the term in x^3 in its simplest form. **(2 marks)**

E/P **6** **a** Use the binomial expansion to expand $(8-5x)^{\frac{1}{3}}$, $|x| < \frac{8}{5}$, in ascending powers of x, up to and including the term in x^2, giving each term as a simplified fraction. **(5 marks)**

b Use your expansion, with a suitable value of x, to obtain an approximation for $\sqrt[3]{7}$.
Give your answer to 3 decimal places. **(2 marks)**

E/P **7** $g(x) = \frac{4}{2-4x} - \frac{2}{3-5x}$

a Find the series expansion of $g(x)$ in ascending powers of x, up to and including the term in x^2.
Simplify each term. **(6 marks)**

b State the range of values of x for which the expansion of $g(x)$ is valid. **(1 mark)**

c Find the exact value of $g(0.01)$. Round your answer to 7 decimal places. **(2 marks)**

d Find the percentage error made in using your expansion from part **a** to estimate the value of $g(0.01)$. Give your answer to 2 significant figures. **(3 marks)**

E/P **8** **a** Use the binomial expansion to expand $\sqrt[3]{\frac{1+x}{8-3x}}$ in ascending powers of x, up to and including the term in x^2, giving each term as a simplified fraction. **(8 marks)**

b State the range of values of x for which the expansion is valid. **(1 mark)**

c By substituting $x = 0.1$ into your expansion, find an approximation for $\sqrt[3]{7}$, giving your answer to 5 decimal places. **(3 marks)**

4.3 Using partial fractions

1 **a** Express $\frac{4x+1}{(1+x)(2-x)}$ as partial fractions.

b Hence, or otherwise, expand $\frac{4x+1}{(1+x)(2-x)}$ in ascending powers of x, up to and including the term in x^2.

c State the range of values of x for which the expansion is valid.

Hint Partial fractions can be used to simplify more complicated algebraic fractions and make them easier to expand using the binomial expansion. ← Section 1.3

Hint Choose a range of values for x that is valid for all the binomial expansions that you use.

2 a Express $\frac{3x}{(3+x)^2}$ as partial fractions.

b Use the binomial expansion to show that $\frac{3x}{(3+x)^2} \approx \frac{1}{3}x + Bx^2 + Cx^3$, where B and C are constants to be determined.

c State the range of values of x for which the expansion is valid.

Hint As $(3 + x)$ is a repeated linear factor, use two partial fractions with denominators $(3 + x)$ and $(3 + x)^2$ respectively. ← Section 1.4

3 a Express $\frac{2x^2+5x-8}{(x-5)(x+4)}$ using partial fractions.

b Hence, or otherwise, expand $\frac{2x^2+5x-8}{(x-5)(x+4)}$ in ascending powers of x, up to and including the term in x^2.

c State the range of values for x for which the expansion is valid.

Hint As the degree of the numerator is the same as the degree of the denominator, first divide the numerator by the denominator. ← Section 1.5

E/P 4 a Express $f(x) = \frac{8x-1}{(1-2x)(1+4x)}$ as partial fractions. **(3 marks)**

b Hence, or otherwise, expand $\frac{8x-1}{(1-2x)(1+4x)}$ in ascending powers of x, up to and including the term in x^2. **(6 marks)**

c State the range of values for x for which the expansion is valid. **(1 mark)**

E/P 5 $\frac{10x+4}{(1+2x)^2} \equiv \frac{A}{1+2x} + \frac{B}{(1+2x)^2}$, $|x| < \frac{1}{2}$, where A and B are constants.

a Find the values of A and B. **(3 marks)**

b Hence, or otherwise, find the first three terms in the expansion of $\frac{10x+4}{(1+2x)^2}$ **(6 marks)**

E/P 6 $\frac{3x^2+5x-7}{(x+4)(x-3)} \equiv A + \frac{B}{x+4} + \frac{C}{x-3}$, where A, B and C are constants.

a Find the values of A, B and C. **(4 marks)**

b Hence, or otherwise, find the first three terms in the expansion of $\frac{3x^2+5x-7}{(x+4)(x-3)}$ **(6 marks)**

c State the range of values for x for which the expansion is valid. **(1 mark)**

E/P 7 $f(x) = \frac{2x^2+5x+12}{(3x-1)^2(x-2)} \equiv \frac{A}{3x-1} + \frac{B}{(3x-1)^2} + \frac{C}{x-2}$

a Find the values of A, B and C. **(4 marks)**

b Hence, or otherwise, find the series expansion of $f(x)$, in ascending powers of x, up to and including the term in x^2. Simplify each term. **(6 marks)**

c Explain why the expansion is not valid for $x = 0.5$. **(1 mark)**

Problem solving Set A

Bronze

The binomial expansion of $(1 + 10x)^{\frac{1}{2}}$ in ascending powers of x, up to and including the term in x^3, is $1 + 5x + px^2 + qx^3$, $|10x| < 1$.

a Find the value of p and the value of q. **(4 marks)**

b Use this expansion with your values of p and q together with an appropriate value of x to obtain an estimate of $(1.5)^{\frac{1}{2}}$. **(3 marks)**

c Find the percentage error made in using your expansion to estimate the value of $(1.5)^{\frac{1}{2}}$. Give your answer to 2 significant figures. **(3 marks)**

Silver

a Find the binomial expansion of $\sqrt{1 - 6x}$ in ascending powers of x, up to and including the term in x^3, simplifying each term. **(4 marks)**

b Substitute $x = \frac{1}{9}$ into the binomial expansion to find an approximation for $\sqrt{3}$. Give your answer as a fraction in its simplest form. **(5 marks)**

c Explain why the expansion is valid for this value of x. **(1 mark)**

Gold

a Use binomial expansions to show that $\sqrt{\frac{1 + 3x}{1 - x}} \approx 1 + 2x + 2x^3$. **(6 marks)**

A student attempts to use this expansion to find an approximation for $\sqrt{5}$. The first few steps of the student's working are shown below.

$$\frac{1 + 3x}{1 - x} = 5$$
$$1 + 3x = 5 - 5x$$
$$x = \frac{1}{2}$$
Substitute $x = \frac{1}{2}$ into expansion

b Explain the error in the student's working. **(2 marks)**

c By substituting a suitable value of x into the approximation, obtain an approximation for $\sqrt{5}$, giving your answer to 5 decimal places. You must state the value of x you chose and justify your choice. **(1 mark)**

Problem solving Set B

Bronze

a Use the binomial expansion to show that $\frac{1}{2-3x} \approx \frac{1}{2} + \frac{3x}{4} + \frac{9x^2}{8}$ and state the range of values of x for which the expansion is valid. **(5 marks)**

b Obtain the binomial expansion of $\frac{1}{(1-x)^2}$ up to and including the term in x^2. **(2 marks)**

c Given that $\frac{3x^2-4}{(2-3x)(1-x)^2}$ can be written in the form $\frac{A}{(2-3x)} + \frac{B}{(1-x)} + \frac{C}{(1-x)^2}$, find the values of the constants A, B and C. **(5 marks)**

d Hence find the binomial expansion of $\frac{3x^2-4}{(2-3x)(1-x)^2}$ up to and including the term in x^2. **(3 marks)**

e State the range of values of x for which this expansion is valid. **(1 mark)**

Silver

a Express $f(x) = \frac{8x^2+12x+4}{x^2+x-6}$ using partial fractions. **(5 marks)**

b Hence, or otherwise, find the series expansion of $f(x)$ in ascending powers of x, up to and including the term in x^2. Simplify each term. **(5 marks)**

c State the range of values of x for which the expansion is valid. **(1 mark)**

Gold

By considering the series expansion of $\frac{1}{2x^2+5x+3}$, or otherwise, use binomial expansions to show that $\frac{\sqrt{1+3x}}{2x^2+5x+3} \approx \frac{1}{3} - \frac{x}{18} - \frac{109x^2}{216}$ **(10 marks)**

Now try this → Exam question bank Q14, Q33, Q51, Q57, Q60, Q70, Q81

5.1 Radian measure

1 Convert these angles from radians to degrees, giving your answers to 1 decimal place, where appropriate.

Hint To convert radians to degrees multiply by $\frac{180}{\pi}$

a $\frac{5\pi}{6}$ b $\frac{\pi}{8}$ c 4π d 0.34 rad e $\sqrt{2}$ rad f 1.9 rad

2 a Convert the following angles to radians, giving your answers as multiples of π.

i 18° ii 32.5° iii 320°

Hint To convert degrees to radians multiply by $\frac{\pi}{180}$

b Convert the following angles to radians, giving your answers to 3 significant figures.

i 16° ii 124° iii 260°

3 Sketch the following graphs, marking any points where the graphs intersect with the coordinate axes.

a $y = \tan 2x$ for $0 \leqslant x \leqslant \pi$

b $y = \cos(x + \pi)$ for $0 \leqslant x \leqslant 2\pi$

c $y = \sin\left(\frac{1}{2}x\right) + 1$ for $-\pi \leqslant x \leqslant \pi$

Hint Take note of the domain given for each graph. When the domain includes values in terms of π, you must sketch the graph in radians.

4 Without using a calculator find the exact values of these trigonometric ratios.

a $\cos\left(\frac{9\pi}{3}\right)$ b $\tan\left(-\frac{3\pi}{4}\right)$ c $\sin\left(-\frac{11\pi}{6}\right)$

Hint Start by expressing each part in terms of trigonometric ratios of values between 0 and π.

E/P 5 Sketch the following graphs on separate sets of axes, marking any points where the graph intersects with the coordinate axes.

a $y = 2\cos 2x$ for $-2\pi \leqslant x \leqslant 0$ **(3 marks)**

b $y = \sin\left(x - \frac{\pi}{4}\right)$ for $-\pi \leqslant x \leqslant \pi$ **(3 marks)**

E 6 In the triangle PQR, $PQ = 12$ cm, $QR = 8$ cm and $RP = 9$ cm.

a Find the size of angle QRP, giving your answer in radians to 3 significant figures. **(3 marks)**

b Find the area of triangle PQR, giving your answer in cm^2 to 3 significant figures. **(3 marks)**

E/P 7 The diagram shows the curve with equation

$y = \sin\left(x + \frac{5\pi}{6}\right)$, $0 \leqslant x \leqslant 4\pi$

Write down the exact coordinates of the points where the curve intersects with:

a the x-axis **(3 marks)**

b the y-axis. **(1 mark)**

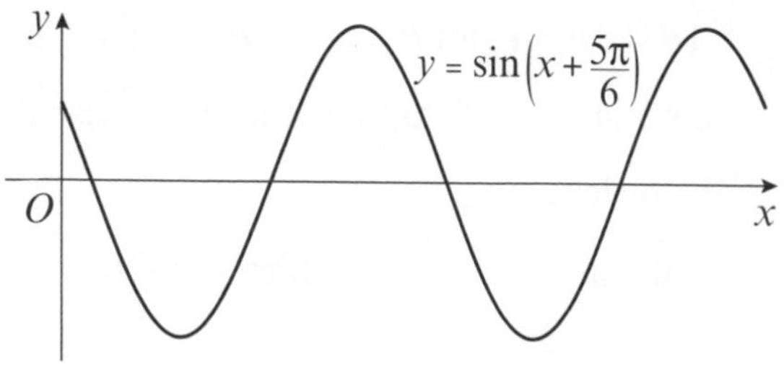

E/P **8** The diagram shows three ships A, B and C. The ships are in the same horizontal plane.

Ship B is 600 m due north of ship A.

Ship C is 800 m from ship A on a bearing of $\frac{\pi}{9}$ radians.

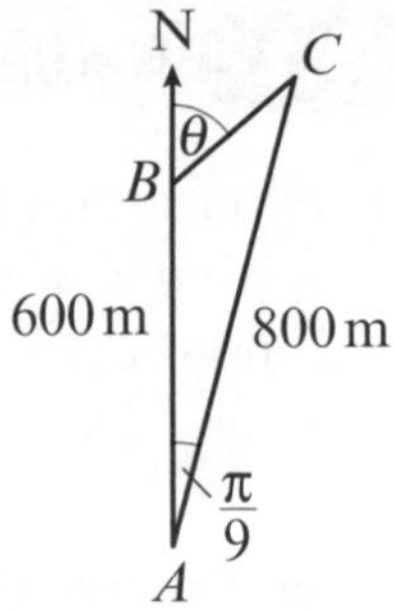

a Find the distance between ship B and ship C in metres to 3 significant figures. **(3 marks)**

b The bearing of ship C from ship B is θ. Find the value of θ in degrees to 3 significant figures. **(3 marks)**

5.2 Arc length

1 An arc AB of a circle, with centre O and radius r cm, subtends an angle θ radians at O. Giving exact values where possible, find the length of AB, l cm, when:

a $r = 18$, $\theta = 2.5$ rad **b** $r = 6.5$, $\theta = \frac{2\pi}{3}$

c $r = 2.3$, $\theta = 0.35$ rad

Hint Use $l = r\theta$ to find the arc length.

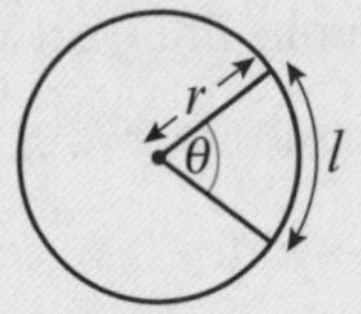

2 An arc AB of a circle, with centre O and radius r cm, subtends an angle θ radians at O. The length of AB is l cm.

Hint Make sure your calculator is in radians mode when using the formula for arc length.

Giving your answers to 3 significant figures, find the radius, r cm, when:

a $l = 5\sqrt{3}$, $\theta = \frac{\pi}{6}$ **b** $l = 20$, $\theta = 1.8$ rad **c** $l = 9.25$, $\theta = 0.45$ rad

3 An arc AB of a circle, with centre O and radius r cm, subtends an angle θ radians at O. The length of AB is l cm.

Giving your answers to 3 significant figures, find the angle, θ radians, when:

a $l = 12.1$, $r = 3.4$ **b** $l = 7.235$, $r = 0.92$ **c** $l = \sqrt{5}$, $r = \sqrt{2}$

E/P **4** The shape $ABCD$ consists of a triangle ABC joined to a sector ACD of a circle with radius r cm and centre A. The lines $AB = 8.6$ cm and $BC = 7.3$ cm, and angle $DAC = 1.52$ radians.

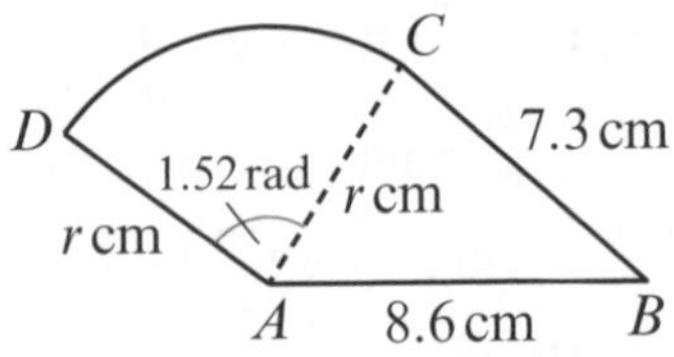

Given that the length of the arc DC is 6.08 cm, find:

a the length r **(2 marks)**

b the perimeter of the shape $ABCD$. **(2 marks)**

(E/P) **5** The shape $ABCDEA$ consists of a right-angled triangle BCD joined to a sector $ABDEA$ of a circle with radius 8 cm and centre B.

The points A, B and C lie on a straight line with $AB = 8$ cm and the size of the angle ABD is $\frac{7\pi}{9}$ radians.

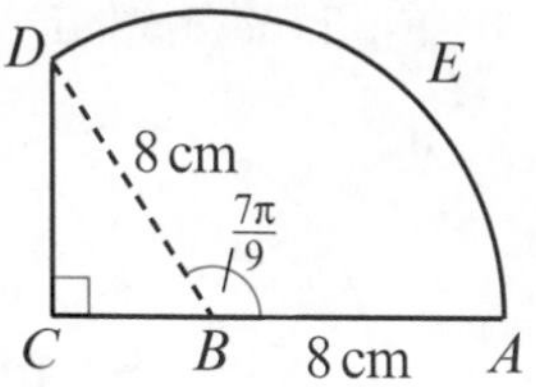

a Calculate the exact length of the arc DEA, giving your answer as a multiple of π. **(2 marks)**

b Calculate the perimeter of the shape $ABCDEA$ to 3 significant figures. **(4 marks)**

(E/P) **6** The shape comprises a triangle XYZ, with $XY = 6$ cm and $ZX = 4$ cm, and part of a circle. The circular arc ZW is a major arc of the circle with centre X and radius 4 cm. The point W lies on the line XY and the angle $ZXW = \alpha$ radians.

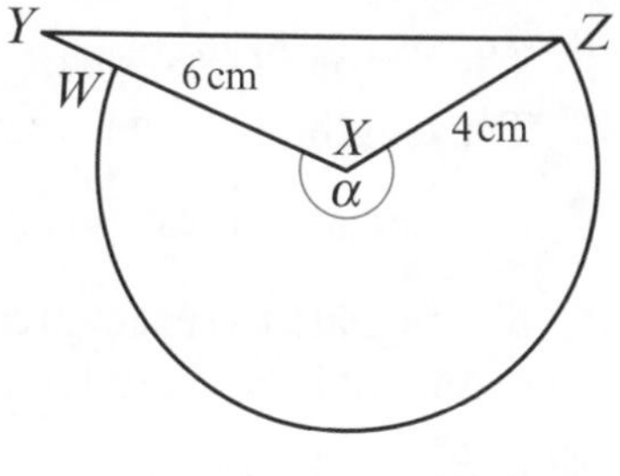

Given that the exact length of arc ZW is $\frac{40\pi}{9}$ cm, find:

a the exact value of α in radians **(2 marks)**

b the area of triangle XYZ, giving your answer to 1 decimal place. **(3 marks)**

(E/P) **7** A circular cake is cut into 12 exactly equal slices, so that the horizontal cross-section of each slice is a sector of a circle.

Given that the arc length of the cross section of each slice is $\frac{5\pi}{3}$ cm, find:

a the diameter of the cake **(2 marks)**

b the exact angle, in radians, between the two straight edges of each slice. **(1 mark)**

5.3 Areas of sectors and segments

1 a Find the area of the sector of a circle of radius 5 cm, given that the sector subtends an angle of 0.45 radians at the centre of the circle.

b Find the area of the sector of a circle of radius 7.3 cm, given that the sector subtends an angle of 1.2 radians at the centre of the circle.

c Find the radius, r cm, of a circle, given that a sector of the circle has an area of $\frac{9\pi}{8}$ cm^2 and the sector subtends an angle of $\frac{\pi}{4}$ radians at the centre of the circle.

d Find the angle, θ radians, subtended by a sector at the centre of a circle, given that the circle has radius 7.2 cm and the sector has an area of 33.696 cm^2.

Hint Draw a diagram of each sector with the given information.

Use $A = \frac{1}{2}r^2\theta$ to find sector area.

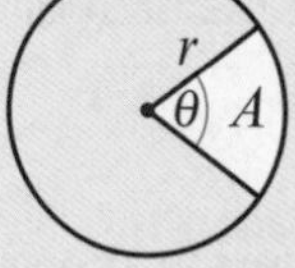

2 Find the area of the shaded segment in each of these sectors.

a

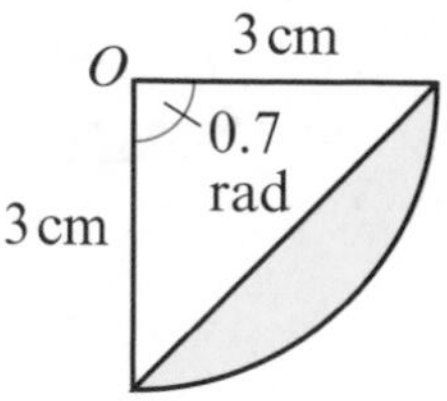

b

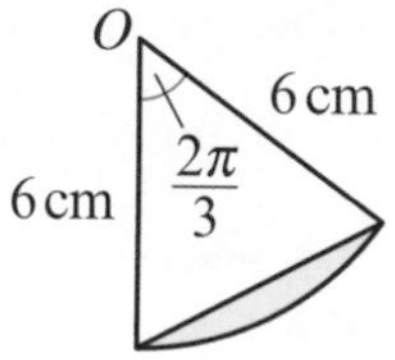

c

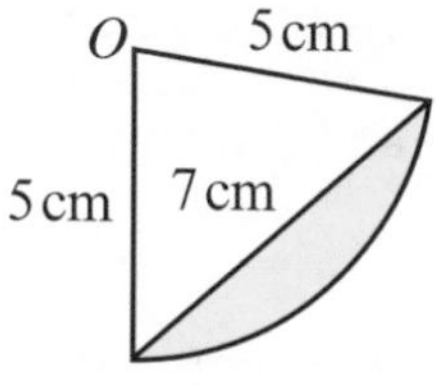

Hint Use the formula $A = \frac{1}{2}r^2(\theta - \sin\theta)$

In part **c** you need to find θ first. You can do this by using the cosine rule.

3 Find the shaded area in each of these circles with centre C.

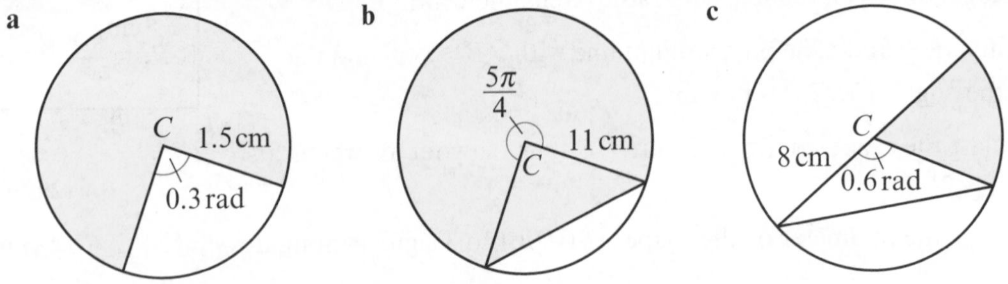

(E) 4 The sector $PQRS$ is part of a circle with centre Q and radius 5 m. The length of the line segment PR is $5\sqrt{3}$ m.

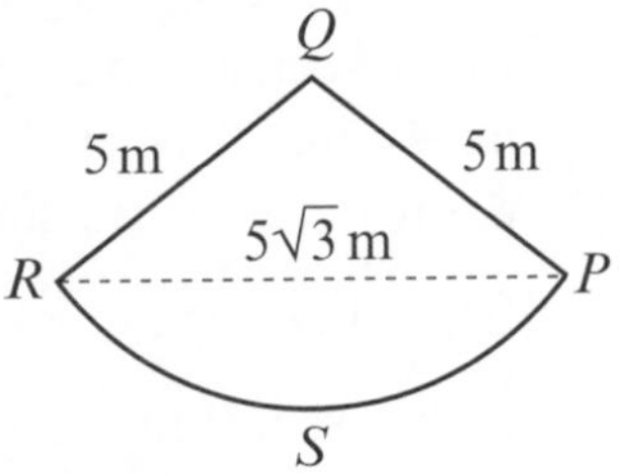

a Calculate the exact size of angle PQR in radians. **(3 marks)**

b Calculate the exact area of the sector, giving your answer as a multiple of π. **(3 marks)**

c Calculate the area of the segment PRS, giving your answer to 3 significant figures. **(3 marks)**

(E/P) 5 The shape consists of a triangle ABE joined to a sector $BCDE$ of a circle with radius 8 cm and centre B. The points A, B and C lie on a straight line with $AB = 19$ cm and $BC = 8$ cm.

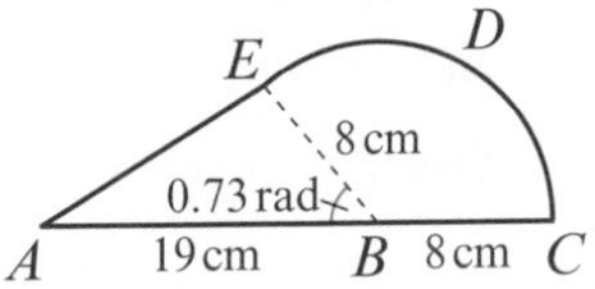

Given that the size of angle ABE is exactly 0.73 radians, find, giving your answers to 3 significant figures:

a the area of the shape **(4 marks)**

b the perimeter of the shape. **(5 marks)**

(E/P) 6 The diagram shows the sector OAB of a circle of radius r cm.

The area of the sector is 37.8 cm^2 and angle AOB is 1.2 radians.

a Show that $r = 3\sqrt{7}$ cm. **(3 marks)**

The shaded segment R is enclosed by the arc AB and the straight line AB.

b Find the area of R, giving your answer to 1 decimal place. **(3 marks)**

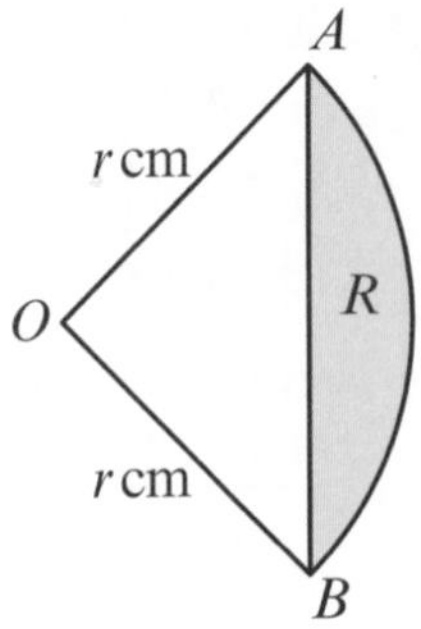

(E/P) 7 The diagram shows a sector AOB of a circle with centre O and radius r cm. The angle AOB is θ radians. The area of the sector AOB is 12 cm^2.

a Given that the perimeter of the sector is 6 times the length of the arc AB, find the exact values of θ and r. **(4 marks)**

The shaded segment T is enclosed by the straight line AB and the arc AB.

b Use your values of θ and r to find the area of T, giving your answer to 3 significant figures. **(3 marks)**

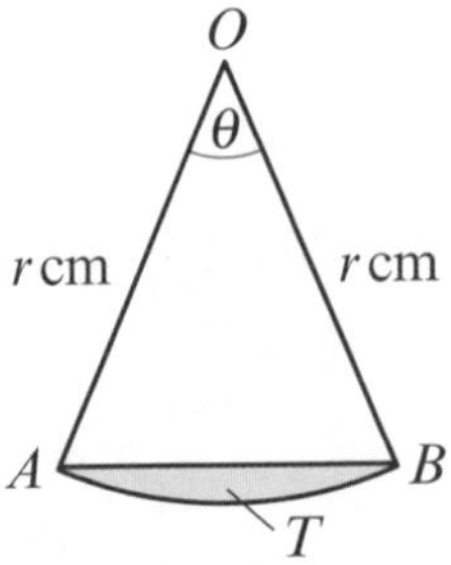

5.4 Solving trigonometric equations

1 Solve these equations for θ in the interval $0 \leqslant \theta \leqslant 2\pi$, giving your answers to 3 significant figures when they are not exact.

Hint Make sure your calculator is in radians mode.

a $\sin\theta = 0.5$ **b** $\tan\theta = -2$

c $5\cos\theta = 3$ **d** $\sqrt{2}\sin\theta + 1 = 2$

Hint For parts **c** and **d**, rewrite the equations in the forms $\cos\theta = \ldots$ and $\sin\theta = \ldots$

2 Solve these equations for θ in the given intervals, giving your answers to 3 significant figures when they are not exact.

Hint Check that your final values are within the given range.

a $2 + 3\sin\theta = 4,\ 0 \leqslant \theta \leqslant \pi$

b $6\cos\theta - 1 = -4,\ -\pi \leqslant \theta \leqslant 2\pi$

c $\sqrt{2}\tan\theta - 7 = -5,\ -2\pi \leqslant \theta \leqslant \pi$

d $\sqrt{2}\cos 2\theta - 0.6 = 0.4,\ \pi \leqslant \theta \leqslant 3\pi$

3 Solve these equations for θ in the interval $0 \leqslant \theta \leqslant 2\pi$, giving your answers to 3 significant figures.

a $\tan^2\theta + 3\tan\theta = -2$

b $3\sin^2\theta - 2\cos\theta + 1 = 0$

c $\cos\left(\theta + \frac{\pi}{4}\right) = 0.5$

d $\sin(2\theta + 0.6) = 1$

Hint For part **a**, use the substitution $u = \tan\theta$ to form a quadratic equation.
For part **b**, you need to use the identity $\sin^2\theta + \cos^2\theta \equiv 1$

(E/P) 4 Find all the values of θ in the interval $0 \leqslant \theta \leqslant 2\pi$ for which:

a $\cos\left(\theta - \frac{\pi}{18}\right) = \cos\left(\frac{\pi}{12}\right)$ **(3 marks)**

b $\tan 2\theta = 0.6$ **(3 marks)**

Give your answers to 3 significant figures where they are not exact.

(E/P) 5 **a** Given that $4\sin x = 3\cos x$, find the value of $\tan x$. **(1 mark)**

b Solve $4\sin 2x = 3\cos 2x$ for $-\pi \leqslant x \leqslant \pi$, giving your answers to 1 decimal place. **(5 marks)**

(E/P) 6 **a** Show that the equation $2\cos^2 x + 3\sin x = 3$ can be written in the form

$2\sin^2 x - 3\sin x + 1 = 0$ **(2 marks)**

b Solve $2\sin^2 x - 3\sin x + 1 = 0$ for $0 \leqslant x \leqslant \pi$, giving your answers exactly. **(4 marks)**

(E/P) 7 **a** Solve $\sin\left(3\theta + \frac{\pi}{4}\right) = -0.2$ in the range $0 \leqslant \theta \leqslant \frac{3\pi}{2}$

Give your answers to 3 significant figures. **(4 marks)**

b Find the exact values of θ in the interval $0 \leqslant \theta \leqslant \pi$ for which $4\cos x = 6\tan x$. **(6 marks)**

5.5 Small angle approximations

1 When θ is small, find the approximate values of:

a $\dfrac{\sin 3\theta}{\theta}$ b $\dfrac{\tan 4\theta}{\sin 2\theta}$ c $\dfrac{5\tan\theta - \theta}{\sin 4\theta}$

Hint When θ is small and measured in radians, $\sin\theta \approx \theta$ and $\tan\theta \approx \theta$.

2 When θ is small, find the approximate values of:

a $\dfrac{1 - \cos 2\theta}{\theta \sin\theta}$ b $\dfrac{\cos 6\theta - 1}{\sin 3\theta \tan\theta}$ c $\dfrac{\theta \tan\theta}{1 - \cos\theta}$

Hint When θ is small and measured in radians, $\cos\theta = 1 - \dfrac{\theta^2}{2}$

3 When θ is small, show that:

a $\dfrac{2\theta - \sin 3\theta}{\theta \tan 4\theta} = -\dfrac{1}{4}\theta$ b $\dfrac{\cos\theta - 1}{\sin\theta} = -\dfrac{1}{2}\theta$

c $\dfrac{\sin\theta + \tan\theta}{1 - \cos 2\theta} = \dfrac{1}{\theta}$

Hint Use the small angle approximations and then simplify.

(E) 4 Given that θ is small and is measured in radians, use the small angle approximations to find an approximate value of

$\dfrac{1 - \cos 2\theta}{3\theta \sin 2\theta}$ **(3 marks)**

(E/P) 5 Given that θ is small, use the small angle approximations for $\sin\theta$, $\cos\theta$ and $\tan\theta$ to show that

$\dfrac{3\tan\theta - 4\cos\theta + 5}{\sin\theta + 1} \approx 2\theta + 1$ **(3 marks)**

(E/P) 6 a Given that θ is small, use the small angle approximation for $\cos\theta$ to show that

$5\cos^2\theta + 6\cos\theta + 1 \approx 12 - 8\theta^2$ **(3 marks)**

Josh tests the approximation in part **a** on his calculator by using $\theta = 10°$, and his working is shown below.

> $5\cos^2 10° + 6\cos 10° + 1 = 11.76$, to 4 significant figures.
>
> The approximation gives $12 - 8(10)^2 = -788$
>
> Therefore, $5\cos^2\theta + 6\cos\theta + 1 \approx 12 - 8\theta^2$ is not true for $\theta = 10°$.

b Is Josh correct? Give full reasons for your answer. **(2 marks)**

Problem solving Set A

Bronze

The diagram shows an equilateral triangle ABC with side length 6 cm. A segment of a circle with centre C is attached to AB, and an identical segment of a circle with centre A is attached to BC.

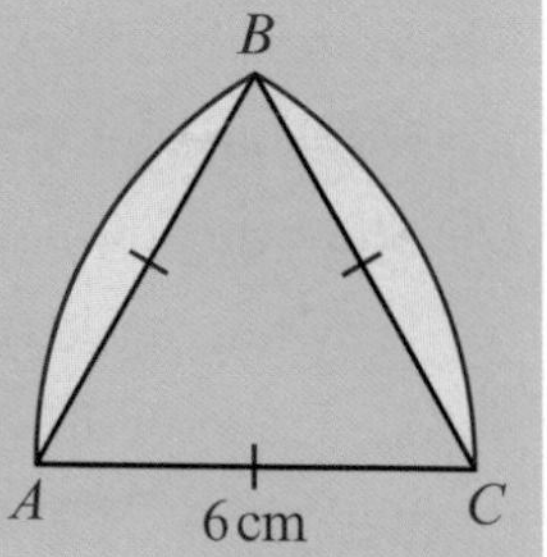

a Write down the exact size of angle CAB in radians. **(1 mark)**

b Find the exact area of triangle ABC. **(2 marks)**

c Find the exact area of the sector with centre A and arc BC, giving your answer as a multiple of π. **(2 marks)**

d Hence show that the shaded area of the shape is $(12\pi - 18\sqrt{3})$ cm^2. **(2 marks)**

Silver

A shape is comprised of a rhombus enclosed by two arcs of circles. Arc BAD has centre C and arc BCD has centre A. Some of the dimensions of the shape are shown in the diagram.

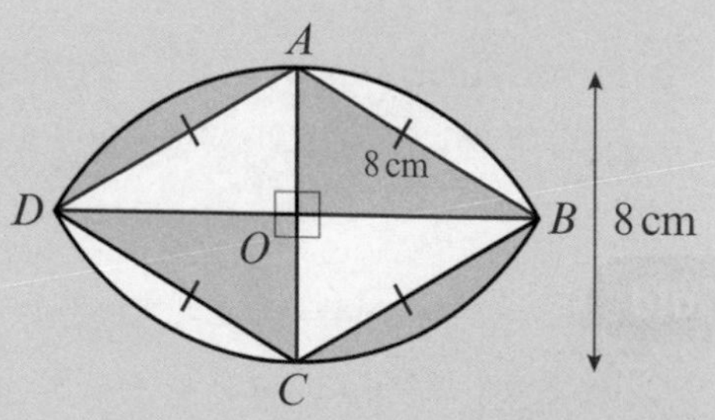

a Find the exact area of the rhombus $ABCD$. **(3 marks)**

b Find the exact area of the sector with centre A and arc BCD, giving your answer as a multiple of π. **(3 marks)**

c Hence show that the shaded area of the shape is $\frac{1}{3}(128\pi - 96\sqrt{3})$ cm^2. **(2 marks)**

Gold

A shape is comprised of a rhombus surrounded by two arcs. Arc BAD has centre C and arc BCD has centre A. Angle DAB is θ radians.

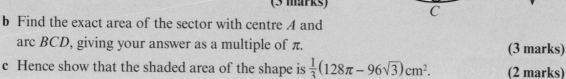

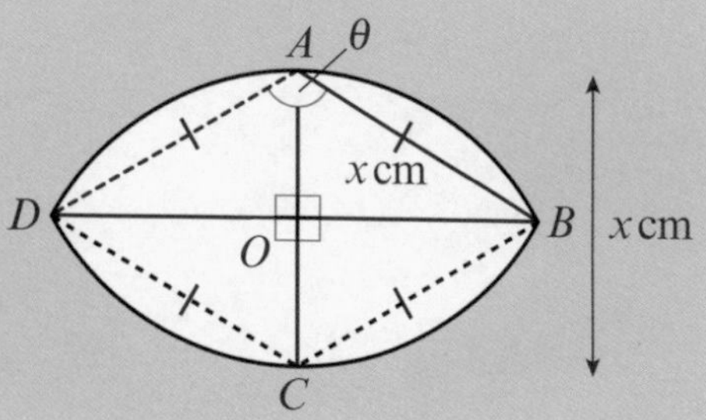

Show that the area of the shape is

$$\left(\theta - \frac{\sqrt{a}}{b}\right)x^2$$

where a and b are integers to be found. **(8 marks)**

Problem solving Set B

Bronze

a Sketch the following graphs on the same set of axes:

i $y = \tan x$ for $0 \leqslant x \leqslant 2\pi$ **ii** $y = \frac{1}{3}$ **iii** $y = -3$ **(3 marks)**

b Show that the equation $3\tan^2 x + 8\tan x - 3 = 0$ can be written as

$(3\tan x - 1)(\tan x + 3) = 0$ **(1 mark)**

c Hence solve the equation $3\tan^2 x + 8\tan x - 3 = 0$ for $0 \leqslant x \leqslant 2\pi$, giving your answers to 3 significant figures. **(3 marks)**

Silver

a Show that $3\cos^2 x = 5(1 - \sin x)$ can be written as

$3\sin^2 x - 5\sin x + 2 = 0$ **(3 marks)**

b Hence solve $3\cos^2 x = 5(1 - \sin x)$ for $-\pi \leqslant x \leqslant \pi$, giving your answers to 3 significant figures where they are not exact. **(4 marks)**

Gold

Solve $\cos x = 3\tan x$ for $0 \leqslant x \leqslant 3\pi$, giving your answers to 3 significant figures. **(8 marks)**

Now try this → Exam question bank Q25, Q30, Q35, Q41, Q44, Q46

6.1 Secant, cosecant and cotangent

1 Without using your calculator, work out the exact values of:

a $\sec 30°$ b $\text{cosec}\frac{5\pi}{4}$ c $\cot\frac{7\pi}{6}$

Hint $\sec x = \frac{1}{\cos x}$, $\text{cosec}\, x = \frac{1}{\sin x}$, $\cot x = \frac{1}{\tan x}$ and $\cot x = \frac{\cos x}{\sin x}$

2 Use your calculator to find the values of the following, giving your answers to 3 significant figures:

a $\cot 3.6$ rad b $\text{cosec}\, 153°$ c $\sec\frac{7\pi}{4}$

Hint Your calculator may not have keys for these functions. For example, for part **a**, find $\tan 3.6$ rad, then find its reciprocal.

3 Find the exact values of:

a $\sec 150°$ b $\cot(-135°)$ c $\text{cosec}\,\frac{3\pi}{2}$

(P) 4 Show that:

a $\frac{\sec 60°}{\text{cosec}\, 270°} = -2$ b $\text{cosec}\frac{3\pi}{4}\cot\frac{\pi}{6} = \sqrt{6}$

(P) 5 Prove that:

a $\sec(-\theta) \equiv \sec\theta$ b $\cot(\theta + \pi) \equiv \cot\theta$

(P) 6 ABC is a right-angled triangle, with angle $ACB = x$, and sides $AC = 5$ cm and $BC = 4$ cm.

Write down the exact value of:

a $\sec x$ b $\text{cosec}\, x$ c $\cot x$

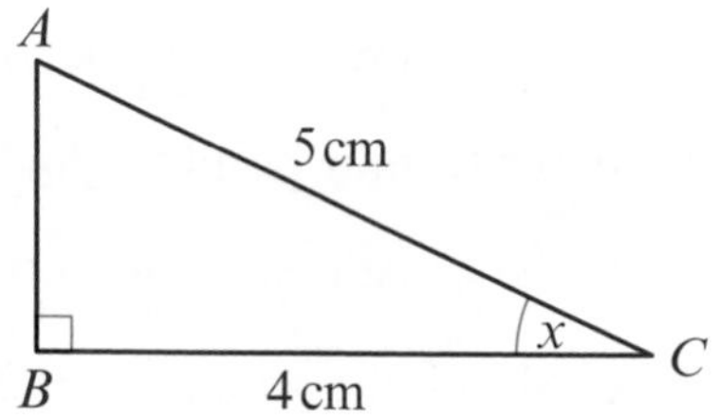

(E/P) 7 Show that $\cot\frac{\pi}{3} - \text{cosec}\frac{\pi}{4} = \frac{\sqrt{a} - a\sqrt{b}}{a}$, where a and b are integers to be found. **(2 marks)**

6.2 Graphs of sec *x*, cosec *x* and cot *x*

1 a i On the same set of axes, sketch the graphs of $y = \sec x$ and $y = 3$ in the interval $0 \leqslant x \leqslant 2\pi$.

ii State the number of solutions to the equation $\sec x - 3 = 0$ for $0 \leqslant x \leqslant 2\pi$.

b i On the same set of axes, sketch the graphs of $y = \text{cosec}\, x$ and $y = -\sin x$ in the interval $-180° \leqslant x \leqslant 180°$

ii Explain how your graphs show that there are no real solutions to $\text{cosec}\, x = -\sin x$.

Hint The number of solutions to the equation is the same as the number of points of intersection of the graphs.

The graph of $y = \sec x$ is undefined for values of x for which $\cos x = 0$. It has vertical asymptotes at these points.

Hint The graph of $y = \text{cosec}\, x$ is undefined for values of x for which $\sin x = 0$, and has vertical asymptotes at these points.

2 **a i** On separate sets of axes, sketch the graphs of $y = \cot x$ and $y = -\tan x$ in the interval $-360° \leqslant x \leqslant 360°$.

Hint The graph of $y = \cot x$, is undefined for values of x for which $\tan x = 0$, and has vertical asymptotes at these points.

ii Hence state a relationship between $\cot x$ and $-\tan x$.

b i On the same set of axes, sketch the graphs of $y = \sec x$ and $y = \operatorname{cosec} x$ in the interval $-\pi \leqslant x \leqslant \frac{3\pi}{2}$

ii Hence state a relationship between $\sec x$ and $\operatorname{cosec} x$.

3 Sketch the following graphs on separate sets of axes in the interval $0 \leqslant x \leqslant 360°$, showing the coordinates of any maximum and minimum points, and any points of intersection with the coordinate axes.

Hint Start by sketching the graph of $\sec x$, $\operatorname{cosec} x$ or $\cot x$, and then apply each stretch or translation to transform the graph.

a $y = 1 + \operatorname{cosec} x$ **b** $y = -\cot \frac{1}{2}x$ **c** $y = 3\sec 2x$

(P) 4 The graph shows the curve $y = \operatorname{cosec}\left(x + \frac{\pi}{4}\right)$ in the interval $0 \leqslant x \leqslant 4\pi$.

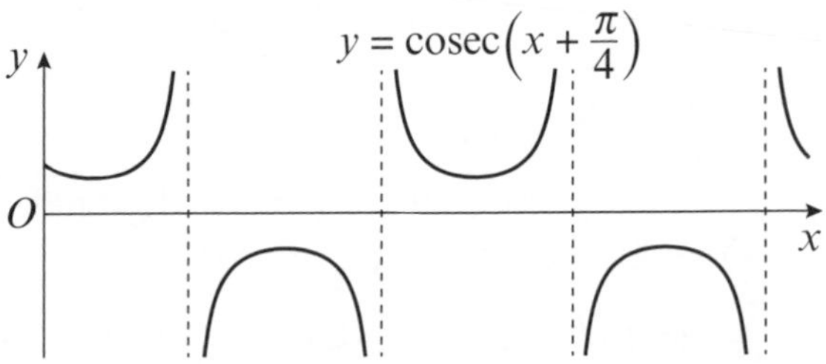

Write down:

a the coordinates of the y-intercept

b the turning points of the curve

c the equations of any vertical asymptotes.

(E/P) 5 **a** Sketch the graph of $y = 2 + 4\sec x$ in the interval $-360° \leqslant x \leqslant 360°$. **(3 marks)**

b Given that the equation $2 + 4\sec x = a$ has no real solutions, find the range of possible values for a. **(1 mark)**

(E/P) 6 The diagram shows a sketch of the curve $y = \mathrm{f}(x)$, where $\mathrm{f}(x) = \cot 3x$, for $0 \leqslant x < 180°$, $x \neq 60°, 120°$.

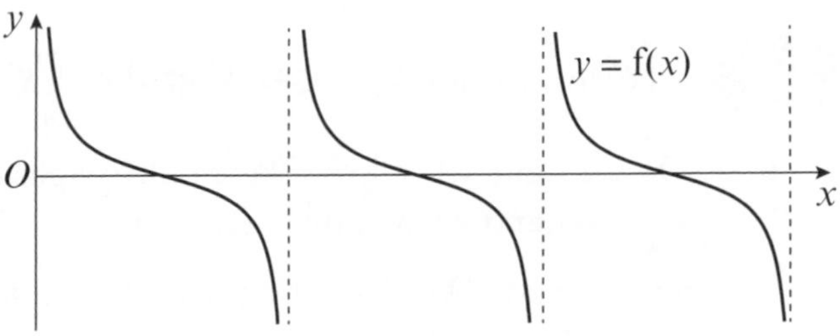

a Write down the number of solutions to the equation $\mathrm{f}(x) = x$. **(1 mark)**

b Write down the solutions to the equation $\mathrm{f}(x) = 0$. **(2 marks)**

(E/P) 7 **a** On the same set of axes, sketch the graphs of $y = 2 + 3\operatorname{cosec} x$ and $y = -x$ in the interval $-\pi \leqslant x \leqslant \pi$. **(3 marks)**

b Write down the number of solutions to the equation $2 + 3\operatorname{cosec} x + x = 0$ in the interval $-\pi \leqslant x \leqslant \pi$. **(1 mark)**

c Deduce the maximum value of $\dfrac{1}{2 + 3\operatorname{cosec} x}$ and give the smallest positive value of x at which this occurs. **(2 marks)**

6.3 Using sec x, cosec x and cot x

1 Write down the value of:

a $\sec x$ given that $\cos x = \frac{1}{4}$

b $\operatorname{cosec} x$ given that $\frac{3}{\sin x} = 5$

c $\cot x$ given that $2\cos x = 3\sin x$

Hint For part **c**, use $\frac{\sin x}{\cos x} = \tan x$

← **Year 1, Section 10.3**

2 Simplify each expression, writing your answer as a single trigonometric function.

a $\cos x \cot x + \sin x$ **b** $\frac{1}{\cos x \tan x}$

c $\cot 3x \sec 3x$

Hint Start by writing $\sec x$, $\operatorname{cosec} x$ or $\cot x$ in terms of $\sin x$, $\cos x$ or $\tan x$ and then simplify.

3 Solve the following equations for values of x in the interval $0 \leqslant x \leqslant 360°$, giving your answers to 3 significant figures where necessary.

a $\operatorname{cosec} x = 2$ **b** $\sqrt{3}\sec x = 4$

c $3\cot x = -2.5$

Hint Write the equivalent equation for $\sin x$, $\cos x$ or $\tan x$, then solve.

(E/P) **4** **a** Prove that $\frac{\cot x + \tan x}{\sec x} \equiv \operatorname{cosec} x$ **(4 marks)**

b Hence solve in the interval $0 \leqslant x \leqslant 360°$, the equation $\frac{\cot x + \tan x}{\sec x} = 4$ **(3 marks)**

(E/P) **5** **a** Prove that $\cos 3\theta + \sin 3\theta \tan 3\theta \equiv \sec 3\theta$ **(4 marks)**

b Explain why the equation $2\cos 3\theta + 2\sin 3\theta \tan 3\theta = -1$ has no solutions. **(2 marks)**

(E/P) **6** Solve $3\sin x = 8\cot x$ in the interval $0 \leqslant x \leqslant 2\pi$. **(4 marks)**

(E/P) **7** **a** Prove that $\frac{\sin x}{1 + \cos x} + \frac{1 + \cos x}{\sin x} \equiv 2\operatorname{cosec} x$ **(4 marks)**

b Hence solve in the interval $0 \leqslant x \leqslant 2\pi$, the equation

$$\frac{\sin\left(x - \frac{\pi}{6}\right)}{1 + \cos\left(x - \frac{\pi}{6}\right)} + \frac{1 + \cos\left(x - \frac{\pi}{6}\right)}{\sin\left(x - \frac{\pi}{6}\right)} = 5$$

(4 marks)

6.4 Trigonometric identities

1 Show that:

a $\operatorname{cosec}^2 x + \tan^2 x \equiv \sec^2 x + \cot^2 x$

b $\cot^2 x + \cos^2 x \equiv (\operatorname{cosec} x - \sin x)(\operatorname{cosec} x + \sin x)$

c $\frac{1}{1 + \sin x} + \frac{1}{1 - \sin x} \equiv 2 + 2\tan^2 x$

Hint Use these identities:

$1 + \tan^2 x \equiv \sec^2 x$

$1 + \cot^2 x \equiv \operatorname{cosec}^2 x$

$\sin^2 x + \cos^2 x \equiv 1$

2 Given that $\sin x = \frac{4}{5}$ and that $90° \leqslant x \leqslant 180°$, find the exact values of:

a $\cos x$ b $\cot x$ c $\operatorname{cosec} x$

Hint The interval $90° \leqslant x \leqslant 180°$ means that x lies in the second quadrant, where $\cos x$ and $\tan x$ are negative.

3 Solve these equations in the given intervals. Give your answers to 3 significant figures when they are not exact.

a $\sec^2 x + \tan x = 1$ for $-\pi \leqslant x \leqslant \pi$

b $3\cot^2 x + 9\operatorname{cosec} x + 1 = 0$ for $0 \leqslant x \leqslant 2\pi$

c $\operatorname{cosec}^2 x + \cot^2 x = 3$ for $0 \leqslant x \leqslant 2\pi$

Hint Use the identities $1 + \tan^2 x \equiv \sec^2 x$ and $1 + \cot^2 x \equiv \operatorname{cosec}^2 x$ to write each equation in terms of one trigonometrical function only, and then factorise and solve.

(E/P) 4 Given that $7\cot^2 x - 5\operatorname{cosec}^2 x = 2$, and that x is obtuse, find the exact value of $\cos x$. **(3 marks)**

(E/P) 5 Solve $\sec^2 x = 5 + 3\tan x$ in the interval $0 \leqslant x \leqslant 360°$, giving your answers to 1 decimal place where necessary. **(4 marks)**

(E/P) 6 Given that $\cot^2 p = -4\operatorname{cosec} p$,

a find the value of $\operatorname{cosec} p$ **(4 marks)**

b show that $\sin p = 2 - \sqrt{5}$. **(2 marks)**

c Hence solve $\cot^2 p = -4\operatorname{cosec} p$ in the interval $0 \leqslant p \leqslant 2\pi$, giving your answers to 1 decimal place. **(3 marks)**

(E/P) 7 Solve $2\operatorname{cosec}^2 x + 5\cot x = 5$ in the interval $-\pi \leqslant x \leqslant \pi$, giving your answers to 2 decimal places. **(4 marks)**

6.5 Inverse trigonometric functions

1 In each of the following cases, sketch $y = f(x)$, showing any points where the curve intersects the coordinate axes, and the domain and range of each function.

a $f(x) = \arcsin x$ b $f(x) = \arccos x$

c $f(x) = \arctan x$

Hint $\arcsin x$, $\arccos x$ and $\arctan x$ are the inverse functions of $\sin x$, $\cos x$ and $\tan x$ respectively. These inverse functions have a restricted domain to ensure they are one-to-one functions.

2 Without using a calculator work out the following, giving your answer in terms of π.

a $\arctan(1)$ b $\arcsin\left(-\frac{\sqrt{3}}{2}\right)$

c $\arccos\left(\frac{1}{2}\right)$

Hint You can work these out without a calculator by considering exact values of sin, cos and tan.

3 Without using a calculator work out the values of:

a $\arcsin\left(\sin\frac{\pi}{2}\right)$

b $\arccos(\cos 3\pi)$

c $\arctan\left(\tan\frac{5\pi}{4}\right)$

Hint Make sure you give your answers in the appropriate ranges for arcsin, arccos and arctan.

E/P **4** **a** Sketch the graph of $y = \frac{\pi}{3} + \arcsin\left(x - \frac{1}{2}\right)$, clearly showing the exact coordinates of the endpoints of the curve. **(4 marks)**

b Find the exact coordinates of the point where the curve crosses the x-axis. **(3 marks)**

E/P **5** Find in terms of π, the value of $\arccos\left(\frac{\sqrt{3}}{2}\right) + \arccos\left(-\frac{1}{2}\right)$ **(2 marks)**

E/P **6** The diagram shows the graph of $y = a\arctan(x + b)$, where a and b are constants to be determined.

a Find a and b. **(3 marks)**

b Find the coordinates of the point where the curve crosses the y-axis, giving your answer to 3 decimal places. **(2 marks)**

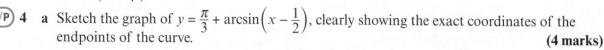

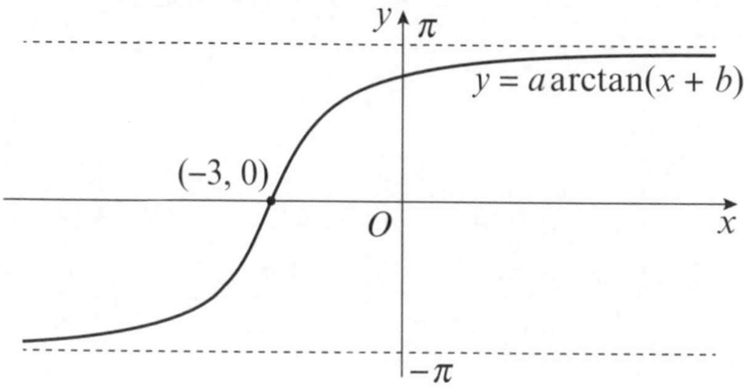

E/P **7** Given that $\arccos(x - 3) = -\frac{\pi}{4}$, find the exact value of x. **(3 marks)**

Problem solving Set A

Bronze

a Given that $\frac{\cos x}{1 - \sin x} + \frac{1 - \sin x}{\cos x} = p$, show that

$$\frac{\cos^2 x + (1 - 2\sin x + \sin^2 x)}{(1 - \sin x)(\cos x)} = p$$ **(2 marks)**

b Hence show that $\sec x = \frac{p}{2}$ **(3 marks)**

Silver

a Given that $\cot^2 x + \operatorname{cosec}^2 x = a$, show that $\operatorname{cosec}^2 x = \frac{a+1}{2}$ **(2 marks)**

b Hence show that $\sec^2 x = \frac{a+1}{a-1}$, $a \neq 1$. **(3 marks)**

Gold

Given that $\frac{1 - \tan^2 x}{1 + \tan^2 x} = z$, show that $\operatorname{cosec}^2 x = \frac{2}{1 - z}$, $z \neq 1$. **(5 marks)**

Problem solving Set B

Bronze

a **i** Sketch the curve $y = \tan 2x$ in the interval $0 \leqslant x \leqslant \pi$, showing the points where the curve crosses the x-axis.

ii Write down the period of $\tan 2x$. **(3 marks)**

b **i** Show that the equation $\cot^2 2x - 4\cot 2x + 4 = 0$ can be written as $(\cot 2x - a)^2 = 0$, where a is a constant to be found.

ii Write down the value of $\tan 2x$, and hence solve the equation $\cot^2 2x - 4\cot 2x = -4$ in the interval $0 \leqslant x \leqslant \pi$, giving your answers to 2 decimal places. **(4 marks)**

Silver

a Given $4\cot^2 2x + 12\operatorname{cosec} 2x + 9 = 0$, show that $\sin 2x = -\frac{2}{5}$ **(4 marks)**

b Hence solve $4\cot^2 2x + 12\operatorname{cosec} 2x + 9 = 0$ in the interval $0 \leqslant x \leqslant 360°$, giving your answers to 1 decimal place. **(3 marks)**

Gold

Solve $5 + 2\cot^2 a = 7(1 + \operatorname{cosec} a)$, where $a = 2x + \frac{\pi}{3}$, in the interval $0 \leqslant x \leqslant 2\pi$.
Give your answers to 2 decimal places. **(7 marks)**

Now try this → Exam question bank Q3, Q6, Q15, Q21, Q42, Q58

7.1 Addition formulae

1 **a** By substituting $x = 90° - A$ and $y = B$ into the expansion of $\sin(x + y)$, show that $\cos(A - B) = \cos A \cos B + \sin A \sin B$

b By substituting $x = A$ and $y = -B$ into the expansion of $\cos(x - y)$, show that $\cos(A + B) = \cos A \cos B - \sin A \sin B$

Hint $\sin(90° - x) = \cos x$ and $\cos(90° - x) = \sin x$
$\cos(-y) = \cos y$ and $\sin(-y) = -\sin y$
← **Year 1, Section 9.6**

2 **a** Write $\sin\left(x - \frac{\pi}{3}\right)$ in the form $a \sin x + b \cos x$, where a and b are constants to be found.

b Write $\cos\left(x - \frac{\pi}{6}\right)$ in the form $p \cos x + q \sin x$, where p and q are constants to be found.

c Write $\tan\left(x + \frac{\pi}{3}\right)$ in the form $\frac{\tan x + m}{1 - m \tan x}$, where m is a constant to be found.

Hint The addition formulae for sin, cos and tan are given in the formulae booklet:
$\sin(A \pm B) = \sin A \cos B \pm \cos A \sin B$
$\cos(A \pm B) = \cos A \cos B \mp \sin A \sin B$
$\tan(A \pm B) = \frac{\tan A \pm \tan B}{1 \mp \tan A \tan B}$

3 Express each of the following as a single trigonometric function:

a $\frac{\tan 7\theta - \tan 3\theta}{1 + \tan 7\theta \tan 3\theta}$

b $\cos\left(\frac{3a + 5b}{3}\right)\cos\left(\frac{3a - 5b}{3}\right) - \sin\left(\frac{3a + 5b}{3}\right)\sin\left(\frac{3a - 5b}{3}\right)$

c $\frac{\sqrt{2}}{2}\sin x - \frac{\sqrt{2}}{2}\cos x$

Hint Match each expansion to the correct addition formula and write the resulting expression as simply as possible.

(E/P) **4** Express $\frac{\cos(x - y)}{\sin(x + y)}$ in terms of $\tan x$ and $\tan y$. **(3 marks)**

(P) **5** Use the addition formulae to write:

a $\frac{1}{2}(\cos x - \sqrt{3}\sin x)$ in the form $\cos(x \pm \theta)$, where $0 < \theta < \frac{\pi}{2}$

b $\frac{1}{2}(\sqrt{3}\sin x - \cos x)$ in the form $\sin(x \pm \theta)$, where $0 < \theta < \frac{\pi}{2}$

(E/P) **6** Given that $\sin\left(x + \frac{\pi}{6}\right) = \cos x$, show that $\tan x = \frac{1}{\sqrt{3}}$ **(3 marks)**

(E/P) **7** Show that $2\sin\left(x + \frac{5\pi}{6}\right) + 2\sin\left(x + \frac{10\pi}{6}\right) = (1 - \sqrt{3})\sin x + (1 - \sqrt{3})\cos x$. **(4 marks)**

7.2 Using the angle addition formulae

1 Without using your calculator find the exact value of:

a $\sin\frac{\pi}{12}\cos\frac{\pi}{4} + \cos\frac{\pi}{12}\sin\frac{\pi}{4}$

b $\cos 96° \cos 51° + \sin 96° \sin 51°$

c $\frac{\tan\frac{\pi}{18} + \tan\frac{\pi}{9}}{1 - \tan\frac{\pi}{18}\tan\frac{\pi}{9}}$

Hint Use the addition formulae in reverse and your knowledge of exact values of trigonometric ratios.

2 **a** Use the formula for $\sin(A+B)$ to show that $\sin 135° = \frac{\sqrt{2}}{2}$

Hint For part **a**, write 135° as 90° + 45°.

b Use the formula for $\cos(A-B)$ to show that $\cos 15° = \frac{\sqrt{6}+\sqrt{2}}{4}$

c Use the formula for $\tan(A+B)$ to show that $\tan 75° = 2+\sqrt{3}$

3 Given that $\cos A = \frac{3}{5}$ and $\sin B = \frac{8}{17}$, where A and B are both acute angles, calculate the exact value of:

Hint You can find the values of $\sin A$ and $\cos B$ using $\sin^2 x + \cos^2 x \equiv 1$.

a $\cos(A+B)$ **b** $\tan(A-B)$

c $\text{cosec}(A+B)$

(P) 4 Given that $\cos A = \frac{1}{2}$, and that A is acute, find the exact value of:

a $\cos\left(\frac{\pi}{6} - A\right)$ **b** $\tan\left(\frac{\pi}{3} + A\right)$ **c** $\sin\left(\frac{\pi}{2} - A\right)$

(P) 5 Given that $\sin A = \frac{24}{25}$, where A is obtuse and $\cos B = -\frac{5}{13}$, where B is reflex, calculate the exact value of:

a $\sin(A+B)$ **b** $\tan(A-B)$ **c** $\sec(A+B)$

(E/P) 6 **a** Express $\tan\left(\frac{\pi}{4} - \frac{\pi}{6}\right)$ in terms of $\tan\frac{\pi}{4}$ and $\tan\frac{\pi}{6}$ **(2 marks)**

b Hence show that $\tan\frac{\pi}{12} = 2 - \sqrt{3}$. **(2 marks)**

(E/P) 7 **a** Use $\sin(x+\alpha) \equiv \sin x \cos\alpha + \cos x \sin\alpha$ to show that $\sin 105° = \frac{\sqrt{6}+\sqrt{2}}{4}$ **(4 marks)**

b Hence, or otherwise, show that $\text{cosec}\,105° = \sqrt{6} - \sqrt{2}$ **(3 marks)**

7.3 Double-angle formulae

1 Write each of the following expressions as a single trigonometric ratio.

Hint $\sin 2A \equiv 2\sin A\cos A$

$\cos 2A \equiv \cos^2 A - \sin^2 A \equiv 2\cos^2 A - 1 \equiv 1 - 2\sin^2 A$

$\tan 2A \equiv \frac{2\tan A}{1-\tan^2 A}$

a $2\sin\frac{\pi}{3}\cos\frac{\pi}{3}$ **b** $4\cos^2 7° - 2$

c $\frac{1-\tan^2 13.5°}{2\tan 13.5°}$

2 Write each of the following in terms of a single trigonometric function.

a $6\sin 5\theta\cos 5\theta$ **b** $\tan\theta(1+\cos 2\theta)$ **c** $\frac{\sin 2\theta}{1-\cos 2\theta}$

3 Given that $\sin A = \frac{5}{13}$, and that A is obtuse, find the exact value of:

a $\tan 2A$ **b** $\cos 2A$

c $\text{cosec}\,2A$

Hint A is in the second quadrant, so only $\sin A$ will be positive.

(P) 4 Eliminate θ from the following pairs of equations and express y in terms of x.

a $x = 5\sin\theta$, $y = 2 - 10\cos 2\theta$

b $x = \cos 2\theta$, $y = 4\sec\theta$

(E/P) 5 a Show that $\cos^4 x - \sin^4 x \equiv \cos 2x$. **(2 marks)**

b Hence find the exact value of $\cos^4 \frac{\pi}{12} - \sin^4 \frac{\pi}{12}$ **(2 marks)**

(E/P) 6 Given that $a = 2\sin x$, $b = 2\cos x$, $c = \cos 2x$ and $d = \tan 2x$,

a express c in terms of a **(2 marks)**

b show that $d = \frac{2ab}{b^2 - a^2}$ **(3 marks)**

(E/P) 7 Given that $\pi < \theta < \frac{3\pi}{2}$, find the value of $\sin\frac{\theta}{2}$ when $\cos\theta = \frac{24}{25}$ **(4 marks)**

7.4 Solving trigonometric equations

1 Solve in the interval $0 \leqslant x \leqslant 2\pi$, giving your answers to 1 decimal place:

a $\sin\left(x + \frac{\pi}{3}\right) + 4\sin x = 0$

b $\cos\left(\frac{\pi}{6} + x\right) = \sin x$

c $\cos\left(x + \frac{\pi}{4}\right) + \sin\left(x + \frac{\pi}{4}\right) = \frac{1}{2}$

Hint Use the addition formulae to expand and simplify the left-hand side of each equation. Then write an equation in $\tan x$ and solve.

2 Solve in the interval $0 \leqslant \theta \leqslant 180°$, giving your answers to 1 decimal place where necessary:

a $1 + \cos 2\theta = 7\cos^2\theta - 1$

b $\sin 2\theta = \frac{1}{4}\sin\theta$

c $\tan\theta\tan 2\theta = 3$

Hint Start by using the double-angle formulae to write the terms involving 2θ in terms of θ.

3 a Show that $\cos\left(x - \frac{\pi}{6}\right) \equiv \frac{1}{2}(\sqrt{3}\cos x + \sin x)$.

b Hence solve the equation $\sqrt{3}\cos x + \sin x = 1$ in the interval $0 \leqslant x \leqslant 2\pi$, giving your answers in terms of π.

Hint For part **b**, solve $\cos\left(x - \frac{\pi}{6}\right) = \frac{1}{2}$

(E/P) 4 a Show that $\sin(x - 45°) = \cos x$ can be written as $\tan x = a + \sqrt{b}$, where a and b are real constants to be found. **(3 marks)**

b Hence, or otherwise, solve $\sin(x - 45°) = \cos x$ in the interval $0 \leqslant x \leqslant 360°$, giving your answers to 1 decimal place. **(3 marks)**

(E/P) 5 a Show that $2\sin\left(x-\frac{\pi}{6}\right)=\sin\left(x+\frac{\pi}{2}\right)$ can be written in the form $\sqrt{3}\sin x-2\cos x=0$. **(3 marks)**

b Hence solve $2\sin\left(x-\frac{\pi}{6}\right)=\sin\left(x+\frac{\pi}{2}\right)$ in the interval $-\pi\leqslant x\leqslant\pi$.

Give your answers to 2 decimal places. **(3 marks)**

(E/P) 6 a Given that $\tan 2x-\tan x=0$, show that $\tan x+\tan^3 x=0$. **(3 marks)**

b Hence solve $\tan 2x=\tan x$ in the interval $0\leqslant x\leqslant 2\pi$. Give your answers in terms of π. **(3 marks)**

(E/P) 7 a Express $2\sin^2 x-\cos 2x-\cos x=0$ in the form $a\cos^2 x+\cos x-b=0$. **(3 marks)**

b Hence solve the equation $2\sin^2 x-\cos 2x-\cos x=0$ in the interval $-\pi\leqslant x\leqslant\pi$. Give your answers to 2 decimal places when they are not exact. **(4 marks)**

(E/P) 8 Solve the equation $\cos^2 x-2\sin^2 x-\sin 2x=1$ in the interval $-\pi\leqslant x<\pi$.

Give your answers to 2 decimal places when they are not exact. **(6 marks)**

7.5 Simplifying $a\cos x\pm b\sin x$

Unless otherwise stated, give all angles to 1 decimal place and write non-integer values of R in surd form.

1 Find the value of R, $R>0$, and the value of $\tan\alpha$, given that:

a $20\sin\theta+21\cos\theta\equiv R\sin(\theta+\alpha)$

b $\sqrt{3}\cos\theta-\sqrt{5}\sin\theta\equiv R\cos(\theta+\alpha)$

c $2\sin\theta-3\cos\theta\equiv R\sin(\theta-\alpha)$

Hint Expand the right-hand side and equate the coefficients of $\sin\theta$ and $\cos\theta$ to obtain two equations in R and α. Divide the equations to eliminate R and find the value of $\tan\alpha$. Square and add the equations to eliminate α and find the value of R.

2 Find the value of R, $R>0$, and α, where $0<\alpha<90°$, given that:

a $2\sin\theta+\cos\theta\equiv R\cos(\theta-\alpha)$

b $12\cos\theta-5\sin\theta\equiv R\cos(\theta+\alpha)$

c $4\sin\theta-2\cos\theta\equiv R\sin(\theta-\alpha)$

Hint Use the $\tan^{-1}$ function on your calculator to find the value of α in each case.

3 a i Express $\sqrt{3}\sin\theta-\cos\theta$ in the form $R\sin(\theta-\alpha)$, where $R>0$, $0<\alpha<\frac{\pi}{2}$

ii Hence sketch the graph of $y=\sqrt{3}\sin\theta-\cos\theta$ in the interval $0\leqslant\theta\leqslant 2\pi$.

Hint The graph of $y=R\sin(\theta-\alpha)$ is the graph of $y=\sin x$ stretched by scale factor R in the vertical direction, and translated by the vector $\begin{pmatrix}\alpha\\0\end{pmatrix}$.

b i Express $2\cos\theta-\sqrt{12}\sin\theta$ in the form $R\cos(\theta+\alpha)$, where $R>0$, $0<\alpha<\frac{\pi}{2}$

ii Hence sketch the graph of $y=2\cos\theta-\sqrt{12}\sin\theta$ in the interval $0\leqslant\theta\leqslant 2\pi$.

c i Express $2\sin\theta+2\cos\theta$ in the form $R\sin(\theta+\alpha)$, where $R>0$, $0<\alpha<\frac{\pi}{2}$

ii Hence sketch the graph of $y=2\sin\theta+2\cos\theta$ in the interval $0\leqslant\theta\leqslant 2\pi$.

E/P **4** $h(\theta) = 2\sin\theta + 4\cos\theta$

a Given that $h(\theta) = R\sin(\theta + \alpha)$, where $R > 0$ and $0 < \alpha < 90°$, find the exact value of R and the value of α to 2 decimal places. **(3 marks)**

b Hence solve $2\sin\theta + 4\cos\theta = 3$, for $0 \leqslant \theta \leqslant 360°$, giving your answers to 1 decimal place. **(3 marks)**

E/P **5** **a** Express $3\cos 2\theta + 2\sin 2\theta$ in the form $R\cos(2\theta - \alpha)$, where $R > 0$ and $0 < \alpha < \frac{\pi}{2}$, giving the value of α to 3 decimal places. **(3 marks)**

b Hence solve $3\cos 2\theta + 2\sin 2\theta = 1$, for $-\pi \leqslant \theta \leqslant \pi$, giving your answers to 2 decimal places. **(5 marks)**

c Given that k is a constant and the equation $3\cos 2\theta + 2\sin 2\theta = k$ has no solutions, state the range of possible values of k. **(2 marks)**

E/P **6** **a** Express $8\sin\theta - 15\cos\theta$ in the form $R\sin(\theta - \alpha)$, where R and a are constants, $R > 0$ and $0 < \alpha < \frac{\pi}{2}$. Give the value of α to 2 decimal places. **(3 marks)**

$$g(\theta) = \frac{10}{23 + 8\sin\theta - 15\cos\theta}$$

b **i** Find the maximum value of $g(\theta)$.

ii Find the value of θ, in the interval $0 \leqslant \theta \leqslant 2\pi$, at which this maximum value occurs, giving your answer to 2 decimal places. **(3 marks)**

c **i** Find the minimum value of $g(\theta)$.

ii Find the value of θ, for $0 \leqslant \theta \leqslant 2\pi$, at which this minimum value occurs, giving your answer to 2 decimal places. **(3 marks)**

E/P **7** **a** Show that that $2\sin\left(x - \frac{\pi}{6}\right) - (\sqrt{3} - 2)\sin x$ can be written as $2\sin x - \cos x$. **(3 marks)**

b Solve $2\sin\left(x - \frac{\pi}{6}\right) - (\sqrt{3} - 2)\sin x = \frac{1}{2}$ in the interval $-\pi \leqslant x \leqslant 2\pi$. Give your answers to 2 decimal places. **(4 marks)**

c Find the maximum value of $\left(2\sin\left(x - \frac{\pi}{6}\right) - (\sqrt{3} - 2)\sin x\right)^4$ **(2 marks)**

7.6 Proving trigonometric identities

1 Prove the following identities.

a $\dfrac{\sin 2x - \tan x}{\tan x} \equiv \cos 2x$

b $\dfrac{\sin 6\theta}{1 - \cos 6\theta} \equiv \cot 3\theta$

c $\frac{1}{4}\sec x \tan 2x \equiv \frac{1}{2}\sec 2x \sin x$

Hint Use the double-angle formulae.

For part **b**, write $A = 3\theta$.

For part **c**, write the left-hand side in terms of $\sin x$ and $\cos x$. Dividing the numerator and denominator by a common term might be helpful.

2 Prove the following identities.

Hint Use the addition formulae.

a $\cos(x - 30°) - \cos(x + 30°) \equiv \sin x$

b $\dfrac{\sin(a+b)}{\sin(a-b)} \equiv \dfrac{\cot b + \cot a}{\cot b - \cot a}$

c $\cot\left(\frac{\pi}{4} - \theta\right) \equiv \dfrac{\cos\theta + \sin\theta}{\cos\theta - \sin\theta}$

3 Prove the following identities.

a $2\sin\left(3\theta + \frac{\pi}{3}\right) \equiv \sin 3\theta + \sqrt{3}\cos 3\theta$

b $\cos 3A \equiv 4\cos^3 A - 3\cos A$

Hint For part **b**, write $\cos 3A$ as $\cos(2A + A)$.

c $\cot 2x + \tan x \equiv \operatorname{cosec} 2x$

E/P 4 Prove that $\sqrt{3}\cos x - \sin x \equiv 2\cos(x + 30°)$. **(4 marks)**

E/P 5 a Prove that $\dfrac{\sin 2x}{1 + \cos 2x} \equiv \tan x$. **(3 marks)**

b Hence find the value of $\dfrac{\sin\frac{2\pi}{3}}{1 + \cos\frac{2\pi}{3}}$ **(2 marks)**

E/P 6 Prove that $2\sin\left(2\theta - \frac{\pi}{4}\right) \equiv 2\sqrt{2}\sin\theta\cos\theta - \sqrt{2} + 2\sqrt{2}\sin^2\theta$. **(4 marks)**

E/P 7 a Prove that $\cos^4 x - \sin^4 x \equiv \cos 2x$. **(3 marks)**

b Hence, or otherwise, given that x is acute and $\tan x = \frac{1}{\sqrt{3}}$, find the value of $\cos 2x$. **(2 marks)**

7.7 Modelling with trigonometric functions

1 Georgia performs somersaults in the air while trampolining. Georgia's height above the trampoline, h metres, at time t seconds after she begins performing somersaults can be modelled by the equation

$h = 0.3 - 0.3\cos(240t)°$

a State the maximum height Georgia reaches above the trampoline.

b State the time it takes Georgia to reach this maximum height for the first time.

Hint For part **a**, $\cos\theta$ has a maximum value of 1 and a minimum value of −1. So the maximum value of h occurs when $\cos(240t)° = -1$.

c Given that Georgia performs one somersault every time she jumps, find according to the model, how many somersaults she will complete in 30 seconds.

Hint For part **c**, start by using the period of curve to find out how long it takes to complete one somersault.

d Criticise the model with respect to Georgia's path through the air.

2 The depth of water beneath a toy boat floating in a stream can be modelled by the equation

$d = 40.5 + 2.5\sin(\pi t)$

where d cm is the depth of the water and t is time in seconds.

a Calculate the depth of water beneath the boat after 3 seconds.

b Find the maximum depth of water beneath the boat according to this model.

c Calculate the times that the depth of water reaches this maximum in the first 5 seconds.

Hint For part **b**, use the maximum value of the sine function to find the maximum depth of water.

d A larger toy boat needs a minimum depth of 40 cm of water to be able to float properly. State whether the water in the stream is deep enough.

3 Charlotte's blood pressure can be modelled by the function

$P = 105 + 25\sin(450t)°$

where P is blood pressure in mm Hg and t is time in seconds.

a Write down Charlotte's maximum blood pressure. This is known as systolic pressure.

b Write down Charlotte's minimum blood pressure. This is known as diastolic pressure.

c Calculate Charlotte's blood pressure after 4 seconds.

d Find the times that Charlotte's blood pressure is 110 mm Hg during the first 2 seconds. Give your answers in seconds to 2 decimal places.

Hint There are six different times in part **d**.

E/P 4 A toy company records the average daily sales of a new toy during its first year of production. It models the data with the equation

$S = 6 - 3\sin(0.5t + 3), 0 \leqslant t \leqslant 12$

where S is the number of toys sold in thousands, and t is time in months after 1 January 2018.

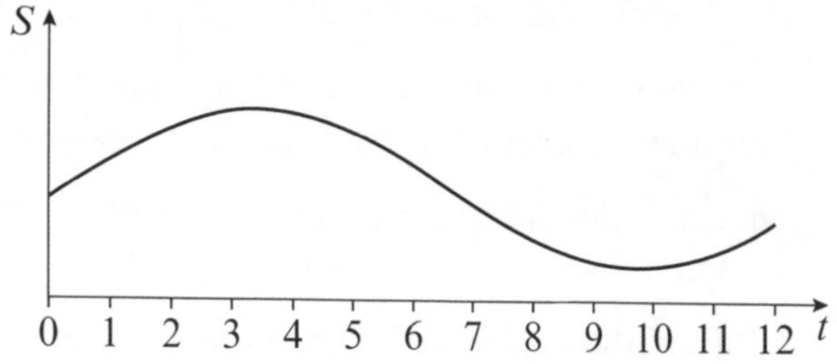

The graph shows sales over the year.

a Write down the maximum number of recorded sales, and state in which month this occurred. **(2 marks)**

The employees of the company are paid a bonus in any month during which the daily sales average exceeds 8500 on any day.

b State the months in which a bonus was paid. **(4 marks)**

c Calculate the average daily sales on the final day in December. **(2 marks)**

d Tom says that the model predicts that sales will increase during the first few months of 2019. State whether you think he is correct. **(1 mark)**

(E/P) 5 **a** Express $\frac{5\sqrt{2}}{2}\cos\theta - \frac{5\sqrt{2}}{2}\sin\theta$ in the form $R\cos(\theta + \alpha)°$, where $R > 0$ and $0 < \alpha < 90°$. **(4 marks)**

b i Find the minimum value of $\frac{5\sqrt{2}}{2}\cos\theta - \frac{5\sqrt{2}}{2}\sin\theta$.

ii Find the value of θ for $0 < \theta < 360°$ at which the minimum occurs. **(3 marks)**

The height of water at the entrance to a harbour over a period of 24 hours can be modelled by the equation

$$h = 9 - \frac{5\sqrt{2}}{2}\cos(30t) + \frac{5\sqrt{2}}{2}\sin(30t)$$

where h, metres, is the height of the water and t is the number of hours after midnight.

c Write down the maximum height of water over the 24 hours, and the first time that this occurs. **(3 marks)**

d Write down the minimum height of water over the 24 hours, and the final time this occurs. **(3 marks)**

e Find:

i the first time after which the water rises above 9 metres

ii the first time after which the water falls below 9 metres. **(4 marks)**

(E/P) 6 **a** Express $0.2\cos x + 0.35\sin x$ in the form $R\cos(x - \alpha)$, where $R > 0$ and $0 < \alpha < \frac{\pi}{2}$. Give α to 1 decimal place. **(4 marks)**

The temperature of an electric heater can be modelled by the equation

$$T = 30 + 0.2\cos 2m + 0.35\sin 2m$$

where T is the temperature in Celsius and m is the time in minutes after the heater reaches the required temperature. All angles are measured in radians.

b Calculate the temperature of the heater 1 minute after it has reached the required temperature. **(2 marks)**

c Find the difference between the maximum and minimum temperatures of the heater after it has reached the required temperature. **(2 marks)**

d Calculate the times during the first 8 minutes, after the heater has reached the required temperature, when it reaches maximum temperature. **(4 marks)**

(E/P) 7 **a** Express $132\sin x - 72\cos x$ in the form $R\sin(x - \alpha)$, where $R > 0$ and $0 < \alpha < \frac{\pi}{2}$. Give α to 1 decimal place. **(4 marks)**

The share price of a company during the first year after it is floated on the stock exchange can be modelled by the equation

$$P = 200 + 132\sin(0.8t) - 72\cos(0.8t)$$

where P is the share price in pence and t is the time in months since the company was floated (assuming it was floated on the 1st of January). All terms in t are measured in radians.

b Write down the maximum share price and the month in which this first occurred. **(3 marks)**

c Write down the month in which the shares were at their lowest price, and find the lowest share price. **(3 marks)**

d State during which month the share price fell below 100p. **(2 marks)**

Luke purchased 2000 shares in the company at its flotation price, and sold them at the end of 12 months.

e Find the profit or loss made by Luke. Give your answer to 2 significant figures. **(2 marks)**

Problem solving Set A

Bronze

The graph shows a curve that models the blood pressure of a patient during the first 5 seconds of measurement.

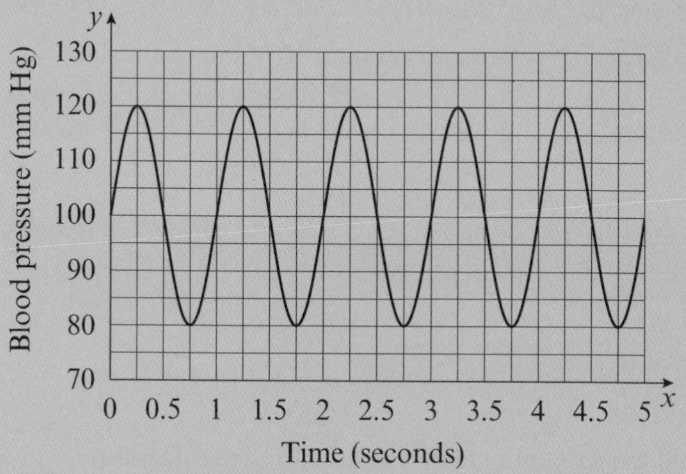

The model has the equation

$$y = a + b\sin(cx)^\circ$$

where y is blood pressure in mm Hg and x is time in seconds, and a, b and c are real constants.

a By considering the maximum and minimum values of y, find the values of a and b. **(3 marks)**

b By considering the period of the curve, find the value of c, and hence write the equation of the curve. **(2 marks)**

Silver

The graph shows a curve that models daylight hours on any day of the year in a particular city.

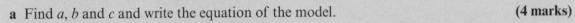

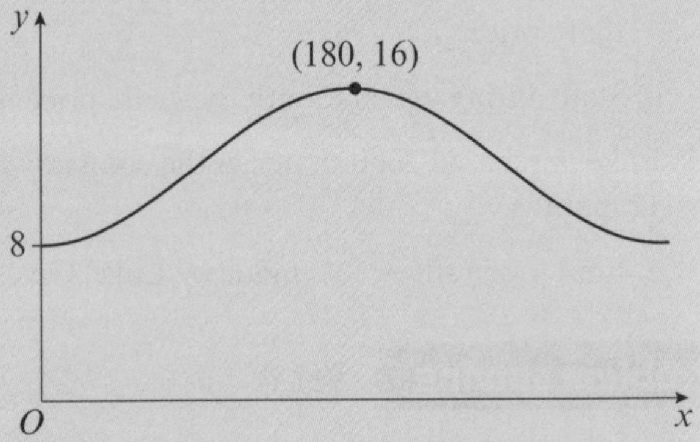

The model has the equation

$y = a + b\sin(x - c)°$

where y is the number of daylight hours, and x is the number of days after 1 January, and a, b and c are real constants.

There are a minimum of 8 daylight hours at the start of the year, rising to a maximum of 16 daylight hours on day 180.

a Find a, b and c and write the equation of the model. **(4 marks)**

b Describe two transformations that could be made to the curve with equation $y = \sin x$ to obtain the curve given in the model. **(2 marks)**

c Find the number of days in the year which experience more than 14 hours of sunshine. **(2 marks)**

Gold

The height of a car on a big wheel is modelled by the equation

$h = a + b\cos(ct - d)°$

where h is the height of the car above ground in metres, t is time after the ride starts, in seconds, and a, b, c and d are real constants.

The initial height of the car is 2 m, and the maximum height reached on the ride is 22 m, which occurs 90 seconds after the start of the ride. The car completes four full revolutions, and the ride ends with the car in its initial position after 12 minutes.

a Find the values of a, b, c and d and hence write the equation of the curve. **(5 marks)**

The fairground operator decides to increase the speed of the wheel so that it completes five full revolutions in 12 minutes.

b Amend the model to reflect this change. **(2 marks)**

Revathi says that the length of time the car is more than 20 m above the ground will be the same for both models.

c Determine whether Revathi is correct. **(2 marks)**

Problem solving Set B

Bronze

a Express $12\sin 2x - 5\cos 2x$ in the form $R\sin(2x - \alpha)$, with $R > 0$ and $0 < \alpha < \frac{\pi}{2}$
Give the value of α in radians to 3 decimal places. **(4 marks)**

b Show that $12 - 3\operatorname{cosec} 2x = 5\cot 2x$ can be written as $12\sin 2x - 5\cos 2x = k$, where k is a positive constant to be determined. **(2 marks)**

c Hence solve $12 - 3\operatorname{cosec} 2x = 5\cot 2x$ in the interval $0 \leqslant x \leqslant 2\pi$ giving your answers to 1 decimal place. **(4 marks)**

Silver

a Express $7\cos^2 x - 3\sin^2 x - 8\sin x\cos x$ in the form $a\cos 2x - b\sin 2x + c$, where a, b and c are constants to be found. **(3 marks)**

b Solve the equation $7\cos^2 x - 3\sin^2 x - 8\sin x\cos x = 4$ in the interval $0 \leqslant x \leqslant 2\pi$. Give your answers to 2 decimal places. **(4 marks)**

c i Show that $10\cos^2 x - 8\sin x\cos x$ can be written in the form $a\cos 2x - b\sin 2x + k$, stating the values of a, b, and k.

ii Hence deduce the exact maximum value of $10\cos^2 x - 8\sin x\cos x$. **(4 marks)**

Gold

a Express $\frac{15}{2}\sin 4x - 4\cos 4x - 4\cos 2x - 4$ in the form $\cos 2x(a\sin 2x - b\cos 2x - c)$, where a, b and c are constants to be found. **(3 marks)**

Hence or otherwise:

b solve $\frac{15}{2}\sin 4x = 4(\cos 4x + \cos 2x + 1)$ in the interval $0 \leqslant x \leqslant \pi$, giving your answers to 2 decimal places **(4 marks)**

c deduce the maximum value of $\dfrac{1}{30\sin x\cos x - 16\cos^2 x}$ **(4 marks)**

Now try this → **Exam question bank Q11, Q17, Q36, Q40, Q50, Q59, Q71, Q83**

8 Parametric equations

8.1 Parametric equations

1 For each of the following parametric equations, find a Cartesian equation, giving your answer in the form $y = \text{f}(x)$. In each case find the domain and range of $\text{f}(x)$.

Hint A Cartesian equation in two dimensions involves the variables x and y only. Rearrange one parametric equation into the form $t = \ldots$, and then substitute into the other equation to eliminate t.

a $x = t - 3,\ y = t^2 - 1,\ -3 \leqslant t \leqslant 3$

b $x = \frac{2}{t},\ y = t^2 + 1,\ t > 0$

c $x = 2t - 1,\ y = \frac{3}{t^2},\ t \geqslant 1$

2 For each of the following parametric curves, find a Cartesian equation, giving your answer in the form $y = \text{f}(x)$. In each case find the domain and range of $\text{f}(x)$.

Hint To find the domain of $\text{f}(x)$, consider the range of values of x for the given domain of t. To find the range of $\text{f}(x)$, consider the range of values of y for the given domain of t.

a $x = \ln(t + 2),\ y = \frac{1}{t + 3},\ t > -1$

b $x = \ln(4 + t),\ y = t^2 + 10t + 25,\ t > -3$

c $x = \text{e}^{2t},\ y = \text{e}^{6t} + 2\text{e}^{4t},\ t \in \mathbb{R}$

3 For each of these parametric curves:

i find a Cartesian equation for the curve in the form $y = \text{f}(x)$

ii find the domain and range of $\text{f}(x)$

iii sketch the curve within the given domain of t.

a $x = t^{\frac{1}{2}} + 1,\ y = 2t^{\frac{1}{2}} + 7,\ 0 < t \leqslant 16$

b $x = 2t + 1,\ y = 4t^2 + 14t + 12,\ -3 \leqslant t \leqslant 0$

c $x = \ln(2 - t),\ y = 5 - t,\ t < 1$

(E) 4 The parametric equations $x = 3t,\ y = (1 - t)(9 - t),\ 0 \leqslant t \leqslant 8$ define a curve A.

a Find the Cartesian equation of the curve in the form $y = \text{f}(x)$, and state the domain and range of $\text{f}(x)$. **(3 marks)**

b Sketch the curve A, clearly showing the coordinates of any points of intersection with the axes, turning points or endpoints. **(3 marks)**

(E/P) 5 A curve C is defined by the parametric equations $x = \ln(t + 5),\ y = 2t + 12,\ t \geqslant -4$.

a Find the Cartesian equation of the curve in the form $y = \text{f}(x)$. **(2 marks)**

b Write down the minimum value of x and the minimum value of y. **(2 marks)**

(E/P) 6 A curve M has parametric equations $x = \text{e}^{3t},\ y = \text{e}^{9t} - 2\text{e}^{6t} - 5\text{e}^{3t} + 6,\ t \in \mathbb{R}$.

a Show that the Cartesian equation of M can be written in the form $y = (x + a)(x - b)(x - c)$, where a, b, and c are integers to be determined. **(4 marks)**

b Hence write down the coordinates of the points where the curve crosses each axis. **(3 marks)**

(E/P) 7 The curves C_1 and C_2 are defined parametrically as follows:

$C_1: x = 5t^2,\ y = 3t^2 + 2,\ 0 \leqslant t \leqslant 2$

$C_2: x = 3\sqrt{t} - 3,\ y = 9 - 5\sqrt{t},\ 0 \leqslant t \leqslant 4$

a Show that the curves are line segments which are perpendicular to each other. **(3 marks)**

b Find the exact length of each line segment. **(2 marks)**

(E/P) 8 The curve C has parametric equations $x = 4t^2,\ y = 8t^3,\ -1 \leqslant t \leqslant 1$.

Find a Cartesian equation of C in the form $y^2 = \text{f}(x)$. **(4 marks)**

8.2 Using trigonometric identities

1 Find the Cartesian equations of the curves given by the following parametric equations:

a $x = \sin t - 1,\ y = \cos t + 3,\ 0 < t < 2\pi$

b $x = 2\sin t,\ y = 3\cos t,\ 0 < t < \pi$

c $x = 2 + 2\cos t,\ y = 5 + 2\sin t,\ 0 < t < 2\pi$

> **Hint** Use $\sin^2 t + \cos^2 t \equiv 1$. You do not need to give the equations in the form $y = \text{f}(x)$.
> ← **Year 1, Section 10.3**

2 Find the Cartesian equations of the curves given by the following parametric equations:

a $x = \sin t,\ y = \cos 2t,\ 0 < t < 2\pi$

b $x = 4\sec t,\ y = 2\tan t,\ 0 < t < 2\pi$

c $x = \sin t,\ y = \sin^2 2t,\ 0 < t < 2\pi$

> **Hint** $\cos 2t \equiv 1 - 2\sin^2 t$ ← **Section 7.3**
> $1 + \tan^2 t \equiv \sec^2 t$ ← **Section 6.4**
> $\sin 2t \equiv 2\sin t\cos t$ ← **Section 7.3**

3 For each of these parametric curves:

i find a Cartesian equation in the form $y = \text{f}(x)$

ii sketch the curve within the given domain of t.

a $x = \sin t + 3,\ y = \cos t - 4,\ 0 < t < 2\pi$

b $x = \dfrac{2}{\tan t},\ y = 4\operatorname{cosec}^2 t - 8,\ 0 < t < \pi$

c $x = 10\sin t,\ y = \frac{1}{5}\operatorname{cosec}^2 t,\ 0 < t < \frac{\pi}{2}$

> **Hint** $(x - a)^2 + (y - b)^2 = r^2$ is the equation of a circle with centre (a, b) and radius r.
> ← **Year 1, Section 6.2**

(P) 4 A curve C has parametric equations

$x = 6\cos t + 5,\ y = 6\sin t - 2,\ 0 \leqslant t \leqslant k$

When $k = 2\pi$, C is a circle.

a Write a Cartesian equation for the circle, and hence state its radius and the coordinates of its centre.

b Write down a value of k such that C is a semicircle.

(E/P) **5** A curve C has parametric equations

$x = 5\sec^2 2t,\ y = 2\cot^2 2t,\ 0 < t \leqslant \frac{\pi}{4}$

a Find a Cartesian equation of the curve, expressing y in terms of x. **(5 marks)**

b State the range of possible values of x for the given domain of t. **(1 mark)**

(E/P) **6** Show that the curve with parametric equations $x = 2\sin t,\ y = \cos\left(t + \frac{\pi}{3}\right),\ -\frac{\pi}{2} < t < \frac{\pi}{2}$, can be written in the form $y = \frac{1}{4}(\sqrt{4 - x^2} - \sqrt{3}x),\ -k < x < k$, where k is a real constant to be found. **(6 marks)**

(E/P) **7** A curve has parametric equations

$x = \cot^2 t + 3,\ y = 3\cos t,\ 0 < t < \frac{\pi}{2}$

a Find the Cartesian equation of the curve in the form $y = f(x)$. **(4 marks)**

b Find the domain and range of $y = f(x)$ in the given domain of t. **(2 marks)**

8.3 Curve sketching

1 A curve is given by the parametric equations

$x = 2t + 2,\ y = t^2,\ -2 \leqslant t \leqslant 3$

Copy and complete the table and draw a graph of the curve.

Hint For each value of t, substitute into the parametric equations to find the corresponding values of x and y.

t	−2	−1.5	−1	−0.5	0	0.5	1	1.5	2	2.5	3
$x = 2t + 2$	−2	−1			2						
$y = t^2$	4	2.25		0.25							

2 A curve is given by the parametric equations

$x = 3\sin t,\ y = 5\cos t,\ 0 \leqslant t \leqslant 2\pi$

Hint Make sure you plot x against y. Do not plot any values of t.

Copy and complete the table and draw a graph of the curve for $0 \leqslant t \leqslant 2\pi$.

t	0	$\frac{\pi}{4}$	$\frac{\pi}{2}$	$\frac{3\pi}{4}$	π	$\frac{5\pi}{4}$	$\frac{3\pi}{2}$	$\frac{7\pi}{4}$	2π
$x = 3\sin t$	0	2.12							
$y = 5\cos t$	5	3.54							

3 By using a table of values, or otherwise, sketch the curves given by these parametric equations:

a $x = 2t^2,\ y = 4t,\ -2 \leqslant t \leqslant 2$

b $x = 3\operatorname{cosec} t,\ y = 3\cot t,\ 0 \leqslant t \leqslant 2\pi$

c $x = t + 5,\ y = \frac{1}{t},\ 0 \leqslant t \leqslant 8$

(P) 4 The curves C_1, C_2 and C_3 are defined parametrically as follows:

$C_1 : x = 2t,\ y = 2.5 - t, 0.5 \leqslant t \leqslant 2.5$

$C_2 : x = \frac{1}{t},\ y = \frac{2}{t}, \frac{1}{3} \leqslant t \leqslant 1$

$C_3 : x = 2t + 1,\ y = 12 - 6t, 1 \leqslant t \leqslant 2$

a Find Cartesian equations of C_1, C_2 and C_3 in the form $y = f(x)$.

b On the same set of coordinate axes, sketch C_1, C_2 and C_3 on their given domains.

c Find the area of the shape enclosed by C_1, C_2 and C_3.

(E/P) 5 The curve C is defined by the parametric equations

$x = t + 2,\ y = -5t - t^2, -5 \leqslant t \leqslant 1$

a Find a Cartesian equation of C in the form $y = (a - x)(x + b)$, where a and b are integers to be found. **(4 marks)**

b Sketch the curve C on the given domain of t. **(3 marks)**

(E/P) 6 The curve C is defined by the parametric equations

$x = 10\cos t + 3,\ y = 10\sin t - 2, -\frac{\pi}{2} \leqslant t \leqslant \frac{\pi}{2}$

a Find a Cartesian equation of C in the form $(x + a)^2 + (y + b)^2 = c$, stating the values of a, b and c. **(4 marks)**

b Sketch the curve C on the appropriate domain. **(3 marks)**

c Find the exact length of the curve C. **(3 marks)**

8.4 Points of intersection

1 Find the coordinates of the point(s) where the following curves meet the x-axis and the y-axis.

a $x = t - 3,\ y = t + 4, \in \mathbb{R}$

b $x = 3t,\ y = 3(t + 2)(t - 1), \in \mathbb{R}$

c $x = 2t^2 - 2,\ y = t^2 - 4t, \in \mathbb{R}$

Hint Substitute $y = 0$ or $x = 0$ into the parametric equations to find the value(s) of t when the curve crosses the x-axis and the y-axis respectively. Then find the corresponding coordinates.

2 Find the coordinates of the point(s) where the following curves meet the x-axis and the y-axis.

a $x = \sin 2t + 1,\ y = 2\tan^2 t, -\frac{\pi}{4} \leqslant t \leqslant \frac{\pi}{4}$

b $x = 2t,\ y = \cos t, -\pi \leqslant t \leqslant \pi$

c $x = e^t - 3,\ y = e^{2t} - 2, t > 0$

Hint The curve in part **b** intersects the x-axis twice within the given domain of t.

3 The line L is defined parametrically by

$x = t + 1, y = t + 3, t \in \mathbb{R}$

The circle C has equation $x^2 + y^2 + 6x - 4 = 0$.

a Find the values of t at the points of intersection of L and C.

b Hence find the coordinates of these points.

Hint Substitute the expressions for x and y in the parametric equations for L into the equation for C, then solve the resulting quadratic equation to find two possible values for t.

4 **a** A curve has parametric equations $x = p(1 + 2t), y = p(1 - 2t)^2, t \in \mathbb{R}$ where p is a constant. The curve passes through the point (6, 0). Find the value of p.

b A curve has parametric equations $x = qt^2 - 2q, y = q(t - 1)(t - 3)^2, t > 1$, where q is a constant. The curve passes through the point $\left(\frac{7}{2}, 0\right)$. Find the value of q.

E/P 5 A curve C has parametric equations $x = e^{2t}, y = 4e^t - 4, t \in \mathbb{R}$.

a Find the values of t where the line $y = x - 1$ crosses the curve C. **(3 marks)**

b Hence determine the coordinates of the points where the line $y = x - 1$ intersects the curve C. **(2 marks)**

E/P 6 A curve C is defined by the parametric equations

$x = \cos t, y = 2\sin 2t + 1, \frac{\pi}{4} < t < \frac{3\pi}{2}$

a Determine the coordinates of the points where the line $y = 1$ crosses the curve C. **(5 marks)**

b Show that the curve cuts the x-axis where $t = \frac{7\pi}{12}$ and $t = \frac{11\pi}{12}$ **(3 marks)**

c Hence determine the exact coordinates of the points where the curve cuts the x-axis. **(2 marks)**

E/P 7 A curve C has parametric equations $x = 4\sin t, y = 8\cos t, 0 < t < 2\pi$.

The points P and Q lie on C where $t = \frac{\pi}{6}$ and $t = \frac{3\pi}{2}$ respectively.

Find an equation of the straight line through P and Q, giving your answer in the form $ay + bx + c = 0$. **(5 marks)**

E/P 8 A curve has parametric equations $x = \ln(t + 2), y = \ln(t - 1), t > 1$.

a Show that the line $y = 2x - \ln 18$ crosses the curve at the points where $t = a \pm b\sqrt{3}$, where a and b are integers to be found. **(4 marks)**

b Hence determine the exact coordinates of the points where the line $y = 2x - \ln 18$ intersects the curve. **(3 marks)**

8.5 Modelling with parametric equations

(P) **1** A ski lift lifts a skier from ground level to an elevation of 450 m.

The position of the skier at time t seconds is modelled by the parametric equations

$x = 3.6t\,\text{m},\ y = 2.7t\,\text{m}$

where x is the distance travelled horizontally and y is the distance travelled vertically.

a Find the time taken to travel to the top of the ski lift.

b Show that the motion of the skier is a straight line.

c Hence find the total distance travelled by the skier in travelling from ground level to the top of the ski lift.

d Determine the speed of the ski lift.

e Criticise the model in relation to: **i** the path of the skier **ii** the speed of the ski lift.

(P) **2** Adam's position as he travels down a water slide at time t can be modelled by the parametric equations $x = 8t$, $y = 16 - 7.6t - \cos 8t$, $0 < t < k$, where x is the horizontal distance travelled (in metres) and y is Adam's vertical height above ground level (in metres).

a Find Adam's initial height above ground level.

b Find Adam's vertical height above ground level after $\frac{17}{8}$ seconds.

c State the horizontal distance that Adam has travelled after $\frac{17}{8}$ seconds, giving your answer to the nearest metre.

(P) **3** A ball is kicked from the ground with an initial speed of $18\,\text{m}\,\text{s}^{-1}$ at an angle of 45°.

Its position after t seconds can be described using the parametric equations

$x = 9\sqrt{2}t$ m, $y = (-kt^2 + 9\sqrt{2}t)$ m, where k is a constant

a Given that ball travels a horizontal distance of 33 m before hitting the ground, find the time of flight of the ball.

b Hence find the value of k.

c Show that the path of the ball is modelled by a quadratic curve.

(P) **4** The path of a kangaroo as it jumps can be modelled by the parametric equations

$x = 5.6t\,\text{m},\ y = -4.9t^2 + 2.1t\,\text{m}$

where x is the horizontal distance from the point the kangaroo jumps off the ground, y is the height above the ground and t is the time in seconds after the kangaroo has started its jump.

a Find the time the kangaroo takes to complete a single jump.

b Find the horizontal distance the kangaroo travels during a single jump.

c The kangaroo jumps over a log that is 20 cm high. Find the range of the distances from the log that the kangaroo must jump from in order to clear it.

E/P **5** The cross-section of a vase design is given by the parametric equations

$x = (18t - 32\sin t)\,\text{cm},\ y = (8 - 16\cos t)\,\text{cm},\ -\frac{\pi}{2} \leqslant t \leqslant \frac{\pi}{2}$

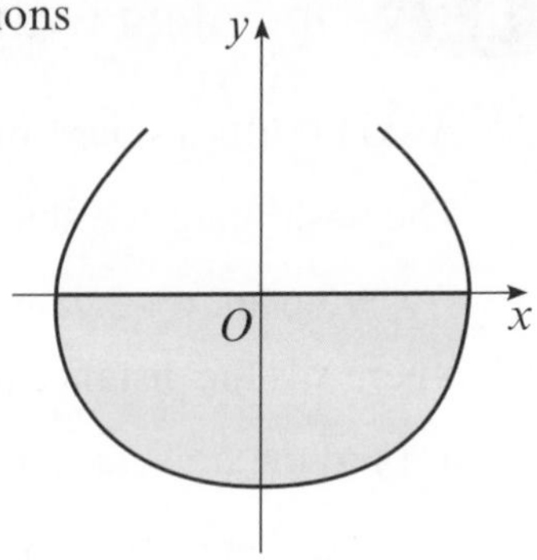

a Find the width of the opening of the vase. **(3 marks)**

b The vase is filled with water up to the level of the x-axis. Find the radius of the vase at the surface of the water. **(3 marks)**

c Given that the cross-section of the vase crosses the y-axis at its deepest point, find the depth of the water in the vase. **(3 marks)**

E/P **6** Particle A is moving in the xy-plane such that its position relative to a fixed origin O at time t seconds is given by the parametric equations

$x = \frac{t^2 - 6t + 5}{t + 1},\ y = t - 2,\ t \geqslant 0$

The diagram shows the path of the particle.

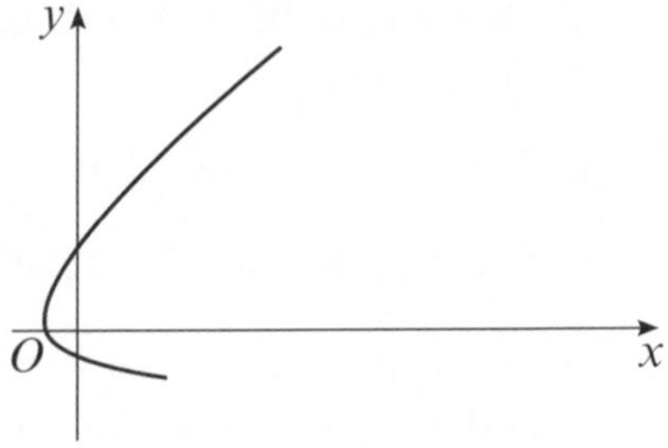

Particle B is moving in the xy-plane such that its position relative to the same fixed origin O at time t seconds is given by the parametric equations

$x = t + 5,\ y = 5t - 2,\ t \geqslant 0$

a Show that the path of particle B is a straight line. **(2 marks)**

Both particles are at $(5, -2)$ when $t = 0$.

b Find the exact coordinates of the other point where the paths of the particles intersect. **(3 marks)**

Adam states that the particles will collide at this point.

c State whether you agree with Adam's statement, giving a reason for your answer. **(2 marks)**

E/P **7** A walker travels around one loop of a path in a park. The position of the walker relative to the entrance of the park, O, at time t minutes, is modelled using the parametric equations

$x = 400\cos\left(\frac{1}{5}\left(t - \frac{\pi}{3}\right)\right),\ y = 400\sin^2\frac{t}{5} - 200\sin\frac{t}{5},\ t \geqslant 0$

where x and y are measured in metres, and the positive y-axis is the north direction.

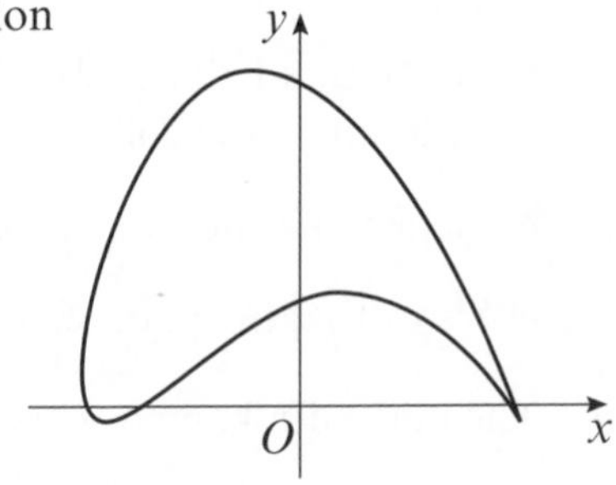

a Find the distance of the walker from the park entrance at the beginning of his motion. **(3 marks)**

b Find the distances of the walker from the park entrance at the times when he is due north of the park entrance. **(4 marks)**

c Determine how long it takes the walker to complete one loop of the path to the nearest minute. **(3 marks)**

E/P **8** The diagram shows the profile of a hill modelled by the parametric equations $x = t^2 + 16t$, $y = 20\sin t$, $0 < t < k$, where x represents the distance in metres measured horizontally from a fixed point, and y represents the height above sea level in metres.

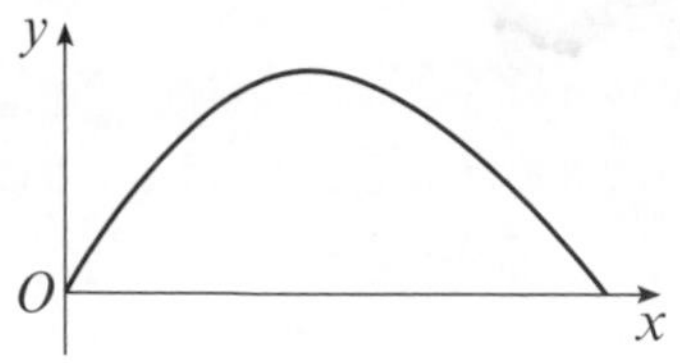

a Find the height of the hill. **(3 marks)**

b Find the value of k and hence find the average gradient of the descent away from the origin. **(4 marks)**

Problem solving Set A

Bronze

A curve C has parametric equations

$x = 10\sin t$, $y = 5\sin 2t$, $0 \leqslant t \leqslant \frac{\pi}{2}$

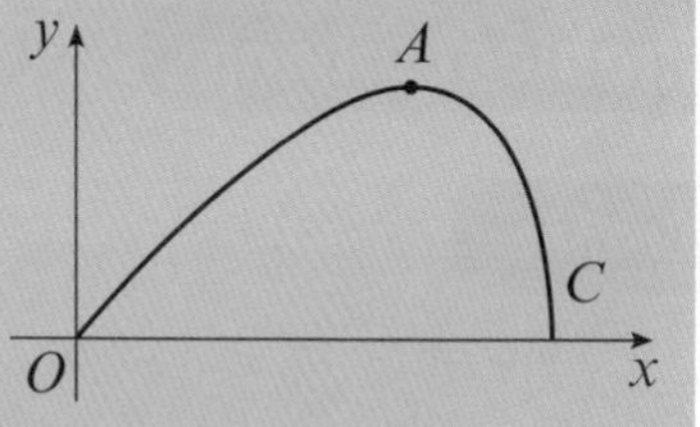

a i Show that $y = x\cos t$.

ii Hence show that a Cartesian equation of C can be written as $100(y^2 - x^2) + x^4 = 0$. **(4 marks)**

The point A lies on C at the point where $t = \frac{\pi}{4}$

The line with equation $y = x + k$, where k is a constant, intersects the curve at point A.

b Find:

i the coordinates of point A

ii the exact value of k. **(4 marks)**

Silver

A curve C has parametric equations

$x = \frac{2}{\sqrt{3}}\sin t$, $y = 4\cos\left(t + \frac{\pi}{3}\right)$, $0 \leqslant t \leqslant 2\pi$

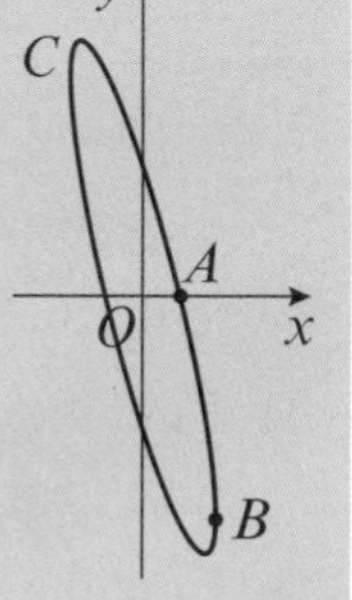

a Show that all points on C satisfy $(3x + y)^2 + 3x^2 - 4 = 0$. **(5 marks)**

A straight line l passes through the points A and B on curve C where $t = \frac{\pi}{6}$ and $t = \frac{\pi}{2}$ respectively.

b i Show that the gradient of line l is -6.

ii Hence find the equation for line l in the form $ax + by + c = 0$. **(4 marks)**

Gold

A curve C has parametric equations

$x = 2 + 2\cos t,\ y = 2\sin t + \sin 2t,\ 0 \leqslant t \leqslant \frac{3\pi}{4}$

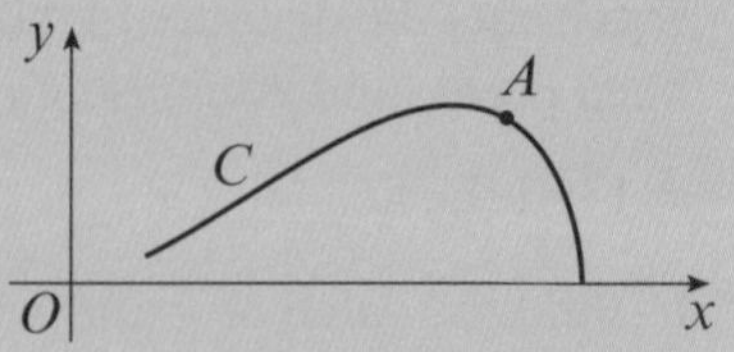

a Show that all points on C satisfy $y^2 = x^3\left(1 - \frac{1}{4}x\right)$, $a \leqslant x \leqslant b$, stating the exact values of a and b. **(6 marks)**

The line with equation $x + y = p$, where p is a constant, is a tangent to C at point A, where $t = \frac{\pi}{4}$

b Find the value of p. **(2 marks)**

c Given that the line $x + y = q$ intersects curve C at least once, find the exact range of possible values of q, writing your answer in set notation. **(2 marks)**

Problem solving Set B

Bronze

The motion of a football as it is kicked is modelled using the parametric equations

$x = 7.6t,\quad y = -4.9t^2 + 16.3t$

where x m is the horizontal distance travelled and y m is the height of the ball above the ground after t seconds.

a Find the two values of x for which the football is exactly 10 m above the ground. **(4 marks)**

b Show that the path of the ball is a parabola and work out the maximum height of the ball above the ground. **(5 marks)**

Silver

The motion of a dancer relative to a fixed origin O at time t minutes is modelled using the parametric equations

$x = 16\sin 4t,\ y = 32\cos\left(8t - \frac{8\pi}{3}\right),\ t \geqslant 0$

where x and y are measured in metres.

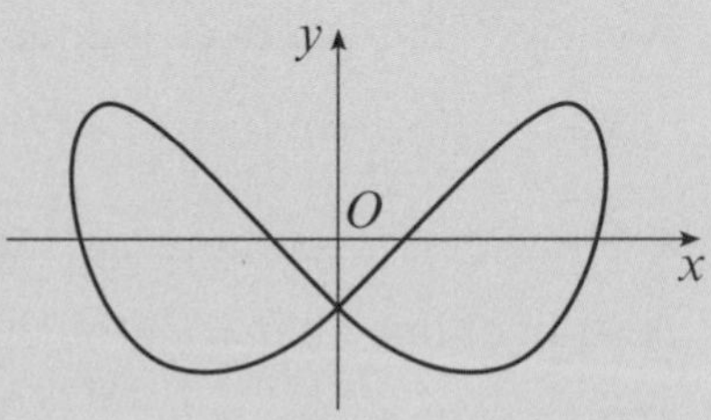

a Find the distance of the dancer from the origin at time $t = 1$. **(2 marks)**

b Find the coordinates of the point where the dancer intersects his own path. **(4 marks)**

c Determine how long it takes the dancer to complete one complete figure-of-eight motion. **(4 marks)**

Gold

A particle is moving in the xy-plane such that its position after time t seconds relative to a fixed origin O is given by the parametric equations

$$x = \frac{t^2 - 7t + 10}{t},\ y = t\ln t,\ t > 0$$

The diagram shows the path of the particle.

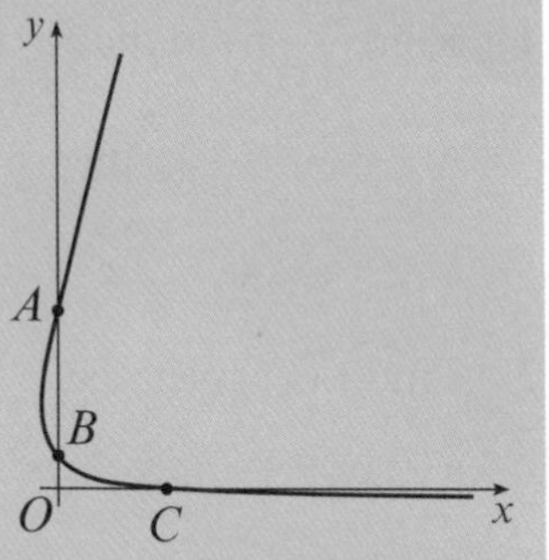

The particle crosses the y-axis at points A and B, and the x-axis at point C as shown on the diagram.

a Find the area of triangle ABC, giving your answer in the form $\ln k$ where k is a rational number to be found. **(5 marks)**

b Given that the line with equation $x = k$ intersects the curve exactly once, determine the value of k. **(3 marks)**

Now try this → **Exam question bank Q10, Q31, Q34, Q45, Q48, Q54, Q72, Q86**

9.1 Differentiating $\sin x$ and $\cos x$

1 Find $\frac{dy}{dx}$ given that:

a $y = 6\sin x$ **b** $y = -3\sin\frac{1}{2}x$ **c** $y = \frac{1}{3}\sin 5x$

d $y = \cos 4x$ **e** $y = 5\cos 6x$ **f** $y = -\frac{1}{2}\cos 7x$

Hint If $y = \sin kx$, then $\frac{dy}{dx} = k\cos kx$

If $y = \cos kx$, then $\frac{dy}{dx} = -k\sin kx$

2 Find $f'(x)$ given that:

Hint Differentiate each term separately.

a $f(x) = 4\sin x - 3\cos x$

b $f(x) = \frac{1}{2}\sin 2x + 4\cos x - 6\sin\frac{1}{4}x$

c $f(x) = 5x^{\frac{3}{2}} - \frac{4}{x^2} - 6\sin\frac{1}{3}x$ **d** $f(x) = \frac{8}{\sqrt{x}} + 3\cos\frac{1}{6}x$

3 $f(x) = 5\sin x - 3\cos x$. Find the x-coordinates of the stationary points on the curve with equation $y = f(x)$ in the interval $-180° \leqslant x \leqslant 180°$.

Hint Stationary points occur when the gradient is equal to zero.

4 $f(x) = x - \cos 2x$. Find the equation of the tangent to the curve at the point $\left(\frac{\pi}{4}, \frac{\pi}{4}\right)$.

Hint First differentiate to find the gradient, m. Then find the equation of the tangent using the equation $y - y_1 = m(x - x_1)$

← Year 1, Section 12.6

(E) **5** $f(x) = 6\sin x - 3\cos 2x$
Find the stationary points of the curve $y = f(x)$ in the interval $0 \leqslant x \leqslant 2\pi$. **(6 marks)**

(E/P) **6** $g(x) = 6\sin 2x - 4\cos 2x$. Find the equation of the normal to the curve with equation $y = g(x)$ at the point $(\pi, -4)$. **(5 marks)**

(E/P) **7** $h(x) = 3\sin x - 4\cos x + \frac{1}{2}x^2$. Show that the equation of the tangent to the curve with equation $y = h(x)$ at the point with x-coordinate $\frac{\pi}{2}$ is $8y - (32 + 4\pi)x = 24 - 16\pi - \pi^2$. **(6 marks)**

(E/P) **8** Prove from first principles that the derivative of $\cos x$ is $-\sin x$. **(5 marks)**

9.2 Differentiating exponentials and logarithms

1 Differentiate:

Hint If $y = e^{kx}$, then $\frac{dy}{dx} = ke^{kx}$

a $6e^{-3x}$ **b** $5e^{2x} - 7e^{-x}$

c $\frac{7}{e^{5x}}$ **d** $\frac{(1 - e^{2x})^2}{e^{2x}}$

2 Find $f'(x)$ given that:

Hint If $y = \ln x$, then $\frac{dy}{dx} = \frac{1}{x}$
First expand the expression using laws of logarithms. ← Year 1, Section 14.5

a $f(x) = \ln 2x$ **b** $f(x) = \ln x^2$

c $f(x) = \ln\left(\frac{7}{x}\right)$ **d** $f(x) = \ln(4x^3)$

3 Find $\frac{dy}{dx}$ given that:

a $y = 3^x$ b $y = 5^{2x}$

c $y = \left(\frac{2}{5}\right)^{4x}$ d 8^{-x}

Hint If $y = a^{kx}$, where k is a real constant and $a > 0$, then $\frac{dy}{dx} = a^{kx} k \ln a$.

4 Find the equation of the tangent to the curve $y = 4^x$ at the point with x-coordinate $-\frac{1}{2}$

(E) 5 Given $f(x) = e^{-x} + 2\ln x^3$, find $f'(x)$. **(3 marks)**

(E/P) 6 A curve has equation $y = 3e^x - \ln x^2$. Show that the equation of the normal at the point with x-coordinate 1 is $x + (3e - 2)y - 9e^2 + 6e - 1 = 0$. **(6 marks)**

(E/P) 7 $f(x) = 4^x + 4^{-x}$. Show that the equation of the of the tangent to the curve with equation $y = f(x)$ at the point with x-coordinate $\frac{1}{2}$ is $y = (\ln 8)x + \frac{5}{2} - \frac{1}{2}\ln 8$. **(6 marks)**

(E/P) 8 $f(x) = 9^{3x} + 3^{6x}$

a Demonstrate, clearly showing all your steps, that $f(x)$ can be written in the form $a(3^{kx})$ where a and k are constants to be found. **(2 marks)**

b Hence, or otherwise, show that $f'(x) = (4\ln 3)(3^{6x+1})$ **(3 marks)**

9.3 The chain rule

1 Find $\frac{dy}{dx}$ for each of the following:

a $y = (4 - 3x)^3$ b $y = (6 + 5x)^{\frac{1}{2}}$

c $y = (5 + 2x^3)^4$ d $y = (7 + 3x^2)^{-5}$

e $y = \frac{6}{\sqrt{4 - 5x}}$ f $y = \frac{1}{6 - x}$

g $y = \sqrt[3]{3 + 2x^4}$ h $y = \sqrt{7x^3 - 4}$

Hint If $y = (f(x))^n$, then $\frac{dy}{dx} = n(f(x))^{n-1}f'(x)$.

2 Differentiate:

a $y = \sin^3 x$ b $y = \ln x^4$

c $y = e^{\cos 4x}$ d $y = (\ln x)^2$

e $y = \ln(\cos x)$ f $y = \sin(e^{-3x})$

Hint You can use the chain rule to differentiate a function of a function. If $y = f(g(x))$, then $\frac{dy}{dx} = f'(g(x))g'(x)$.

3 $f(x) = (3 - \ln 6x)^2$

a Find $f'(x)$. b Evaluate $f'\left(\frac{e^2}{6}\right)$.

4 Find the value of $\frac{dy}{dx}$ at the point (3, 6) on the curve with equation $2y^2 - 4y = x$.

Hint First find $\frac{dx}{dy}$
Then use the fact that $\frac{dy}{dx} = \frac{1}{\frac{dx}{dy}}$

(E/P) 5 A curve has equation $y = (2x - 3)^5$. Find the equation of the normal to the curve at the point P with x-coordinate 2. **(5 marks)**

(E/P) 6 $f(x) = \frac{3}{(6 - x)^3}$, $x \neq 6$. Find the tangent to the curve with equation $y = f(x)$ at the point P with x-coordinate 4. Give your answer in the form $ax + by + c = 0$. **(7 marks)**

(E/P) 7 $f(x) = 3\sin^2 x - 2\cos^2 x$. Show that the equation of the tangent to the curve with equation $y = f(x)$ at the point Q with x-coordinate $-\frac{5\pi}{6}$ is $12y - 30\sqrt{3}x - 25\pi\sqrt{3} + 9 = 0$. **(6 marks)**

(E/P) 8 The curve C has equation $x = -2\sin 4y$. Show that the equation of the normal to C at the point A with y-coordinate $\frac{2\pi}{3}$ is $4x + y + 4\sqrt{3} - \frac{2\pi}{3} = 0$. **(6 marks)**

(E/P) 9 Find the equation of the tangent to the curve with equation $y = 2^{(x^4)}$ at the point with coordinates (−1, 2). Give your answer in the form $ax + by + c = 0$, where a, b and c are exact values to be found. **(6 marks)**

9.4 The product rule

1 Find $\frac{dy}{dx}$ for each of the following:

a $y = x(4 - 5x)^3$ **b** $y = 3x^3(2x - 1)^6$

c $y = \frac{4}{x^2}(6x - 7)^4$ **d** $y = 8x^2(2x^3 - 4)^{-3}$

Hint If $y = uv$, then $\frac{dy}{dx} = u\frac{dv}{dx} + v\frac{du}{dx}$, where u and v are functions of x.

2 Find $f'(x)$ given that:

a $f(x) = x^2\cos 2x$ **b** $f(x) = e^{3x}\sin 5x$

c $f(x) = e^{-x}(2x^2 + 3)^3$ **d** $f(x) = -3\cos 4x \sin 2x$

e $f(x) = x^2 \ln x$ **f** $f(x) = e^{4x}\ln(\cos 3x)$

Hint If $f(x) = g(x)h(x)$ then $f'(x) = g(x)h'(x) + h(x)g'(x)$

3 Find the value of $\frac{dy}{dx}$ at the point (1, 4) on the curve with equation $y = 4x^3(1 - 2x^2)^4$.

Hint Evaluate $\frac{dy}{dx}$ when $x = 1$.

4 Differentiate with respect to x:

a $(x^4 - 3x^2)e^{-2x}$ **b** $(4\cos 2x - \sin x)e^{3x}$ **c** $\left(x^2 - 5\cos\frac{1}{2}x\right)\ln 4x$

(E) 5 Differentiate with respect to x:

a $e^{-x}\cos 3x$ **(2 marks)**

b $x^4\ln(\sin x)$ **(2 marks)**

(E/P) 6 **a** A curve C has equation $y = 2x^4(2 - 5x^2)^3$. Show that $\frac{dy}{dx} = x^3(2 - 5x)^n(ax^2 + bx + c)$, where n, a, b and c are constants to be found. **(4 marks)**

b Hence find the exact x-coordinates of the stationary points of C. **(4 marks)**

(E/P) 7 The curve C has equation $f(x) = e^{4x}\sin x$.

a Show that the turning points of C occur when $\tan x = -\frac{1}{4}$ **(3 marks)**

b Show that the equation of the normal to C at the point where $x = \frac{\pi}{2}$ is $x + 4e^{2\pi}y - 4e^{4\pi} - \frac{\pi}{2} = 0$ **(3 marks)**

(E/P) 8 A curve has equation $y = (x - \pi)\sin 2x$. Show that the equation of the tangent to the curve at the point with x-coordinate $\frac{3\pi}{4}$ is $x + y = \pi$. **(6 marks)**

9.5 The quotient rule

1 Find $f'(x)$ given that:

a $f(x) = \frac{4x + 3}{2x - 9}$ **b** $f(x) = \frac{6x^2}{3 - 5x}$

c $f(x) = \frac{1 - 8x}{(3x^3 + 2)^2}$ **d** $f(x) = \frac{7x^2 - 9x}{\sqrt{x^2 + 6}}$

Hint If $f(x) = \frac{g(x)}{h(x)}$ then $f'(x) = \frac{h(x)g'(x) - g(x)h'(x)}{(h(x))^2}$

2 Find $\frac{dy}{dx}$ for each of the following:

a $y = \frac{4x^2}{\cos 2x}$ **b** $y = \frac{x - e^{-x}}{\ln x}$

c $y = \frac{e^x}{\cos^2 x}$ **d** $y = \frac{5 - e^{-x}}{\sin 4x}$

Hint If $y = \frac{u}{v}$ then $\frac{dy}{dx} = \frac{v\frac{du}{dx} - u\frac{dv}{dx}}{v^2}$ where u and v are functions of x.

3 Find the gradient of the curve with equation $y = \frac{8 - 2x}{4x + 1}$ at the point $\left(\frac{1}{2}, \frac{7}{3}\right)$

4 The curve C has equation $y = \frac{x^2 - 6x}{e^{2x}}$

a Find $\frac{dy}{dx}$. **b** Find the equation of the normal to C at $\left(1, -\frac{5}{e^2}\right)$.

(E) 5 Given $y = \frac{\sin^2 x}{e^{2x}}$, find $\frac{dy}{dx}$ **(4 marks)**

(E) 6 Differentiate $\frac{e^{4x}}{x(x - 5)}$ with respect to x. **(4 marks)**

(E/P) 7 The curve C has equation $x = \frac{\cos 2y}{e^y}$. Find the equation of the tangent to the curve at the point where $y = \frac{\pi}{8}$ in the form $ax + by + c = 0$. **(6 marks)**

(E/P) 8 The diagram shows part of the graph with equation $y = f(x)$, where $f(x) = \frac{\cos^2 x}{e^x}$

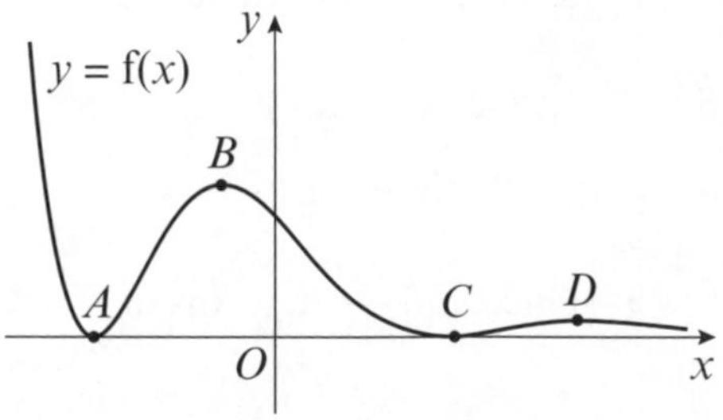

a Show that at the stationary points A, B, C and D, either $\cos x = 0$ or $\tan x = -\frac{1}{2}$ **(4 marks)**

b Hence, or otherwise, find the x-coordinates of the points A, B, C and D, giving your answers in radians to 2 decimal places. **(2 marks)**

9.6 Differentiating trigonometric functions

1 Find $\frac{dy}{dx}$ given:

a $y = \tan 4x$ **b** $y = 7\cot 2x$

c $y = \cot^5 x$ **d** $y = -3\tan^2 x$

Hint If $y = \tan kx$, then $\frac{dy}{dx} = k\sec^2 kx$

If $y = \cot kx$, then $\frac{dy}{dx} = -k\operatorname{cosec}^2 kx$

2 Find $\frac{dy}{dx}$ given:

a $y = \operatorname{cosec} 6x$ **b** $y = -4\sec 5x$

c $y = (\operatorname{cosec} x)^{\frac{4}{3}}$ **d** $y = -2\sec^3 4x$

Hint If $y = \operatorname{cosec} kx$, then $\frac{dy}{dx} = -k\operatorname{cosec} kx \cot kx$

If $y = \sec kx$, then $\frac{dy}{dx} = k\sec kx\tan kx$

3 Find $f'(x)$ when $f(x)$ is:

a $x^2\tan 3x$ **b** $\frac{e^{\sec x}}{x^2+1}$

c $\ln(\operatorname{cosec}^2 x)$ **d** $e^{-x}\cot 4x$

e $\frac{\sec^2 x}{\ln x}$ **f** $\frac{(4x-1)^3}{\cot^2 x}$

Hint Use the product rule or quotient rule in addition to the chain rule and standard rules for differentiating trigonometric functions.

4 Given that $x = \sin 2y$,

a find $\frac{dx}{dy}$ in terms of y.

b Hence find $\frac{dy}{dx}$ in terms of x.

Hint Use the identity $\sin^2 A + \cos^2 A \equiv 1$ to write $\cos 2y$ in terms of x.

← Year 1, Section 10.3

(E) **5** Show that if $y = \operatorname{cosec} x$, then $\frac{dy}{dx} = -\operatorname{cosec} x \cot x$. **(5 marks)**

(E/P) **6** $f(x) = \ln(\cot 2x)$

a Show that $f'(x) = -4\operatorname{cosec} 4x$. **(5 marks)**

b Find the equation of the normal to the curve $y = f(x)$ at the point with x-coordinate $\frac{\pi}{8}$ **(3 marks)**

(E/P) **7** The diagram shows part of the curve $y = f(x)$, where

$f(x) = e^{\tan\frac{1}{2}x}$

Point A is the y-intercept of $y = f(x)$. The tangent and normal to the curve $y = f(x)$ at A intersect the x-axis at the points B and C respectively.
Find the area of triangle ABC. **(8 marks)**

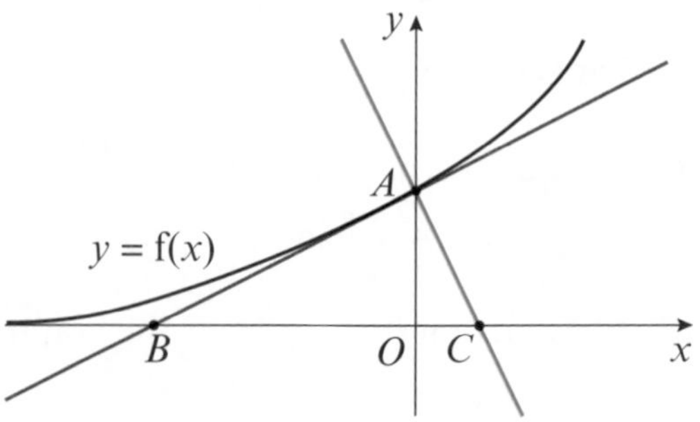

(E/P) **8** Given that $x = \sec 4y$,

a find $\frac{dx}{dy}$ in terms of y. **(2 marks)**

b Hence find $\frac{dy}{dx}$ in terms of x. **(4 marks)**

9.7 Parametric differentiation

1 Find $\frac{dy}{dx}$ for each of the following, leaving your answers in terms of the parameter t.

Hint If x and y are given as functions of a parameter, t, then $\frac{dy}{dx} = \frac{\frac{dy}{dt}}{\frac{dx}{dt}}$

a $x = 4t - 1, y = 2t^3$

b $x = \frac{2}{t^2}, y = 4 - t^2$

c $x = 3t, y = te^{4t}$

d $x = 4\sin t, y = 5\tan t$ **e** $x = 4e^{3t} - 1, y = 2e^t + 4$ **f** $x = 2t^3 - 1, y = \ln t$

2 A curve C has parametric equations $x = \tan t, y = \sec t$. Find:

a $\frac{dy}{dx}$ in terms of the parameter t

b the equation of the tangent to the curve at the point P, where $t = \frac{\pi}{4}$

Hint Substitute $t = \frac{\pi}{4}$ into the original equations to find the coordinates of P.

3 A curve C has parametric equations $x = 1 - t^2, y = t^3 + 2t^2$. Find:

a $\frac{dy}{dx}$ in terms of the parameter t

b the equation of the normal to the curve at the point P, where $t = -3$.
Give your answer in the form $ax + by + c = 0$, where a, b and c are constants to be found.

4 A curve C has parametric equations $x = 1 - \cos 2\theta, y = 4\sin 2\theta, -\pi \leqslant \theta \leqslant \pi$. Find:

a $\frac{dy}{dx}$ in terms of the parameter θ

b the coordinates of the points with zero gradient on the curve C.

Hint Solve $\frac{dy}{dx} = 0$ to find the values of θ at the points with zero gradient, then substitute into the original parametric equations to find the coordinates.

E/P 5 The curve C has parametric equations $x = 2\sec\theta, y = 4\cos^2\theta, -\pi \leqslant \theta \leqslant \pi$.

a Find an expression for $\frac{dy}{dx}$ in terms of the parameter θ. **(4 marks)**

b Find an equation of the normal to the curve at the point where $\theta = \frac{\pi}{3}$ **(4 marks)**

E/P 6 The curve C has parametric equations $x = (t - 2)^2, y = t^2 + 4t, t \in \mathbb{R}$.

The line l is a tangent to C and is parallel to the line with equation $y = 2x - 9$.

Find the equation of l. **(6 marks)**

E/P 7 The curve C has parametric equations $x = -2\sec 2t, y = 2\cot t, -\frac{\pi}{2} \leqslant \theta \leqslant \frac{\pi}{2}$

a Find an expression for $\frac{dy}{dx}$ in terms of the parameter t. **(4 marks)**

The point A with coordinates $(-4, -2\sqrt{3})$ lies on the curve C. The line l is tangent to C at A.

b Show that an equation for l is $x\sqrt{3} + 3y + 10\sqrt{3} = 0$. **(4 marks)**

E/P **8** The curve C has parametric equations $x = \frac{t}{1-t}$, $y = \frac{1}{1+t^2}$, $-1 < t < 1$.
The line l is normal to C at the point where $t = -\frac{1}{2}$

a Find an equation for the line l. **(6 marks)**

b Show that a Cartesian equation for the curve C is $y = \frac{x^2 + 2x + 1}{2x^2 + 2x + 1}$ **(4 marks)**

9.8 Implicit differentiation

1 By writing $u = y^5$ and using the chain rule, show that $\frac{d}{dx}(y^5) = 5y^4\frac{dy}{dx}$

Hint Use $\frac{du}{dx} = \frac{du}{dy} \times \frac{dy}{dx}$

2 Show that $\frac{d}{dx}(x^3y^2) = 2x^3y\frac{dy}{dx} + 3x^2y^2$

Hint Use the product rule and the fact that $\frac{d}{dx}(y^n) = ny^{n-1}\frac{dy}{dx}$

3 Find $\frac{dy}{dx}$ in terms of x and y where:

a $x^4 - y^3 = 3$

b $3x^2 + 4y^2 - 5x^2y = 2$

c $y = \frac{5y^2}{x^2 - y^2}$

d $4\ln(x-5) - \ln(y^3) = 0$ **e** $\cos x + \sin^2 y = 1$ **f** $xe^{-y} + ye^{2x} - 7 = 0$

Hint When you differentiate implicitly, your expression for $\frac{dy}{dx}$ will usually involve both x and y.

4 The curve C is described by the equation
$x^2 - 4x^2y + y^2 = 21$

a Find $\frac{dy}{dx}$

b Evaluate $\frac{dy}{dx}$ at the point $(2, -1)$.

c Find an equation of the tangent to C at the point $(2, -1)$.

Hint For part **b**, substitute $x = 2$ and $y = -1$ into your expression for $\frac{dy}{dx}$

E **5** Find the gradient of the curve with equation $3x^2 - y^3 - 5xy = 1$ at the point $(2, 1)$. **(5 marks)**

E **6** Given that $e^{-3y} - e^{-2x} = 4xy$, find $\frac{dy}{dx}$ in terms of x and y. **(5 marks)**

E/P **7** The curve C satisfies $\cos 2x + \sin 2y = 1$, where $-\frac{\pi}{4} < x < \frac{\pi}{4}$ and $0 < y < \frac{\pi}{6}$

a Find an expression for $\frac{dy}{dx}$ **(3 marks)**

b Find an equation of the tangent to C at the point P with x-coordinate $-\frac{\pi}{6}$, giving your answer in the form $ax + by + c = 0$, where a, b and c are constants to be found. **(5 marks)**

E/P **8** A curve C is described by the equation $4x^2 + y^2 + 6x - 8y - 10 = 0$.
Find an equation of the normal to C at the point $(1, 8)$, giving your answer in the form $ax + by + c = 0$, where a, b and c are constants to be found. **(7 marks)**

9.9 Using second derivatives

1 $f(x) = e^{-x}\cos 2x$

a Find $f'(x)$. **b** Find $f''(x)$.

Hint To find $f''(x)$, differentiate $f'(x)$.

2 $f(x) = 8x^2 + 3e^{4x}$

a Find $f''(x)$.

b Hence show that $f(x)$ is a convex function for all real values of x.

Hint The function $f(x)$ is convex on the interval $[a, b]$ if and only if $f''(x) \geqslant 0$ for every value of x in that interval.

3 $f(x) = \cos 2x, -\frac{\pi}{2} \leqslant x \leqslant \frac{\pi}{2}$

a Find $f''(x)$.

b Find the range of values for which $f(x)$ is concave.

Hint The function $f(x)$ is concave on the interval $[a, b]$ if and only if $f''(x) \leqslant 0$ for every value of x in that interval.

4 $f(x) = x(2x - 1)^5$

a Find $f'(x)$ and $f''(x)$.

b Show that $f''(x) = 0$ at $x = \frac{1}{6}$ and $x = \frac{1}{2}$

c Show that $x = \frac{1}{6}$ is a point of inflection by demonstrating that $f''(0.1)$ and $f''(0.2)$ have different signs.

Hint A point of inflection is a point at which $f''(x)$ changes sign. To find the point of inflection, solve $f''(x) = 0$, then check that $f''(x)$ has different signs on either side of that point.

(E) 5 Find the interval on which the function $f(x) = x^3 - 8x^2 + 6x - 2$ is convex. **(4 marks)**

(E) 6 $f(x) = x(2x - 5)^4$

a Find $f'(x)$ and $f''(x)$. **(4 marks)**

b Show that $f(x)$ has a point of inflection at $x = 1$. **(3 marks)**

(E/P) 7 The curve C has equation $y = f(x)$ where $f(x) = \frac{\sin 4x}{e^{2x}}, 0 \leqslant x \leqslant \frac{\pi}{4}$

Determine the range of values for which $f(x)$ is convex. Give your answer to 2 decimal places where necessary. **(6 marks)**

(E/P) 8 $f(x) = x^3e^x$. Find the exact range of values for which the curve C with equation $y = f(x)$ is concave. **(6 marks)**

9.10 Rates of change

1 Given that $S = 6x^2$ and that $\frac{dx}{dt} = \frac{2}{3}$,

a find $\frac{dS}{dt}$

b evaluate $\frac{dS}{dt}$ when $x = 3$.

Hint You can use the chain rule to connect rates of change in situations involving two or more variables. Here $\frac{dS}{dt} = \frac{dS}{dx} \times \frac{dx}{dt}$

2 Given that $y = x\cos 4x$ and that $\frac{\mathrm{d}x}{\mathrm{d}t} = 3$, find $\frac{\mathrm{d}y}{\mathrm{d}t}$ when $x = \frac{5\pi}{16}$

3 Given that $y = \frac{e^{2x}}{x^2}$ and that $\frac{\mathrm{d}x}{\mathrm{d}t} = -\frac{1}{2}$, find $\frac{\mathrm{d}y}{\mathrm{d}t}$ when $x = 4$.

4 The volume of a sphere $V\,\text{cm}^3$ is related to its radius by the formula $V = \frac{4}{3}\pi r^3$.

a Find $\frac{\mathrm{d}V}{\mathrm{d}r}$

b Given that the rate of change of the radius in cm s^{-1} is given by $\frac{\mathrm{d}r}{\mathrm{d}t} = 3$, find $\frac{\mathrm{d}V}{\mathrm{d}t}$

Hint For part **b**, r varies with t, so you cannot treat it as a constant when you differentiate V with respect to t. You need to use the chain rule:
$$\frac{\mathrm{d}V}{\mathrm{d}t} = \frac{\mathrm{d}V}{\mathrm{d}r} \times \frac{\mathrm{d}r}{\mathrm{d}t}$$

(E) 5 At any given time, the rate of population growth in a small town is modelled as being proportional to the current population, P.

a Write a differential equation to describe this model. **(1 mark)**

b Explain how this model could be adapted if the population is declining at a rate proportional to its size. **(1 mark)**

(E) 6 At time t years after monitoring began, the area covered by Arctic ice is $I\,\text{km}^2$.

The rate of decay of ice coverage is directly proportional to the square root of the existing area covered. Write down a differential equation in terms of I and t. **(2 marks)**

(E) 7 The value, V in £s, of a car t years after it is purchased is modelled by the equation

$V = 23500\,e^{-0.25t}, t \geqslant 0$

a Find the value of the car 7 years after it was purchased. **(1 mark)**

b Find the rate of change of value of the car after 10 years. **(3 marks)**

(E) 8 The volume, $V\,\text{cm}^3$, of a sphere is given by $V = \frac{4}{3}\pi r^3$ and the surface area, $S\,\text{cm}^2$, of a sphere is given by $S = 4\pi r^2$.

a Show that $V = \frac{1}{6\sqrt{\pi}}S^{\frac{3}{2}}$ **(2 marks)**

The surface area of the sphere is expanding at a constant rate of $4\,\text{cm s}^{-1}$.

b Show that $\frac{\mathrm{d}V}{\mathrm{d}t} = \sqrt{\frac{S}{\pi}}$ **(2 marks)**

Problem solving Set A

Bronze

The curve C has equation $y = x^4 - \frac{20}{3}x^3 + 14x^2 + 6x - 4$.

a Find $\frac{dy}{dx}$ and $\frac{d^2y}{dx^2}$ **(3 marks)**

b Show that the curve C is concave in the interval $\left[1, \frac{7}{3}\right]$. **(3 marks)**

Silver

The curve C has equation $y = 4x^3 \ln x^2, x > 0$.

Show that the curve C is convex when $x \geqslant e^{-\frac{5}{6}}$. **(6 marks)**

Gold

$f(x) = ax^4 + 2x^3 + 3x^2 - 10x + 5$. Given that $f(x)$ is convex for all real values of x, find the range of possible values of a. **(6 marks)**

Problem solving Set B

Bronze

The curve C is described by $x^2 + y = (2 - x)(y - 1)$.

a Find $\frac{dy}{dx}$ **(4 marks)**

b Find the equation of the normal to C at the point with x-coordinate 0. **(4 marks)**

Silver

Circle C has parametric equations

$x = 2\sin t - 1, y = 2\cos t + 3, 0 \leqslant t \leqslant 2\pi$

The line l_1 is normal to C at the point B, which lies on the y-axis.

a Find the Cartesian equation of the circle, clearly stating the centre and radius. **(3 marks)**

b Show clearly that B has coordinates $(0, 3 + \sqrt{3})$. **(2 marks)**

The line l_1 intersects the x-axis at the point A.

c Find the area of triangle AOB. **(7 marks)**

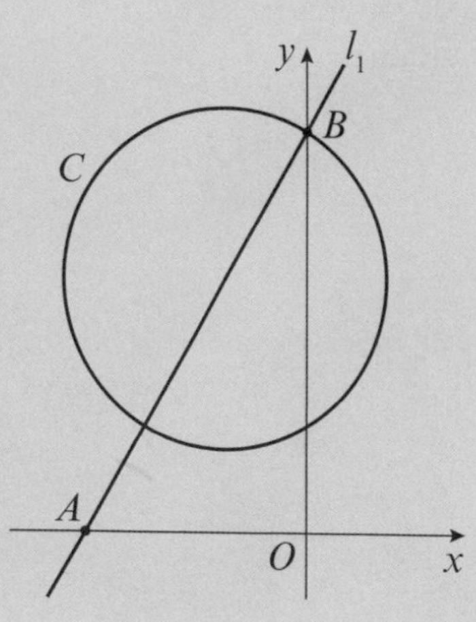

Gold

The diagram shows the curve C given by the equation

$\cos y + \sin x = 1,\ 0 \leqslant x \leqslant \pi,\ -\frac{\pi}{2} \leqslant y \leqslant \frac{\pi}{2}$

Find the equations of the tangents to the curve that are parallel to the line $y = x$. You must show clear algebraic working. Solutions based on graphical or numerical approaches are not acceptable. **(9 marks)**

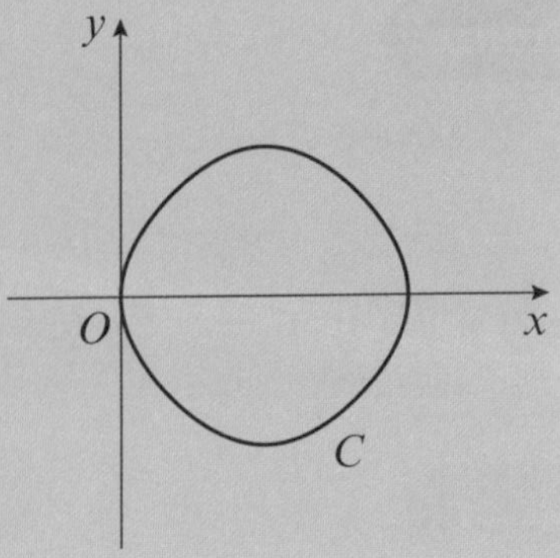

Now try this → **Exam question bank Q4, Q7, Q28, Q39, Q43, Q52, Q67, Q77**

10.1 Locating roots

1 The diagram shows a sketch of the curve $y = f(x)$, where $f(x) = 2x^3 - 4x^2 - 2x + 2$.

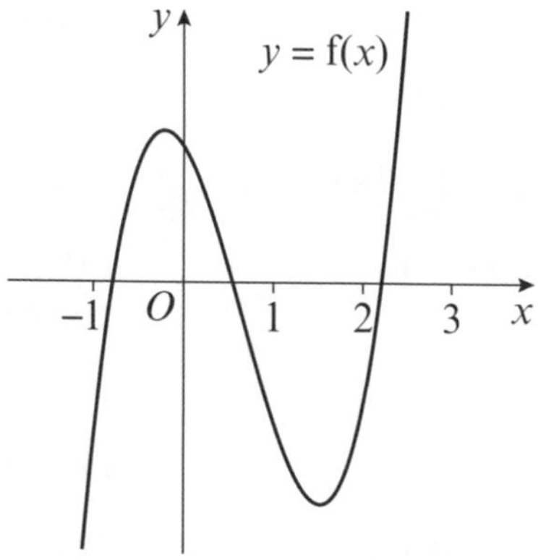

Hint If the function $f(x)$ is continuous on the interval $[a, b]$ and $f(a)$ and $f(b)$ have opposite signs, then $f(x)$ has at least one root, x, which satisfies $a < x < b$.

a Explain how the graph shows that $f(x)$ has a root between $x = -1$ and $x = 0$.

b Calculate:

i $f(2.2)$ **ii** $f(2.3)$

c Explain how your answer to part **b** shows that $f(x)$ has a root between $x = 2.2$ and $x = 2.3$.

2 Show that each of these functions has at least one root in the given interval.

a $f(x) = 4 - \frac{1}{2}x^2 + 2x^3$, $-1.2 < x < -1.1$

b $f(x) = x^2 \ln x - 2e^x + 4$, $0.6 < x < 0.7$

c $f(x) = 3x^2 + \dfrac{5}{x^3}$, $-1.11 < x < -1.10$

d $f(x) = 9 + \frac{3}{4}x - 7\sqrt{x}$, $2.37 < x < 2.38$

Hint Evaluate $f(x)$ at the endpoints of the given interval and show that $f(x)$ changes sign in that interval.

3 **a** On the same set of axes, sketch the graphs of $y = \ln x$ and $y = -(x + 1)^2 + 6$.

b Explain why the function $f(x) = \ln x + (x + 1)^2 - 6$ has only one root.

Hint If $\ln x + (x + 1)^2 - 6 = 0$, then $\ln x = -(x + 1)^2 + 6$.

c Show that the function $f(x) = \ln x + (x + 1)^2 - 6$ has a root between $x = 1.3$ and $x = 1.4$.

4 $f(x) = \cos^2 x - e^{-2x}$, where x is in radians.

a Find $f'(x)$.

b Show that there is a stationary point, α, of $y = f(x)$ in the interval $[3.1, 3.2]$.

c By considering a change in sign of $f'(x)$ in a suitable interval, verify that $\alpha = 3.143$ to 3 decimal places.

Hint A stationary point occurs where the gradient is zero, so look for a sign change in the gradient. ← Year 1, Section 12.9

Hint To determine a root to a given degree of accuracy you need to show it lies within the range of values that all round to the given value. Here consider $f'(3.1425)$ and $f'(3.1435)$.

(E) **5** $g(x) = \frac{1}{2}x^3 - 2\cos x$, where x is in radians.

a Show that $g(x)$ has a root, α, in the interval $1.1 < x < 1.2$. **(2 marks)**

b By considering a change of sign of $g(x)$ in a suitable interval, verify that $\alpha = 1.165$ correct to 3 decimal places. **(3 marks)**

(E/P) **6** **a** On the same set of axes, sketch the graphs of $y = (x + 2)^2 - 1$ and $y = 2^x$. **(2 marks)**

b With reference to your sketch explain why $f(x) = 2^x + 1 - (x + 2)^2$ has two roots. **(2 marks)**

c Show that the function $f(x) = 2^x + 1 - (x + 2)^2$ has a root in the interval $-0.8 < x < -0.7$. **(3 marks)**

(E/P) **7** $f(x) = \frac{2}{6 - 3x} - 4$

a Calculate f(1.9) and f(2.1). **(2 marks)**

b Explain why the equation $f(x) = 0$ does not have a root in the interval $1.9 < x < 2.1$. **(2 marks)**

The equation $f(x) = 0$ has a single root α.

c Use algebra to find the exact value of α. **(2 marks)**

(E/P) **8** **a** On the same set of axes, sketch the graphs of $y = \frac{1}{4}\sin 2x$ and $y = \ln x$. **(2 marks)**

b With reference to your sketch explain why $h(x) = \sin 2x - 4\ln x$ has only one root. **(2 marks)**

c Show that the function $h(x) = \sin 2x - 4\ln x$ has a root in the interval [1.18, 1.19]. **(3 marks)**

10.2 Iteration

1 $f(x) = x^2 - 8x + 3$

Show that $f(x) = 0$ can be written as:

a $x = \sqrt{8x - 3}$ **b** $x = 8 - \frac{3}{x}, x \neq 0$

c $x = \frac{x^2 - 3}{8}$

Hint Rearrange $x^2 - 8x + 3 = 0$ to obtain each answer.

2 $f(x) = x^2 - 4x - 2$

a Show that $f(x) = 0$ can be written as $x = \sqrt{4x + 2}$.

b Use the iterative formula $x_{n+1} = \sqrt{4x_n + 2}$, $x_0 = 5$, to find, to 3 decimal places, the values of x_1, x_2, x_3 and x_4.

Hint Use your calculator to find the values of x_1, x_2, x_3 and x_4 efficiently.

3 $h(x) = -x^3 + 3x^2 - 1$

a Show that $h(x) = 0$ can be written as:

i $x = \sqrt[3]{3x^2 - 1}$ **ii** $x = \sqrt{\frac{x^3 + 1}{3}}$

b Use the iterative formula $x_{n+1} = \sqrt[3]{3x_n^2 - 1}$, $x_0 = 1$, to find, to 3 decimal places, the values of x_1, x_2, x_3 and x_4.

c Use the iterative formula $x_{n+1} = \sqrt{\frac{x_n^3 + 1}{3}}$, $x_0 = 1$, to find, to 3 decimal places, the values of x_1, x_2, x_3 and x_4.

d Use your answers to parts **b** and **c** to explain why there could be more than one solution to the equation $\text{h}(x) = 0$.

(E/P) **4** $\text{f}(x) = 2\sin x - \frac{1}{2}x^2$

a Show that the equation $\text{f}(x) = 0$ can be written as $x = \sqrt{4\sin x}$. **(2 marks)**

b Let $x_0 = 1.5$. Use the iterative formula $x_{n+1} = \sqrt{4\sin x_n}$ to find, to 3 decimal places, the values of x_1, x_2 and x_3. **(3 marks)**

The root of $\text{f}(x)$ is α.

c By considering the change of sign of $\text{f}(x)$ in a suitable interval, prove that $\alpha = 1.934$ to 3 decimal places. **(3 marks)**

(E/P) **5** The diagram shows a sketch of the curve $y = \text{f}(x)$, where $\text{f}(x) = x^5 - 5x^2 + 2$.

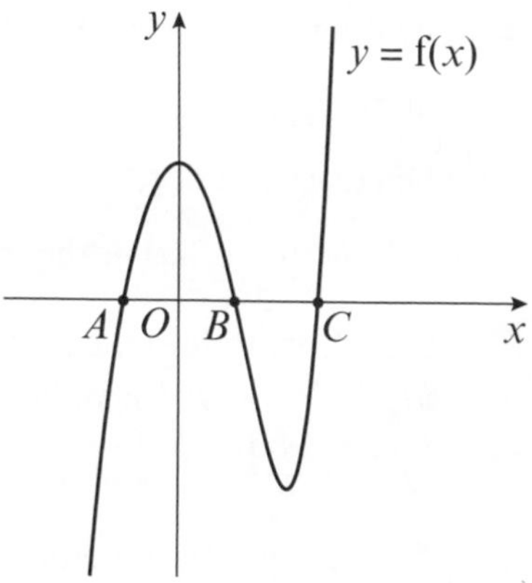

The x-coordinates of the points A and C are also solutions to the equation $x^2 - x - 1 = 0$.

a Find the exact coordinates of the points A and C. **(3 marks)**

b Show that the equation $\text{f}(x) = 0$ can be written as

$$x = \sqrt{\frac{x^5 + 2}{5}}$$ **(2 marks)**

c Let $x_0 = 0.5$. Use the iterative formula $x_{n+1} = \sqrt{\frac{x_n^5 + 2}{5}}$ to find, to 3 decimal places, the values of x_1, x_2 and x_3. **(3 marks)**

The root of $\text{f}(x)$ at point B is α.

d By considering a suitable interval, prove that $\alpha = 0.651$ to 3 decimal places. **(3 marks)**

(E/P) **6** $\text{f}(x) = \text{e}^{x+4} + \frac{1}{2}x^2 - 10$

a Show that there is a root α of $\text{f}(x)$ in the interval $[-1.9, -1.8]$. **(2 marks)**

b Show that the equation $\text{f}(x) = 0$ can be written as $x = \ln\left(10 - \frac{1}{2}x^2\right) - 4$. **(2 marks)**

c Let $x_0 = -3$. Use the iterative formula $x_{n+1} = \ln\left(10 - \frac{1}{2}x_n^2\right) - 4$ to find, to 3 decimal places, the values of x_1, x_2 and x_3. **(3 marks)**

d By considering a suitable interval, prove that $\alpha = -1.8954$ to 4 decimal places. **(3 marks)**

E/P **7** The diagram shows the part of the graph of $y = f(x)$ where $f(x) = x\sin^2 x$. The curve touches the x-axis at A and B and has a turning point at P.

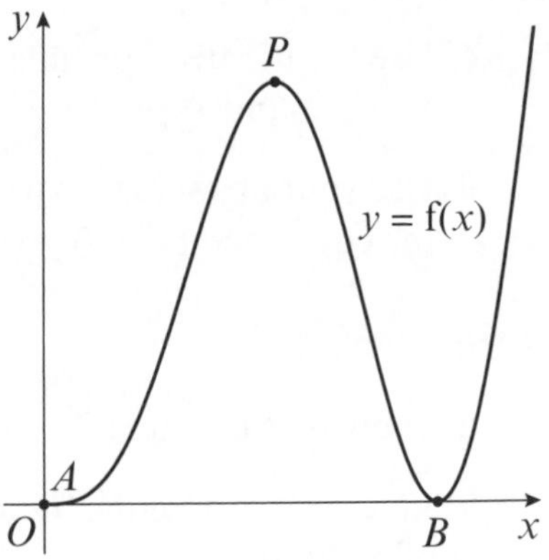

a Verify that the coordinates of A and B are $(0, 0)$ and $(\pi, 0)$ respectively. **(1 mark)**

b Find $f'(x)$. **(3 marks)**

c Show that the x-coordinate of P lies in the interval $[1.8, 1.9]$. **(2 marks)**

d Show that the x-coordinate of P is the solution to the equation $x = \arccos\left(\frac{-\sin x}{2x}\right)$. **(2 marks)**

e Use the iterative formula $x_{n+1} = \arccos\left(\frac{-\sin x_n}{2x_n}\right)$, $x_0 = 1.8$ to calculate the values of x_1, x_2 and x_3, giving your answers to 3 decimal places. **(3 marks)**

E/P **8** The diagram shows part of the curve with equation

$$y = \frac{1}{x+1}$$

The curve intersects the line $y = x$ at the point where $x = \alpha$.

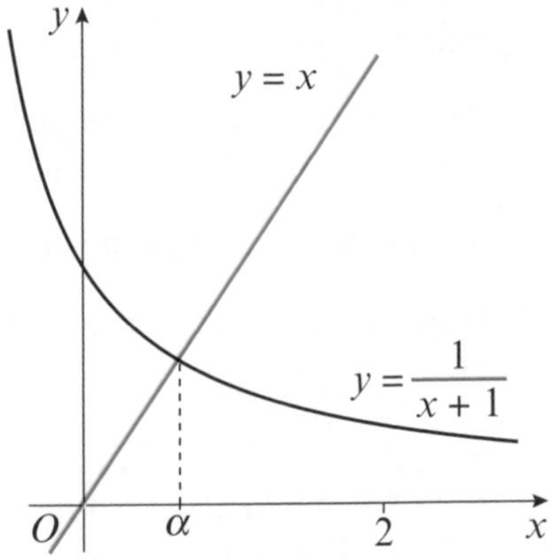

a Show that α lies in the interval $\left[\frac{1}{2}, 1\right]$. **(2 marks)**

In an effort to find a better approximation to α, a student uses the iterative formula

$$x_{n+1} = \frac{1}{x_n + 1}$$

b Use the graph, together with $x_0 = 2$, to explain whether the iteration will converge or diverge. **(2 marks)**

10.3 The Newton–Raphson method

1 $f(x) = x^2 - 6x + 7$

a Show that the equation $f(x) = 0$ has a root, α, in the interval $[1.5, 1.6]$.

b Calculate $f'(1.6)$.

c Work out the value of $1.6 - \frac{f(1.6)}{f'(1.6)}$, giving your answer correct to 6 decimal places.

d Use algebra to find the exact values of the roots of $f(x)$.

e Comment on the accuracy of your answer from part **c**.

2 $f(x) = x^4 - 3x^2 + x + 1$

Hint The Newton–Raphson formula is $x_{n+1} = x_n - \frac{f(x_n)}{f'(x_n)}$

a Show that the equation $f(x) = 0$ has a root α in the interval $1.2 < \alpha < 1.3$.

b Using $x_0 = 1.3$ as a first approximation to α, apply the Newton–Raphson procedure once to $f(x)$ to find a second approximation to α, giving your answer to 3 decimal places.

3 The diagram shows part of the curve $y = f(x)$.

The x-coordinates of which points would not be valid as a first approximation when applying the Newton–Raphson method to find the roots of $f(x) = 0$?

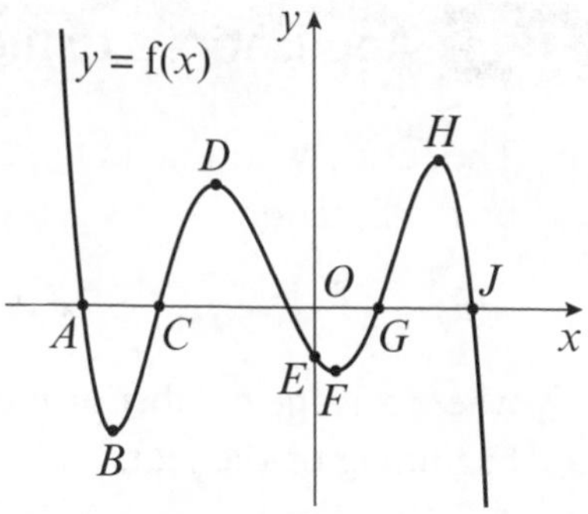

Hint If any value, x_i, in the Newton–Raphson method is at a turning point, the method will fail because $f'(x_i) = 0$ and the formula would result in division by zero, which is not valid.

(E) **4** $f(x) = 4\cos^2 x - e^{-x}$

a Show that the equation $f(x) = 0$ has a root α in the interval [1.3, 1.4]. **(1 mark)**

b Find $f'(x)$. **(2 marks)**

c Using $x_0 = 1.3$ as a first approximation to α, apply the Newton–Raphson procedure once to $f(x)$ to find a second approximation to α, giving your answer to 3 decimal places. **(3 marks)**

(E) **5** $f(x) = e^{-\frac{1}{4}x} + \frac{3}{4}x - \frac{1}{4}x^2$

a Show that the equation $f(x) = 0$ has a root α in the interval [3.4, 3.5]. **(1 mark)**

b Using $x_0 = 3.5$ as a first approximation to α, apply the Newton–Raphson procedure once to $f(x)$ to find a second approximation to α, giving your answer to 3 decimal places. **(4 marks)**

c By considering the change of sign of $f(x)$ over an appropriate interval, show that your answer to part **b** is correct to 3 decimal places. **(2 marks)**

(E) **6** $f(x) = \dfrac{\cos^2 x}{x} - \frac{1}{4}\ln x$

a Show that $f(x) = 0$ has a root α in the interval $1.2 < \alpha < 1.3$. **(2 marks)**

b Find $f'(x)$. **(2 marks)**

c Taking 1.3 as a first approximation to α, apply the Newton–Raphson procedure once to $f(x)$ to obtain a second approximation for α, giving your answer to 3 decimal places. **(3 marks)**

(E/P) **7** $f(x) = x - \dfrac{4}{x^2} + 5$

The diagram shows part of the curve with equation $y = f(x)$.

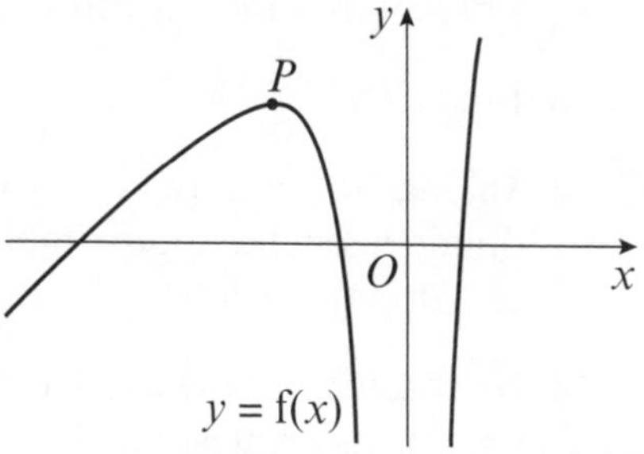

The coordinates of the point P are (p, q).

a Find the value of p and explain clearly why $x_0 = p$ is not suitable to use as a first approximation when applying the Newton–Raphson method. **(3 marks)**

b Show that $f(x) = 0$ has a root α in the interval [0.8, 0.9]. **(1 mark)**

$f(x) = 0$ also has a root β in the interval [–5, –4].

c Taking $x_0 = -5$ as a first approximation, apply the Newton–Raphson process once to $f(x)$ to obtain a second approximation to β. Give your answer to 3 decimal places. **(4 marks)**

10.4 Applications to modelling

1 The future world ranking position of a tennis player during a calendar year can be modelled by the function

$w(x) = -\frac{1}{50}x^4 + \frac{7}{10}x^3 - 7x^2 + 17x + 40,\ 0 \leqslant x \leqslant 12$

where x is the number of months since the beginning of the year.

The diagram shows the graph with equation $y = w(x)$. The graph has a local maximum at A and local minimum at B.

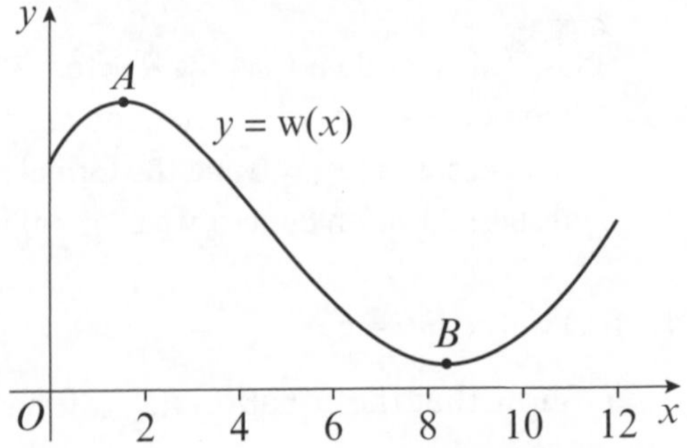

a Find $w'(x)$.

b Show that the player reaches a minimum ranking between 8.3 and 8.4 months after the beginning of the year.

c Show that the turning points of the graph correspond to the equation

$$x = \pm\sqrt{\frac{10}{21}\left(\frac{2}{25}x^3 + 14x - 17\right)}$$

Hint The turning points occur when $w'(x) = 0$ so rearrange your answer from part **a**.

Let $x_0 = 8.3$ and $x_{n+1} = \sqrt{\frac{10}{21}\left(\frac{2}{25}x_n^3 + 14x_n - 17\right)}$

d Find the values of x_1, x_2, x_3 and x_4, giving your answers to 3 decimal places.

(E) **2** A boomerang is thrown from a point on level ground. The height in metres of the boomerang above the ground t seconds after it is thrown can be modelled by the function

$$h(t) = 50\sin\left(\frac{t^2}{36}\right),\ t \geqslant 0$$

The diagram shows the sketch of $y = h(t)$.

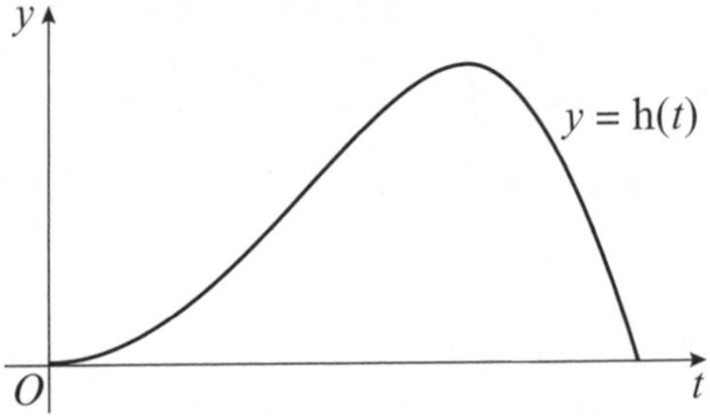

a Show that the boomerang lands between 10 and 11 seconds after it is thrown. **(1 mark)**

b Find $h'(t)$. **(2 marks)**

c Taking 10.5 as a first approximation, apply the Newton–Raphson process once to $h(t)$ to obtain a second approximation for the time when the boomerang lands. Give your answer to 2 decimal places. **(3 marks)**

d By considering the change of sign of $h'(t)$ in a suitable interval, verify that the boomerang reaches its greatest height 7.52 seconds after it is thrown, correct to 2 decimal places. **(2 marks)**

E/P **3** The trading price, £p, of a stock during a 8-hour trading window can be modelled by the function

$$p(x) = \frac{1}{3}\cos\left(\frac{x}{3}\right) + \frac{x^2}{100} + 1.29, 0 \leqslant x \leqslant 8$$

The diagram shows a sketch of $y = p(x)$.

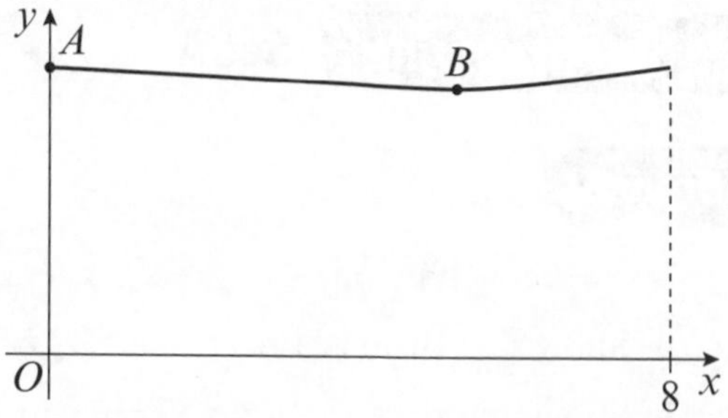

a State the price of the stock, to the nearest penny, when trading begins. **(1 mark)**

b Find $p'(x)$. **(2 marks)**

c Show that the price of the stock reaches a minimum at point B between 5 and 5.5 hours after trading opens. **(2 marks)**

d Show that the x-coordinate of B is the solution to the equation $x = \frac{50}{9}\sin\left(\frac{x}{3}\right)$. **(2 marks)**

e Use the iterative formula $x_{n+1} = \frac{50}{9}\sin\left(\frac{x_n}{3}\right)$, $0 \leqslant x \leqslant 8$, with $x_0 = 5.3$, to calculate the values of x_1, x_2 and x_3, giving your answers to 3 decimal places. **(3 marks)**

E/P **4** The value of a mobile phone, t years after purchase, is modelled by the function

$v(t) = 450e^{-0.5t} - 40\cos t, t > 0$

a Show that $v(t)$ has a root in the interval [5, 6]. **(1 mark)**

b Find $v'(t)$. **(2 marks)**

c Taking 5 as a first approximation, apply the Newton–Raphson process once to $v(t)$ to obtain a second approximation for the time when the value of the mobile phone is zero. Give your answer to 2 decimal places. **(3 marks)**

d Criticise this model with respect to the value of the phone as it gets older. **(1 mark)**

E/P **5** The height of a bungee jumper above the ground can be modelled by the equation $h = 40\cos t + 50 - 4t^{\frac{2}{3}}$, $0 \leqslant t \leqslant 6$ where t seconds is the time since the person jumped and h is the height, in metres, above the ground. The bungee jump is considered to be safe if the jumper does not get closer than 10 m to the ground.

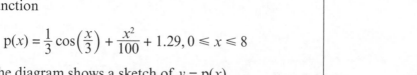

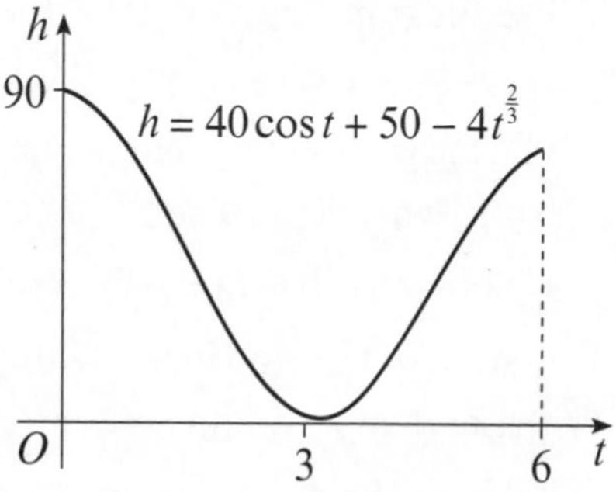

a Show that, some time between 2 and 3 seconds after the person jumps, the bungee jumper is exactly 10 m from the ground. **(2 marks)**

b Comment on whether the jump is safe according to this model. **(1 mark)**

c Show that the equation $40\cos t + 50 - 4t^{\frac{2}{3}} = 10$ can be written as

$$t = \arccos\left(\frac{4t^{\frac{2}{3}} - 40}{40}\right)$$ **(2 marks)**

d Using $t_0 = 2.5$, and the iterative formula $t_{n+1} = \arccos\left(\frac{4t_n^{\frac{2}{3}} - 40}{40}\right)$, find, to 5 decimal places, the values of t_1, t_2, t_3 and t_4. **(3 marks)**

Problem solving Set A

Bronze

$f(x) = \frac{1}{2}\cos(x^2) - \frac{1}{2}x + 1$

a Show that there is a root α of $f(x) = 0$ in the interval [1, 1.5]. **(2 marks)**

b Show that the equation $f(x) = 0$ can be written as $x = \sqrt{\arccos(x - 2)}$ **(2 marks)**

c Let $x_0 = 1.5$. Use the iterative formula $x_{n+1} = \sqrt{\arccos(x_n - 2)}$ to find, to 3 decimal places, the values of x_1, x_2 and x_3. **(3 marks)**

Silver

The diagram shows part of the curve with equation

$y = 3\cos\left(\frac{1}{3}x\right)$

The curve meets the line $y = x$ at a single point, $x = \alpha$.

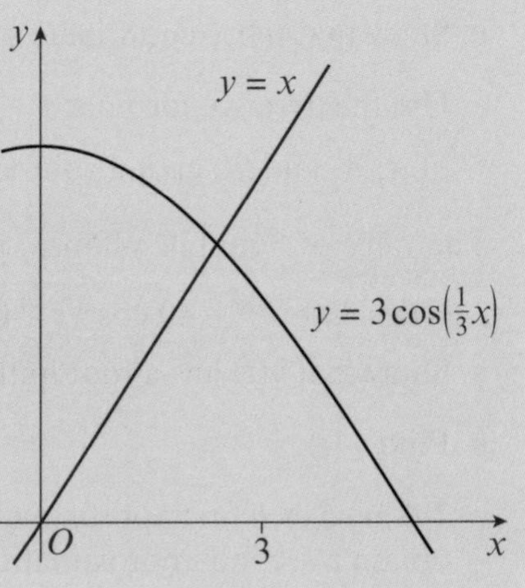

a Show that α is in the interval [2, 3]. **(2 marks)**

A student uses the iterative formula $x_{n+1} = 3\cos\left(\frac{1}{3}x_n\right)$ in an attempt to find an approximation for α.

b Using the graph and starting with $x_0 = 3$, explain why the iteration will converge to α. **(2 marks)**

c Find x_1, x_2 and x_3, giving your answers to 3 decimal places. **(2 marks)**

Gold

The diagram shows part of the curve with equation

$y = (x - 1)e^x$

The curve meets the line $y = x$ at a two points, $x = \alpha$ and $x = \beta$, where $\alpha < 0$ and $\beta > 0$.

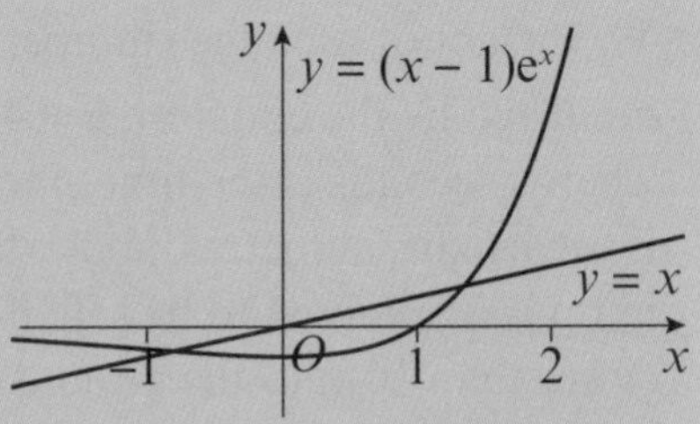

a Show that β is in the interval $1 < \beta < 2$. **(2 marks)**

A student uses the iterative formula $x_{n+1} = (x_n - 1)e^{x_n}$ in an attempt to find an approximation for β.

b Using the graph, describe what will happen for the following starting values.

i $x_0 = \frac{1}{2}$ **ii** $x_0 = 2$ **(4 marks)**

c By choosing a suitable interval, show that $\alpha = -0.806$ correct to 3 decimal places. **(2 marks)**

Problem solving Set B

Bronze

$f(x) = -\frac{4}{3}x + 3x^{\frac{4}{3}} - 2$

a Show that there is a root α of $f(x) = 0$ in the interval $[1.1, 1.2]$. **(2 marks)**

b Taking $x_0 = 1.2$ as a first approximation to α, apply the Newton–Raphson process once to $f(x)$ to obtain a second approximation to α. Give your answer to 3 decimal places. **(2 marks)**

c By considering a change of sign of $f(x)$ in a suitable interval, verify that your answer to part **b** is correct to 2 decimal places. **(2 marks)**

Silver

$f(x) = e^{-x}\sin(x^2)$

a Show that there is a root α of $f(x) = 0$ in the interval $1.5 < \alpha < 2$. **(2 marks)**

b Taking $x_0 = 1.75$ as a first approximation to α, apply the Newton–Raphson process once to $f(x)$ to obtain a second approximation to α. Give your answer to 3 decimal places. **(2 marks)**

c By considering a change of sign of $f(x)$ in a suitable interval, show that your answer to part **b** is correct to 3 decimal places. **(2 marks)**

Gold

The diagram shows the curve with equation $y = f(x)$, where $f(x) = 12xe^{-2x} - 1$.

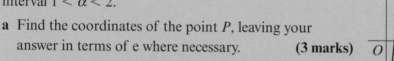

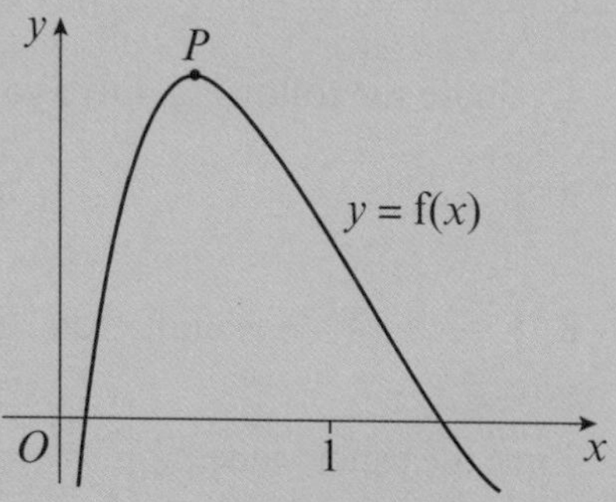

The point P, with coordinates (p, q), is a stationary point on the curve. The equation $f(x) = 0$ has a root α in the interval $1 < \alpha < 2$.

a Find the coordinates of the point P, leaving your answer in terms of e where necessary. **(3 marks)**

b Explain why $x_0 = p$ is not suitable to use as a first approximation if using the Newton–Raphson process to find an approximation for α. **(1 mark)**

c Taking $x_0 = 1.5$ as a first approximation to α, apply the Newton–Raphson process once to $f(x)$ to obtain a second approximation to α. Give your answer to 2 decimal places. **(2 marks)**

Now try this → Exam question bank Q2, Q12, Q18, Q22, Q29, Q37

11.1 Integrating standard functions

1 Integrate the following with respect to x.

a $e^x + 2\sin x$

b $4\cos x - \frac{3}{x^2}$

c $\frac{5}{x} - 2e^x$

d $\sqrt{x} + \frac{3}{4}\sin x$

e $11x^2 + \frac{1}{2}e^x - \frac{6}{x}$

f $3\cos x - \frac{1}{\sqrt{x}}$

Hint Use the following standard integrals to help:

$\int x^n \, dx = \frac{x^{n+1}}{n+1} + c$

$\int e^x \, dx = e^x + c$

$\int \frac{1}{x} \, dx = \ln|x| + c$

$\int \sin x \, dx = -\cos x + c$

$\int \cos x \, dx = \sin x + c$

2 Find the following integrals.

a $\int \frac{1}{\sin^2 x} \, dx$

b $\int \frac{\sin x}{\cos^2 x} \, dx$

c $\int \frac{\cos x}{\sin^2 x} \, dx$

d $\int \frac{4}{\cos^2 x} \, dx$

e $\int \frac{4}{1 - \cos^2 x} \, dx$

f $\int \frac{8\cos x}{\cos^2 x - 1} \, dx$

Hint Use the following standard integrals to help:

$\int \sec^2 x \, dx = \tan x + c$

$\int \operatorname{cosec} x \cot x \, dx = -\operatorname{cosec} x + c$

$\int \operatorname{cosec}^2 x \, dx = -\cot x + c$

$\int \sec x \tan x \, dx = \sec x + c$

3 Find the following integrals.

a $\int \sec x(\sec x + \tan x) \, dx$

b $\int \frac{7x^2 - 5}{x} \, dx$

c $\int \operatorname{cosec}^2 x(3e^x \sin^2 x - 5) \, dx$

d $\int \frac{x^2 - x + 1}{x} \, dx$

Hint Simplify each expression so it forms one or more standard integral.

4 Evaluate the following. Give your answers as exact values.

a $\int_{\ln 5}^{\ln 20} e^x \, dx$

b $\int_2^5 \frac{1 - 3x^3}{x} \, dx$

c $\int_0^{\frac{\pi}{3}} \left(\frac{\sin x}{\cos^2 x} + 4e^x\right) dx$

d $\int_0^{\frac{\pi}{4}} \sec^2 x(4 - \cos x \tan x) \, dx$

e $\int_{\ln 2}^{\ln 6} (e^x + e^{2x}) \, dx$

(E) 5 Find the exact value of $\int_4^9 \frac{x(1 + x)}{x^2} \, dx$, leaving your answer in the form $a + \ln b$, where a and b are rational numbers. **(4 marks)**

(E/P) 6 $\int_3^9 \frac{p}{x} \, dx = \ln 81$, where p is a positive constant.

Find the value of p. **(4 marks)**

(E) 7 Find the exact value of $\int_{\frac{\pi}{6}}^{\frac{\pi}{3}} \sec^2 x(\cot^2 x - 3e^x \cos^2 x - 1) \, dx$ **(5 marks)**

(E/P) 8 Given that a is a real constant, and that

$$\int_{2a}^{5a} \frac{2x + 3}{x} \, dx = \ln 1000$$

show that $a = \ln k$, where k is a constant to be found. **(5 marks)**

11.2 Integrating f(*ax* + *b*)

1 **a** Differentiate:

i $(4x-5)^4$ **ii** $(3-2x)^6$

b Find:

i $\int 16(4x-5)^3\,dx$ **ii** $\int (4x-5)^3\,dx$

iii $\int \left(-12(3-2x)^5\right)dx$ **iv** $\int 2(3-2x)^5\,dx$

Hint Integration is the reverse process of differentiation, so use your answers to part **a** to help.

2 Integrate the following with respect to x.

a $6e^{3x}$ **b** $\cos(3x+2)$

c $(4x+1)^5$ **d** $\operatorname{cosec} 4x \cot 4x$

e $\sec^2(8x-1)$ **f** $\operatorname{cosec}^2(1-5x)$

g $\frac{5}{2x-3}$ **h** $11e^{4-x}$

Hint In general, $\int f'(ax+b)\,dx = \frac{1}{a}f(ax+b) + c$

3 Find the following integrals.

a $\int \left(\frac{1}{(4x-3)^2} - (4x-3)^2\right)dx$

b $\int \sec^2 3x\left(\frac{1}{2}e^{5x}\cos^2 3x - 2\right)dx$

c $\int \left(e^{2x} - \frac{1}{e^{2x}}\right)^2 dx$ **d** $\int \frac{5-3\cos 2x}{\sin^2 2x}\,dx$

Hint First simplify each expression and then apply the integration rule in question 2 to each term separately.

4 Find the exact value of:

a $\int_{-2}^{0} \frac{4}{6-4x}\,dx$

b $\int_{-\frac{\pi}{8}}^{\frac{\pi}{8}} \operatorname{cosec}^2 2x(1-\cos 2x)\,dx$

c $\int_{0}^{\ln 4} (e^x-4)^2\,dx$ **d** $\int_{\frac{5\pi}{8}}^{\frac{3\pi}{4}} \frac{1}{\sin^2(2\pi - x)}\,dx$

Hint Integrate each expression and then apply the limits to evaluate the integral.

E/P **5** Given that a is a positive constant and $\int_1^a (2x+1)^2\,dx = 117$, find the value of a. **(4 marks)**

E/P **6** $\int_1^4 \frac{k}{2x-1}\,dx = \ln 25$, where k is a real constant.

Find the value of k. **(4 marks)**

E/P **7** Find the exact value of $\int_{\ln 2}^{\ln 8} (e^x+2)^2\,dx$, giving your answer in the form $p + \ln q$, where p and q are integers. **(4 marks)**

E/P **8** Given that $\int_{\frac{\pi}{6k}}^{\frac{\pi}{3k}} \frac{\pi}{2}\cos kx\,dx = \frac{9\pi}{4}(1-\sqrt{3})$, where k is a real constant, find the value of k. **(5 marks)**

11.3 Using trigonometric identities

1 Integrate the following with respect to x.

a $\sin^2 x$ b $3\cot^2 x$

c $(1 + \cos x)^2$ d $\dfrac{\sin^2 x}{\cos^2 x}$

Hint Use a trigonometric identity to transform each expression into a sum of standard integrals. ← **Sections 6.4, 7.3**

2 Find the exact value of:

a $\displaystyle\int_{\frac{\pi}{6}}^{\frac{\pi}{4}} \frac{\cos 2x}{\sin^2 x}\,dx$

b $\displaystyle\int_{\frac{\pi}{4}}^{\frac{3\pi}{4}} (\sin x - \operatorname{cosec} x)^2\,dx$

c $\displaystyle\int_{\frac{\pi}{3}}^{\frac{2\pi}{3}} \frac{(1-\cos x)^2}{\sin^2 x}\,dx$ d $\displaystyle\int_0^{\frac{\pi}{4}} (\sec x - \tan x)^2\,dx$

Hint In part **a**, use $\cos 2A \equiv 1 - 2\sin^2 A$ together with the standard result for integrating $\operatorname{cosec}^2 x$. ← **Section 7.3**

3 a Using the addition formula, expand:

i $\cos(5x + 2x)$ ii $\cos(5x - 2x)$

b By adding parts **a i** and **a ii** together, show that

$\cos 7x + \cos 3x = 2\cos 5x \cos 2x$

c Use your answer to part **b** to find $\displaystyle\int 4\cos 5x \cos 2x\,dx$.

Hint $\cos(A + B) \equiv \cos A \cos B - \sin A \sin B$

$\cos(A - B) \equiv \cos A \cos B + \sin A \sin B$

← **Section 7.1**

E/P 4 Show that $\displaystyle\int_{\frac{\pi}{6}}^{\frac{\pi}{2}} \cos^2 x\,dx = \frac{\pi}{6} - \frac{\sqrt{3}}{8}$ **(4 marks)**

E/P 5 Show that $\displaystyle\int_{\frac{\pi}{12}}^{\frac{\pi}{6}} \tan^2 2x\,dx = \frac{\sqrt{3}}{3} - \frac{\pi}{12}$ **(5 marks)**

E/P 6 a By considering $\sin(6x + x)$ and $\sin(6x - x)$, or otherwise, show that

$\sin 7x + \sin 5x = 2\sin 6x \cos x$ **(3 marks)**

b Hence find $\displaystyle\int 3\sin 6x \cos x\,dx$. **(3 marks)**

11.4 Reverse chain rule

1 a Differentiate:

i $(x^2 - 4)^3$ ii $(x^2 + 4x - 5)^4$

b Find:

i $\displaystyle\int 6x(x^2 - 4)^2\,dx$ ii $\displaystyle\int 15x(x^2 - 4)^2\,dx$

iii $\displaystyle\int -8(x + 2)(x^2 + 4x - 5)^2\,dx$

Hint Integration is the reverse process of differentiation, so use your answers to part **a** to help.

2 Find the following integrals.

a $\displaystyle\int 6x(x^2 - 7)^{\frac{1}{2}}\,dx$ b $\displaystyle\int 5\sin 2x\, e^{\cos 2x}\,dx$

c $\displaystyle\int (6x^2 + 8)(4x^3 + 16x - 5)^{\frac{3}{2}}\,dx$

Hint To integrate an expression in the form $\int k\mathrm{f}'(x)(\mathrm{f}(x))^n\,dx$, try differentiating $(\mathrm{f}(x))^{n+1}$, then adjust for a constant if necessary.

d $\int \sec^2 x\sqrt{1+\tan x}\,dx$ **e** $\int \mathrm{cosec}^2 3x\, e^{\cot 3x}\,dx$ **f** $\int \cos^4 5x \sin 5x\,dx$

3 Find the following integrals.

a $\int \frac{4x}{2-x^2}\,dx$ **b** $\int \frac{\sin x}{4-3\cos x}\,dx$

c $\int \frac{6x^2-9}{14+9x-2x^3}\,dx$ **d** $\int \frac{\sin 2x}{\cos^2 x}\,dx$

e $\int \frac{\frac{1}{2}\sin x\cos x}{4-\cos 2x}\,dx$ **f** $\int \frac{e^{-3x}}{1+e^{-3x}}\,dx$

Hint To integrate an expression in the form $\int k\frac{f'(x)}{f(x)}\,dx$, try differentiating $\ln(f(x))$, then adjust for a constant if necessary.

4 Find the exact value of:

a $\int_{\frac{3\pi}{8}}^{\frac{\pi}{2}} \sin^2 4x\cos 4x\,dx$ **b** $\int_0^{\frac{\pi}{9}} \frac{\sec^2 3x\tan 3x}{\sec^2 3x}\,dx$

c $\int_{\ln 2}^{\ln 3} \frac{6e^{3x}}{e^{3x}+1}\,dx$

d $\int_{\frac{\pi}{6}}^{\frac{\pi}{4}} \mathrm{cosec}\, 3x\cot 3x\, e^{\mathrm{cosec}\, 3x}\,dx$

Hint Decide carefully whether each expression is in the form $kf'(x)\,(f(x))^n$ or $k\frac{f'(x)}{f(x)}$
Then integrate and apply the limits to evaluate each integrand.

E/P **5** Evaluate $\int_{\frac{\pi}{6}}^{\frac{\pi}{4}} (1+\cot x)^3\mathrm{cosec}^2 x\,dx$, leaving your answer in the form $a+b\sqrt{3}$. **(5 marks)**

E/P **6** **a** Show that $\sin^5 x \equiv \sin x - 2\sin x\cos^2 x + \sin x\cos^4 x$ **(3 marks)**

b Hence find $\int \sin^5 x\,dx$. **(3 marks)**

E **7** Evaluate $\int_0^4 (x+1)\sqrt{2x^2+4x}\,dx$, leaving your answer in the form $k\sqrt{3}$. **(3 marks)**

E **8** Find the exact value of $\int_0^{\frac{\pi}{8}} \sin 4x\,(e^{\cos 4x})\,dx$. **(4 marks)**

E **9** Find the exact value of $\int_0^{\frac{\pi}{4}} \frac{\sec^2 x}{(3-\tan x)^4}\,dx$, leaving your answer as a simplified fraction. **(5 marks)**

E/P **10** Given that $\int_1^k \frac{x}{x^2+3}\,dx = \ln\frac{3}{2}$ and $k > 0$, find the exact value of k. **(4 marks)**

11.5 Integration by substitution

1 Complete the following steps to find $\int 2x(x+2)^4\,dx$ using integration by substitution.

a Given $u = x+2$, find $\frac{du}{dx}$

b Given $u = x+2$, write $2x$ in terms of u.

c Use your answers to parts **a** and **b** to show that $\int 2x(x+2)^4\,dx = \int 2(u-2)u^4\,du$.

d Show that $\int 2(u-2)u^4\,du = \frac{1}{3}u^6 - \frac{4}{5}u^5 + c$

e Use the substitution in part **a** to write your answer in part **d** in terms of x.

2 Use the given substitution to find:

a $\int x(x-8)^4\,dx;\ u = x-8$

b $\int \sin x \cos x(1+\cos x)^5\,dx;\ u = 1+\cos x$

c $\int \operatorname{cosec}^2 x \cot x\sqrt{2+\cot x}\,dx;\ u = 2+\cot x$

d $\int \frac{\sqrt{x^2+1}}{x}\,dx;\ u = \sqrt{x^2+1}$

Hint Use $\frac{du}{dx}$ to replace dx with an expression involving du. Then write the integrand in terms of u and integrate. Remember to use the substitution to write your final answer in terms of x.

3 Use the given substitution to evaluate:

a $\int_{\frac{1}{2}}^{\frac{5}{4}} x\sqrt{4x-1}\,dx;\ u = 4x-1$

b $\int_{16}^{25} \frac{4}{\sqrt{x}(\sqrt{x}-9)}\,dx;\ u = \sqrt{x}$

c $\int_{\frac{2\pi}{3}}^{\frac{3\pi}{4}} \frac{\sin x}{\cos^3 x}\,dx;\ u = \cos x$

d $\int_0^{\frac{\pi}{2}} \frac{\sin 2x}{1+\sin x}\,dx;\ u = \sin x$

(E/P) 4 Using the substitution $u = 1+x^2$ or otherwise, find the exact value of $\int_0^2 x^3\sqrt{1+x^2}\,dx$. **(6 marks)**

(E/P) 5 Using the substitution $u = e^x$, or otherwise, find the exact value of $\int_{\ln 2}^{\ln 6} \frac{1}{1+e^x}\,dx$, leaving your answer in the form $\ln a$, where a is a rational number to be found. **(6 marks)**

(E) 6 a Using the substitution $x = \tan\theta$, or otherwise, show that $\int \frac{1}{1+x^2}\,dx = \arctan x + c$. **(4 marks)**

b Hence evaluate $\int_{\frac{\sqrt{3}}{3}}^{1} \frac{1}{1+x^2}\,dx$. **(2 marks)**

(E/P) 7 Using the substitution $u^2 = 2x+1$ or otherwise, show that the exact value of $\int_0^4 \frac{5x}{\sqrt{2x+1}}\,dx$ is $\frac{370\sqrt{3}-20}{21}$ **(6 marks)**

(E/P) 8 By using a suitable substitution, or otherwise, find $\int \frac{2\sin 2x}{1+\sin x}\,dx$. **(5 marks)**

11.6 Integration by parts

1 Find the following integrals.

a $\int x\cos x\,dx$

b $\int x\sec^2 x\,dx$

c $\int xe^{2x}\,dx$

d $\int x\operatorname{cosec}^2 4x\,dx$

e $\int xe^{-4x}\,dx$

f $\int x\sin 5x\,dx$

Hint $\int u\frac{dv}{dx}\,dx = uv - \int v\frac{du}{dx}\,dx$

In part **a**, let $u = x$ and $\frac{dv}{dx} = \cos x$.

2 Find the following integrals.

a $\int x\ln x\,dx$

b $\int x^3\ln x\,dx$

c $\int \ln x\,dx$

Hint In part **a**, let $u = \ln x$ and $\frac{dv}{dx} = x$.

In part **c**, write $\int \ln x\,dx$ as $\int 1\times\ln x\,dx$.

3 Find the following integrals.

a $\int x^2 \sin 2x \, dx$ b $\int x^2 e^{-3x} \, dx$

c $\int 2x^2 (1 + x)^3 \, dx$

Hint You will need to apply integration by parts twice to answer each part of this question.

4 Evaluate:

a $\int_0^{\frac{\pi}{4}} x \sin x \, dx$ b $\int_2^5 x\sqrt{6 - x} \, dx$ c $\int_{\frac{\pi}{4}}^{\frac{3\pi}{4}} x \operatorname{cosec}^2 x \, dx$

d $\int_0^{\frac{\pi}{6}} x \sec^2 2x \, dx$ e $\int_0^{\frac{\pi}{4}} x^2 \cos 4x \, dx$ f $\int_0^3 x^3 e^{-x} \, dx$

(E) 5 Find the exact value of $\int_{\frac{1}{2}}^{2} 6x \ln 4x \, dx$. **(5 marks)**

(E) 6 Show that $\int_1^2 x^2 e^{2x} \, dx = \frac{e^2}{4}(5e^2 - 1)$. **(6 marks)**

(E) 7 a Use integration to find $\int x \sin \pi x \, dx$. **(3 marks)**

b Hence, or otherwise, evaluate $\int_{\frac{3}{2}}^{\frac{5}{2}} x^2 \cos \pi x \, dx$, leaving your answer as an exact value in terms of π. **(5 marks)**

(E) 8 Find $\int_{\frac{\pi}{4}}^{\frac{\pi}{2}} 2x^2 \operatorname{cosec}^2 x \cot x \, dx$, leaving your answer in exact form. **(5 marks)**

(E/P) 9 a Find $\int x \cos 2x \, dx$. **(3 marks)**

b Hence, using a suitable trigonometric identity, find $\int x \sin^2 x \, dx$. **(3 marks)**

11.7 Partial fractions

1 $\frac{8x - 4}{(x + 2)(x - 4)} \equiv \frac{A}{x + 2} + \frac{B}{x - 4}$

a Find the values of the constants A and B.

b Hence find $\int \frac{8x - 4}{(x + 2)(x - 4)} \, dx$.

Hint Write the integral using the expression you found in part **a**, then use integrate each term using

$\int \frac{1}{ax + b} \, dx = \frac{1}{a} \ln |ax + b| + c$

2 Use partial fractions to integrate:

a $\int \frac{4x + 17}{(x + 5)(x + 2)} \, dx$ b $\int \frac{7x + 6}{(x + 3)(2 - x)} \, dx$

c $\int \frac{x + 17}{(x - 1)(x + 2)} \, dx$ d $\int \frac{6}{(x - 4)(2x - 1)} \, dx$

Hint First rewrite each expression using partial fractions. ← **Section 1.3**

3 $f(x) = \frac{-2x^2 + 14}{(x + 4)(2x - 1)}, x \in \mathbb{R}, x \neq -4, x \neq \frac{1}{2}$

a Use algebraic long division to show that $f(x) \equiv \frac{7x + 10}{(x + 4)(2x - 1)} - 1$.

b Use partial fractions to find values A and B such that $f(x) \equiv \frac{A}{x + 4} + \frac{B}{2x - 1} - 1$.

c Hence find $\int \frac{-2x^2 + 14}{(x + 4)(2x - 1)} \, dx$.

4 a Show that $\dfrac{16x^2 - 37x + 17}{(4 - x)(2x - 3)^2} \equiv \dfrac{5}{4 - x} + \dfrac{2}{2x - 3} - \dfrac{1}{(2x - 3)^2}$

b Hence find $\displaystyle\int \frac{16x^2 - 37x + 17}{(4 - x)(2x - 3)^2}\,dx$.

Hint $2x - 3$ is a repeated factor, so the partial fraction expansion includes separate denominators of $(2x - 3)$ and $(2x - 3)^2$.

← Section 1.4

(E) 5 $f(x) = \dfrac{3x + 15}{(x - 1)(x + 2)}, x > 1$

a Express f(x) in partial fractions. **(3 marks)**

b Find $\displaystyle\int_2^3 f(x)\,dx$, giving your answer in the form $\ln k$, where k is a rational constant. **(5 marks)**

(E) 6 $f(x) = \dfrac{2x^2 - 5x + 5}{2x^2 - 5x + 2}, x > 1$

a Given that $f(x) = \dfrac{A}{x - 2} + \dfrac{B}{2x - 1} + C$, find the values of the constants A, B and C. **(4 marks)**

b Hence find the exact value of $\displaystyle\int_3^5 \frac{2x^2 - 5x + 5}{2x^2 - 5x + 2}\,dx$, writing your answer in the form $a + \ln b$, where a and b are rational constants to be found. **(5 marks)**

(E) 7 $f(x) = \dfrac{12x + 6}{(2x + 1)^2(x + 3)}, x > 0$

a Express f(x) in partial fractions. **(5 marks)**

b Find $\displaystyle\int_1^2 f(x)\,dx$, giving your answer in the form $a\ln b$, where a and b are rational constants. **(5 marks)**

(E) 8 $f(x) = \dfrac{x^2 + 4}{x^2 - 1}, x > 1$

a Given that $f(x) = A + \dfrac{B}{x + 1} + \dfrac{C}{x - 1}$, find the values of the constants A, B and C. **(5 marks)**

b Find $\displaystyle\int_2^4 f(x)\,dx$, giving your answer in the form $a + b\ln c$, where a, b and c are rational constants. **(5 marks)**

11.8 Finding areas

1 The diagram shows part of the curve $y = \dfrac{4}{(1 + 2x)^2}$

The shaded region is bounded by the curve, the coordinate axes and the line with equation $x = 2$.

Find the exact area of the shaded region.

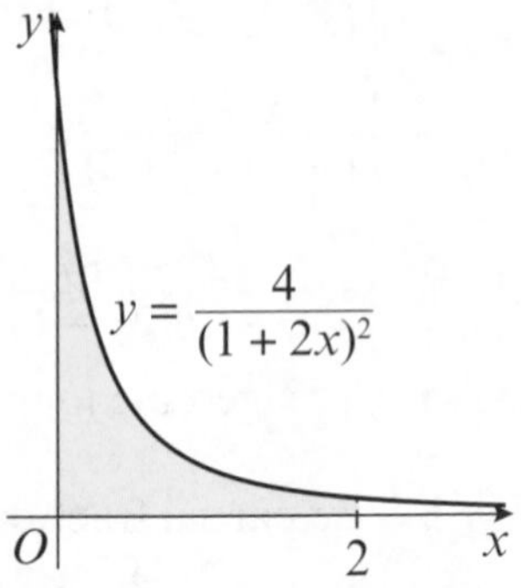

Hint The area under the curve between $x = 0$ and $x = 2$ is given by $\displaystyle\int_0^2 \frac{4}{(1 + 2x)^2}\,dx$

2 The diagram shows a sketch of part of the curve with equation

$y = x\ln\left(\frac{1}{2}x\right), x \geqslant 0$

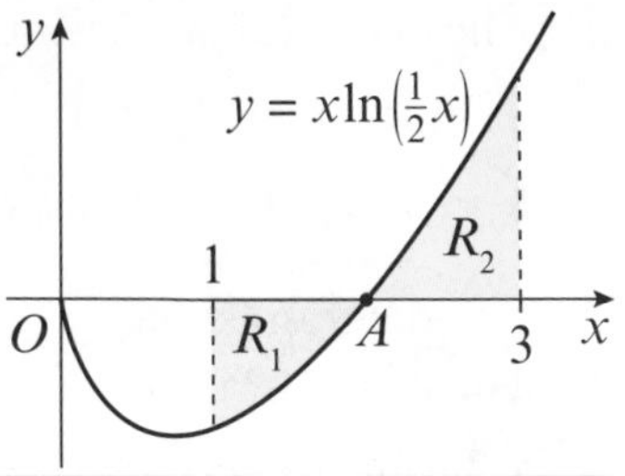

a Verify that A has coordinates (2, 0).

b Show that the exact area of the shaded region R_1 is

$\frac{3}{4} - \frac{1}{2}\ln 2$

Hint In part **b**, the value of the integral will be negative as the area is below the x-axis. Remember to give a positive answer for the shaded area.

c Show that the total shaded area is

$\frac{9}{2}\ln\frac{3}{2} - \frac{1}{2}\ln 2 - \frac{1}{2}$

Hint To find the total area you need to consider R_1 and R_2 separately.

3 The diagram shows part of the curve $y = \text{f}(x)$ and the line $y = \text{g}(x)$, where $\text{f}(x) = 2\cos\frac{1}{2}x + 1$ and $\text{g}(x) = -\frac{1}{\pi}x + 2$.

The region R is bounded by the curve, the line and the y-axis.

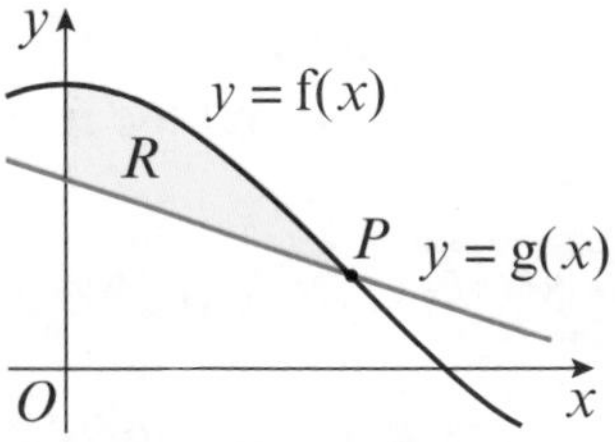

a Show that the coordinates of point P are $(\pi, 1)$.

b Use integration to find the exact area of R.

Hint You could consider the total area under $y = \text{f}(x)$ between $x = 0$ and $x = \pi$, then subtract the area of the trapezium under $y = \text{g}(x)$. Or you could use the formula for the area between two curves: $\int_a^b (\text{f}(x) - \text{g}(x))\,\text{d}x$

4 The curve C has parametric equations $x = t^2, y = 2t + 1, t \geqslant 0$.

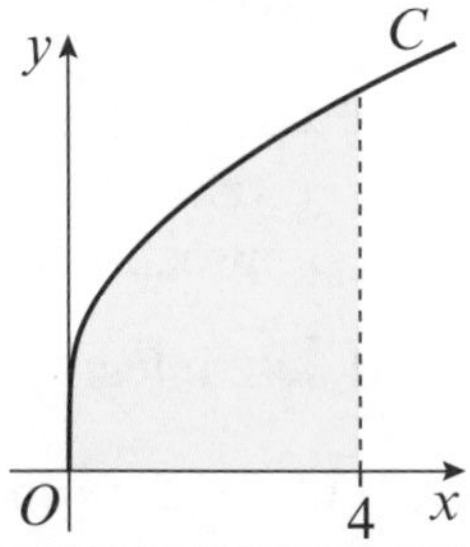

a Write down $\frac{\text{d}x}{\text{d}t}$

b Find the value of t when $x = 0$.

c Explain why $t = 2$, and not -2, when $x = 4$.

d Find the exact area of the region bounded by the curve, the x-axis, the y-axis and the line $x = 4$.

Hint When a curve is defined parametrically, you can find the area bounded by the curve, the x-axis and the lines $x = a$ and $x = b$ using $\int_a^b y\frac{\text{d}x}{\text{d}t}\,\text{d}t$

E/P **5** The diagram shows part of the curve $y = \text{f}(x)$ where $\text{f}(x) = \frac{1}{2}x\cos x$.

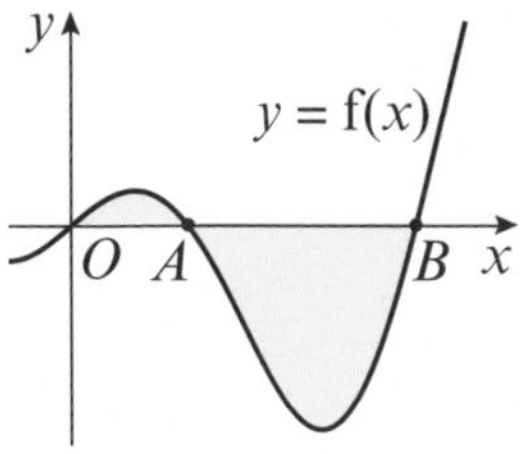

a Verify that points A and B have coordinates $\left(\frac{\pi}{2}, 0\right)$ and $\left(\frac{3\pi}{2}, 0\right)$ respectively. **(1 mark)**

b Find the exact area of the shaded region. **(7 marks)**

E/P **6** The curve C has parametric equations $x = t^2, y = 4\sin t, t \geqslant 0$.

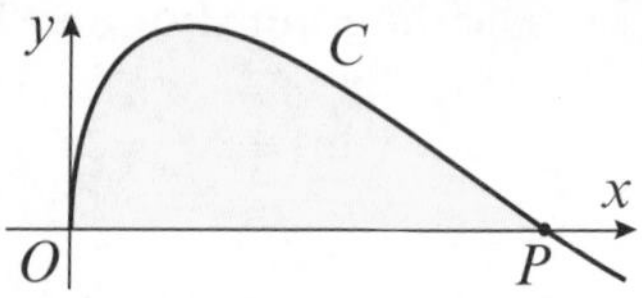

a Find the coordinates of point P. **(1 mark)**

b Find the area of the shaded region. **(5 marks)**

E/P **7** The diagram shows part of the curves $y = \sin x$ and $y = -\cos 2x + 1$. The region R is bounded by the two curves.

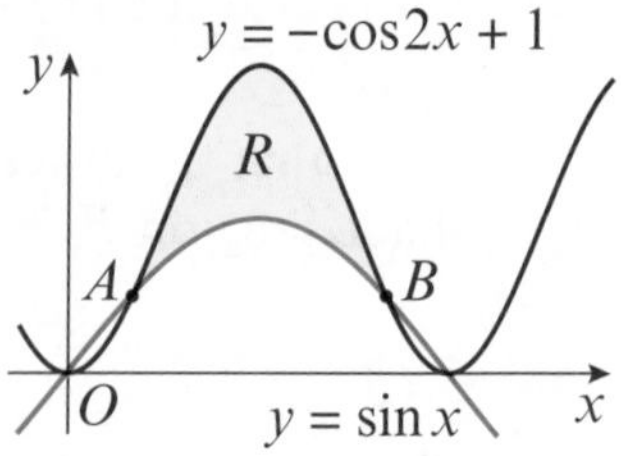

a Using an appropriate trigonometric identity, show that point A has x-coordinate $\frac{\pi}{6}$, and find the x-coordinate of point B. **(3 marks)**

b Use calculus to find the exact area of R. **(6 marks)**

E/P **8** The diagram shows the curve with parametric equations

$$x = 12\cos\theta, y = 5\sin\theta, 0 \leqslant \theta \leqslant 2\pi$$

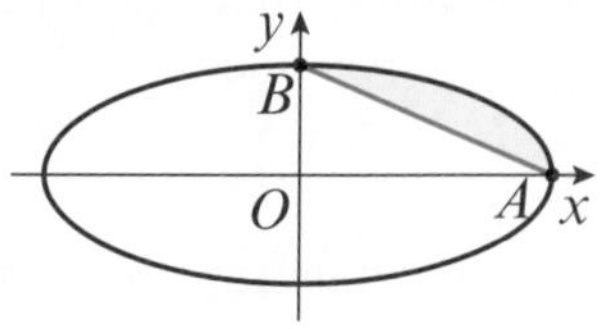

The curve intersects the positive x- and y-axes at points A and B respectively. Find the exact area of the shaded region enclosed by the curve and the line segment AB. **(7 marks)**

11.9 The trapezium rule

1 The diagram shows a sketch of part of the curve with equation $y = 2x^2 - x^3$.

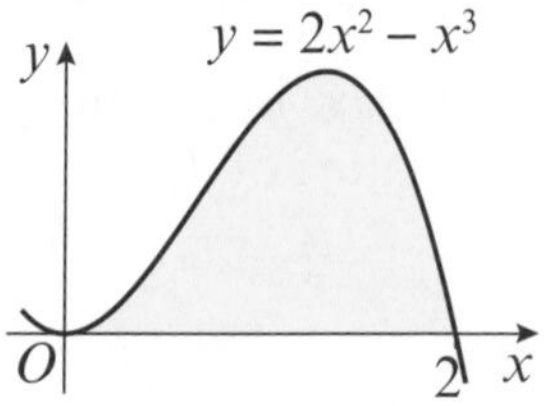

a Copy and complete the table.

x	0	0.5	1	1.5	2
y	0				0

b Explain why $h = 0.5$.

Hint $\int_a^b y\,dx = \frac{1}{2}h(y_0 + 2(y_1 + y_2 + \ldots + y_{n-1}) + y_n)$ where $h = \frac{b-a}{n}$ and $y_i = f(a + ih)$.

c Use the trapezium rule, with all the y-values in the completed table, to find an approximate value for the area of the shaded region.

d Use integration to calculate the exact value of $\int_0^2 (2x^2 - x^3)\,dx$.

2 The diagram shows a sketch of part of the curve with equation $y = e^{-4x} + x - \frac{1}{10}x^2$

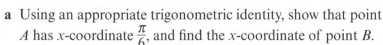

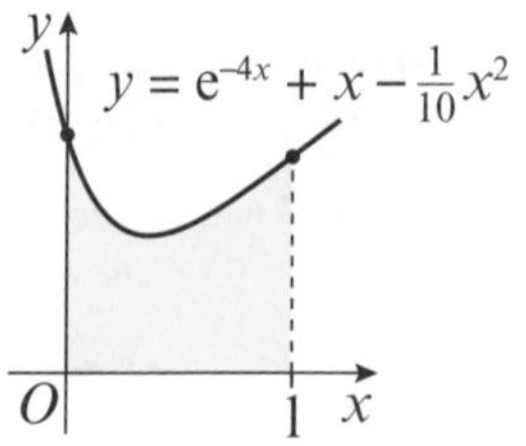

a Copy and complete the table.

x	0	0.25	0.5	0.75	1
y	1	0.6116		0.7435	0.9183

b Use the trapezium rule, with all the y-values in the completed table, to obtain an estimate for the area of the shaded region, giving your answer to 3 decimal places.

c Use integration to calculate the exact value of $\int_0^1 (e^{-4x} + x - \frac{1}{10}x^2)\,dx$.

d Use the shape of the curve in the diagram to explain why the answer in part **b** was an overestimate.

e Explain how the accuracy of your approximation in part **b** could be improved.

Hint The trapezium rule will overestimate a convex curve and underestimate a concave curve.

(E) **3** The diagram shows part of the curve with equation $y = x^2 \cos x$.

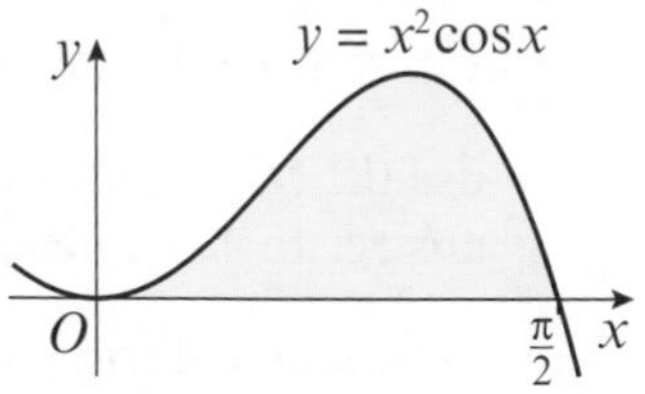

a Copy and complete the table with the corresponding y-value for $x = \frac{3\pi}{8}$

x	0	$\frac{\pi}{8}$	$\frac{\pi}{4}$	$\frac{3\pi}{8}$	$\frac{\pi}{2}$
y	0	0.142	0.436		0

(1 mark)

Given that $I = \int_0^{\frac{\pi}{2}} x^2 \cos x\,dx$,

b use the trapezium rule, with four strips to find an approximate value for I, giving your answer to 3 significant figures. **(4 marks)**

c Use integration to calculate the exact value of I. **(5 marks)**

d Calculate the percentage error of the approximation in part **b**. **(1 mark)**

(E/P) **4** The diagram shows part of the curve with equation
$$y = \frac{x - 15}{(2x + 3)(x - 4)}$$

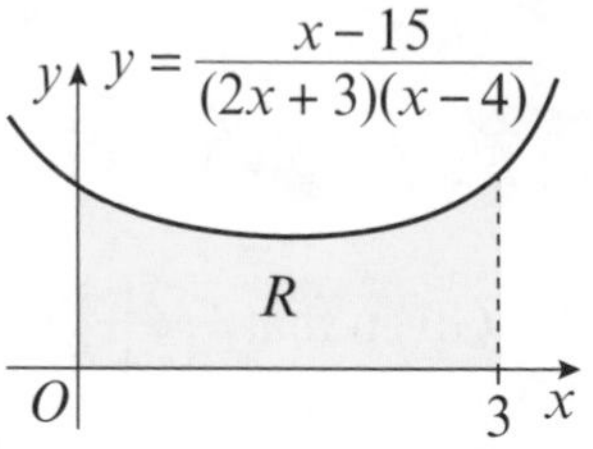

a Copy and complete with the y-value corresponding to $x = 1.5$.

x	0	0.5	1	1.5	2	2.5	3
y	1.25	1.038	0.933		0.929	1.041	1.333

(1 mark)

b Use the trapezium rule, with all the values from your table, to estimate the area of the region R, giving your answer to 2 decimal places. **(4 marks)**

c Find the exact value of $\int_0^3 \frac{x - 15}{(2x + 3)(x - 4)}\,dx$, giving your answer in the form $\ln a$, where a is an exact value to be found. **(5 marks)**

d Calculate the percentage error of the approximation in part **b**. **(1 mark)**

E/P **5** The diagram shows part of the curve with equation

$y = \sin^2 x \cos^3 x$

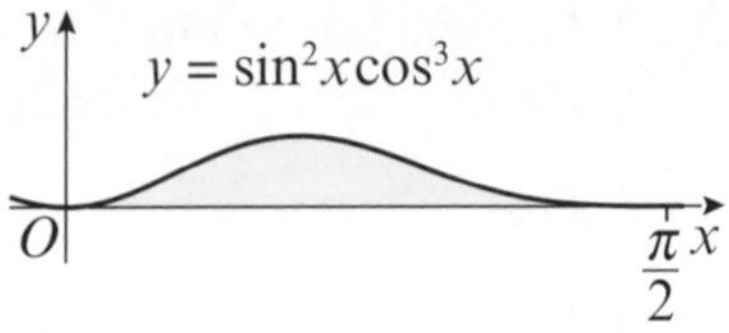

a Copy and complete the table with the corresponding y-value for $x = \frac{\pi}{8}$

x	0	$\frac{\pi}{8}$	$\frac{\pi}{4}$	$\frac{3\pi}{8}$	$\frac{\pi}{2}$
y	0		0.1768	0.0478	0

(1 mark)

Given that $I = \int_0^{\frac{\pi}{2}} \sin^2 x \cos^3 x \, dx$,

b use the trapezium rule, with four strips to find an approximate value for I, giving your answer to 4 significant figures **(4 marks)**

c use a suitable trigonometric substitution to calculate the exact value of I. **(5 marks)**

E/P **6** The diagram shows part of the curve with equation $y = \frac{1}{4}x^2 \ln x + 1$.

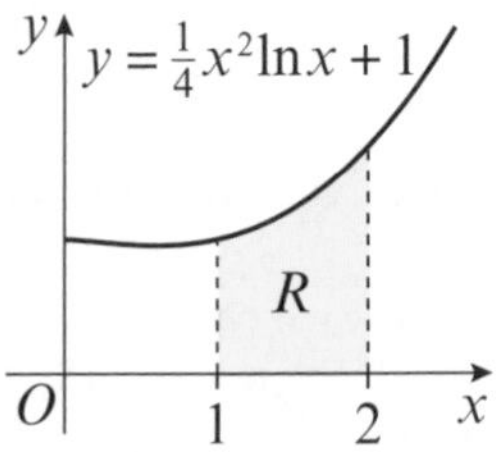

a Complete the table with the y-value corresponding to $x = 1.25$.

x	1	1.25	1.5	1.75	2
y	1		1.2281	1.4285	1.6931

(1 mark)

b Use the trapezium rule, with all the y-values from the completed table, to obtain an estimate for the area of the shaded region R. **(4 marks)**

c Show by integration that the exact value of $\int_1^2 \left(\frac{1}{4}x^2 \ln x + 1\right) dx$ is $\frac{2}{3}\ln 2 + \frac{29}{36}$ **(5 marks)**

11.10 Solving differential equations

1 Given that $\frac{1}{(x^2+6)^5} \times \frac{dy}{dx} = \frac{x}{y}$

a show that $\int y \, dy = \int x(x^2+6)^5 \, dx$.

b Hence show that $\frac{1}{2}y^2 = \frac{1}{12}(x^2+6)^6 + c$.

Hint When $\frac{dy}{dx} = f(x)g(y)$, you can write $\int \frac{1}{g(y)} dy = \int f(x) \, dx$.
This method is called separating the variables.

2 Find the general solution to the following differential equations, giving your answers in the form $y = f(x)$.

a $\frac{dy}{dx} = e^{4x-3y}$

b $\frac{dy}{dx} = \sin^2 x \sec y$

c $\frac{dy}{dx} = 6xy(x+1)$

d $\frac{dy}{dx} = e^{2y} \sin x \cos^2 x$

Hint Use the method of separating the variables, and remember to rearrange your integrated expression so it is in the form $y = f(x)$.

3 Find particular solutions to the following differential equations using the given boundary conditions.

a $(x+1)(x+2)\frac{dy}{dx} = xy + 3y$; $x = 1, y = 1$

b $\frac{dy}{dx} = \sin^2 y + e^x \sin^2 y$; $x = \ln 2, y = \frac{\pi}{4}$

c $\operatorname{cosec} y \cos^2 x \frac{dy}{dx} = \sin y$; $x = \frac{\pi}{4}, y = \frac{\pi}{4}$

d $\frac{2}{x} \times \frac{dy}{dx} = -\frac{2}{y}$; $x = 12, y = -5$

Hint Substitute the boundary conditions into your integrated expression to find the value of the constant c.

4 **a** Find the general solution to $\frac{dy}{dx} = 4x - 1$.

b On the same set of axes, sketch the particular solutions to this differential equation when $c = -10$, -3 and 0, where c is the constant of integration.

Hint The general solution provides a family of solutions. Choosing some values of c will allow you to see what this family of curves look like.

E/P **5** Given that $y = 0$ when $x = 1$, find the particular solution to the differential equation $xy\frac{dy}{dx} = (1 + x^2)(1 - y^2)$, giving your answer in the form $y^2 = f(x)$. **(6 marks)**

E/P **6** Find the particular solution to the differential equation $\sec y \frac{dy}{dx} = 2\cot y \sin^2 x + \cot y$, with the boundary condition $y = \frac{\pi}{4}$ at $x = \frac{\pi}{4}$. Give your answer in the form $\sec y = f(x)$. **(8 marks)**

E/P **7** Find the general solution to the differential equation $e^{2y-x}\frac{dy}{dx} = xe^{2y} - 4x$, leaving your answer in the form $\ln|g(y)| = f(x)$. **(6 marks)**

E/P **8** **a** Express $\frac{8x - 11}{(2x - 5)(x + 2)}$ in partial fractions. **(3 marks)**

b Given that $x > \frac{5}{2}$, find the general solution to the differential equation

$$(2x - 5)(x + 2)\frac{dy}{dx} = y(8x - 11)$$ **(5 marks)**

c Hence find the particular solution to the differential equation that satisfies $x = 3$, $y = 25$, giving your answer in the form $y = f(x)$. **(4 marks)**

11.11 Modelling with differential equations

1 The population of wild geese at time t years is given by $\frac{dP}{dt} = 3P^{\frac{1}{3}}$.

a Show that $\frac{3}{2}P^{\frac{2}{3}} = 3t + c$.

Given that initially the population of wild geese is 1000,

b find the value of the constant c.

c Hence show that $P = (2t + 100)^{\frac{3}{2}}$.

d Find the time taken for the population to reach 2500.

Hint Solve the differential equation using the method of separating the variables.

2 The value, £V, of a laptop decreases at a rate proportional to the current value of the laptop.

The differential equation that models this situation is $\frac{dV}{dt} = -kV$, where t is the time in years since the laptop was purchased.

Hint You might need to form differential equations based on a proportionality relationship. Read the question carefully: in this case the **rate** of decrease is proportional to the value.

a Explain:

i the meaning of $\frac{dV}{dt}$ in the context of this question

ii the significance of the negative sign

iii the meaning of kV.

b Solve the differential equation to show that $V = V_0 e^{-kt}$ where V_0 is the initial value of the laptop.

c Given that initially the value of the laptop is £800, state the value of V_0.

d Given further that after 4 years, the value of the laptop is £550, find the value of k to 2 significant figures.

(E/P) 3 The rate of increase of the world's population, P, in millions, t years after 1900 is proportional to the existing population.

Given that in 1900 the world's population was 1600 million and by 1950 the world's population was 2600 million,

a show that $P = Ae^{kt}$, stating the exact values of the constants A and k. **(5 marks)**

b Find the time when, according to the model, the world's population will be exactly three times the population in 1900. **(2 marks)**

In November 2018 the population of the world was 7700 million.

c Evaluate the model based on this information. **(1 mark)**

(E/P) 4 A bowl of hot soup, with a temperature of T °C is left to cool for t minutes in a room with a temperature of 20 °C. The rate at which the soup cools is proportional to the difference in temperature between the soup and the room.

a Explain clearly why the differential equation $\frac{dT}{dt} = -k(T - 20)$, where k is a positive constant, models this situation. **(3 marks)**

Initially the temperature of the soup is 75 °C. After five minutes the soup has cooled to 65 °C.

b Find, to 1 decimal place, the time when the soup reaches a temperature of 50 °C. **(7 marks)**

(E/P) 5 Water enters a large cylindrical rain barrel, with diameter 60 cm, at a rate of $100\pi \text{ cm}^3 \text{ s}^{-1}$. Water flows out of the bottom of the barrel at a rate of $3\pi h \text{ cm}^3 \text{ s}^{-1}$.

a Show that this situation can be modelled by the differential equation $900\frac{dh}{dt} = 100 - 3h$. **(3 marks)**

b Given that initially the water level is 20 cm, find the exact time when the water level is 30 cm. **(5 marks)**

E/P **6** Following a robbery, a circular police cordon is formed to capture the criminal. The circle has a radius of r km and an area of A km². The radius is gradually decreased in an effort to capture the criminal.

The rate of decrease of the area, in km² per minute, at time t minutes after the cordon is initially formed can be modelled as $\frac{\mathrm{d}A}{\mathrm{d}t} = -k\sin\left(\frac{t}{4\pi}\right)$, $t \geqslant 0$, where k is a positive constant.

a Show that $\frac{\mathrm{d}r}{\mathrm{d}t} = -\frac{k}{2\pi r}\sin\left(\frac{t}{4\pi}\right)$. **(2 marks)**

Given that the initial radius of the cordon is 10 km and after $2\pi^2$ minutes the radius is 5 km,

b find an expression for r^2 in terms of t **(6 marks)**

c find the time when the radius is reduced to 0 km. **(3 marks)**

Problem solving Set A

Bronze

The diagram shows a sketch of the curve with equation

$y = \mathrm{e}^{5x} - x\mathrm{e}^{5x}$, $x > 0$

The region R is bounded by the curve and the coordinate axes.

Use calculus to find the exact area of R. **(5 marks)**

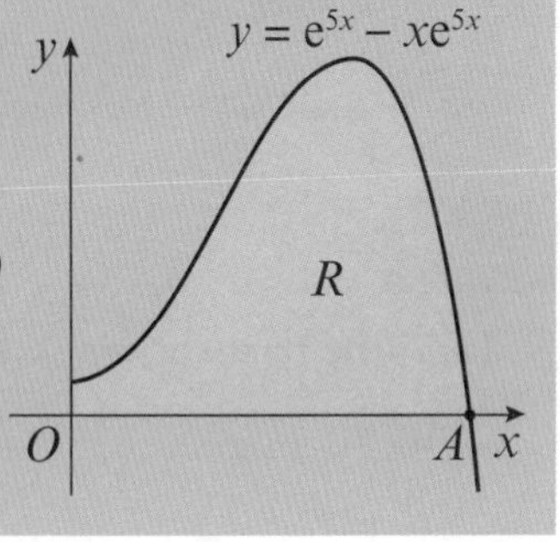

Silver

The diagram shows part of the curve with equation $y = \mathrm{f}(x)$, where

$\mathrm{f}(x) = 2\sin x\cos x(1 + \sin x)^4$, $x \geqslant 0$

By means of a suitable substitution, or otherwise, find the exact area of the shaded region bounded by the curve and the x-axis.

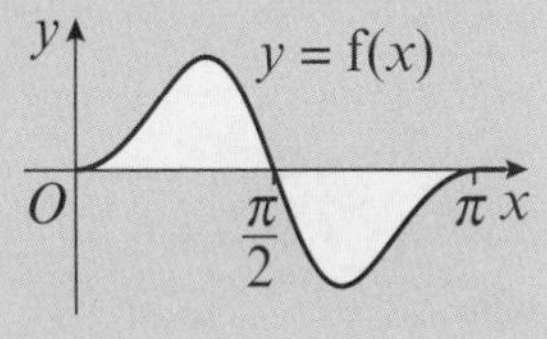

(6 marks)

Gold

The curve C has parametric equations

$$x = 6\cos t,\ y = 4\sin^2 t,\ 0 \leqslant t \leqslant \frac{\pi}{2}$$

P is the point on the curve where $t = \frac{\pi}{6}$

Line PQ is the normal to C at point P.

Find the exact area of the shaded region bounded by PQ, the curve and the x-axis. **(10 marks)**

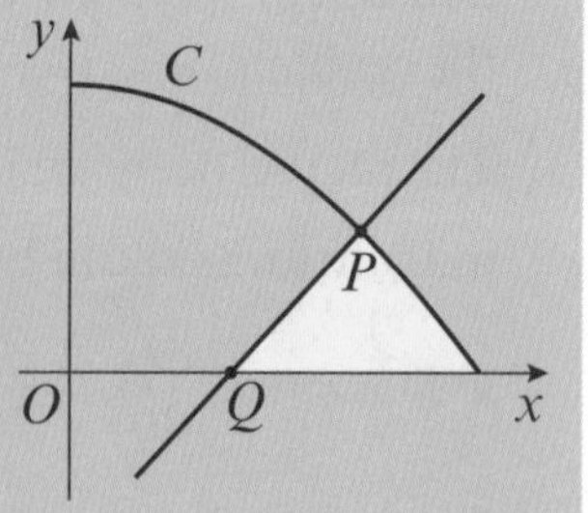

Problem solving Set B

Bronze

a Find the general solution to the differential equation $(x^2 + x + 2)\frac{\mathrm{d}y}{\mathrm{d}x} = 4xy + 2y$. **(3 marks)**

b Find the particular solution to this differential equation that satisfies $y = 1$ at $x = 0$. **(3 marks)**

Silver

Find the particular solution to the differential equation $e^{2y-x}\frac{\mathrm{d}y}{\mathrm{d}x} = x(e^{2y} - 1)$ with boundary conditions $x = 0$, $y = \ln 2$, giving your answer in the form $\ln|f(y)| = g(x)$. **(6 marks)**

Gold

The sale of tickets for a cup final can be modelled by the differential equation

$$\frac{\mathrm{d}T}{\mathrm{d}t} = \frac{1}{120\,000}T(80\,000 - T)$$

where T is the number of tickets sold and t is the time in days since the tickets first went on sale.

Given that before tickets went on sale (at time $t = 0$), 16 000 tickets were given away to corporate sponsors,

a solve the differential equation giving your answer in the form $T = \frac{a}{b + ce^{-\frac{2}{3}t}}$ **(7 marks)**

b Assuming the stadium sells out as $t \to \infty$, state the capacity of the stadium. **(1 mark)**

Now try this → **Exam question bank Q8, Q20, Q23, Q38, Q47, Q53, Q56, Q74**

12.1 3D coordinates

1 The rectangular prism *OABCDEFG* is shown in the diagram, positioned so that *O* lies at the point (0, 0, 0).

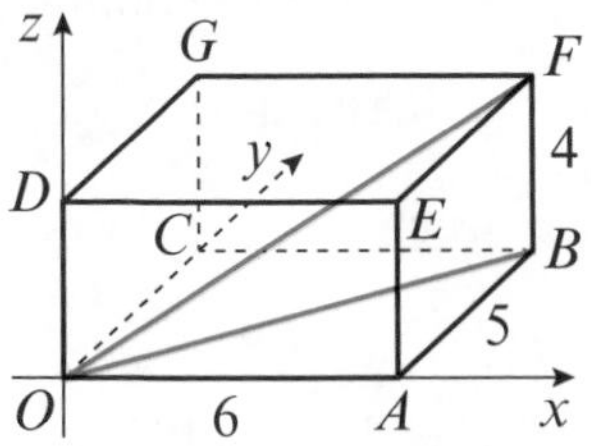

a Use Pythagoras' theorem to calculate the exact length of:

i *OB* **ii** *OF*

The coordinates of point *F* are (p, q, r).

b Write down the values of p, q and r.

c Calculate $\sqrt{p^2 + q^2 + r^2}$.

d Compare your answers to parts **a ii** and **c**.

2 Calculate, leaving your answer as a simplified surd, the distance from the origin to the point:

Hint The distance between the origin and the point (x, y, z) is $\sqrt{x^2 + y^2 + z^2}$

a $A(4, 10, 3)$ **b** $B(6, 4, -8)$

c $C(-2, -4, 15)$

3 In each case, calculate the distance between the points *P* and *Q*:

a $P(5, 3, -2)$ and $Q(-4, 5, 4)$

b $P(-1, -3, 6)$ and $Q(9, -14, 4)$

c $P(11, -2, -1)$ and $Q(7, 0, 4)$.

Hint The distance between points (x_1, y_1, z_1) and (x_2, y_2, z_2) is $\sqrt{(x_1 - x_2)^2 + (y_1 - y_2)^2 + (z_1 - z_2)^2}$

4 The coordinates of *A* and *B* are $(6, -1, 3)$ and $(3, 5, k)$ respectively.

Given that the distance from *A* to *B* is 7 units,

a show that $(3 - k)^2 = 4$.

b Hence find the possible values of k.

Hint Substitute your coordinates for *A* and *B* into the formula for the distance between two points.

(E) 5 The coordinates of *A* and *B* are $(-2, 4, 8)$ and $(0, k, 7)$ respectively.

Given that the distance from *A* to *B* is 3 units, find the possible values of k. **(3 marks)**

(E) 6 The coordinates of *A* and *B* are $(2, -5, k)$ and $(-2, -1, 3)$ respectively.

Given that the distance from *A* to *B* is 9 units, find the possible values of k. **(3 marks)**

(E) 7 The coordinates of *A* and *B* are $(k, -4, 6)$ and $(8, -5, -1)$ respectively.

Given that the distance from *A* to *B* is $5\sqrt{3}$ units, find the possible values of k. **(3 marks)**

(E) 8 The coordinates of *A* and *B* are $(4, -4, 3)$ and $(k, 4, 4)$ respectively.

Given that the distance from *A* to *B* is $3\sqrt{10}$ units, find the possible values of k. **(3 marks)**

12.2 Vectors in 3D

1 Consider the points $A(4, -3, 1)$ and $B(-2, 6, 5)$.

a Write the position vector of A in the form $p\mathbf{i} + q\mathbf{j} + r\mathbf{k}$.

b Write the position vector of B in the form $\begin{pmatrix} p \\ q \\ r \end{pmatrix}$.

Hint $\mathbf{i}$, $\mathbf{j}$ and $\mathbf{k}$ are the unit vectors along the x-, y- and z-axes.

$$p\mathbf{i} + q\mathbf{j} + r\mathbf{k} = \begin{pmatrix} p \\ q \\ r \end{pmatrix}$$

2 P is the point $(5, 2, 1)$ and Q is the point $(3, 7, -2)$.

a Find the vector $\overrightarrow{PQ}$ giving your answer:

i in **ijk** notation **ii** as a column vector.

b Find the distance between P and Q.

c Find the unit vector in the direction of $\overrightarrow{PQ}$.

Hint For the vector $\mathbf{a}$, where $\mathbf{a} = p\mathbf{i} + q\mathbf{j} + r\mathbf{k}$, the unit vector, $\hat{\mathbf{a}}$, is given by $\hat{\mathbf{a}} = \dfrac{p\mathbf{i} + q\mathbf{j} + r\mathbf{k}}{\sqrt{p^2 + q^2 + r^2}}$

3 The vectors $\mathbf{m}$ and $\mathbf{n}$ are defined by $\mathbf{m} = \begin{pmatrix} 2 \\ -2 \\ 3 \end{pmatrix}$ and $\mathbf{n} = \begin{pmatrix} -4 \\ -5 \\ 6 \end{pmatrix}$.

a Find, giving your answer in the form $p\mathbf{i} + q\mathbf{j} + r\mathbf{k}$:

i $\mathbf{m} + 2\mathbf{n}$ **ii** $-\mathbf{m} - \mathbf{n}$

b Show that the vector $4\mathbf{m} - \mathbf{n}$ is parallel to the vector $4\mathbf{i} - \mathbf{j} + 2\mathbf{k}$.

Hint Two vectors are parallel if one is a scalar multiple of the other.

4 Find, to one decimal place, the angle that the vector $\mathbf{a} = 2\mathbf{i} - \mathbf{j} - 2\mathbf{k}$ makes with:

a the positive x-axis **b** the positive y-axis

c the positive z-axis.

Hint If the vector $\mathbf{a} = x\mathbf{i} + y\mathbf{j} + z\mathbf{k}$ makes an angle θ_x with the positive x-axis then $\cos\theta_x = \dfrac{x}{|\mathbf{a}|}$ and similarly for the angles θ_y and θ_z.

(P) 5 Given that $\overrightarrow{OA} = 2\mathbf{i} + 3\mathbf{j} - 5\mathbf{k}$ and $\overrightarrow{OB} = -\mathbf{i} + 4\mathbf{j} + 2\mathbf{k}$,

a find $\overrightarrow{AB}$ **b** show that the triangle OAB is scalene.

(E) 6 Given $\overrightarrow{AB} = 4\mathbf{i} + \mathbf{j} + 3\mathbf{k}$ and $\overrightarrow{AC} = 5\mathbf{i} - 6\mathbf{j} - \mathbf{k}$, find the unit vector in the direction $\overrightarrow{BC}$. **(3 marks)**

(E/P) 7 The points A, B and C have position vectors $\begin{pmatrix} 4 \\ 4 \\ -3 \end{pmatrix}$, $\begin{pmatrix} 7 \\ -1 \\ 0 \end{pmatrix}$ and $\begin{pmatrix} -1 \\ 1 \\ -6 \end{pmatrix}$ respectively.

a Find the vectors $\overrightarrow{AB}$, $\overrightarrow{AC}$ and $\overrightarrow{BC}$. **(3 marks)**

b Find $|\overrightarrow{AB}|$, $|\overrightarrow{AC}|$ and $|\overrightarrow{BC}|$ giving your answers in exact form. **(3 marks)**

c Describe the triangle ABC. **(1 mark)**

(E/P) 8 Triangle PQR has vertices $P(1, 2, -3)$, $Q(1, 2, 3)$ and $R(-2, -2, -3)$.

a Find $|\overrightarrow{PQ}|$, $|\overrightarrow{QR}|$ and $|\overrightarrow{PR}|$ giving your answers in exact form. **(3 marks)**

b Use your answer to part **a** to explain why $\angle RPQ$ is a right angle. **(2 marks)**

c Find the size of angle PRQ, giving your answer to one decimal place. **(2 marks)**

(E) 9 Given $\overrightarrow{AB} = -\mathbf{i} + 2\mathbf{j} + \mathbf{k}$ and $\overrightarrow{AC} = -8\mathbf{i} + 7\mathbf{j} + 2\mathbf{k}$ in triangle ABC, find $\angle ABC$, giving your answer in degrees to one decimal place. **(6 marks)**

12.3 Solving geometric problems

1 The diagram shows a rectangular prism.

The vectors $\overrightarrow{OA}$, $\overrightarrow{OB}$ and $\overrightarrow{OC}$ are equal to **a**, **b** and **c** respectively. M and N are the midpoints of CF and AF respectively. Express in terms of **a**, **b** and **c**:

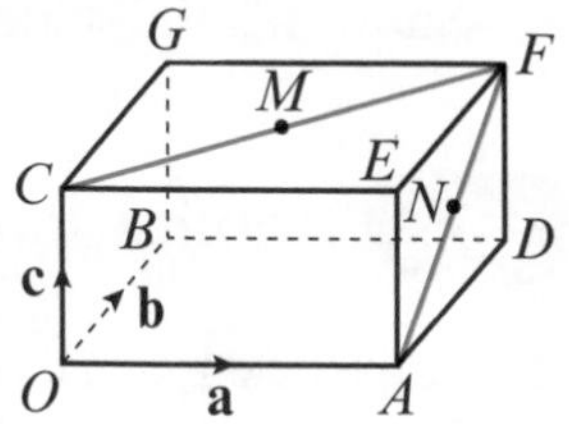

a $\overrightarrow{OF}$ **b** $\overrightarrow{DC}$ **c** $\overrightarrow{AG}$ **d** $\overrightarrow{CF}$

e $\overrightarrow{OM}$ **f** $\overrightarrow{AM}$ **g** $\overrightarrow{AN}$ **h** $\overrightarrow{NM}$

Hint Use the rules for vector addition, working in three dimensions.

2 The diagram shows a quadrilateral $PQRS$, where P, Q, R and S are the points (7, 6, 3), (4, 10, −4), (3, 15, −12) and (6, 11, −5) respectively.

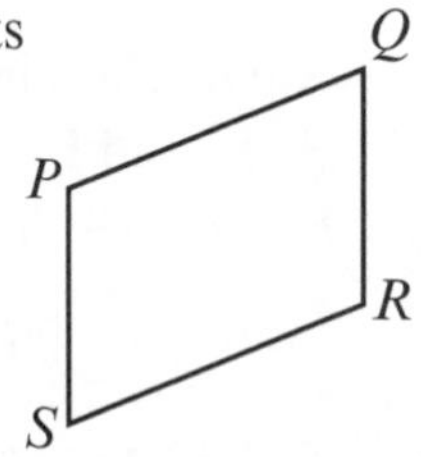

Find:

a $\overrightarrow{PQ}$ and $\overrightarrow{SR}$ **b** $\overrightarrow{SP}$ and $\overrightarrow{RQ}$

c Describe the quadrilateral $PQRS$.

3 Given that

$(2q - 3p)\mathbf{i} + 5\mathbf{j} + r\mathbf{k} = 13\mathbf{i} + (4q + p)\mathbf{j} + (2q - p)\mathbf{k}$

find the values of p, q and r.

Hint As the vectors **i**, **j** and **k** are non-coplanar, you can compare coefficients.

If $a\mathbf{i} + b\mathbf{j} + c\mathbf{k} = d\mathbf{i} + e\mathbf{j} + f\mathbf{k}$, then $a = d$, $b = e$ and $c = f$.

4 A rectangle $OACB$ has an area of 20. A new rectangle $OPRQ$ is formed, such that $\overrightarrow{OP} = 3\overrightarrow{OA}$ and $\overrightarrow{OQ} = 2\overrightarrow{OB}$.

Find the area of the new rectangle.

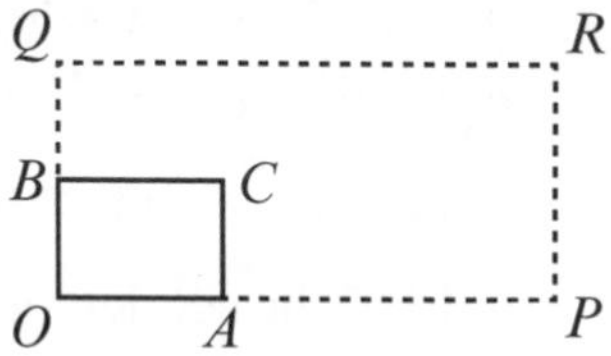

(E) 5 Given that $-a\mathbf{i} - 6\mathbf{j} + (3a + 2b)\mathbf{k} = 2b\mathbf{i} + bc\mathbf{j} + 8\mathbf{k}$, find the values of a, b and c. **(4 marks)**

(E) 6 The diagram shows the parallelogram $PQRS$.

Given that $\overrightarrow{PQ} = \mathbf{i} + 10\mathbf{j} - 3\mathbf{k}$ and $\overrightarrow{QR} = 8\mathbf{i} + 3\mathbf{j} + 2\mathbf{k}$, find the area of the quadrilateral, giving your answer to one decimal place. **(6 marks)**

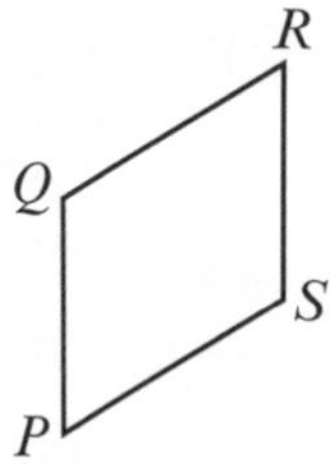

(P) 7 The vertices of triangle ABC have coordinates $A(2, 11, 4)$, $B(6, k, -6)$ and $C(12, 6, 1)$. Given that triangle ABC is isosceles, and k is a positive integer, find the value of k.

(E/P) 8 A student makes the following hypothesis:

> It is not possible to have an equilateral triangle in 3 dimensions with each vertex having integer coordinates.

Show that the student's hypothesis is incorrect. **(5 marks)**

12.4 Applications to mechanics

1 A particle is acted on by three forces $\mathbf{F}_1 = (-5\mathbf{i} + 3\mathbf{j} + \mathbf{k})$N, $\mathbf{F}_2 = (2\mathbf{i} - 5\mathbf{k})$N and $\mathbf{F}_3 = (-4\mathbf{j} + 3\mathbf{k})$N.

a Find the resultant force **R**.

b Find the magnitude of the resultant force.

> **Hint** The resultant force can be found by summing all three forces. The magnitude of the force $\mathbf{F} = a\mathbf{i} + b\mathbf{j} + c\mathbf{k}$ is $\sqrt{a^2 + b^2 + c^2}$.

2 A particle is in equilibrium and is acted on by three forces $\mathbf{F}_1$, $\mathbf{F}_2$ and $\mathbf{F}_3$, where $\mathbf{F}_1 = (2b\mathbf{i} - b\mathbf{j} + 5\mathbf{k})$N, $\mathbf{F}_2 = (-4\mathbf{i} + 7\mathbf{j} - 8\mathbf{k})$N and $\mathbf{F}_3 = (a\mathbf{i} + 2a\mathbf{j} + 3\mathbf{k})$N.

Find the values of a and b.

> **Hint** If the particle is in equilibrium, the resultant force will be zero.

3 A particle, initially at rest at O, is acted on by a force that causes the particle to accelerate at $(-3\mathbf{i} + 6\mathbf{j} - \mathbf{k})\,\text{m s}^{-2}$ for 2 seconds.

a Find the magnitude of the acceleration of the particle.

b Find the distance of the particle from O after 2 seconds.

> **Hint** Use the *suvat* equations to find the position of the particle. Here, $s = ut + \frac{1}{2}at^2$ is the correct formula to use.
> ← **Statistics and Mechanics Year 1, Chapter 9**

4 A particle of mass 4 kg is acted on by two forces, $\mathbf{F}_1 = (8\mathbf{i} - 3\mathbf{j} + 6\mathbf{k})$N and $\mathbf{F}_2 = (-6\mathbf{i} + 9\mathbf{j} + 4\mathbf{k})$N.

a Find the resultant force acting on the particle.

b Find the acceleration of the particle, giving your answer as a vector.

> **Hint** Use the vector form of Newton's second law: $\mathbf{F} = m\mathbf{a}$.
> ← **Statistics and Mechanics Year 1, Section 10.4**

(E) 5 A particle, initially at rest at O, accelerates at $(5\mathbf{i} - 11\mathbf{j} + 2\mathbf{k})\,\text{m s}^{-2}$ for 4 seconds.

Find:

a the speed of the particle after 4 seconds, giving your answer in the form $a\sqrt{6}\,\text{m s}^{-1}$, where a is a constant **(3 marks)**

b the distance travelled by the particle in the first 4 seconds of its motion. **(2 marks)**

(E) 6 Given that a force of $(5\mathbf{i} - 6\mathbf{j} + 12\mathbf{k})$N acts on a particle of mass 4 kg, find:

a the acceleration of the particle **(2 marks)**

b the angle the acceleration vector makes with **i**. **(3 marks)**

E/P **7** A particle of mass 3 kg is in static equilibrium and is acted on by three forces $\mathbf{F}_1 = (2\mathbf{i} + 3\mathbf{j} + b\mathbf{k})$ N, $\mathbf{F}_2 = (a\mathbf{j} + 4\mathbf{k})$ N and $\mathbf{F}_3 = (-2\mathbf{i} - 5\mathbf{j} + 3\mathbf{k})$ N.

a Find the values of the constants a and b. **(2 marks)**

The force $\mathbf{F}_3$ is removed. Find:

b the resultant force $\mathbf{R}$ **(1 mark)**

c the acceleration of the particle, giving your answer in the form $(p\mathbf{i} + q\mathbf{j} + r\mathbf{k})\,\text{m s}^{-2}$ **(2 marks)**

d the magnitude of the acceleration. **(2 marks)**

E/P **8** A particle of mass 5 kg is acted on by three forces, $\mathbf{F}_1 = (2\mathbf{i} + p\mathbf{j} - \mathbf{k})$ N, $\mathbf{F}_2 = (p\mathbf{i} + 5\mathbf{j} + 2\mathbf{k})$ N and $\mathbf{F}_3 = (\mathbf{i} + \mathbf{j} - p\mathbf{k})$ N. Given that the particle is accelerating and that the magnitude of that acceleration is $5\,\text{m s}^{-2}$, find the possible values of p. **(5 marks)**

Problem solving Set A

Bronze

The coordinates of A and B are $(8, -6, 4)$ and $(k, -4, -7)$ respectively.

Given that the distance from A to B is 15 units, find the possible values of k. **(3 marks)**

Silver

Given that $\mathbf{a} = 4p\mathbf{i} - 5p\mathbf{j} + 3p\mathbf{k}$, and that $|\mathbf{a}| = 10\sqrt{6}$, find the possible values of p. **(3 marks)**

Gold

A particle of mass 3 kg is acted on by three forces:

$\mathbf{F}_1 = (4\mathbf{i} + q\mathbf{j} + 2\mathbf{k})$ N, $\mathbf{F}_2 = (-q\mathbf{i} + 2\mathbf{j} - \mathbf{k})$ N and $\mathbf{F}_3 = (-\mathbf{i} + 3\mathbf{j} - q\mathbf{k})$ N.

Given that the particle is accelerating and that the magnitude of that acceleration is $2\,\text{m s}^{-2}$, find the possible values of q. **(5 marks)**

Problem solving Set B

Bronze

A, B, C and D are the points $(7, 4, -1)$, $(11, -2, 3)$, $(6, -15, 16)$ and $(-2, -3, 8)$ respectively.

a Find $\overrightarrow{AB}$ and $\overrightarrow{DC}$, giving your answers in the form $p\mathbf{i} + q\mathbf{j} + r\mathbf{k}$. **(2 marks)**

b Prove that $\overrightarrow{AB}$ and $\overrightarrow{DC}$ are parallel. **(2 marks)**

c Find k such that $|AB| = k|DC|$. **(1 mark)**

d Hence describe quadrilateral $ABCD$. **(1 mark)**

Silver

$ABCD$ is a quadrilateral and A, B, C are the points (6, −8, 4), (−3, −4, 2) and (−7, 9, −3) respectively. Find the coordinates of D such that $ABCD$ is a parallelogram. **(4 marks)**

Gold

The diagram shows a cuboid whose vertices are O, A, B, C, D, E, F and G.

Vectors **a**, **b** and **c** are equal to $\overrightarrow{OA}$, $\overrightarrow{OB}$ and $\overrightarrow{OC}$ respectively.

The points M, N, P and Q lie on OA, AD, FG and GC such that

$OM : MA = AN : ND = FP : PG = GQ : QC = 4 : 1$.

Prove that the lines MP and NQ bisect each other at T. **(10 marks)**

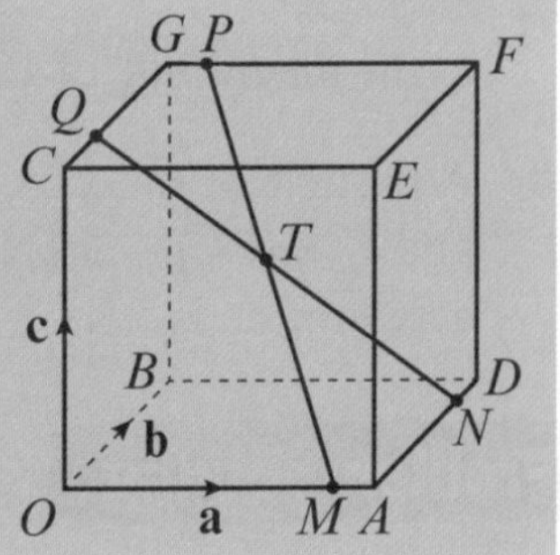

Now try this → Exam question bank Q1, Q13, Q16, Q19, Q65, Q84

Exam question bank

This bank of exam-style questions has not been ordered by topic. Read each question carefully to work out which skills and techniques you will need to apply.

1 The coordinates of A and B are $(6, 3, -3)$ and $(-4, k, 0)$ respectively.
Given that the distance from A to B is $5\sqrt{5}$ units, find the possible values of k. **(3 marks)**

2 $f(x) = \dfrac{1}{3x - 7} - 1$

a Calculate $f(2)$ and $f(2.5)$. **(2 marks)**

A student writes:

> f(x) changes sign in the interval [2, 2.5] so the equation f(x) = 0 must have a root in this interval.

b Explain why the student is incorrect. **(2 marks)**

3 Given that $m = 2\operatorname{cosec} x$ and $n = \frac{1}{5}\sin x$, express m in terms of n. **(4 marks)**

4 The curve C has equation $y = 2x^2 + 2x - e^x$.

a Find $\dfrac{dy}{dx}$ **(2 marks)**

b Find the equation of the tangent to C at the point $(0, -1)$. **(3 marks)**

5 Given that $\dfrac{2x^4 + 3x^2 - 5x + 2}{x^2 - 4} \equiv ax^2 + bx + c + \dfrac{d}{x + 2} + \dfrac{e}{x - 2}$, find the values of the constants a, b, c, d and e. **(6 marks)**

6 Solve $4\cos x = 3\sec x$ in the interval $-180° \leqslant x \leqslant 180°$. **(4 marks)**

7 Given that $x = \dfrac{\ln y}{y}$, $y > 0$,

a find $\dfrac{dy}{dx}$ **(3 marks)**

b Hence, or otherwise, find the value of $\dfrac{dy}{dx}$ at $y = e^{-4}$. **(3 marks)**

8 Find $\displaystyle\int_0^{\frac{\pi}{4}} (6\sec^2 x - 4\tan^2 x)\,dx$. **(3 marks)**

9 Express $\dfrac{7x^2 + 12x}{(x + 1)^2(x + 2)}$ in partial fractions. **(5 marks)**

10 Show that the line with equation $y = 3x + 2$ does not intersect the curve with parametric equations $x = t + 1$, $y = (2t + 2)(2 - t)$, $t \in \mathbb{R}$. **(4 marks)**

11 **a** Use the expansion of $\sin(2x + x)$ to write $\sin 3x$ in terms of $\sin x$. **(3 marks)**

b Hence solve the equation $\sin 3x = \sin x$ in the interval $0 \leqslant x \leqslant \pi$. **(3 marks)**

12 $\text{p}(x) = \frac{1}{3}x^2 - 3\sin x + 1$. The equation $\text{p}(x) = 0$ has a root α between 0 and 1.

a Show that the equation $\text{p}(x) = 0$ can be written as $x = \arcsin\left(\frac{1}{9}x^2 + \frac{1}{3}\right)$. **(2 marks)**

b Use the iterative formula $x_{n+1} = \arcsin\left(\frac{1}{9}x_n{}^2 + \frac{1}{3}\right)$ with $x_0 = 0.5$ to obtain x_1, x_2 and x_3. **(2 marks)**

c Taking 0.4 as a first approximation to α, apply the Newton–Raphson procedure once to obtain a second approximation to α, giving your answer to 3 decimal places. **(3 marks)**

13 Given $\overrightarrow{AB} = 5\mathbf{i} + 2\mathbf{j} - \mathbf{k}$ and $\overrightarrow{BC} = -7\mathbf{i} - 10\mathbf{j} + 4\mathbf{k}$ in triangle ABC, find $\angle BAC$, giving your answer to 1 decimal place. **(6 marks)**

14 **a** Use the binomial expansion, in ascending powers of x, to show that $\sqrt{9 + x} = 3 + \frac{1}{6}x + kx^2 + \ldots$ where k is a rational constant to be found. **(4 marks)**

A student attempts to substitute $x = 1$ into both sides of this equation to find an approximate value for $\sqrt{10}$.

b State, giving a reason, if the expansion is valid for this value of x. **(1 mark)**

15 **a** On the same set of axes, sketch the graphs of $y = 3 + 3\sec x$ and $y = \cot x$ in the interval $-180° \leqslant x \leqslant 180°$. **(3 marks)**

b Write down the number of solutions to the equation $3 + 3\sec x - \cot x = 0$ in the interval $-180° \leqslant x \leqslant 180°$. **(1 mark)**

c Write down the maximum value of $\dfrac{1}{3 + 3\sec x}$ **(1 mark)**

16 Given that a force of $(-2\mathbf{i} - 8\mathbf{j} + 4\mathbf{k})$ N acts on a particle of mass 3 kg, find:

a the acceleration of the particle **(2 marks)**

b the angle the acceleration vector makes with the unit vector $\mathbf{j}$. **(3 marks)**

17 Prove that $\dfrac{1 + \tan^2 x}{1 - \tan^2 x} \equiv \sec 2x$ **(4 marks)**

18 The diagram shows part of the curve with equation

$$y = \frac{4}{5}\sqrt{x + 2}$$

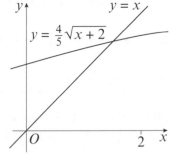

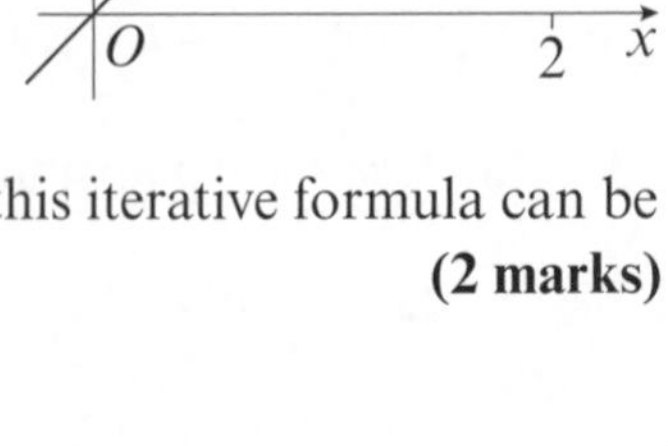

The curve intersects the line $y = x$ at the point $x = \alpha$.

a Show that $1 < \alpha < 2$. **(3 marks)**

A student uses the iterative formula $x_{n+1} = \frac{4}{5}\sqrt{x_n + 2}$ together with $x_0 = 1$ to find a better approximation for α.

b With reference to the graph above, determine whether or not this iterative formula can be used to find an approximation for α, justifying your answer. **(2 marks)**

19 Given that $\mathbf{a} = 2t\mathbf{i} - 4t\mathbf{j} - 2t\mathbf{k}$, and $|\mathbf{a}| = 9\sqrt{6}$, find the possible values of t. **(4 marks)**

20 Find $\int x^3 \ln(x^2 + 1)\,dx$. **(7 marks)**

21 **a** Given that $\cot P = -2$, where $\pi < P < 2\pi$, calculate the exact value of $\sin P$. **(3 marks)**

b Show that $\sec P = \pm\frac{\sqrt{a}}{2}$, where a is an integer to be found. **(3 marks)**

22 The height above ground of a person on a water slide can be modelled by the equation

$$h(t) = 18e^{-0.5t} + 10\sin\left(\frac{t}{3}\right) - \frac{1}{10}t,\ t \geqslant 0$$

where t is the time in seconds since the person began sliding.

The diagram shows the graph of $y = h(t)$.

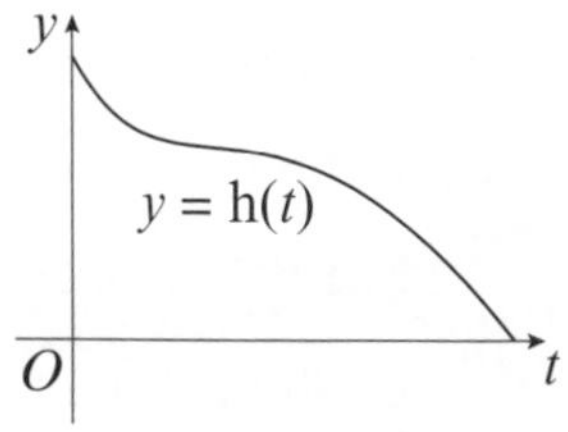

a Show that the person reaches the bottom of the slide between 9 and 10 seconds after they start sliding. **(1 mark)**

b Taking 9 as a first approximation, apply the Newton–Raphson procedure once to $h(t)$ to obtain a second approximation for the time when the person reaches the bottom of the slide, giving your answer to 3 decimal places. **(3 marks)**

c By considering the change of sign of $h(t)$ in a suitable interval, verify that your answer to part **b** is in fact correct to 3 decimal places. **(2 marks)**

23 Given that $\int_{\ln 2}^{\ln a} \frac{2e^x}{e^x + 1}\,dx = \ln 4$, $a > 0$, find the value of a. **(4 marks)**

24 The first term of an arithmetic series is 2. The common difference of the series is 6.

a Find the 20th term of the series. **(2 marks)**

The sum of the first n terms of the series is 7450.

b Find the value of n. **(5 marks)**

25 **a** When θ is small, show that $\frac{1 + \sin 2\theta + \tan 2\theta}{2\cos 4\theta - 1} \approx \frac{1 + 4\theta}{(1 + 2\theta)(1 - 2\theta)}$ **(4 marks)**

b Hence write down an estimate of $\frac{1 + \sin 2\theta + \tan 2\theta}{2\cos 4\theta - 1}$ when $\theta = 0.03$ radians. **(1 mark)**

c Find the percentage error in your estimate, giving your answer to 3 significant figures. **(2 marks)**

26 The function f is defined by $f(x) = 6x^3 - 13x^2 + 4$, $x \in \mathbb{R}$.
Given that $f(2) = 0$, express $f(x)$ as the product of three linear factors and hence sketch the graph of $y = |f(x)|$. Show on your sketch the coordinates of each point at which the graph meets or cuts the coordinate axes. **(7 marks)**

27 A sequence $a_1, a_2, a_3, \ldots$ is defined by $a_1 = k$, $a_{n+1} = 3a_n - 5$, $n \geqslant 1$, where k is a constant.

a Write down an expression for a_2 in terms of k. **(1 mark)**

b Show that $a_3 = 9k - 20$. **(2 marks)**

Given that $\sum_{r=1}^{4} a_r = -30$,

c find the value of k. **(4 marks)**

28 A curve has equation $y = \cos 2x - \sin^2 2x$, $-\pi \leqslant x \leqslant 0$.

a Find $\frac{dy}{dx}$ and $\frac{d^2y}{dx^2}$ **(4 marks)**

b Find the x-coordinates of the stationary points of the curve. **(3 marks)**

c Show that a local maximum occurs at $x = -\frac{\pi}{2}$ **(2 marks)**

29 The diagram shows the part of the graph of $y = f(x)$ where $f(x) = x^3 \ln x$. The curve cuts the x-axis at A and B and has a turning point at P.

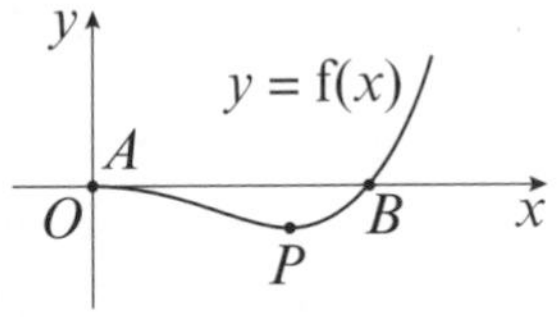

a Work out the coordinates of A and B. **(1 mark)**

b Find $f'(x)$. **(3 marks)**

c By considering the change of sign of $f'(x)$ in a suitable interval, verify that the x-coordinate of P is 0.717 correct to 3 decimal places. **(2 marks)**

d Find the exact value of the x-coordinate of P. **(2 marks)**

30 The diagram shows a circle with centre O. The points A and B lie on the circumference of the circle. The area of the major sector, shown shaded, is 88.725 cm². The reflex angle AOB is 4.2 radians.

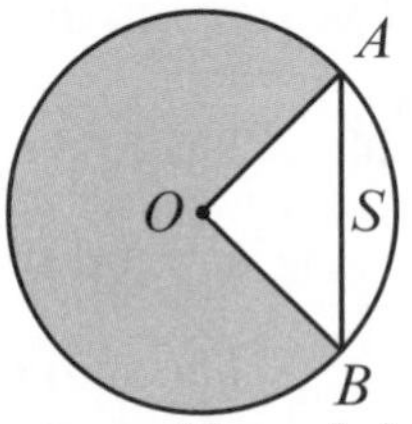

a Find the exact length, in cm, of the minor arc AB, giving your answer in the form $a\pi + b$, where a and b are constants to be found. **(4 marks)**

b Find the area of the segment S, giving your answer to 1 decimal place. **(3 marks)**

31 The curve C has parametric equations $x = 5\cos t - 4$, $y = 5\sin t + 1$, $-\frac{\pi}{2} \leqslant t \leqslant \frac{\pi}{4}$

a Find a Cartesian equation of C in the form $(x + a)^2 + (y + b)^2 = c$, stating the values of a, b and c. **(4 marks)**

b Sketch the curve C on the appropriate domain. **(3 marks)**

c Determine the exact length of curve C. **(2 marks)**

32 The function f is defined by $f(x) = |2x - 7| + 3$.

a Sketch the graph with equation $y = f(x)$, stating the coordinates of any points where the graph cuts or meets the coordinate axes. **(3 marks)**

b State the range of $f(x)$. **(1 mark)**

c Find the values of x which satisfy $f(x) > x + 2$. Write your answer using set notation. **(5 marks)**

33 **a** Expand $\frac{1}{\sqrt{4-3x}}$, where $|x| < \frac{4}{3}$, in ascending powers of x, up to and including the term in x^2. Simplify each term. **(5 marks)**

b Hence, or otherwise, find the first 3 terms in the expansion of $\frac{x+8}{\sqrt{4-3x}}$ as a series in ascending powers of x. **(4 marks)**

34 The motion of a netball as it leaves a player's hand and passes through the net is modelled using the parametric equations $x = 3.8t$, $y = -4.9t^2 + 4.6t + 1.9$, $t \geqslant 0$, where x m is the horizontal distance travelled and y m is the height of the netball above the ground after t seconds.

a Write down the height of the ball when it leaves the player's hand. **(1 mark)**

Given that the height of the net is 2.8 m and that the netball passes through the net as it is travelling downwards,

b find the time at which the netball passes through the net **(3 marks)**

c find the horizontal distance between the player and the net. **(1 mark)**

35 Luke and Isabella were given this question.

Solve the equation $\sqrt{3}\sin\theta = \cos\theta$ for $-\frac{\pi}{2} < \theta < \frac{\pi}{2}$

Their attempts are shown below.

Isabella

$\sqrt{3}\sin\theta = \cos\theta$

$\tan\theta = \sqrt{3}$

$\theta = \frac{\pi}{3}$

Luke

$\sqrt{3}\sin\theta = \cos\theta$

$3\sin^2\theta = \cos^2\theta$

$3\sin^2\theta = 1 - \sin^2\theta$

$\sin^2\theta = \frac{1}{4}$

$\sin\theta = \pm\frac{1}{2}$

$\theta = \pm\frac{\pi}{6}$

a What error has Isabella made? **(1 mark)**

Luke gives $\theta = -\frac{\pi}{6}$ as one of the answers to $\sqrt{3}\sin\theta = \cos\theta$

b Explain why this answer is incorrect and how this answer arose. **(2 marks)**

36 The curve C has parametric equations

$x = \cos t,\ y = \cos\left(t + \frac{\pi}{3}\right),\ 0 < t < \pi$

Show that a Cartesian equation of the curve is $y = \frac{1}{2}x - \frac{\sqrt{3}}{2}\sqrt{1 - x^2}$, for $a < x < b$, stating the values of a and b. **(5 marks)**

37 **a** On the same set of axes, sketch the curve with equation $y = 2\ln x$ and the line with equation $2x + 5y = 10$. **(2 marks)**

b With reference to your sketch, explain why the function $f(x) = 10\ln x + 2x - 10$ has exactly one root. **(2 marks)**

c Show that $f(x)$ has a root between $x = 1.8$ and $x = 1.9$. **(2 marks)**

38 Given that k is a positive integer, show that $\int_{3k}^{4k} \frac{4}{5x + k}\,dx$ is independent of k. **(4 marks)**

39 $f(x) = 2x + 4^{-x}$. Show that the equation of the tangent to the curve with equation $y = f(x)$ at the point with x-coordinate -1 is $(15\ln 2)x + 2y + 15\ln 2 - 9 = 0$. **(6 marks)**

40 **a** Use $\tan(x + \alpha) \equiv \frac{\tan x + \tan\alpha}{1 - \tan x \tan\alpha}$ to show that $\tan 105° = -2 - \sqrt{3}$. **(4 marks)**

b Hence or otherwise, show that $\cot 105° = -2 + \sqrt{3}$. **(3 marks)**

41 The shape $AOBCD$ consists of an isosceles triangle COD joined along its equal sides to sectors OBC and ODA of a circle with centre O and diameter 11 m. Angles AOD and BOC are equal. AOB is a straight line and is parallel to the line DC. DC has length 4 m.

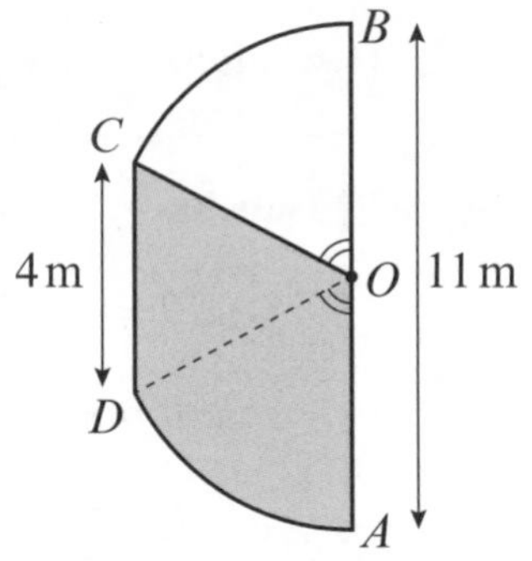

a Find angle COD in radians, correct to 3 decimal places. **(2 marks)**

b Find the shaded area $AOCD$, giving your answer to 1 decimal place. **(3 marks)**

c Find the perimeter of sector COB, giving your answer to 1 decimal place. **(2 marks)**

42 **a** Prove that $\sec^4 x - \tan^4 x \equiv 2\sec^2 x - 1$. **(4 marks)**

b Hence solve the equation $\sec^4 x - \tan^4 x = 24$ in the interval $0 \leqslant x \leqslant 360°$. Give your answers to 4 significant figures. **(4 marks)**

43 A curve has equation $6x^2 - 6y^2 - 4xy + 40 = 0$.

a Find $\frac{dy}{dx}$ in terms of x and y. **(4 marks)**

b Show that line joining the two points on the curve where the gradient is $-\frac{3}{5}$ has equation $9x + 2y = 0$. **(2 marks)**

44 Consider the function $f(x) = -2x^3 + 8x^2 - 7x + 3, x \in \mathbb{R}$.

a Given that $f(3) = 0$, write $f(x)$ as a product of two algebraic factors. **(2 marks)**

b Hence prove that there are exactly two real solutions to the equation

$-2y^6 + 8y^4 - 7y^2 + 3 = 0$ **(2 marks)**

c Deduce the number of real solutions, for $5\pi \leqslant \theta < 8\pi$, to the equation

$2\tan^3\theta - 8\tan^2\theta + 7\tan\theta - 3 = 0$ **(1 mark)**

45 The diagram shows the curve C which is defined by the parametric equations

$x = t^{\frac{1}{2}}, y = 2t^{\frac{1}{2}} - 4t^2, 0 \leqslant t \leqslant 3$

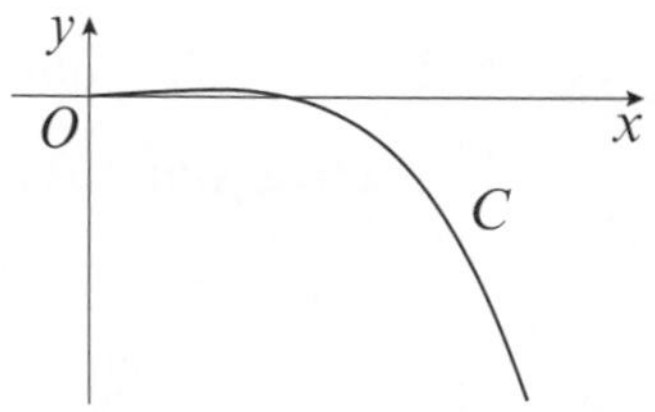

a Find a Cartesian equation of the curve in the form $y = f(x)$ and state the domain of $f(x)$. **(3 marks)**

b Find the value of t when $\frac{dy}{dt} = 0$, and hence determine the exact range of $f(x)$. **(4 marks)**

46 The diagram shows the curve with equation $y = k\sin\left(x + \frac{\pi}{3}\right)$ for $0 \leqslant x \leqslant 2\pi$, where k is a constant.

The curve cuts the y-axis at $(0, 2\sqrt{3})$ and passes through the points $(p, 0)$ and $(q, 0)$.

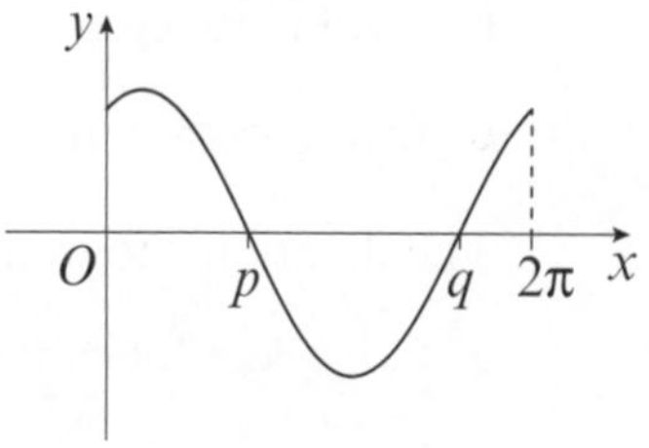

a Show that $k = 4$. **(1 mark)**

b Find p and q. **(2 marks)**

The line $y = -1.2$ meets the curve at the points R and S.

c Find the x-coordinates of R and S, giving your answers to 3 significant figures. **(5 marks)**

47 Using the substitution $u = \operatorname{cosec} x$, or otherwise, find the exact value of $\int_{\frac{\pi}{4}}^{\frac{\pi}{2}} \cot^3 x \, dx$. **(8 marks)**

48 The curve C has parametric equations $x = t - 2, y = \frac{1 - 3t}{t}, t > 0$.

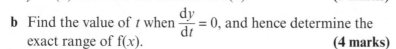

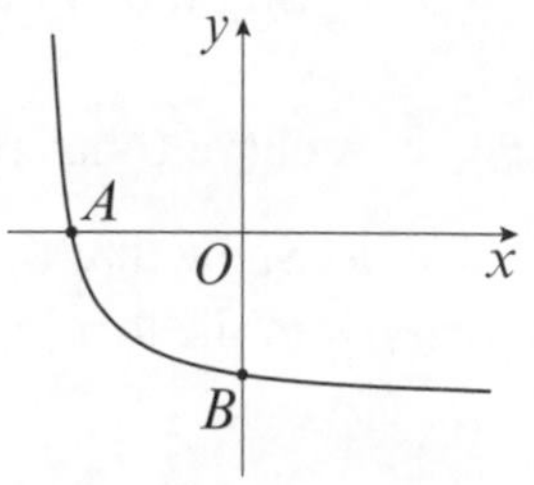

a The curve crosses the x-axis at point A and the y-axis at point B. Find the coordinates of A and B. **(4 marks)**

b A straight line l intersects the curve C at points A and B. Find the equation of the line l in the form $ax + by + c = 0$. **(3 marks)**

49 $f(x) = \frac{12x^2 + 20x + 12}{(3x + 1)(x + 1)(x + 2)} = \frac{A}{3x + 1} + \frac{B}{x + 1} + \frac{C}{x + 2}$

a Find the values of the constants A, B and C. **(3 marks)**

b Hence find the exact value of $\int_0^2 f(x)\,dx$, giving your answer in the form $\ln\frac{a}{b}$ where $\frac{a}{b}$ is a fraction in its simplest form. **(5 marks)**

50 **a** Prove that $\sin 2\theta - \tan\theta \equiv \tan\theta \cos 2\theta$. **(3 marks)**

b Hence solve the following equation in the interval $-\frac{\pi}{2} < x < \frac{\pi}{2}$

$$(\sec^2 x + 3)(\sin 2x - \tan x) = 4\tan^2 x \cos 2x$$

Give your answers to 3 decimal places where necessary. **(6 marks)**

51 **a** Show that the binomial expansion of $(9 + 7x)^{\frac{1}{2}}$ in ascending powers of x up to and including the term in x^2 is $3 + \frac{7}{6}x + kx^2$, giving the value of the constant k as a simplified fraction. **(4 marks)**

b **i** Use the expansion from part **a**, with $x = \frac{9}{25}$, to find an approximate value for $\sqrt{2}$.

Give your answer in the form $\frac{p}{q}$, where p and q are integers.

ii Explain why substituting $x = \frac{9}{25}$ into this binomial expansion leads to a valid approximation. **(4 marks)**

52 $f(x) = x^2(2 - 5x)^5$

a Find $f'(x)$ and $f''(x)$. **(4 marks)**

b Find the x-coordinates of the points where $f''(x) = 0$. **(3 marks)**

c Demonstrate that $x = \frac{2}{5}$ is a point of inflection. **(2 marks)**

53 The diagram shows the part of the curve with equation $y = 3x^2e^{-2x}$.

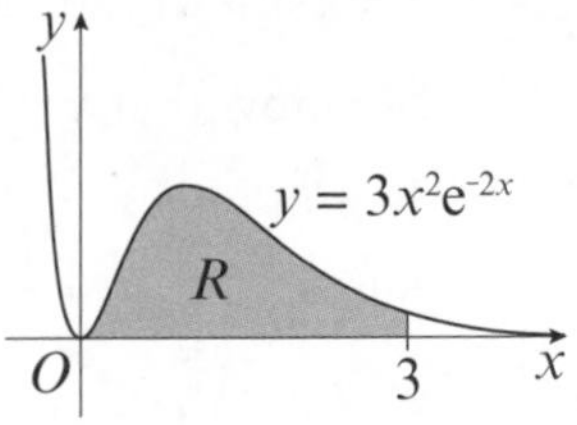

a Complete the table with the y-value corresponding to $x = 1.5$. **(1 mark)**

x	0	0.5	1	1.5	2	2.5	3
y	0	0.2759	0.4060		0.2198	0.1263	0.0669

b Use the trapezium rule, with all your y-values from the completed table, to obtain an estimate for the area of the shaded region R. **(3 marks)**

c Show, by integration, that the exact value of $\int_0^3 3x^2e^{-2x}\,dx$ is $\frac{3}{4} - \frac{75}{4e^6}$ **(5 marks)**

54 A curve C has parametric equations $x = \frac{1}{6}\cos t$, $y = \cos 3t$, $\frac{\pi}{6} \leqslant t \leqslant \frac{5\pi}{6}$

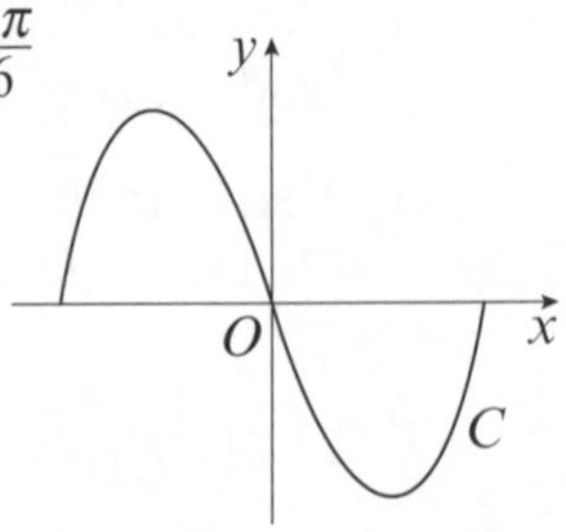

a Show that the Cartesian equation of the curve can be written in the form $y = ax(bx^2 - c)$, stating the values of a, b and c. **(5 marks)**

b Determine the range of possible values of x in the given domain of t. **(1 mark)**

c Find the coordinates of the turning points of the curve, and hence determine the range of possible values of y in the given domain of t. **(3 marks)**

55 **a** Solve the equation $2|x + 4| - 2 = x + 3$. **(4 marks)**

b **i** Sketch the graph of $y = |x| - 4$.

ii Explain why $|x| - 4 \leqslant |x - 4|$ for all real values of x. **(6 marks)**

56 Following heavy rainfall, water flows into a reservoir at a rate $200\,\text{m}^3\,\text{h}^{-1}$. To relieve pressure on the dam, water is released at a rate of $\frac{1}{5}V\,\text{m}^3\text{h}^{-1}$, where V is the volume of the reservoir.

a Show that $-5\dfrac{dV}{dt} = V - 1000$. **(2 marks)**

Given that when the water is initially released, the volume of the dam is $9000\,\text{m}^3$,

b find the solution to the differential equation in the form $V = a + be^{-kt}$, where a, b and k are constants to be found. **(7 marks)**

c State, with a reason, the minimum volume of the reservoir according to the model. **(1 mark)**

57 **a** Use binomial expansions to show that $\sqrt{\dfrac{1 + 6x}{1 - x}} \approx 1 + \dfrac{7x}{2} - \dfrac{21x^2}{8}$ **(6 marks)**

A student substitutes $x = \frac{1}{5}$ into both sides of the approximation shown in part **a** in an attempt to find an approximation to $\sqrt{11}$.

b Give a reason why the student should not use $x = \frac{1}{5}$ **(1 mark)**

c Substitute $x = \dfrac{2}{65}$ into $\sqrt{\dfrac{1 + 6x}{1 - x}} \approx 1 + \dfrac{7x}{2} - \dfrac{21x^2}{8}$ to obtain an approximation to $\sqrt{11}$.
Give your answer to 5 decimal places. **(3 marks)**

58 The function g is defined as $g(x) = \arccos x$, for $-1 \leqslant x \leqslant 1$.
The function h is defined as $h(x) = \frac{1}{2}x$, $x \in \mathbb{R}$.

a Find an expression for $gh(x)$ and state its domain. **(3 marks)**

b Sketch the graph of $y = gh(x)$, clearly showing the exact coordinates of the endpoints of the curve. **(3 marks)**

c Determine $(gh)^{-1}(x)$ and state its domain. **(2 marks)**

59 In triangle ABC, $AB = 3\,\text{cm}$, $BC = 7\,\text{cm}$ and $AC = 8\,\text{cm}$, and $\angle ACB = \dfrac{\theta}{2}$

a Use the cosine rule to show that $\cos\dfrac{\theta}{2} = \dfrac{13}{14}$ **(3 marks)**

b Hence find the exact value of $\cos 2\theta$. **(3 marks)**

60 **a** Expand $\frac{1}{(3-4x)^2}$, $|x| < \frac{3}{4}$, in ascending powers of x up to and including the term in x^2, giving each term as a simplified fraction. **(5 marks)**

Given that the binomial expansion of $\frac{2+kx}{(3-4x)^2}$, $|x| < \frac{3}{4}$, is $\frac{2}{9} + \frac{7x}{27} + Ax^2 + \ldots$

b find the value of the constant k **(2 marks)**

c find the value of the constant A. **(2 marks)**

61 **a** Show that $\sum_{r=1}^{12}(2 + 4r + 3^r) = 797\,496$. **(4 marks)**

b A sequence $u_1, u_2, u_3, \ldots$, is defined by $u_{n+1} = -\frac{1}{u_1}$, $u_1 = \frac{3}{4}$

Find the exact value of $\sum_{r=1}^{200} u_r$. **(3 marks)**

62 **a** "If p and q are irrational numbers, then pq is also an irrational number."
Disprove this statement using a counter example. **(2 marks)**

b Prove that $\sqrt{2}$ is an irrational number. **(6 marks)**

63 The diagram shows a sketch of the curve with equation $y = \mathrm{f}(x)$, $x \in \mathbb{R}$.

The curve passes through the point (0, 4) and has a turning point at $P(3, -5)$.

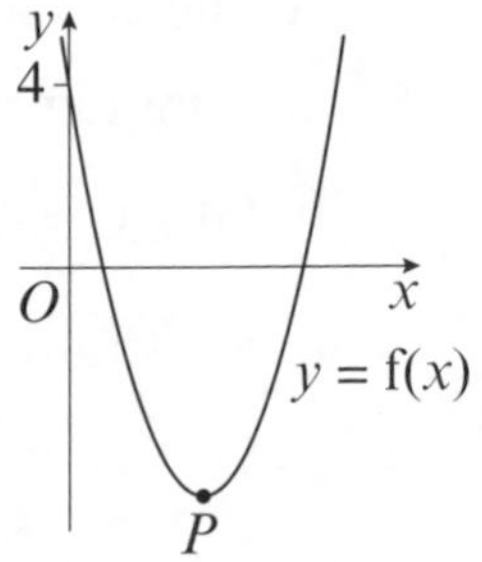

a Write down the coordinates of the point to which P is transformed on the curve with equation:

i $2\mathrm{f}\left(\frac{x}{2}\right)$ **ii** $-\mathrm{f}(-x)$ **(4 marks)**

b Sketch the curve with equation $y = \mathrm{f}(|x|)$.
On your sketch show the coordinates of all turning points and the coordinates of the point at which the curve cuts the y-axis. **(3 marks)**

The curve with equation $y = \mathrm{f}(x)$ is a translation of the curve with equation $y = x^2$.

c Find $\mathrm{f}(x)$. **(2 marks)**

d Explain why the function f does not have an inverse. **(1 mark)**

64 The first term of a geometric series is 30 and the common ratio is $\frac{5}{8}$

a Find, to one decimal place, the value of S_{15}. **(2 marks)**

The sum to infinity of the series is S_∞, and the sum to N terms of the series is S_N.

b Find the smallest value of N, for which $S_\infty - S_N < 0.5$ **(6 marks)**

65 In triangle PQR, $\overrightarrow{PQ} = -3\mathbf{i} + 6\mathbf{j} + \mathbf{k}$ and $\overrightarrow{PR} = 11\mathbf{i} + 7\mathbf{j} - 2\mathbf{k}$.

a Find the area of triangle PQR. **(7 marks)**

The point T is such that $\overrightarrow{PT} = -2\overrightarrow{PQ}$ and the point S is such that $\overrightarrow{PS} = -2\overrightarrow{PR}$.

b Find the area of triangle PST. **(2 marks)**

66 $f(x) = \frac{2x-7}{x-3} + \frac{1}{(x-3)(x-2)}, x > 2$

a Express f(x) as a single fraction in its simplest form. **(5 marks)**

b Hence show that $f(x) = 2 - \frac{1}{x-2}, x > 2$. **(2 marks)**

The curve $y = \frac{1}{x}, x > 0$, is mapped onto the curve $y = f(x)$, using three successive transformations, T_1, T_2 and T_3.

c Describe fully T_1, T_2 and T_3. **(4 marks)**

67 The graph shows part of the curve C with parametric equations

$$x = 2\cos 2\theta, y = \tfrac{1}{2}\sin\theta, 0 \leqslant \theta \leqslant \frac{\pi}{2}$$

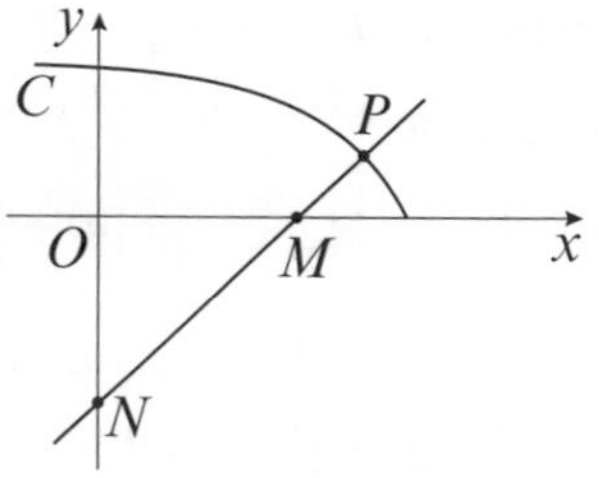

a Find $\frac{dy}{dx}$ giving your answer in terms of θ. **(4 marks)**

P is the point on the curve where $\theta = \frac{\pi}{6}$

b Find an equation of the normal to C at P. **(4 marks)**

The normal to C at P intersects the axes at the points M and N.

c Find the exact area of triangle OMN. **(2 marks)**

68 A geometric series has first term 10 and common ratio $\frac{3}{5}$
Calculate:

a the 20th term of the series, to 3 significant figures **(2 marks)**

b the sum to infinity of the series. **(2 marks)**

Given that the sum to k terms of the series is greater than 24.99,

c show that $k > \frac{\log 0.0004}{\log 0.6}$ **(4 marks)**

d find the smallest possible value of k. **(1 mark)**

69 The function f is defined by f: $x \mapsto \frac{2(x-1)}{x^2-2x-8} - \frac{1}{x-4}, x > 4$

a Show that $f(x) = \frac{1}{x+2}, x > 4$. **(4 marks)**

b Find the range of f(x). **(2 marks)**

c Find $f^{-1}(x)$. State the domain of this inverse function. **(3 marks)**

The function g is defined by g: $x \mapsto 2x^2 + 1, x \in \mathbb{R}$

d Solve $fg(x) = \frac{1}{43}$ **(3 marks)**

70 $f(x) = \frac{5}{3+4x} - \frac{3}{2-5x}, |x| < \frac{2}{5}$

a Show that the first three terms in the series expansion of f(x) can be written as

$\frac{1}{6} - \frac{215x}{36} - \frac{1385x^2}{216}$ **(7 marks)**

b Find the exact value of f(0.01). Round your answer to 7 decimal places. **(2 marks)**

c Find the percentage error made in using the series expansion in part **a** to estimate the value of f(0.01). Give your answer to 2 significant figures. **(3 marks)**

71 **a** Express $\frac{3}{2}\cos\theta + \frac{5}{2}\sin\theta$ in the form $R\cos(\theta - \alpha)$, where $R > 0$ and $0 < \alpha < \frac{\pi}{2}$
Give the value of α to two decimal places. **(3 marks)**

b Hence find the maximum value of $\frac{16}{5} + \left(\frac{3}{2}\cos\theta + \frac{5}{2}\sin\theta\right)^2$. **(2 marks)**

c Solve, for $-\pi < \theta < \frac{\pi}{2}$, the equation $\frac{3}{2}\cos 2\theta + \frac{5}{2}\sin 2\theta = 2$, giving your answers to two decimal places. **(5 marks)**

72 A curve C is defined by the parametric equations $x = e^{2t}$, $y = 6e^t - 2$, $t \in \mathbb{R}$.

a The straight line $y = x + 3$ passes through the points A and B on curve C.
Find the coordinates of A and B. **(6 marks)**

b Another straight line, l, passes through the points P and Q on curve C where $t = \ln 2$ and $t = \ln 3$ respectively. Find an equation for line l in the form $ax + by + c = 0$. **(6 marks)**

73 A company made a profit of £60 000 in 2018 (year 1). Future year-by-year profits are modelled by a geometric sequence with common ratio r, where $r > 1$.

The model predicts that the profits in 2019 (year 2) will be £60 000r.

a Write down an expression for the predicted profit in year n. **(1 mark)**

Given that the model predicts that the profit will exceed £240 000 in year n,

b show that $n > \frac{\log 4}{\log r} + 1$. **(3 marks)**

Using the model with $r = 1.08$,

c find the year in which the profit made will first exceed £240 000 **(2 marks)**

d find the total of the profits that will be made by the company over the 10 years from 2018 to 2027 inclusive, giving your answer to the nearest £10 000. **(3 marks)**

74 The curve C has parametric equations

$x = 6\cos t, y = 2\sin 2t, 0 \leqslant t \leqslant 2\pi$

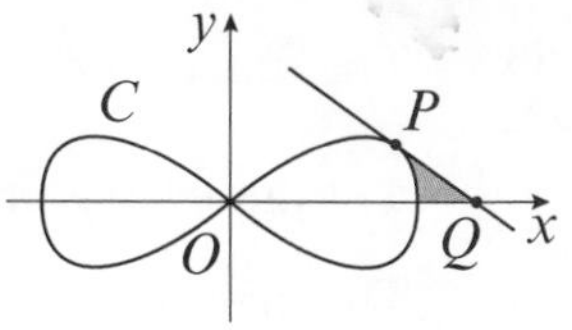

a Find the gradient of the curve at the point P at which $t = \frac{\pi}{6}$ **(3 marks)**

b Find the equation of the tangent to the curve at the point P. **(3 marks)**

c Find the exact area of the shaded region bounded by the tangent PQ, the curve and the x-axis. **(6 marks)**

75 **a** Express $\frac{5x^2 - 4x}{5x^2 + 6x - 8} - \frac{10}{x^2 - x - 6}$ as a single fraction in its simplest form. **(7 marks)**

b Hence write $\frac{5x^2 - 4x}{5x^2 + 6x - 8} - \frac{10}{x^2 - x - 6}$ in the form $A + \frac{B}{x - 3}$, where A and B are constants to be found. **(2 marks)**

$f(x) = \frac{5x^2 - 4x}{5x^2 + 6x - 8} - \frac{10}{x^2 - x - 6}, x \neq 3$

c Use your answer to part **b** to prove that $f(x)$ is an increasing function for all $x > 3$. **(3 marks)**

76 The second and fourth terms of a geometric series are 270 and 120 respectively.

For this series, find:

a the sum to infinity **(6 marks)**

b the smallest value of n for which the sum of the first n terms of the series exceeds 1200. **(4 marks)**

77 The diagram shows part of the curve with the equation $y = f(x)$, where $f(x) = (x^2 - 4x)e^{-x}$.

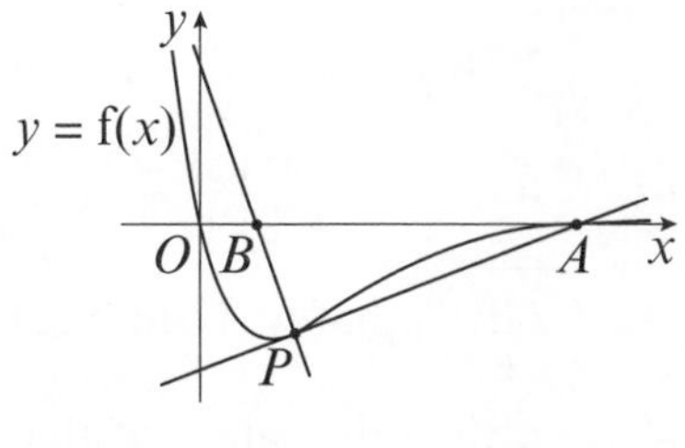

The point P has coordinates $\left(1, -\frac{3}{e}\right)$.

The tangent to the curve at P intersects the x-axis at the point A.

a Find the equation of the tangent. **(4 marks)**

The normal to the curve at P intersects the x-axis at the point B.

b Show that the area of the triangle ABP is $\frac{9(e^2 + 1)}{2e^3}$ **(7 marks)**

78 $\frac{3x^2 - x + 2}{(x + 1)(x - 2)} \equiv A + \frac{B}{x + 1} + \frac{C}{x - 2}$

a Find the values of the constants A, B and C. **(4 marks)**

b Hence, or otherwise, expand $\frac{3x^2 - x + 2}{(x + 1)(x - 2)}$ in ascending powers of x, up to and including the term in x^2. Give each coefficient as a simplified fraction. **(7 marks)**

c State the set of values for which the expansion in part **b** is valid. **(1 mark)**

79 The function f is defined by $f(x) = \dfrac{2 - 3x}{x - 4}$, $x \in \mathbb{R}$, $x \neq 4$.

a Find $f^{-1}(x)$, and state the domain of this inverse function. **(4 marks)**

The diagram shows a sketch of the function g(*x*).
The function g has domain $-2 \leqslant x \leqslant 9$, and is linear from $(-2, -10)$ to $(2, 0)$ and from $(2, 0)$ to $(9, 5)$.

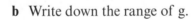

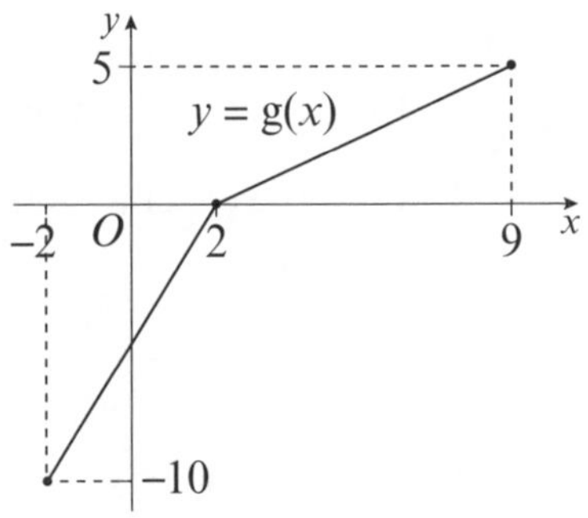

b Write down the range of g. **(1 mark)**

c Find gg(2). **(2 marks)**

d Find fg(9). **(2 marks)**

e On separate diagrams, sketch the graphs with equations:

i $y = |g(x)|$ **ii** $y = g^{-1}(x)$ **(4 marks)**

Show on each sketch the coordinates of each point at which the graph meets or cuts the axes.

f State the domain of the inverse function g^{-1}. **(1 mark)**

80 The first three terms of a geometric sequence are $6k - 5$, $4k - 5$ and $5 - k$, where k is a constant.

Given that $k < 1$,

a show that $k = \frac{10}{11}$ **(6 marks)**

For this value of k,

b i evaluate the fourth term of the sequence, giving your answer as an exact fraction

ii evaluate the sum of the first ten terms of the sequence. **(6 marks)**

81 $f(x) = \dfrac{36x^2 + 15x - 14}{(3x - 2)^2(2 - x)}$, $|x| < \frac{2}{3}$

Given that f(*x*) can be expressed in the form $\dfrac{A}{3x - 2} + \dfrac{B}{(3x - 2)^2} + \dfrac{C}{2 - x}$,

a find the values of the constants A, B and C. **(4 marks)**

b Hence, or otherwise, find the series expansion of f(*x*) in ascending powers of x, up to and including the term in x^2. Simplify each term. **(7 marks)**

c Find the percentage error made in using the series expansion in part **b** to estimate the value of f(0.1). Give your answer to 2 significant figures. **(4 marks)**

82 The functions f and g are defined by $f(x) = 3x + \ln 3,\ x \in \mathbb{R}$ and $g(x) = e^x,\ x \in \mathbb{R}$.

a Prove that the composite function gf is $gf(x) = 3e^{3x},\ x \in \mathbb{R}$. **(4 marks)**

b Sketch the graph of $y = gf(x)$, stating the coordinates of the point where the curve crosses the y-axis. **(2 marks)**

c Write down the range of gf. **(1 mark)**

d Find the value of x for which $\frac{d}{dx}(gf(x)) = 4$, giving your answer to 3 significant figures. **(4 marks)**

83 **a** Express $12.5\cos x + 6.5\sin x$ in the form $R\cos(x - \alpha)$, where $R > 0$ and $0 < \alpha < \frac{\pi}{2}$
Give the value of α to 1 decimal place. **(4 marks)**

b **i** Find the maximum value of $12.5\cos x + 6.5\sin x$.

ii Find the value of x, for $0 < x < \pi$, at which the maximum occurs. **(3 marks)**

The height above ground of a particular car on a Ferris wheel can be modelled by the function

$$H = 16 - 12.5\cos(1.05t) - 6.5\sin(1.05t)$$

where H is the height of the car above ground in metres, and t is time in minutes after the ride begins. All angles are measured in radians. Give your answers to 1 decimal place where necessary.

c State the maximum height of the wheel and the time at which this maximum occurs. **(3 marks)**

d Calculate the height of the car at 4 minutes. **(2 marks)**

e Calculate the times the car reaches a height of 15 metres during the first 6 minutes. **(4 marks)**

f Find the time it takes for the Ferris wheel to complete one rotation. **(2 marks)**

84 The diagram shows a cuboid whose vertices are O, A, B, C, D, E, F and G.

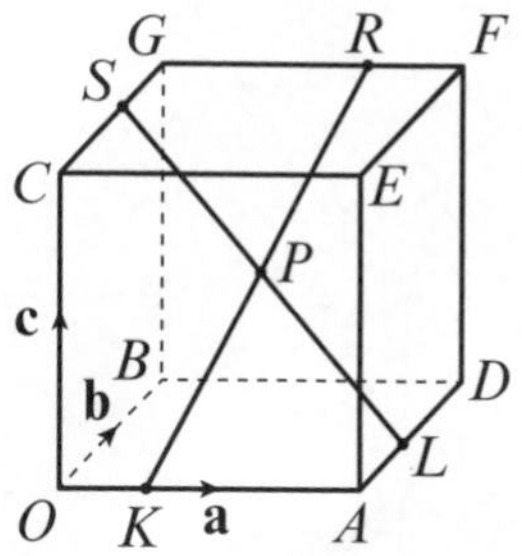

Vectors **a**, **b** and **c** are equal to $\overrightarrow{OA}$, $\overrightarrow{OB}$ and $\overrightarrow{OC}$ respectively.

The points K, L, R and S lie on OA, AD, FG and GC such that $OK : KA = AL : LD = FR : RG = GS : SC = 1 : 2$.

Prove that the lines KR and LS bisect each other at P. **(10 marks)**

85 The function f is defined by $f(x) = e^{-x} + 5, x \in \mathbb{R}$.

a State the range of $f(x)$. **(2 marks)**

b Find $f^{-1}(x)$. State the domain of this inverse function. **(4 marks)**

c Sketch the graphs of $y = f(x)$ and $y = f^{-1}(x)$ on the set of same axes, stating the coordinates of the points where the graphs cross the axes. **(4 marks)**

d Show that the x-coordinate of the point of intersection of $y = f(x)$ and $y = f^{-1}(x)$ is the solution to the equation $e^x(x - 5) = 1$. **(4 marks)**

86 The position of a carriage on a rollercoaster at time t seconds is modelled using the parametric equations

$$x = 40\sqrt{t},\ y = 80t - 20t^2,\ 0 \leqslant t \leqslant T$$

where x represents the distance travelled horizontally in metres and y represents the height above the ground in metres.

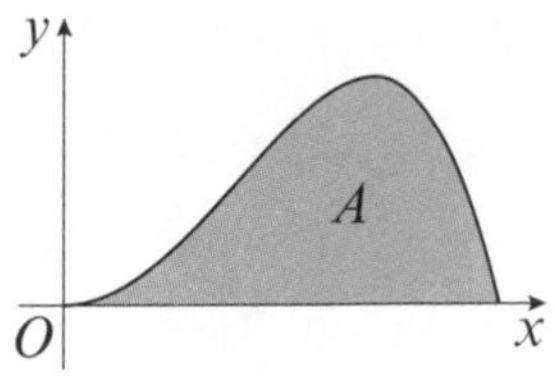

Given that the rollercoaster starts and finishes at ground level,

a find the value of T **(2 marks)**

b find the maximum height of the rollercoaster and the time at which the carriage reaches this height. **(3 marks)**

c **i** Find the angle of descent at the point where the rollercoaster reaches the ground at the end of its path.

ii Hence comment on the validity of the model. **(4 marks)**

d Find the total area bounded by the path of the rollercoaster and the ground, labelled A on the diagram. **(3 marks)**

Answers

CHAPTER 1

1.1 Proof by contradiction

1 **a** There are a finite number of prime numbers.
b There exists an n such that n^2 is even but n is odd.
c There exist p and q such that pq is odd and p and q are both even.

2 Assume that there is a greatest even number, n. Then $n + 2 > n$ and is also even. This contradicts the assumption, so there is no greatest even number.

3 Assume that $a^2 - 4b - 7 = 0$, where a and b are integers. So $a^2 = 4b + 7$. Since $4b + 7$ is odd, a^2 is odd and so a is odd and can be written as $2n + 1$ where n is an integer.
Then $a^2 = (2n + 1)^2 = 4b + 7 \Rightarrow 4n^2 + 4n + 1 = 4b + 7$
Rearranging, $4n^2 + 4n - 4b = 6 \Rightarrow 4(n^2 + n - b) = 6$
So $n^2 + n - b = \frac{3}{2}$, which is not an integer, but as n and b are integers, $n^2 + n - b$ must also be an integer. This contradiction implies that $a^2 - 4b - 7$ cannot be equal to 0.

4 Assume that there is a smallest positive rational number, n. Then $n > 0$ and $n = \frac{a}{b}$ where a and b are integers and $b \neq 0$. Then $\frac{n}{2} = \frac{a}{2b}$, and since b is an integer, $2b$ is also an integer. This means that $\frac{n}{2}$ is rational and as $\frac{n}{2} < n$ this is a contradiction, which implies there is no smallest positive rational number.

5 Assume that n is even. Then $n = 2p$ where p is an integer. $n^3 = (2p)^3 = 8p^3$ which is even. Thus if n^3 is odd, then n must also be odd.

6 Assume that there exist non-zero integers x and y such that $x^2 - y^2 = 1$. Then $(x + y)(x - y) = 1$. The only factor of 1 is 1. There are 2 possibilities using $1 \times 1 = 1$ and $-1 \times -1 = 1$:
$x + y = 1$ and $x - y = 1$ (1)
$x + y = -1$ and $x - y = -1$ (2)
(1) gives $x = 1$ and $y = 0$ and (2) gives $x = -1$ and $y = 0$.
$y = 0$ is a solution in both cases, so there are no non-zero integer solutions to the equation $x^2 - y^2 = 1$.

7 Assume that $\sqrt{5}$ is rational. Then $\sqrt{5} = \frac{a}{b}$, where a and b are integers, $b \neq 0$ and the highest common factor of a and b is 1. Then $a = \sqrt{5}b \Rightarrow a^2 = 5b^2$.
So a^2 is divisible by 5 and it must contain a (repeated) factor of 5, and so a is divisible by 5. So $a = 5p$, where p is an integer.
$\Rightarrow (5p)^2 = 5b^2 \Rightarrow b^2 = 5p^2$. So b^2 is divisible by 5 and so b is divisible by 5. As a and b are both divisible by 5, then the highest common factor of a and b is not 1. This contradiction implies that $\sqrt{5}$ is irrational.

8 Assume that p is rational, q is irrational, and that $p - q$ is rational. Then there exist integers a, b, c and d such that
$p = \frac{a}{b}$ and $p - q = \frac{c}{d}$, $b, d \neq 0$.
So $\frac{a}{b} - q = \frac{c}{d} \Rightarrow q = \frac{a}{b} - \frac{c}{d} = \frac{ad - bc}{bd}$
But $ad - bc$ is an integer as a, b, c and d are all integers and $bd \neq 0$, which means that q is rational. This is a contradiction. So the difference between any rational number and any irrational number is irrational.

1.2 Algebraic fractions

1 **a** $\frac{1}{x+3}$ **b** $\frac{x-1}{3(x+1)}$ **c** $\frac{y(x+5)}{x}$

2 **a** $\frac{x-1}{x^2}$ **b** $\frac{2(3x+4)}{x-2}$ **c** $\frac{2(2x-y)}{y}$

3 **a** $\frac{7x+1}{(x+3)(x-1)}$ **b** $\frac{11x-9}{3(x-3)(x+1)}$
c $\frac{x(25-x)}{(x+5)(x-5)}$ **d** $\frac{2+9x-3x^2}{(2x-3)(x+2)}$

4 **a** $\frac{11x+9}{(2x+3)(2x-3)}$ **b** $\frac{3x}{(x+4)(x-3)(x-2)}$
c $\frac{4x-8}{(2x+1)^2(2x-1)}$ **d** $\frac{7-4x}{(x+2)(x+1)(x-3)}$

5 $\frac{(x+2)(y+3)}{(x-2)(y-3)}$

6 $\frac{x^2(x-5)(x-6)}{2(x^2-6)(x-8)}$

7 $\frac{x(17x-2)}{(5x+1)(5x-1)}$

8 $\frac{13-2x}{(2x+1)(x-3)}$

9 **a** $f(x) = \frac{x(x+3)(x-5) + 5(x-5) + 40}{(x+3)(x-5)}$
$= \frac{x^3 - 2x^2 - 10x + 15}{(x+3)(x-5)}$
b Using the factor theorem, $(x + 3)$ is a factor of
$x^3 - 2x^2 - 10x + 15 = (x + 3)(x^2 - 5x + 5)$
So $f(x) = \frac{x^2 - 5x + 5}{x - 5}$

1.3 Partial fractions

1 **a** $\frac{3}{x+1} + \frac{5}{x-2}$ **b** $\frac{4}{2x-1} - \frac{1}{x+3}$
c $\frac{2}{3x-1} - \frac{5}{2x+1}$

2 **a** $\frac{3}{x} + \frac{4}{x-5}$ **b** $\frac{5}{x-3} - \frac{2}{x+3}$ **c** $\frac{1}{2x+1} + \frac{4}{x-5}$

3 **a** $\frac{5}{x} + \frac{2}{x-2} - \frac{1}{x-5}$ **b** $\frac{2}{x-1} - \frac{1}{x+2} + \frac{3}{x+3}$
c $\frac{2}{x} - \frac{1}{x-3} + \frac{3}{2x-1}$

4 $A = 5, B = 3, C = -4$

5 $A = -\frac{4}{5}, B = \frac{12}{5}$

6 $\frac{13}{x+2} - \frac{21}{2x+3}$

7 $\frac{1}{2(3-y)} + \frac{1}{2(3+y)}$

8 $A = 2, B = -3, C = 1$

9 $A = 2, B = 3, C = -1$

1.4 Repeated factors

1 $A = 2, B = -1, C = 3$

2 $A = 3, B = -4, C = 2$

3 $A = 2, B = -3$

4 $A = 2, B = -1, C = -4$

5 $\frac{1}{x} - \frac{5}{x^2} + \frac{4}{2x-3}$

6 $\frac{4}{x} - \frac{3}{x-2} + \frac{5}{(x-2)^2}$

1.5 Algebraic division

1
$$\begin{array}{r} x - 2 \\ x-3\overline{)\,x^2 - 5x + 7} \\ \underline{x^2 - 3x} \\ -2x + 7 \\ \underline{-2x + 6} \\ 1 \end{array}$$

2 a 15 b $x - 6 + \frac{15}{x+1}$

3 $A = 1, B = -4, C = 12, D = -45$

4 $A = 1, B = 2, C = 8, D = 37$

5 $A = 6, B = -3, C = 1$

6 $A = 2, B = 2, C = 11, D = 32$

7 $A = 1, B = -5, C = 15$

8 $A = 2, B = -2, C = -3$

9 $A = 3, B = -5, C = 0, D = -2, E = 5$

Problem solving: Set A

B a $\frac{3x-2}{x-1}$ b $\frac{3x+1}{x}$

S $\frac{x-3}{x-1}$

G $\frac{2}{3}x - \frac{1}{9} - \frac{52}{27x+18}$

Problem solving: Set B

B $\frac{2}{3x-2} - \frac{1}{(3x-2)^2} + \frac{5}{1-x}$

S $x^2 - x - 6 = (x-3)(x+2)$. $A = 3, B = 5, C = -4$

G $\frac{1}{2(x+1)} - \frac{1}{2x-1} + \frac{3}{2(x-3)}$

CHAPTER 2

2.1 The modulus function

1 a 6 b 14 c 4

2 a 2 b 29 c 6

3 a

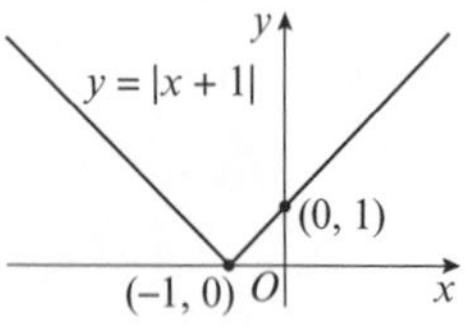

b

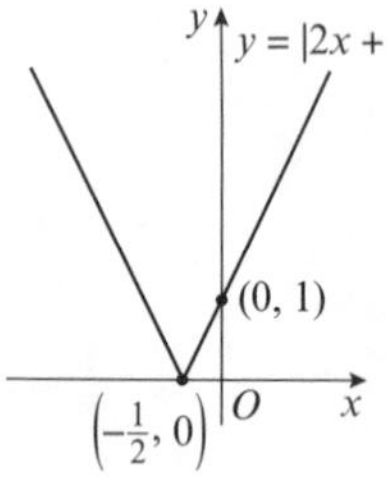

c

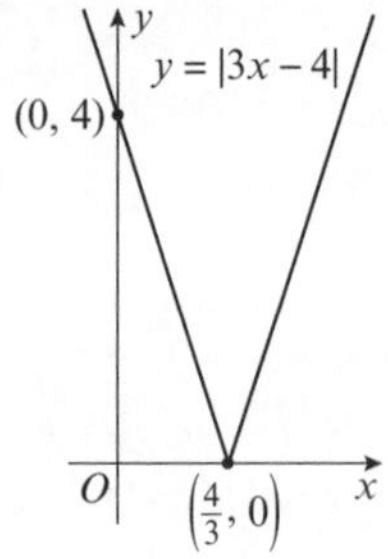

d

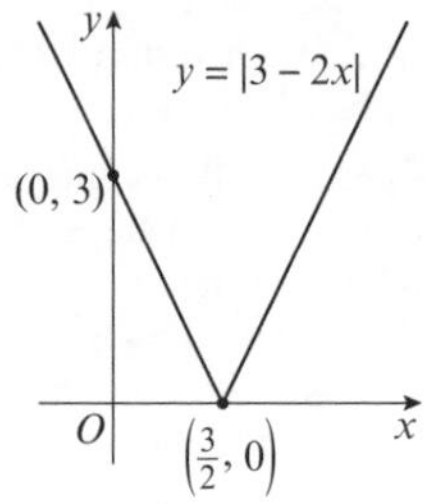

e

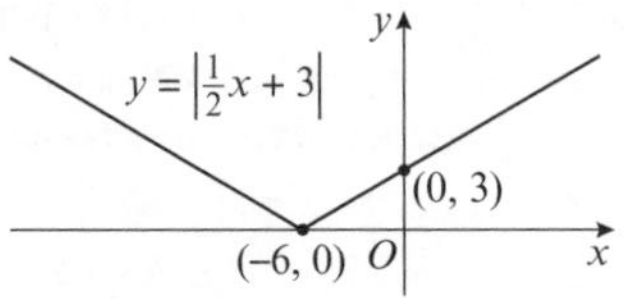

f

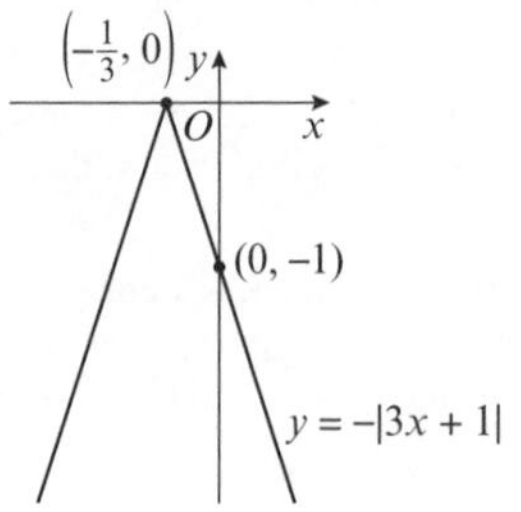

4 a i

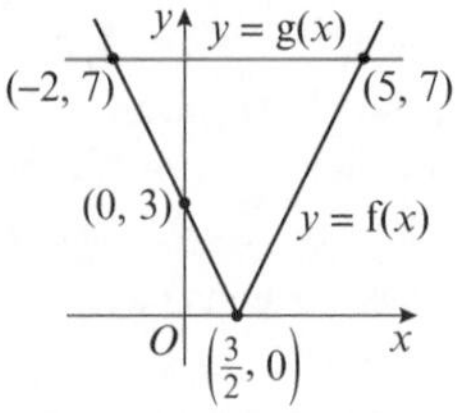

ii $x = -2, 5$

b i

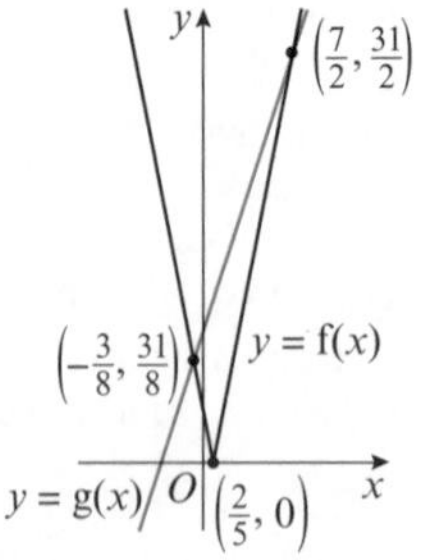

ii $x = -\frac{3}{8}, \frac{7}{2}$

c **i**

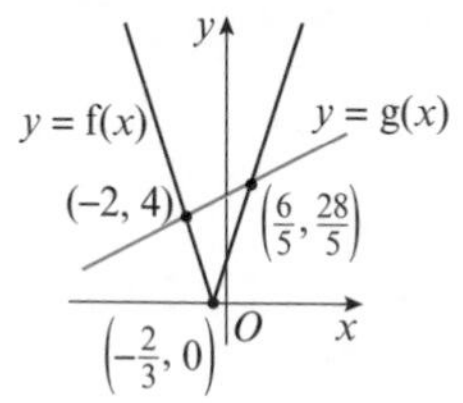

ii $x = -2, \frac{6}{5}$

5 $\left\{x : x < \frac{5}{6}\right\} \cup \left\{x : x > \frac{5}{2}\right\}$

6 **a**

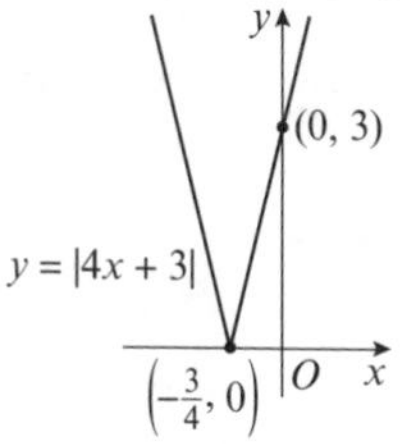

b $-\frac{5}{2} \leqslant x \leqslant 1$

7 **a**

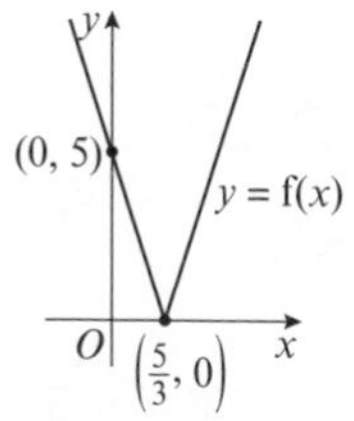

(0, 5) and $\left(\frac{5}{3}, 0\right)$

b $\frac{5}{4}$ and $\frac{5}{2}$

8 $x < 1$ or $x > \frac{11}{3}$

9 **a**

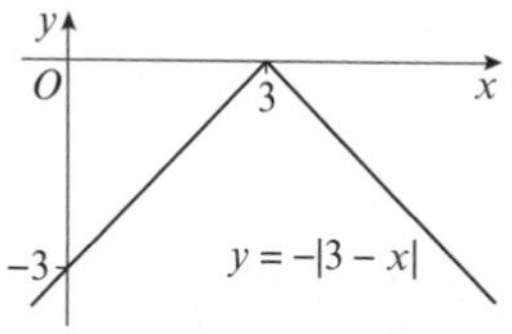

b 1 and 7

2.2 Functions and mappings

1 **a** many-to-one **b** one-to-one
c one-to-many **d** many-to-one

2 **a** $f : x \mapsto \sqrt{x+2}$, $x \in \mathbb{R}$, $x \geqslant -2$
b $f : x \mapsto \frac{1}{x+1}$, $x \in \mathbb{R}$, $x \neq -1$
c $f : x \mapsto \tan x$, $x \in \mathbb{R}$, $-90° < x < 90°$

3 **a** **i**

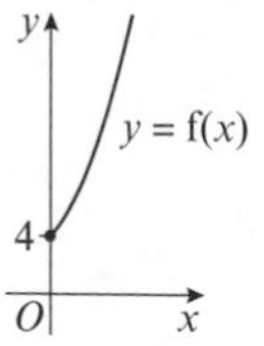

ii $f(x) \geqslant 4$ **iii** one-to-one

b **i**

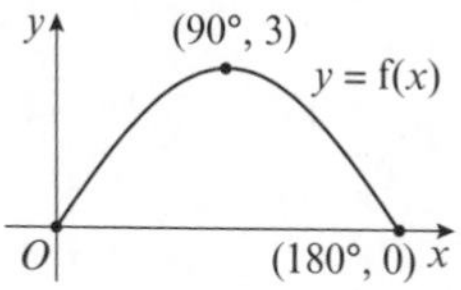

ii $0 \leqslant f(x) \leqslant 3$ **iii** many-to-one

c **i**

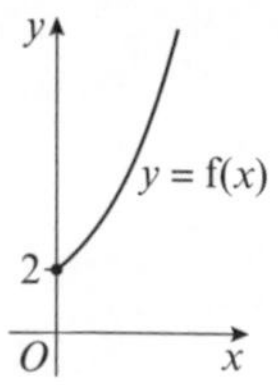

ii $f(x) \geqslant 2$ **iii** one-to-one

d **i**

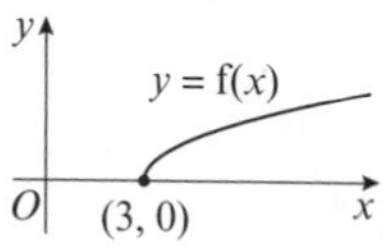

ii $f(x) \geqslant 0$ **iii** one-to-one

4 **a**

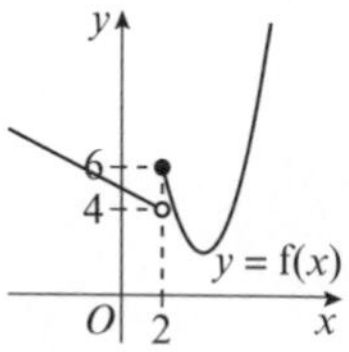

b f(x) is a one-to-one mapping for all $x \in \mathbb{R}$, so it is a function. f(2) = 6

c $f(x) \geqslant 2$ **d** $x = -12$ or $x = 7$

5 **a** $\frac{7}{4} \leqslant f(x) < 8$ **b** many-to-one

6 **a**

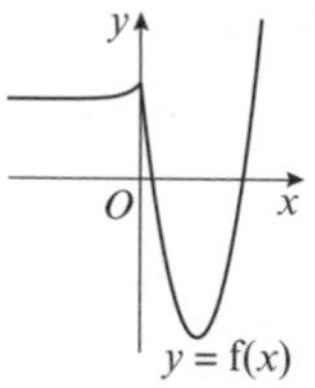

b $f(x) \geqslant -10$

7 $\frac{5}{2}$

8 **a**

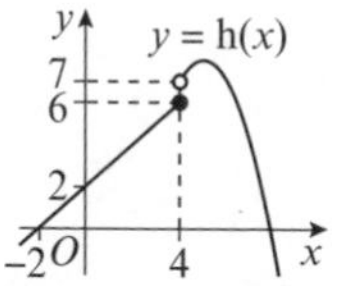

b 6 **c** $h(x) \leqslant 8$ **d** 3 and $5 + \sqrt{3}$

2.3 Composite functions

1 **a** 8 **b** 6 **c** −5
d 1 **e** 27

2 **a** $11 - 3x^2$ **b** $4 - \frac{1}{x^2}$ **c** $9x - 4$
d $\frac{1}{3x-1}$ **e** $11 - \frac{3}{x^2}$

3 **a** 17 **b** $x = \frac{7}{4}$

4 **a** $gf(x) = 2x$
b $fg(x) = x^2$. When $gf(x) = fg(x)$, $2x = x^2$, so $x = 0$ or $x = 2$
As $x = 0$ is not in the domain, $x = 2$.

5 **a** $f(x) \geqslant -4$ **b** $gf(x) = k + 8x - 4x^2$
c $\{k : k \in \mathbb{R}, k < 2\}$

6 **a** $f(x) \leqslant 8$ **b** −92

7 **a** $f(x) \geqslant 0$ **b** $2\left(\frac{1}{x-1}\right)^2$ **c** $x = \frac{2}{3}, \frac{4}{3}$

8 **a** 3^{x-2} **b** $3^x - 2$ **c** $\frac{\ln \frac{9}{4}}{\ln 3}$

2.4 Inverse functions

1 **a** **i** $f^{-1}(x) = \frac{x+5}{2}$

ii

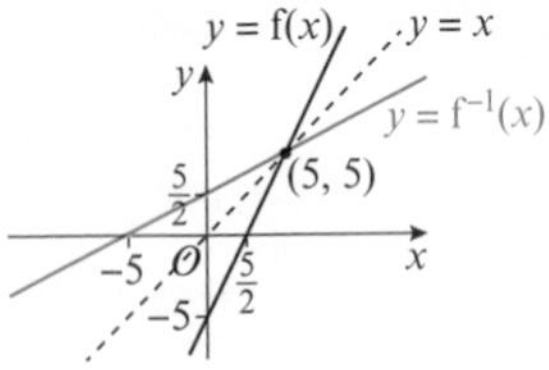

b **i** $f^{-1}(x) = 2x + 3$

ii

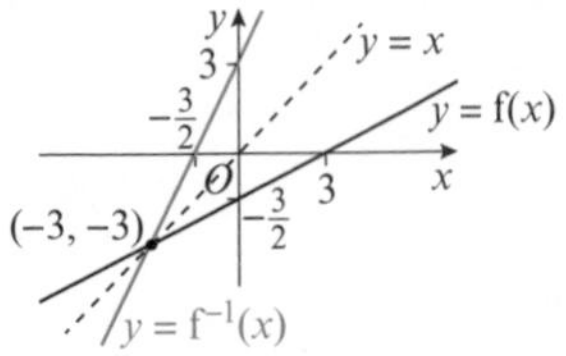

c **i** $f^{-1}(x) = \sqrt[3]{x+1}$

ii

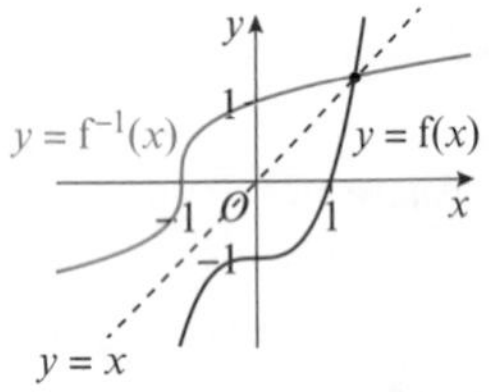

d **i** $f^{-1}(x) = \frac{1-x}{3}$

ii

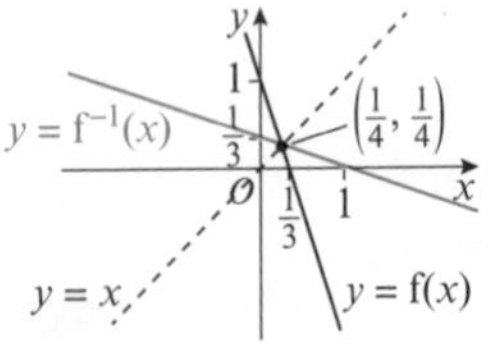

2 **a** **i** $g^{-1}(x) = \frac{x+3}{2}$

ii domain $x \in \mathbb{R}, x \geqslant -3$; range $g^{-1}(x) \geqslant 0$

iii

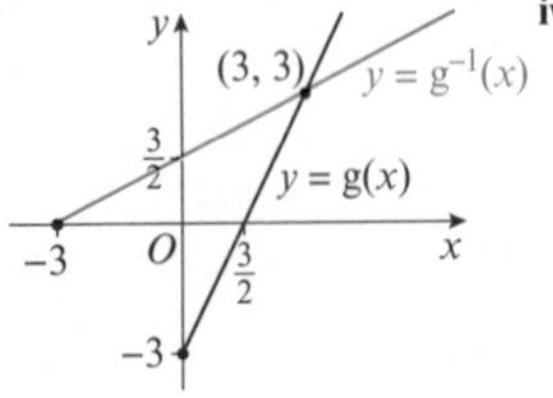

iv $x = 3$

b **i** $g^{-1}(x) = x^2 + 2$

ii domain $x \in \mathbb{R}, x > 0$; range $g^{-1}(x) > 2$

iii

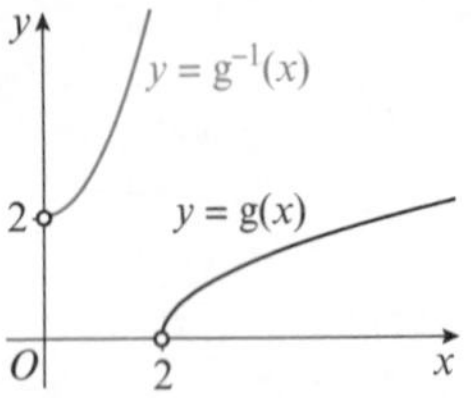

iv no solutions

c **i** $g^{-1}(x) = \frac{4+3x}{x}$

ii domain $x \in \mathbb{R}, x > 0$; range $g^{-1}(x) > 3$

iii

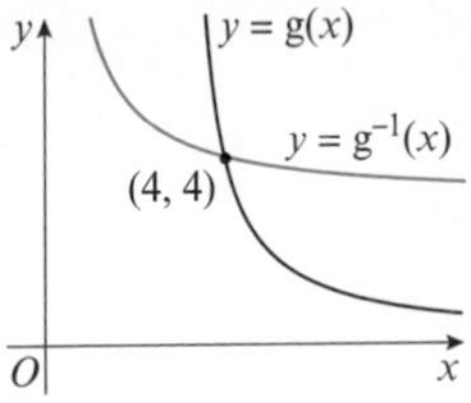

iv $x = 4$

d **i** $g^{-1}(x) = 1 + \sqrt{x+5}$

ii domain $x \in \mathbb{R}, x \geqslant -5$; range $g^{-1}(x) \geqslant 1$

iii

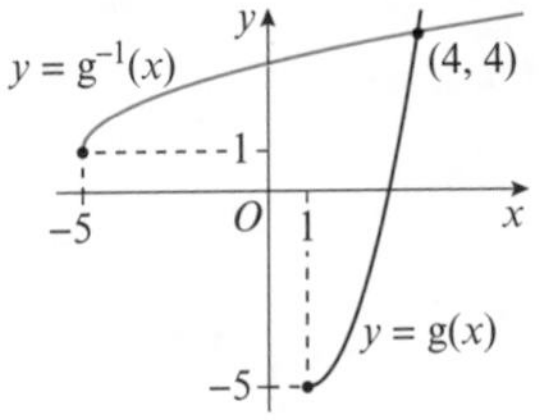

iv $x = 4$

3 **a** Let $f(x) = y = \frac{2}{x}$, then $xy = 2$ and $x = \frac{2}{y}$
so $f^{-1}(x) = \frac{2}{x} = f(x)$ and f is self-inverse.

b x

4 $g(x)$ is not one-to-one in the interval $0 \leqslant x \leqslant 6$

5 **a** $f\left(\frac{3x-5}{x-3}\right) = \frac{3\left(\frac{3x-5}{x-3}\right) - 5}{\left(\frac{3x-5}{x-3}\right) - 3} = \frac{3(3x-5) - 5(x-3)}{3x - 5 - 3(x-3)}$

$= \frac{9x - 15 - 5x + 15}{3x - 5 - 3x + 9} = \frac{4x}{4} = x$

b $f^{-1}(x) = \frac{3x-5}{x-3}, x \in \mathbb{R}, x \neq 3$

6 **a** $f^{-1}(x) = \frac{e^x + 1}{3}, x \in \mathbb{R}; f^{-1}(x) > \frac{1}{3}$

b

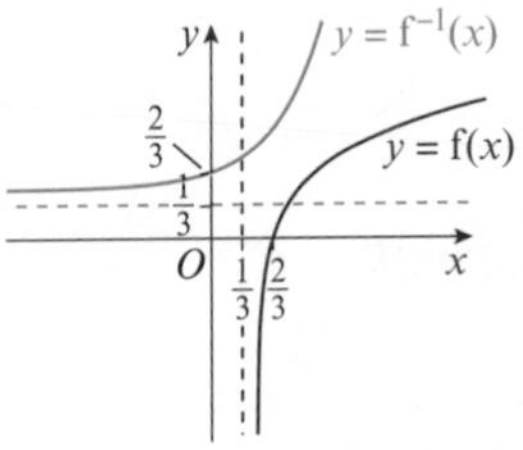

7 **a** $g^{-1}(x) = 3 + \sqrt{x+1}, x \in \mathbb{R}, x > -1; g^{-1}(x) > 3$

b $x = \frac{7 + \sqrt{17}}{2}$

8 **a** $f^{-1}(x) = \frac{3x+1}{x-2}, x \in \mathbb{R}, x > 2; f^{-1}(x) > 3$

b $x = \frac{17}{5}$

2.5 $y = |f(x)|$ and $y = f(|x|)$

1 **a**

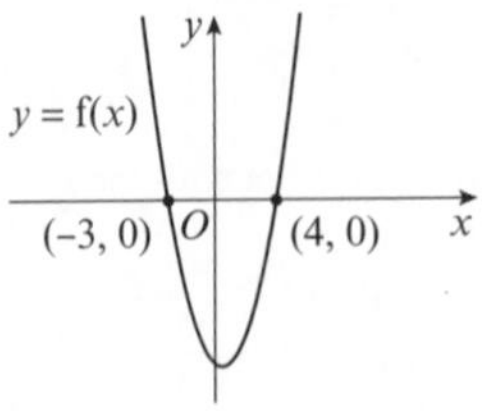

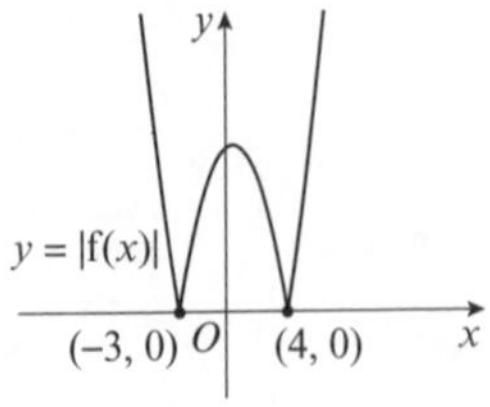

b

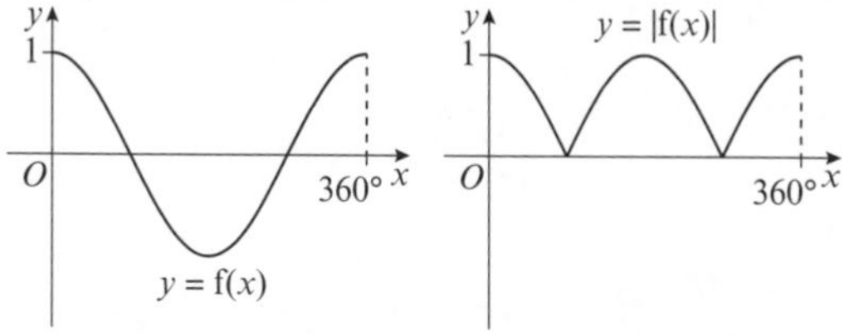

2 a

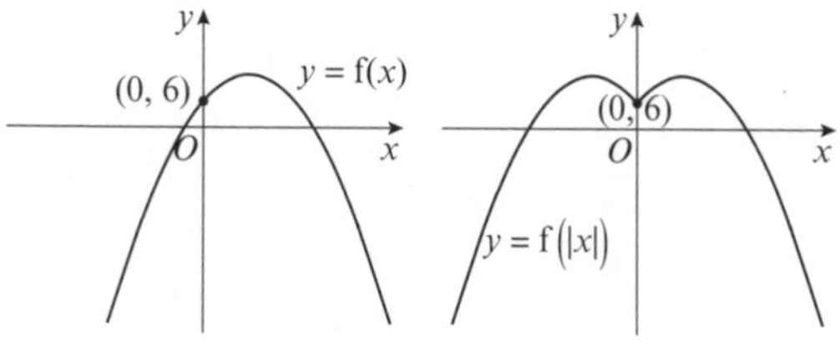

b

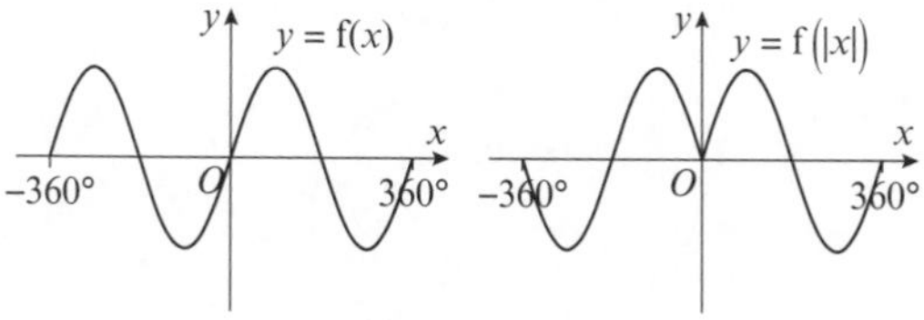

3 a

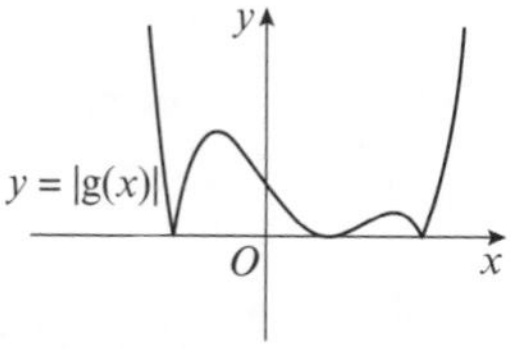

b

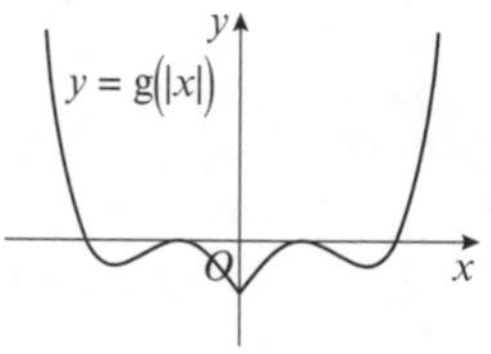

4 a (3, 5)

b

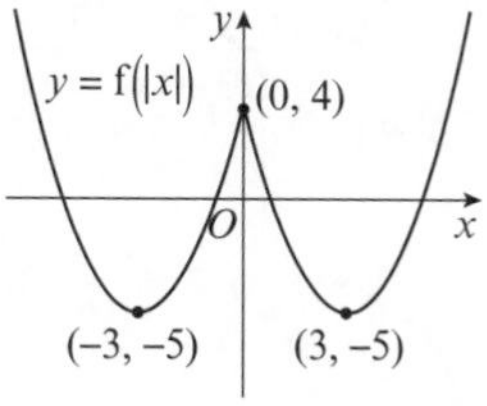

5 a

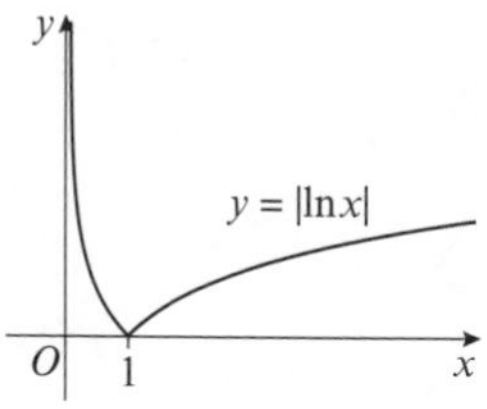

b

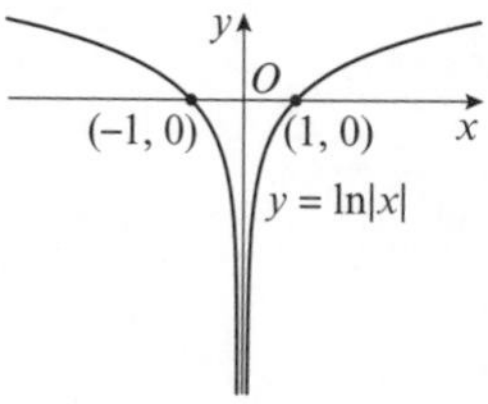

6 a

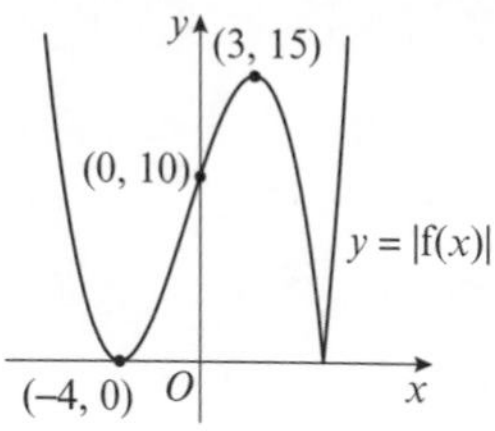

b

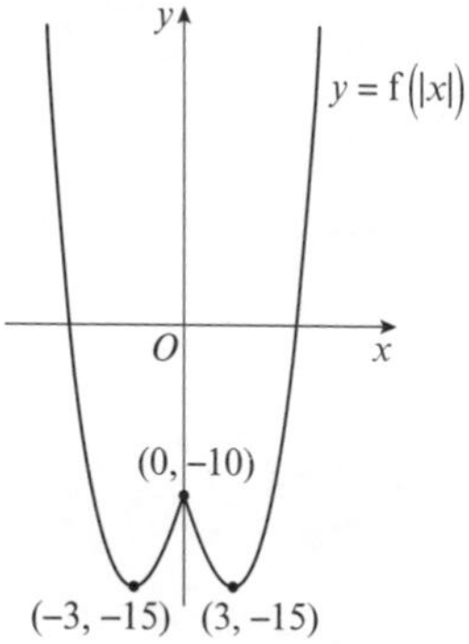

7 a

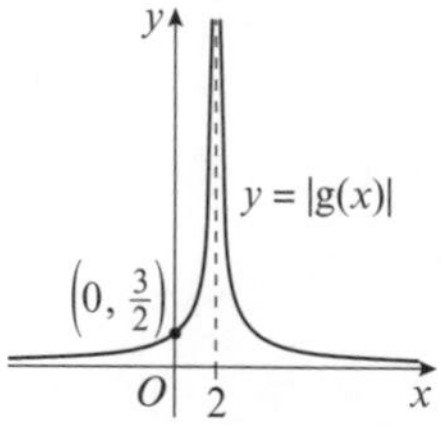

b $\frac{5}{4}$ and $\frac{11}{4}$

2.6 Combining transformations

1

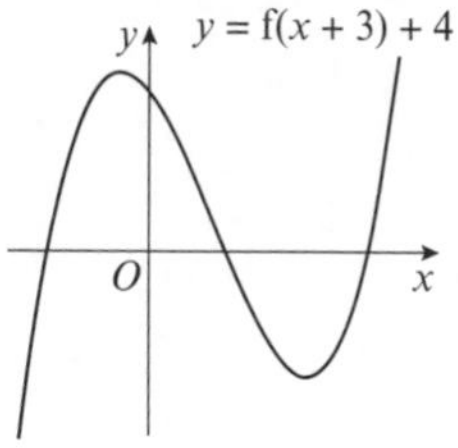

$A'(-1, 12)$, $B'(5, -12)$

2 a $A'(-1, -21)$, $B'(1, -6)$, $C'(3, 12)$

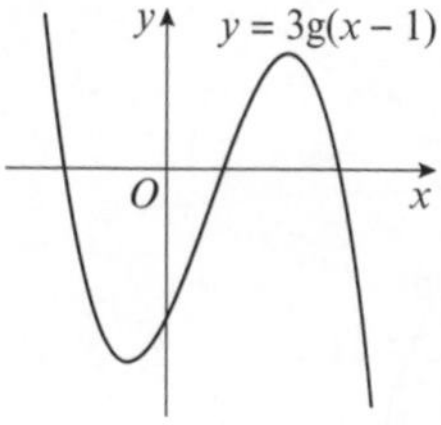

b $A'(-4, -9)$, $B'(0, -4)$, $C'(4, 2)$

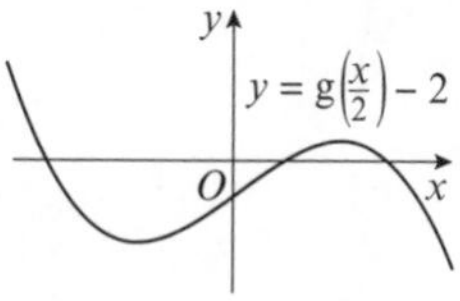

3 a

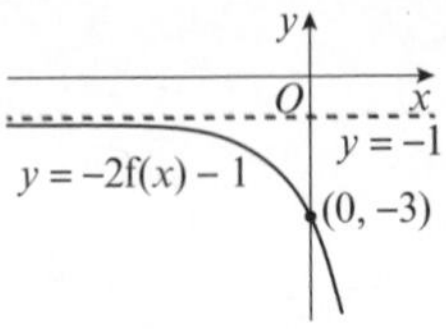

b

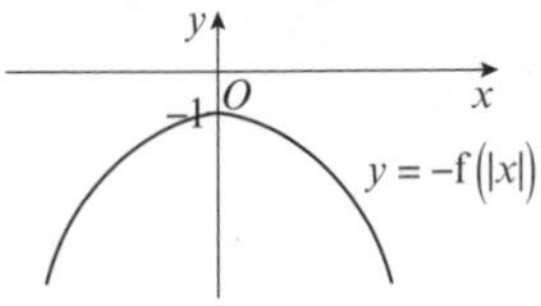

4 a

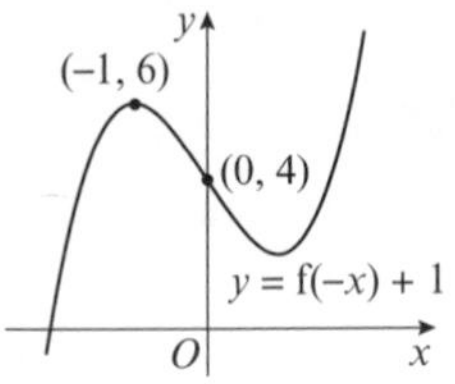

b

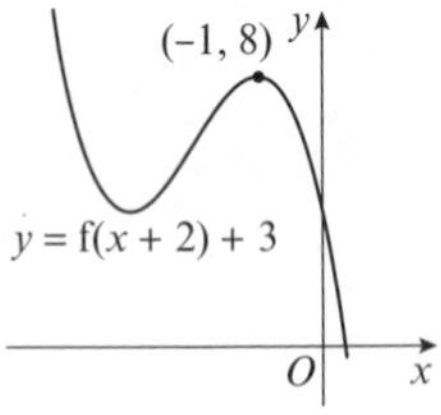

5 a

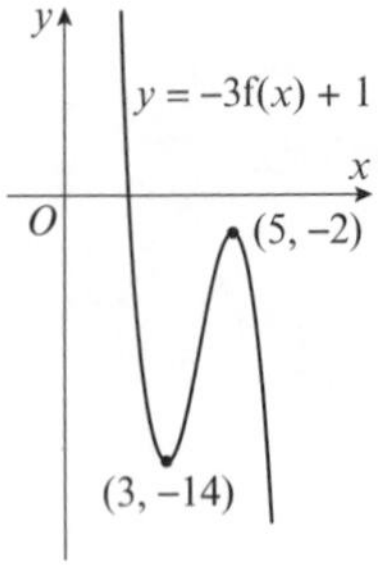

b

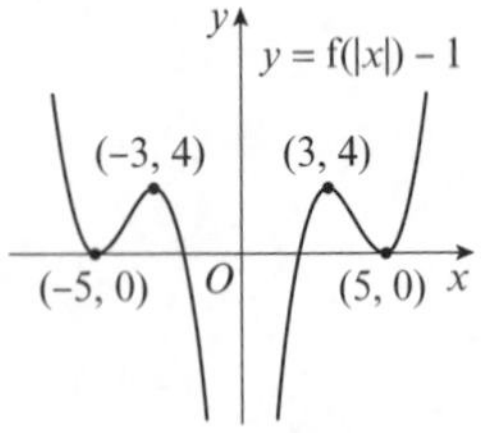

6 a

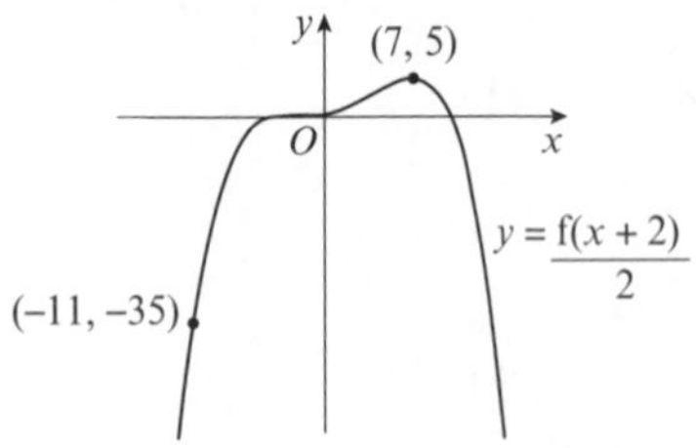

b

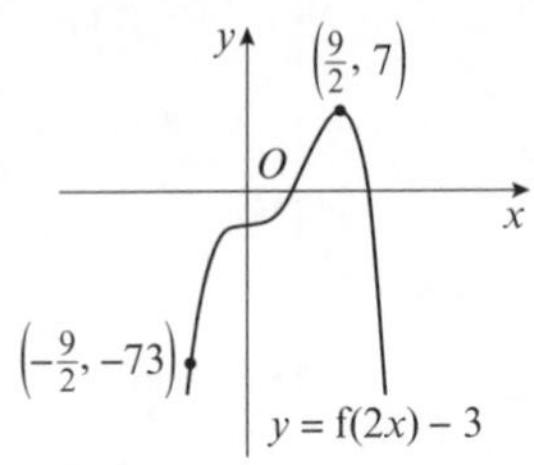

7 a

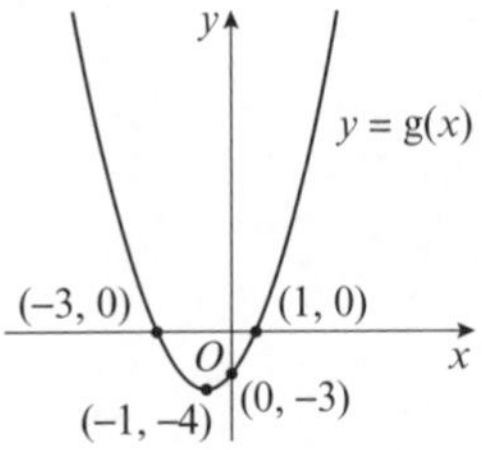

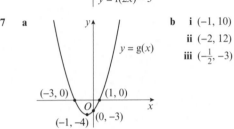

b i $(-1, 10)$

ii $(-2, 12)$

iii $(-\frac{1}{2}, -3)$

8 a

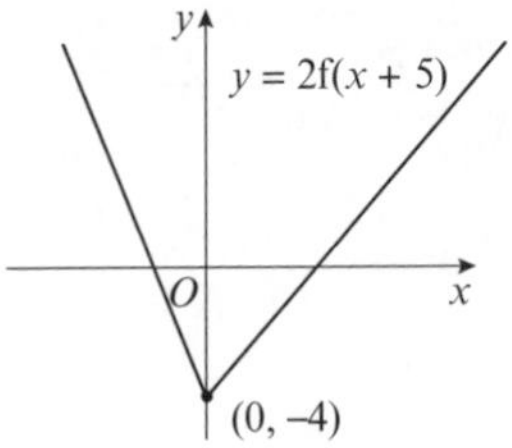

b

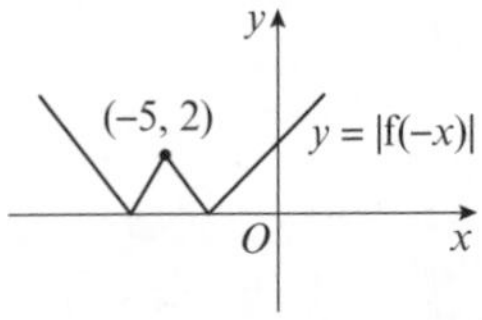

2.7 Solving modulus problems

1 a

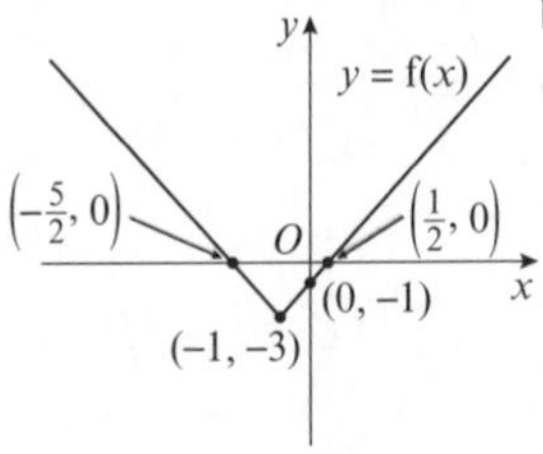

b $f(x) \geqslant -3$

c $x = -3$ or $x = 5$

2 a

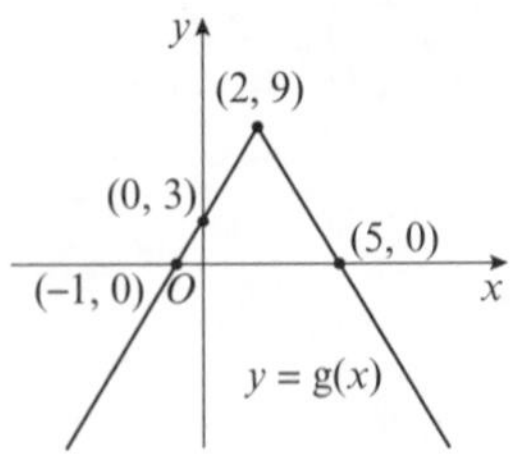

b $g(x) \leqslant 9$

c $g(x)$ is not a one-to-one function

d $\{x : x \leqslant 0\} \cup \{x : x \geqslant 4\}$

3 a i

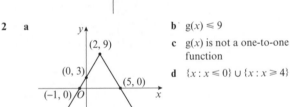

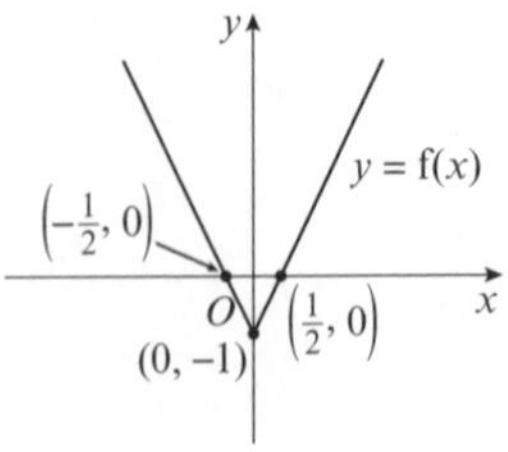

ii $f(x) \geqslant -1$

b **i**

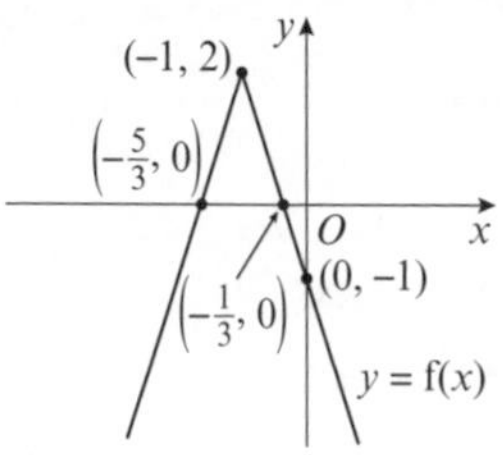

ii $f(x) \leqslant 2$

c **i**

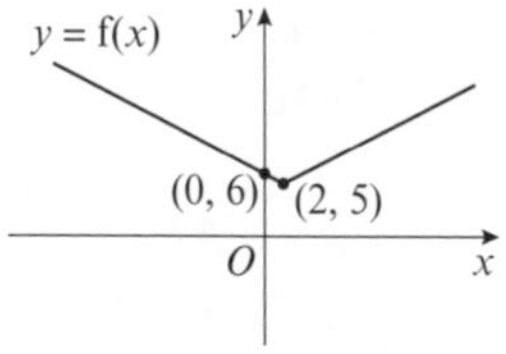

ii $f(x) \geqslant 5$

4 **a** $f(x) \geqslant 4$ **b** $x = 11$ **c** $4 < k \leqslant 10$

5 **a**

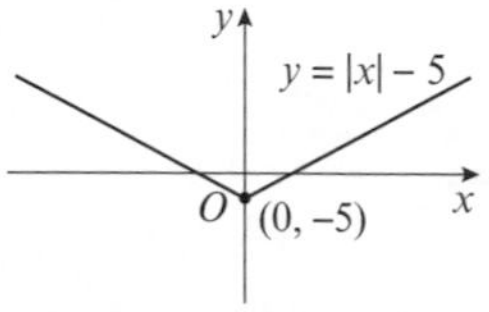

b For $x \geqslant 5$, $|x| - 5 = |x - 5|$. For $x < 5$, $|x| - 5 < |x - 5|$.
So $|x| - 5 \leqslant |x - 5|$ for all real values of x.

6 **a**

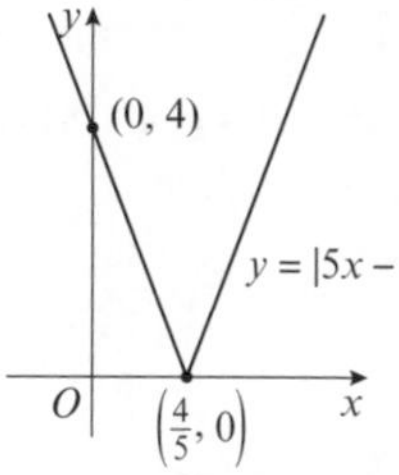

b $\left\{x : x < \frac{1}{3}\right\} \cup \{x : x > 1\}$

c $\left\{x : x < \frac{4}{5}\right\} \cup \left\{x : x > \frac{4}{5}\right\}$

7 **a** **i**

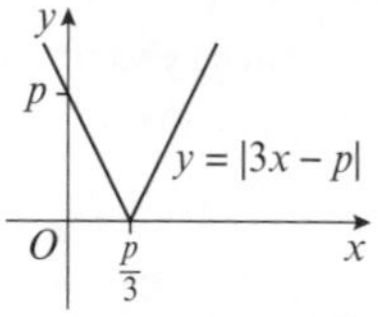

ii

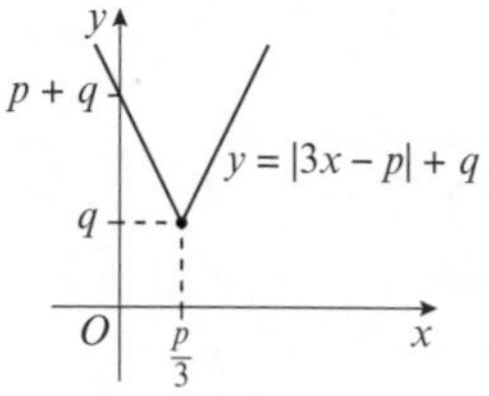

b $k = 2p$

Problem solving: Set A

B **a** $f^{-1}(x) = \sqrt[3]{\frac{3 - x}{2}}$

b $gf(x) = g(3 - 2x^3) = \frac{2}{3 - 2x^3} - 5 = \frac{2 - 5(3 - 2x^3)}{3 - 2x^3}$

$= \frac{2 - 15 + 10x^3}{3 - 2x^3} = \frac{10x^3 - 13}{3 - 2x^3}$

c $x = \sqrt[3]{\frac{4}{3}}$

S **a** $f^{-1}(x) = \frac{\ln(x - 2)}{2}$, $x \in \mathbb{R}$, $x \geqslant 2$

b $fg(x) = (x + 3)^2 + 2$, $fg(x) \geqslant 2$

c $x = -11$ or $x = 5$

G **a** $\frac{x - 5}{x^2 + 2x - 3} - \frac{2}{x + 3} + 2 = \frac{x - 5}{(x + 3)(x - 1)} - \frac{2}{x + 3} + 2$

$= \frac{x - 5 - 2(x - 1) + 2(x + 3)(x - 1)}{(x + 3)(x - 1)}$

$= \frac{x - 5 - 2x - 2 + 2x^2 + 4x - 6}{(x + 3)(x - 1)}$

$= \frac{2x^2 + 3x - 9}{(x + 3)(x - 1)} = \frac{(x + 3)(2x - 3)}{(x + 3)(x - 1)} = \frac{2x - 3}{x - 1}, x > 1$

b $f(x) < 2$

c $f^{-1}(x) = \frac{x - 3}{x - 2}, x < 2$ **d** $x = \pm\frac{5\sqrt{6}}{9}$

Problem solving: Set B

B **a** 6 **b** $f(x) \leqslant 6$

c **i**

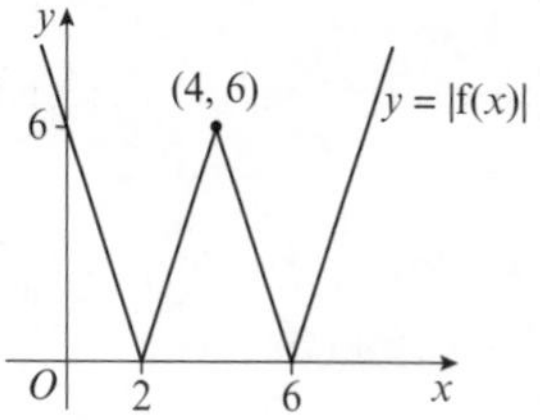

ii

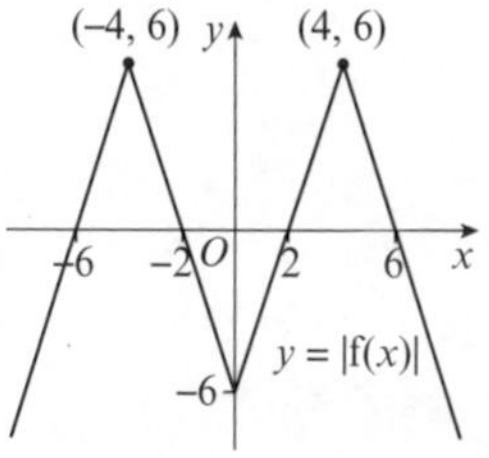

d $x = \frac{14}{5}, \frac{34}{7}$

S **a** $f(x) \geqslant -4$

b **i**

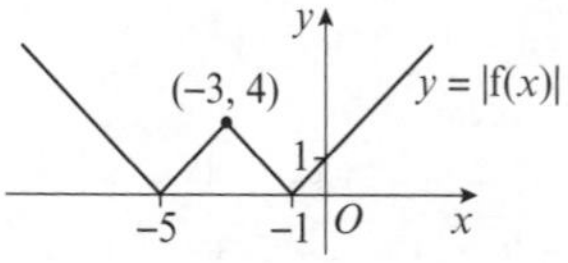

ii

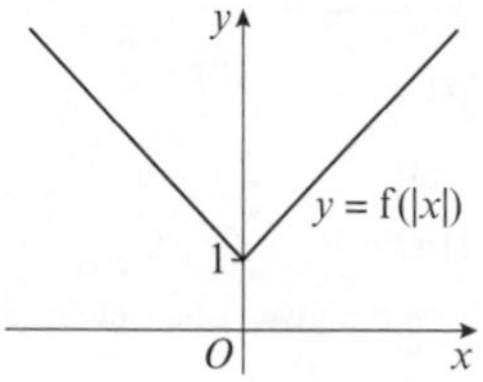

c $\left\{x : -\frac{28}{3} \leqslant x \leqslant \frac{4}{5}\right\}$

d **i** $k < -4$ **ii** $k = -4$ **iii** $k > -4$

G **a** $a = 6, b = 2$

b **i** $\left\{p : -1 \leqslant p < -\frac{1}{2}\right\}$

ii $\left\{-\frac{1}{2}\right\} \cup \{p : p < -1\} \cup \{p : p \geqslant 1\}$

iii $\left\{p : -\frac{1}{2} < p < 1\right\}$

CHAPTER 3

3.1 Arithmetic sequences

1 a i 7, 11, 15, 19 ii $a = 7, d = 4$
b i 4, 1, −2, −5 ii $a = 4, d = -3$
c i 8.5, 9, 9.5, 10 ii $a = 8.5, d = 0.5$
d i −3, −1, 1, 3 ii $a = -3, d = 2$

2 a nth term $= 4n - 2$, 10th term = 38
b nth term $= 7 - 2n$, 10th term = −13
c nth term $= 3n - 5$, 10th term = 25
d nth term $= 11y - 3ny$, 10th term $= -19y$

3 a 33 b 41 c 30 d 53

4 $a = 2, d = 5$

5 a 8 b 41

6 a −1, 2, 5 b 3

7 a $a = 10, d = -4$ b 17

8 a Let the terms be $a = a + kd$, $b = a + (k + 1)d$ and $c = a + (k + 2)d$

$\frac{a+c}{2} = \frac{a + kd + a + (k+2)d}{2}$

$= \frac{2a + 2(k+1)d}{2} = a + (k + 1)d = b$

so $\frac{a+c}{2} = b$

b $p = -3, p = 2.5$

9 a $k = 4$ b 445

3.2 Arithmetic series

1 a 860 b 570 c −1080 d 50

2 a 456 b −816 c 5190 d 960

3 $2S_{60} = 60 \times 61$, so $S_{60} = \frac{60 \times 61}{2} = 1830$

4 25

5 a −1, 3, 7 b 4

c $S_n = \frac{n}{2}(a + l)$ where $a = -1$, $d = 4$ and $l = 4n - 5$

So $S_n = \frac{n}{2}(-1 + 4n - 5) = \frac{n}{2}(4n - 6)$

which shows $S_n = n(2n - 3)$

6 a $S_n = 1 + 2 + 3 + \ldots + (n-2) + (n-1) + n$

$S_n = n + (n-1) + (n-2) + \ldots + 3 + 2 + 1$

$2S_n = n \times (n + 1)$ so $S_n = \frac{n(n+1)}{2}$

b $S = \frac{100 \times 202}{2} = 10\,100$

7 a 40 b 50

8 a $S_{12} = \frac{12}{2}(2a + (12 - 1)d) = 366$

So $6(2a + 11d) = 366$, which gives $12a + 66d = 366$

b $a + 7d = 38$ c $a = 3, d = 5$

9 a Second term $= a + d$, sixth term $= a + 5d$,

so $a + d + a + 5d = 2a + 6d = 14$

so $a + 3d = 7$

b $a = 13, d = -2$

10 a $a + 14d = 11$ (1), $a + 19d = \frac{37}{2}$ (2)

subtracting, (2) − (1) gives $5d = \frac{15}{2}$, so $d = \frac{3}{2}$

substituting into (1) gives $a + 14 \times \frac{3}{2} = 11$

$a = 11 - 21 = -10$

Second term $= -10 + \frac{3}{2} = -\frac{17}{2}$

b $n = 60$

11 $d = k + 5 = 3k - 5$ so $2k = 10$ and $k = 5$.

Terms are 15, 25 and 35 so $d = 10$.

First term = 15 − 10 = 5

$S_n = \frac{n}{2}(10 - 10(n - 1))$

$= \frac{10n}{2}(1 + (n - 1)) = 5n \times n = 5n^2$

12 $d = 4k + 3 - 3k = 6k - 9 - (4k + 3)$,

so $k + 3 = 2k - 12$ and $k = 15$.

$d = k + 3 = 18$

Third term $= 3k = 45 = a + 2d$ so $a = 45 - 36 = 9$

$S_n = \frac{n}{2}(2a + (n - 1)d)$

$= S_n = \frac{n}{2}(18 + (n-1) \times 18) = \frac{n}{2} \times 18n = 9n^2 = (3n)^2$

So the sum of the first n terms of the sequence is a square number.

3.3 Geometric sequences

1 a i $r = 3$ ii $u_n = 2 \times 3^{n-1}$
b i $r = \frac{1}{2}$ ii $u_n = 60 \times \left(\frac{1}{2}\right)^{n-1}$
c i $r = -2$ ii $u_n = 10 \times (-2)^{n-1}$
d i $r = \frac{3}{2}$ ii $u_n = 40 \times \left(\frac{3}{2}\right)^{n-1}$

2 a Part **c**: 10, − 20, 40, −80

b Let the terms be $p = ar^k$, $q = ar^{k+1}$, $r = ar^{k+2}$, then

$pr = ar^k \times ar^{k+2} = a^2r^{2k+2} = (ar^{k+1})^2 = q^2$, so $pr = q^2$

3 a $x = 10$ b 2560

4 2 125 764 (13th term)

5 a $\frac{5}{2}$ b $\frac{128}{125}$

6 $k = \frac{1}{2}$

7 a 0.110 (3 s.f.) b 0.832 (3 s.f.) (15th term)

8 a $a = 150$, $ar^4 = 50$ so $150r^4 = 50$ which gives $r^4 = \frac{1}{3}$

Taking logs on both sides, $4\ln r = -\ln 3$

so $4\ln r + \ln 3 = 0$

b 0.760

9 a $k = \frac{1}{2}$ b 10 240 (13th term)

3.4 Geometric series

1 a 59 048 b 96.0 (3 s.f.)
c −255 d 2370 (3 s.f.)

2 a 1275 b 19 682 c 819 (3 s.f.) d 4118

3 19

4 a 2 b 3 c 3 145 725

5 a 0.101 b 4

6 a $S_k = \frac{20\left(1 - \left(\frac{4}{5}\right)^k\right)}{1 - \frac{4}{5}}$

So $100\left(1 - \left(\frac{4}{5}\right)^k\right) > 50 \Rightarrow 1 - \left(\frac{4}{5}\right)^k > 0.5$

$\Rightarrow 0.5 > \left(\frac{4}{5}\right)^k$

Taking logs gives $\ln 0.5 > k \ln \frac{4}{5}$, so $k > \frac{\ln 0.5}{\ln 0.8}$

b $k = 4$

7 a $k = 10$ b 0.0677 c 63.8

8 536 (3 s.f.)

9 a $a + ar = ar^2$ where a is the first term and r is the common ratio. So $r^2 - r - 1 = 0$, hence r is independent of a.

b $S_{20} = 48\,900$ (3 s.f.)

3.5 Sum to infinity

1 a $r = 0.2 \div 2 = 0.1$

As $|r| < 1$, this means the series is convergent.

b $S_\infty = \frac{20}{9}$

2 a i $|r| = 0.4 < 1$, so the series is convergent.

ii $S_\infty = \frac{25}{3}$

b i Divergent, since $|r| = 3 > 1$

c i Convergent, since $|r| = \frac{1}{3} < 1$

ii $S_\infty = \frac{243}{4}$

d i Not convergent: series is arithmetic.

3 a $ar^4 = 2.4576$, $ar^6 = 1.572\,864$

$\frac{ar^6}{ar^4} = \frac{1.572\,864}{2.4576}$, so $r^2 = 0.64$ and $r = \pm 0.8$

As $|r| < 1$ this means the series is convergent.

b 30 or $\frac{10}{3}$

4 a 0.68 b 32

5 a $r = \pm\frac{1}{3}$ b $a = 54$

6 $\frac{2}{3}$

7 a $|r| < 1$ b $\frac{3}{4}$

8 a 0.9873 b 3.8

9 a $\frac{1}{3}$ b 1.98 c 119.8 (1 d.p.)

10 a $ar = \frac{12}{5}$, $\frac{a}{1-r} = 10$

So $\frac{12}{5} = 10r(1-r)$, which gives $50r^2 - 50r + 12 = 0$

b $r = \frac{2}{5}$ or $r = \frac{3}{5}$ c $a = 6$ or $a = 4$ d $n = 8$

3.6 Sigma notation

1 a i 1, 5, 9, 13, 17, 21 ii 66

b i 2, 16, 54, 128, 250 ii 450

c i 1, 0, −1, 0, 1 ii 1

d i $-\frac{3}{8}, \frac{3}{16}, -\frac{3}{32}, \frac{3}{64}, -\frac{3}{128}$ ii $-\frac{33}{128}$

2 a $a = 4, d = 5$ b 378

3 a $a = 3, r = 2$ b 3 145 725

4 a 185 b 60 c 10

5 a $\sum_{r=1}^{30}(5-2r) = \sum_{r=1}^{7}(5-2r) + \sum_{r=8}^{30}(5-2r)$

so $\sum_{r=8}^{30}(5-2r) = \sum_{r=1}^{30}(5-2r) - \sum_{r=1}^{7}(5-2r)$

b $\sum_{r=1}^{30}(5-2r)$: $a = 3, d = -2, n = 30$,

$S_{30} = \frac{30}{2}(6 + 29 \times (-2)) = -780$

$\sum_{r=1}^{7}(5-2r)$: $a = 3, d = -2, n = 7$,

$S_7 = \frac{7}{2}(6 + 6 \times (-2)) = -21$

$\sum_{r=8}^{30}(5-2r) = -780 - (-21) = -759$

6 28 658 448

7 885 720

8 a $a = 9, d = 3, S_k = \frac{k}{2}(18 + (k-1) \times 3) = 750$,

so $k(18 + 3k - 3) = 1500$, which gives

$3k^2 + 15k - 1500 = 0$

$\Rightarrow (k - 20)(3k + 75) = 0$

b $k = 20$

9 a $a = 8, r = 2$,

$S_k = \frac{8(2^k - 1)}{2 - 1} = 8(2^k - 1) = 262\,136$

So $(2^k - 1) = 32\,767$ and $2^k = 32\,768$

Taking logs gives $k \ln 2 = \ln 32\,768$,

$\Rightarrow k = \frac{\ln 32\,768}{\ln 2}$

b $\sum_{r=1}^{15} 4 \times 2^r = 262\,136$

So $\sum_{r=16}^{20} 4 \times 2^r = \sum_{r=1}^{20} 4 \times 2^r - \sum_{r=1}^{15} 4 \times 2^r$

$= 8\,388\,600 - 262\,136 = 8\,126\,464$

10 a $|x| < \frac{1}{4}$ b $\frac{1}{5}$

11 $\sum_{r=1}^{10} 4 = 4 \times 10 = 40$

$\sum_{r=1}^{10} 3r = 3\sum_{r=1}^{10} r = 3 \times \frac{10 \times 11}{2} = 165$

$\sum_{r=1}^{10} 2^{r-1} = \frac{1(2^{10} - 1)}{2 - 1} = 1023$

$40 + 165 + 1023 = 1228$

3.7 Recurrence relations

1 a 3, 5, 9, 17 b 10, 6, 2, −2 c 4, 8, 32, 512

2 a i increasing

b i periodic ii order 4

c i decreasing

3 a i 2, 5, 8, 11, 14 ii increasing

b i $1, \frac{1}{2}, \frac{1}{4}, \frac{1}{8}, \frac{1}{16}$ ii decreasing

c i $\frac{1}{2}, -\frac{1}{2}, \frac{1}{2}, -\frac{1}{2}, \frac{1}{2}$ ii periodic iii 2

d i 1, 3, 7, 15, 31 ii increasing

e i 8, −4, 8, −4, 8 ii periodic iii 2

f i 10, 6, 2, −2, −6 ii decreasing

4 a $n = 1$: $a_2 = k + (-1)^1 = k - 1$

$n = 2$: $a_3 = k - 1 + (-1)^2 = k - 1 + 1 = k$

$n = 3$: $a_4 = k + (-1)^3 = k - 1$, so $a_2 = a_4 = k - 1$

b 1000

c $a_{399} = 3$

5 $p = 2, q = -5$

6 a $u_1 = 5, u_2 = 5k - 8, u_3 = k(5k - 8) - 8 = 5k^2 - 8k - 8$

b $k = 4$ c 600

7 a 4 b 0

8 a $a_3 = 25k + 24$

b $a_4 = 5(25k + 24) + 4 = 125k + 124$

$\sum_{r=1}^{4} a_r = k + 5k + 4 + 25k + 24 + 125k + 124$

$= 156k + 152 = 4(39k + 38)$, so a multiple of 4

9 a 75 b 150

3.8 Modelling with series

1 a Sundays: first = 6 km, second = 6 + 2 = 8 km, third = 8 + 2 = 10 km, fourth = 10 + 2 = 12 km, fifth = 12 + 2 = 14 km
b $2n + 4$
c 19 weeks
d 500 km

2 a $1.025 \times 28000 = 28700$
b $28000 \times 1.025^{n-1}$
c 34968 (nearest whole number)
d It is unlikely that the adult population will increase by exactly the same percentage each year.

3 a £2.65 b £71.50

4 Option 1 is cheaper. Difference in interest is £207.

5 a $15000 \times 0.75^3 = 6328.125$ = £6328 to the nearest pound
b 10

6 a £289.41
b £3144.47 to the nearest penny
c £2836

7 a 11 b 13.10 m to the nearest cm
c The ball is unlikely to continue to bounce to a height which is $\frac{3}{4}$ of its previous height for a long period of time due to energy losses.

Problem solving: Set A

B a -12.5 b $n = 30$

S 12.5

G $k > -\frac{27}{11}$

Problem solving: Set B

B $\frac{3}{128}$

S $k = 20$

G $k = \frac{9}{2}$

CHAPTER 4

4.1 Expanding $(1+x)^n$

1 a $1 - 2x + 3x^2 - 4x^3$ b $1 + \frac{x}{2} - \frac{x^2}{8} + \frac{x^3}{16}$
c $1 + \frac{4x}{3} + \frac{2x^2}{9} - \frac{4x^3}{81}$ d $1 - \frac{x}{5} + \frac{3x^2}{25} - \frac{11x^3}{125}$
e $1 - 5x + 15x^2 - 35x^3$ f $1 - \frac{5x}{2} + \frac{35x^2}{8} - \frac{105x^3}{16}$

2 a i $1 - 6x + 24x^2 - 80x^3$ ii $|x| < \frac{1}{2}$
b i $1 - \frac{x}{2} - \frac{x^2}{8} - \frac{x^3}{16}$ ii $|x| < 1$
c i $1 + \frac{x}{3} - \frac{x^2}{36} + \frac{x^3}{162}$ ii $|x| < 2$
d i $1 + 20x + 250x^2 + 2500x^3$ ii $|x| < \frac{1}{5}$
e i $1 + \frac{2x}{3} + \frac{8x^2}{9} + \frac{112x^3}{81}$ ii $|x| < \frac{1}{2}$
f i $1 + \frac{2x}{3} + \frac{x^2}{3} + \frac{4x^3}{27}$ ii $|x| < 3$

3 a $1 - 2x - 2x^2 - 4x^3$ b 2.44949
c $\sqrt{1-4x}$ is valid for $|x| < \frac{1}{4}$ and $0.01 < \frac{1}{4}$

4 a $4 - 5x + 12x^2$ b $|x| < \frac{1}{3}$

5 a $\frac{8}{5}$ b $\frac{192}{5}$

6 a $(1 + 3x)^{-1} \approx 1 - 3x + 9x^2 - 27x^3$
So $(1 - x)(1 - 3x + 9x^2 - 27x^3)$
$= 1 - 3x + 9x^2 - 27x^3 - x + 3x^2 - 9x^3$
$= 1 - 4x + 12x^2 - 36x^3$
b $|x| < \frac{1}{3}$

7 a $2 - 26x + 68x^2$ b $|x| < \frac{1}{4}$ c 0.019%

8 a $1 - 3x - \frac{9x^2}{2} - \frac{27x^3}{2}$
b $\frac{7}{10}\sqrt{2} \approx 0.9899495$ gives $\sqrt{2} \approx 1.41421$

9 a $(1 - 5x)^{\frac{1}{2}} \approx 1 - \frac{5x}{2} - \frac{25x^2}{8}$
and $(1 + x)^{-\frac{1}{2}} \approx 1 - \frac{x}{2} + \frac{3x^2}{8}$
$\left(1 - \frac{5x}{2} - \frac{25x^2}{8}\right)\left(1 - \frac{x}{2} + \frac{3x^2}{8}\right)$
$\approx 1 - \frac{x}{2} + \frac{3x^2}{8} - \frac{5x}{2} + \frac{5x^2}{4} - \frac{25x^2}{8} = 1 - 3x - \frac{3x^2}{2}$
b $\frac{128}{77}$

4.2 Expanding $(a + bx)^n$

1 a i $\frac{1}{4} - \frac{3x}{4} + \frac{27x^2}{16} - \frac{27x^3}{8}$ ii $|x| < \frac{2}{3}$
b i $2 - \frac{x}{4} - \frac{x^2}{64} - \frac{x^3}{512}$ ii $|x| < 4$
c i $4 + \frac{2x}{3} - \frac{x^2}{36} + \frac{x^3}{324}$ ii $|x| < 4$

2 a i $\frac{3}{5} + \frac{6x}{25} + \frac{12x^2}{125} + \frac{24x^3}{625}$ ii $|x| < \frac{5}{2}$
b i $\frac{1}{4} - \frac{x^2}{16} - \frac{x^3}{16}$ ii $|x| < 2$
c i $2 + \frac{5x}{4} + \frac{55x^2}{64} + \frac{365x^3}{512}$ ii $|x| < 1$

3 a $\frac{1}{125} + \frac{9x}{625} + \frac{54x^2}{3125} + \frac{54x^3}{3125}$ b $|x| < \frac{5}{3}$

4 a $\frac{1}{\sqrt{6}} - \frac{x}{6\sqrt{6}} + \frac{x^2}{24\sqrt{6}}$ b $-\frac{1}{\sqrt{6}} + \frac{19x}{6\sqrt{6}} - \frac{13x^2}{24\sqrt{6}}$

5 a $a = 9, b = 4$ b $|x| < \frac{9}{4}$ c $-\frac{20}{2187}$

6 a $2 - \frac{5x}{12} - \frac{25x^2}{288}$ b $x = 0.2$: $\sqrt[3]{7} \approx 1.913$

7 a $\frac{4}{3} + \frac{26x}{9} + \frac{166x^2}{27}$ b $|x| < \frac{1}{2}$
c 1.3628502 d 0.00097%

8 a $\frac{1}{2} + \frac{11x}{48} - \frac{11x^2}{576}$ b $|x| < 1$ c 1.91305

4.3 Using partial fractions

1 a $\frac{4x + 1}{(1 + x)(2 - x)} \equiv -\frac{1}{1 + x} + \frac{3}{2 - x}$
b $\frac{1}{2} + \frac{7x}{4} - \frac{5x^2}{8}$ c $|x| < 1$

2 a $\frac{3x}{(3 + x)^2} \equiv \frac{3}{3 + x} - \frac{9}{(3 + x)^2}$
b $\frac{x}{3} - \frac{2x^2}{9} + \frac{x^3}{9}$ c $|x| < 3$

3 a $2 + \frac{67}{9(x - 5)} - \frac{4}{9(x + 4)}$ b $\frac{2}{5} - \frac{27x}{100} - \frac{133x^2}{2000}$
c $|x| < 4$

4 a $\frac{1}{1 - 2x} - \frac{2}{1 + 4x}$ b $-1 + 10x - 28x^2$ c $|x| < \frac{1}{4}$

5 a $A = 5, B = -1$ b $4 - 6x + 8x^2$

6 a $A = 3, B = -3, C = 5$ b $\frac{7}{12} - \frac{53x}{144} - \frac{401x^2}{1728}$
c $|x| < 3$

7 a $A = -\frac{44}{15}, B = -\frac{25}{3}, C = \frac{6}{5}$ b $-6 - \frac{83x}{2} - \frac{795x^2}{4}$
c Expansion of f(x) is valid for $|x| < \frac{1}{3}$
As $0.5 > \frac{1}{3}$, the expansion is not valid for $x = 0.5$

Problem solving: Set A

B **a** $p = -\frac{25}{2}, q = \frac{125}{2}$

b $x = 0.05$: $(1.5)^{\frac{1}{2}} \approx 1.226\,562\,5$ **c** 0.15%

S **a** $1 - 3x - \frac{9x^2}{2} - \frac{27x^3}{2}$ **b** $\sqrt{3} \approx \frac{27}{16}$

c Expansion is valid for $|x| < \frac{1}{6}$ and $\frac{1}{9} < \frac{1}{6}$

G **a** $(1 + 3x)^{\frac{1}{2}} \approx 1 + \frac{3x}{2} - \frac{9x^2}{8} + \frac{27x^3}{16}$

$(1 - x)^{-\frac{1}{2}} \approx 1 + \frac{x}{2} + \frac{3x^2}{8} + \frac{5x^3}{16}$

Multiplying these together gives $1 + 2x + 2x^3 + \dots$

b The expansion is valid for $|x| < \frac{1}{3}$ and $\frac{1}{2} > \frac{1}{3}$

c To ensure $|x| < \frac{1}{3}$, equate the argument to e.g. $\frac{5}{4}$, which gives $x = \frac{1}{17}$. Then $\sqrt{5} \approx 2.236\,11$ to 5 d.p.

Problem solving: Set B

B **a** $\frac{1}{2 - 3x} = (2 - 3x)^{-1} = 2^{-1}\left(1 - \frac{3x}{2}\right)^{-1}$

$= \frac{1}{2}\left(1 + (-1) \times \left(\frac{3x}{2}\right) + \frac{(-1)(-2)}{2!} \times \left(\frac{3x}{2}\right)^2 + \dots\right)$

So $\frac{1}{2 - 3x} \approx \frac{1}{2} + \frac{3x}{4} + \frac{9x^2}{8}$, valid for $|x| < \frac{2}{3}$

b $1 + 2x + 3x^2$ **c** $A = -24, B = 9, C = 1$

d $-2 - 7x - 15x^2$ **e** $|x| < \frac{2}{3}$

S **a** $f(x) = 8 - \frac{8}{x + 3} + \frac{12}{x - 2}$ **b** $-\frac{2}{3} - \frac{19x}{9} - \frac{97x^2}{54}$

c $|x| < 2$

G $\frac{1}{2x^2 + 5x + 3} \equiv \frac{1}{x + 1} - \frac{2}{2x + 3}$

$\frac{\sqrt{1 + 3x}}{2x^2 + 5x + 3} = \frac{\sqrt{1 + 3x}}{x + 1} - \frac{2\sqrt{1 + 3x}}{2x + 3}$

$\frac{1}{x + 1} \approx 1 - x + x^2$ and $-\frac{2}{2x + 3} \approx -\frac{2}{3} + \frac{4x}{9} - \frac{8x^2}{27}$

$\sqrt{1 + 3x} = (1 + 3x)^{\frac{1}{2}} \approx 1 + \frac{3x}{2} - \frac{9x^2}{8}$

$\frac{\sqrt{1 + 3x}}{x + 1} \approx (1 - x + x^2)\left(1 + \frac{3x}{2} - \frac{9x^2}{8}\right) \approx 1 + \frac{x}{2} - \frac{13x^2}{8}$

$-\frac{2\sqrt{1 + 3x}}{2x + 3} \approx \left(1 + \frac{3x}{2} - \frac{9x^2}{8}\right)\left(-\frac{2}{3} + \frac{4x}{9} - \frac{8x^2}{27}\right)$

$\approx -\frac{2}{3} - \frac{5x}{9} + \frac{121x^2}{108}$

$1 + \frac{x}{2} - \frac{13x^2}{8} + \left(-\frac{2}{3} - \frac{5x}{9} + \frac{121x^2}{108}\right) = \frac{1}{3} - \frac{x}{18} - \frac{109x^2}{216}$

CHAPTER 5

5.1 Radian measure

1 **a** 150° **b** 22.5° **c** 720°

d 19.5° **e** 81.0° **f** 108.9°

2 **a** **i** $\frac{\pi}{10}$ **ii** $\frac{13\pi}{72}$ **iii** $\frac{16\pi}{9}$

b **i** 0.279 rad **ii** 2.16 rad **iii** 4.54 rad

3 **a**

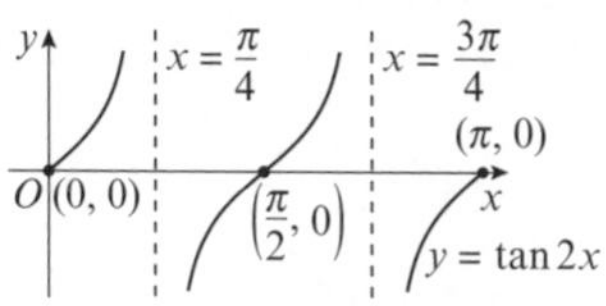

b

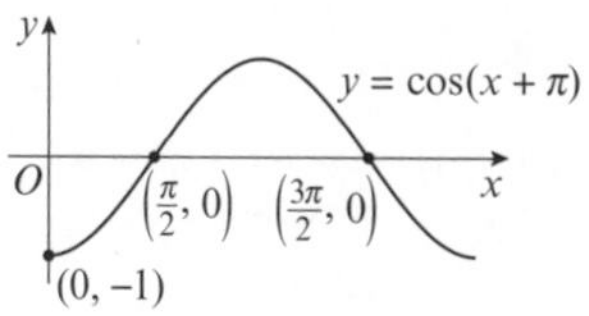

c

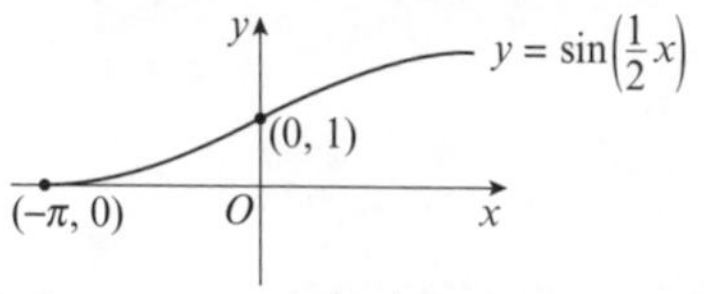

4 **a** –1 **b** 1 **c** $\frac{1}{2}$

5 **a**

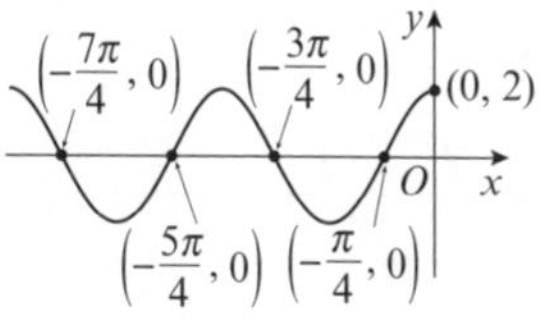

b

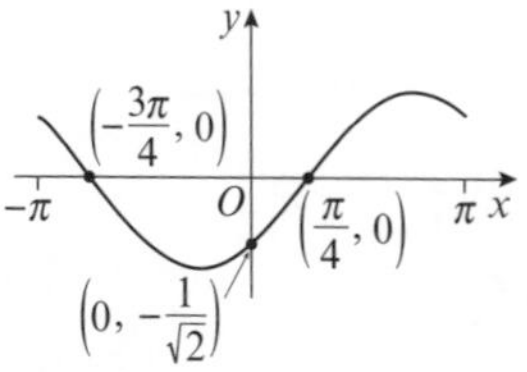

6 **a** 1.56 rad **b** 36.0 cm²

7 **a** $\left(\frac{\pi}{6}, 0\right), \left(\frac{7\pi}{6}, 0\right), \left(\frac{13\pi}{6}, 0\right), \left(\frac{19\pi}{6}, 0\right)$

b $\left(0, \frac{1}{2}\right)$

8 **a** 313 m **b** 061.0°

5.2 Arc length

1 **a** 45 cm **b** $\frac{13\pi}{3}$ cm **c** 0.805 cm

2 **a** 16.5 cm **b** 11.1 cm **c** 20.6 cm

3 **a** 3.56 rad **b** 7.86 rad **c** 1.58 rad

4 **a** 4 cm **b** 25.98 cm

5 **a** $\frac{56\pi}{9}$ cm **b** 38.8 cm

6 **a** $\frac{10\pi}{9}$ **b** 4.1 cm²

7 **a** 20 cm **b** $\frac{\pi}{6}$

5.3 Area of sectors and segments

1 **a** 5.63 cm² (3 s.f.) **b** 32.0 cm² (3 s.f.)

c 3 cm **d** 1.3 rad

2 **a** 0.251 cm² (3 s.f.) **b** 22.1 cm² (3 s.f.)

c 6.89 cm² (3 s.f.)

3 **a** 6.73 cm² (3 s.f.) **b** 280.0 cm² (3 s.f.)

c 81.3 cm² (3 s.f.)

4 **a** $\frac{2\pi}{3}$ **b** $\frac{25\pi}{3}$ m² **c** 15.4 m²

5 **a** 128 cm² **b** 60.4 cm

6 **a** $r = \sqrt{\frac{2 \times 37.8}{1.2}} = 3\sqrt{7}$ cm **b** 8.4 cm²

7 **a** $\theta = \frac{2}{5}$, $r = 2\sqrt{15}$ cm **b** 0.317 cm²

5.4 Solving trigonometric equations

1 **a** $\theta = \frac{\pi}{6}, \frac{5\pi}{6}$ **b** $\theta = 2.03, 5.18$

c $\theta = 0.927, 5.36$ **d** $\theta = \frac{\pi}{4}, \frac{3\pi}{4}$

2 **a** $\theta = 0.730, 2.41$ **b** $\theta = -\frac{2\pi}{3}, \frac{2\pi}{3}, \frac{4\pi}{3}$

c $\theta = -5.33, -2.19, 0.955$ **d** $\theta = \frac{9\pi}{8}, \frac{15\pi}{8}, \frac{17\pi}{8}, \frac{23\pi}{8}$

3 **a** $\theta = 2.03, 2.36, 5.18, 5.50$ **b** $\theta = 0.519, 5.76$

c $\theta = \frac{\pi}{12}, \frac{17\pi}{12}$ **d** $\theta = 0.485, 3.63$

4 **a** $\theta = \frac{5\pi}{36}, \frac{71\pi}{36}$ **b** $\theta = 0.270, 1.84, 3.41, 4.98$

5 **a** $\tan x = \frac{3}{4}$ **b** $x = -2.8, -1.2, 0.3, 1.9$

6 **a** $2(1 - \sin^2 x) + 3\sin x - 3 = 0 \Rightarrow 2\sin^2 x - 3\sin x + 1 = 0$

b $x = \frac{\pi}{6}, \frac{\pi}{2}, \frac{5\pi}{6}$

7 **a** $\theta = 0.853, 1.77, 2.95, 3.86$ **b** $\theta = \frac{\pi}{6}, \frac{5\pi}{6}$

5.5 Small angle approximations

1 **a** 3 **b** 2 **c** 1

2 **a** 2 **b** −6 **c** 2

3 **a** $\frac{-\theta}{4\theta^2} = -\frac{1}{4\theta}$ **b** $\frac{\left(1 - \frac{\theta^2}{2}\right) - 1}{\theta} = \frac{-\frac{\theta^2}{2}}{\theta} = -\frac{1}{2}\theta$

c $\frac{2\theta}{1 - \left(1 - \frac{(2\theta)^2}{2}\right)} = \frac{2\theta}{2\theta^2} = \frac{1}{\theta}$

4 $\frac{1}{3}$

5 $\frac{3\theta - 4\left(1 - \frac{\theta^2}{2}\right) + 5}{\theta + 1} = \frac{3\theta - 4 + 2\theta^2 + 5}{\theta + 1}$

$= \frac{(2\theta + 1)(\theta + 1)}{\theta + 1} = 2\theta + 1$

6 **a** $1 + 6\cos\theta + 5\cos^2\theta \approx 1 + 6\left(1 - \frac{1}{2}\theta^2\right) + 5\left(1 - \frac{1}{2}\theta^2\right)^2$

$= 1 + 6\left(1 - \frac{1}{2}\theta^2\right) + 5\left(1 - \theta^2 + \frac{1}{4}\theta^4\right)$

$= 1 + 6 - 3\theta^2 + 5 - 5\theta^2 + \frac{5}{4}\theta^4$

$= 12 - 8\theta^2$

b Josh is incorrect as he used degrees and not radians. He should substitute $\theta = \frac{10\pi}{180}$ and not $\theta = 10$:

$12 - 8\left(\frac{10\pi}{180}\right)^2 = 11.76$

So $\theta = 10°$ gives a good approximation.

Problem solving: Set A

B **a** $\frac{\pi}{3}$ **b** $9\sqrt{3}\text{ cm}^2$

c $6\pi\text{ cm}^2$ **d** $2(6\pi - 9\sqrt{3}) = (12\pi - 18\sqrt{3})\text{ cm}^2$

S **a** $32\sqrt{3}\text{ cm}^2$ **b** $\frac{64\pi}{3}\text{ cm}^2$

c Area of shaded part of shape

= area of sector $- \frac{1}{2} \times$ area of rhombus

$= \left(\frac{64\pi}{3} - 16\sqrt{3}\right)\text{cm}^2 = \frac{1}{3}(64\pi - 48\sqrt{3})\text{cm}^2$

G Area of the sector $ADCB = \frac{1}{2} \times x^2 \times \theta = \frac{\theta}{2}x^2$

Area of rhombus $= 2\left(\frac{1}{2} \times \sqrt{3}x \times \frac{x}{2}\right) = \frac{\sqrt{3}}{2}x^2$

Total area $= \frac{\theta}{2}x^2 + \left(\frac{\theta}{2}x^2 - \frac{\sqrt{3}}{2}x^2\right) = \left(\theta - \frac{\sqrt{3}}{2}\right)x^2$

Problem solving: Set B

B **a**

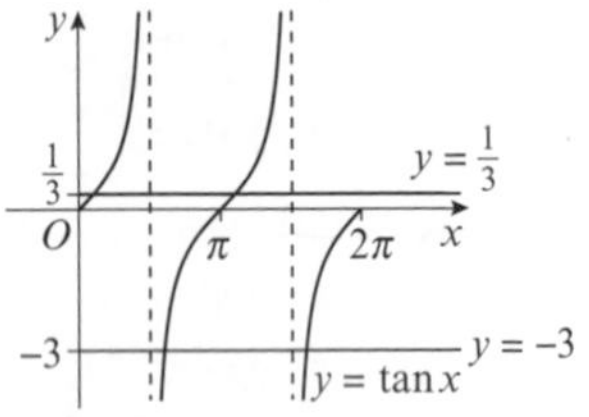

b Factorise $3\tan^2 x + 8\tan x - 3 = 0$ to get

$(3\tan x - 1)(\tan x + 3) = 0$

c 0.322, 1.89, 3.46, 5.03

S **a** $3\cos^2 x = 5(1 - \sin x) \Rightarrow 3(1 - \sin^2 x) = 5(1 - \sin x)$

$\Rightarrow 3 - 3\sin^2 x = 5 - 5\sin x \Rightarrow 3\sin^2 x - 5\sin x + 2 = 0$

b $x = 0.730, 2.41$ and $\frac{\pi}{2}$

G $x = 0.308, 2.83, 6.59, 9.11$

CHAPTER 6

6.1 Secant, cosecant and cotangent

1 **a** $\frac{2\sqrt{3}}{3}$ **b** $-\sqrt{2}$ **c** $\sqrt{3}$

2 **a** 2.03 **b** 2.20 **c** 1.41

3 **a** $-\frac{2\sqrt{3}}{3}$ **b** 1 **c** −1

4 **a** $\frac{\sec 60°}{\text{cosec}\,270°} = \frac{2}{-1} = -2$

b $\text{cosec}\left(\frac{3\pi}{4}\right)\cot\left(\frac{\pi}{6}\right) = \sqrt{2} \times \sqrt{3} = \sqrt{6}$

5 **a** $\sec\theta \equiv \frac{1}{\cos\theta} \equiv \frac{1}{\cos(-\theta)} \equiv \sec(-\theta)$

b $\cot(\theta + \pi) \equiv \frac{1}{\tan(\theta + \pi)} \equiv \frac{1}{\tan\theta} \equiv \cot\theta$

6 **a** $\frac{5}{4}$ **b** $\frac{5}{3}$ **c** $\frac{4}{3}$

7 $\cot\left(\frac{\pi}{3}\right) - \text{cosec}\left(\frac{\pi}{4}\right) = \frac{\sqrt{3}}{3} - \sqrt{2} = \frac{\sqrt{3} - 3\sqrt{2}}{3}$

6.2 Graphs of sec x, cosec x and cot x

1 **a** **i**

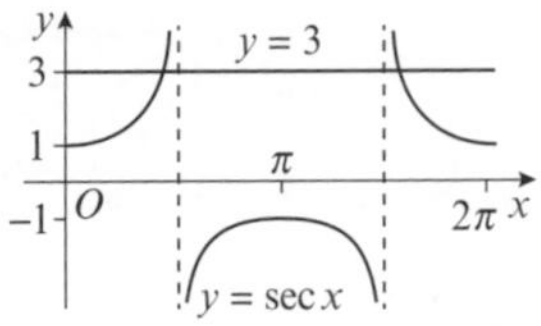

ii 2

b **i**

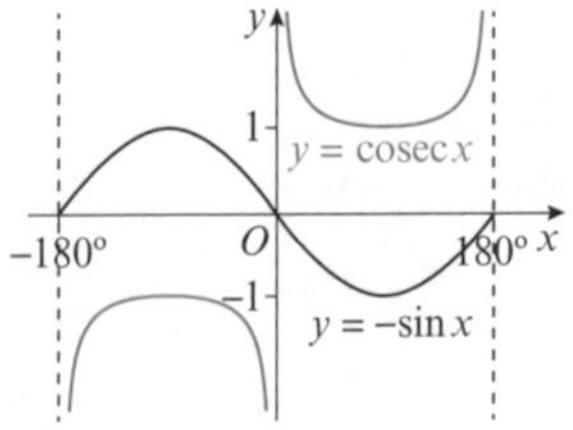

ii Graphs do not intersect.

2 **a** **i**

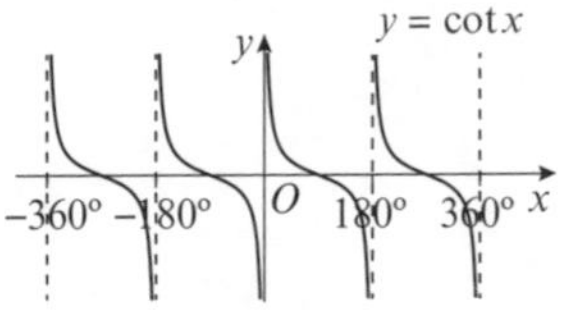

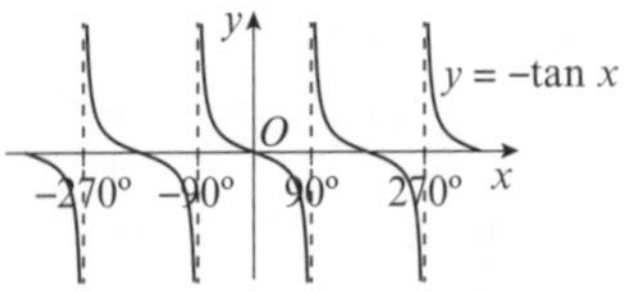

ii The graph of $y = \cot x$ is the same as that of $y = -\tan x$ translated by 90° in the positive or negative x-direction.

b **i**

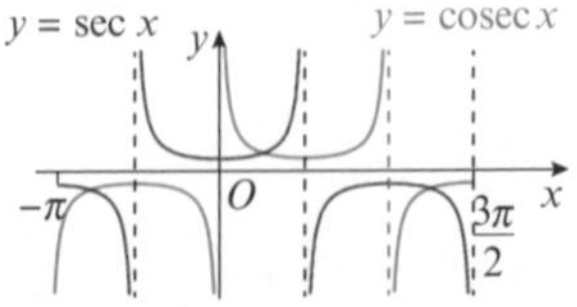

ii The graph of cosec x is the same as that of sec x translated by $\frac{\pi}{2}$ in the positive x-direction.

3 **a**

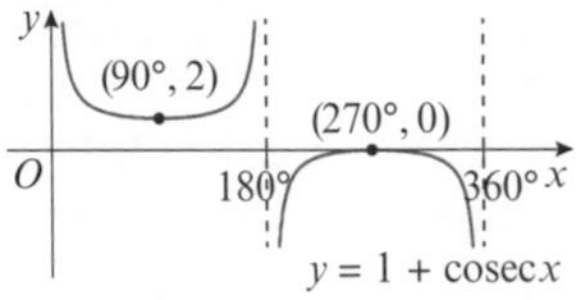

b

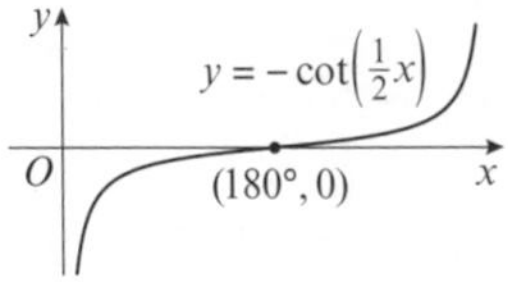

c

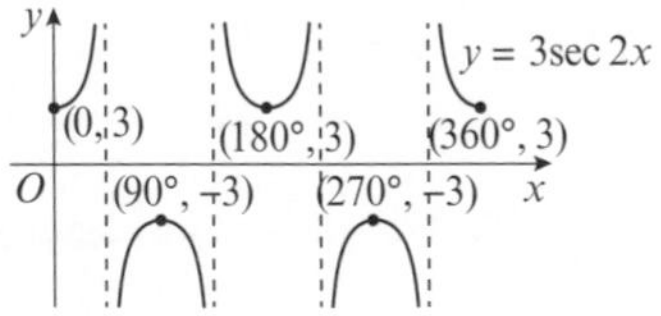

4 **a** $(0, \sqrt{2})$

b $\left(\frac{\pi}{4}, 1\right)$, $\left(\frac{9\pi}{4}, 1\right)$, $\left(\frac{5\pi}{4}, -1\right)$, $\left(\frac{13\pi}{4}, -1\right)$

c $x = \frac{3\pi}{4}$, $x = \frac{7\pi}{4}$, $x = \frac{11\pi}{4}$, $x = \frac{15\pi}{4}$

5 **a**

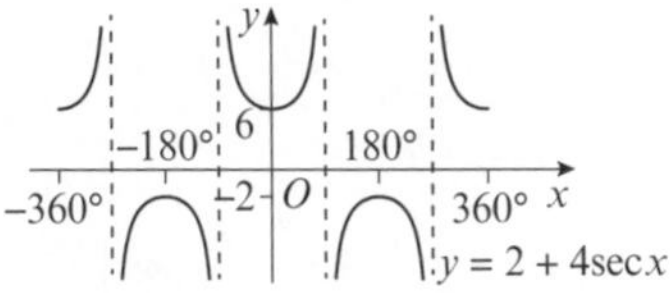

b $-2 < a < 6$

6 **a** 3 **b** $x = 30°, 90°, 150°$

7 **a**

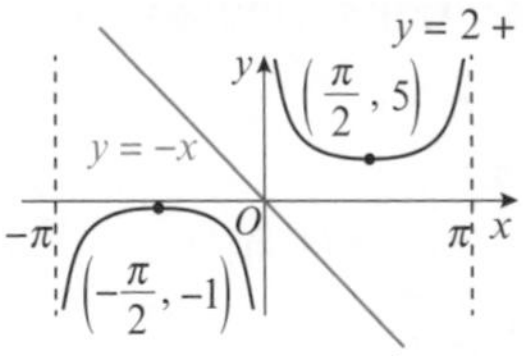

b 0 **c** $\frac{1}{5}$ when $x = \frac{\pi}{2}$

6.3 Using sec x, cosec x and cot x

1 **a** 4 **b** $\frac{5}{3}$ **c** $\frac{3}{2}$

2 **a** cosec x **b** cosec x **c** cosec $3x$

3 **a** $x = 30°, 150°$ **b** $x = 64.3°, 296°$ **c** $x = 130°, 310°$

4 **a** $$\frac{\cot x + \tan x}{\sec x} \equiv \frac{\frac{\cos x}{\sin x} + \frac{\sin x}{\cos x}}{\frac{1}{\cos x}}$$
$$\equiv \frac{\cos^2 x}{\sin x} + \sin x \equiv \frac{1 - \sin^2 x}{\sin x} + \sin x$$
$$\equiv \frac{1 - \sin^2 x + \sin^2 x}{\sin x} \equiv \operatorname{cosec} x$$

b $x = 14.5°, 166°$ (3 s.f.)

5 **a** $$\cos 3\theta + \sin 3\theta \times \frac{\sin 3\theta}{\cos 3\theta} \equiv \cos 3\theta + \frac{1 - \cos^2 3\theta}{\cos 3\theta}$$
$$\equiv \frac{\cos^2 3\theta + 1 - \cos^2 3\theta}{\cos 3\theta} \equiv \sec 3\theta$$

b $2\cos 3\theta + 2\sin 3\theta \tan 3\theta = -1$

$\Rightarrow 2(\cos 3\theta + \sin 3\theta \tan 3\theta) = -1 \Rightarrow 2\sec 3\theta = -1$

$\Rightarrow \sec 3\theta = -\frac{1}{2}$

$\sec 3\theta k$ has no solutions in the range $-1 < k < 1$

6 $x = 1.23, 5.05$ (3 s.f.)

7 **a** $$\text{L.H.S.} \equiv \frac{(\sin x)(\sin x) + (1 + \cos x)(1 + \cos x)}{(1 + \cos x)\sin x}$$
$$\equiv \frac{(1 - \cos^2 x) + 1 + 2\cos x + \cos^2 x}{(1 + \cos x)\sin x}$$
$$\equiv \frac{2(1 + \cos x)}{(1 + \cos x)\sin x} \equiv 2\operatorname{cosec} x$$

b $x = 0.935, 3.25$ (3 s.f.)

6.4 Trigonometric identities

1 **a** $\operatorname{cosec}^2 x + \tan^2 x \equiv (1 + \cot^2 x) + (\sec^2 x - 1)$
$\equiv \sec^2 x + \cot^2 x$

b $\cot^2 x + \cos^2 x \equiv (\operatorname{cosec}^2 x - 1) + (1 - \sin^2 x)$
$\equiv (\operatorname{cosec} x - \sin x)(\operatorname{cosec} x + \sin x)$

c $$\frac{1}{1 + \sin x} + \frac{1}{1 - \sin x} \equiv \frac{1 - \sin x + 1 + \sin x}{(1 + \sin x)(1 - \sin x)}$$
$$\equiv \frac{2}{1 - \sin^2 x} \equiv 2\sec^2 x \equiv 2 + 2\tan^2 x$$

2 **a** $-\frac{3}{5}$ **b** $-\frac{3}{4}$ **c** $\frac{5}{4}$

3 **a** $x = -\pi, -\frac{\pi}{4}, 0, \frac{3\pi}{4}, \pi$ **b** $x = 3.46, 5.97$

c $x = \frac{\pi}{4}, \frac{3\pi}{4}, \frac{5\pi}{4}, \frac{7\pi}{4}$

4 $\cos x = -\frac{\sqrt{7}}{3}$

5 $x = 76.0°, 135°, 256°, 315°$

6 **a** $-2 - \sqrt{5}$

b $\sin p = \frac{1}{-2 - \sqrt{5}} = \frac{-2 + \sqrt{5}}{(-2 - \sqrt{5})(-2 + \sqrt{5})} = 2 - \sqrt{5}$

c $p = 3.4, 6.0$

7 $x = -2.03, -0.32, 1.11, 2.82$

6.5 Inverse trigonometric functions

1 **a**

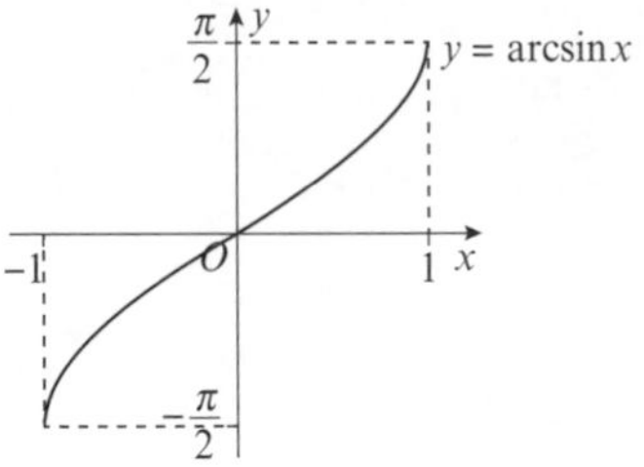

b

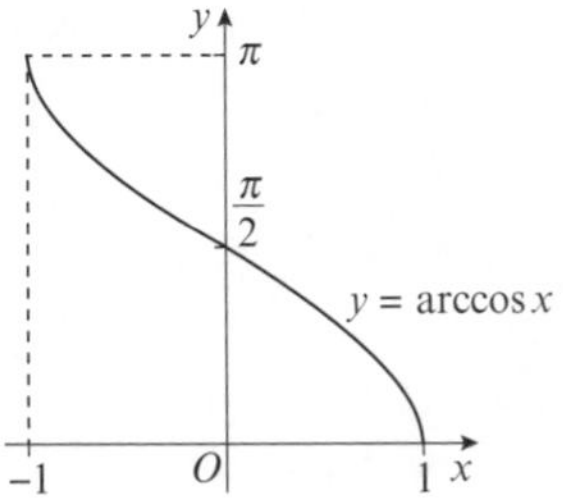

c

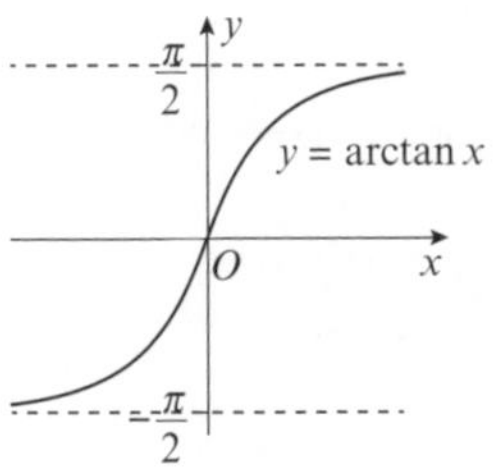

2 a $\frac{\pi}{4}$ b $-\frac{\pi}{3}$ c $\frac{\pi}{3}$

3 a $\frac{\pi}{2}$ b π c $\frac{\pi}{4}$

4 a

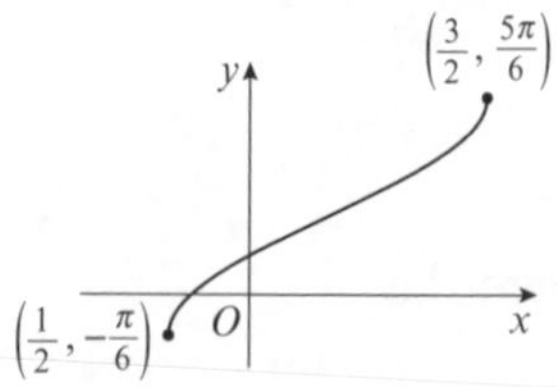

b $\left(\frac{1-\sqrt{3}}{2}, 0\right)$

5 $\frac{5\pi}{6}$

6 a $a = 2, b = 3$ b $(0, 2.498)$

7 $\frac{6+\sqrt{2}}{2}$

Problem solving: Set A

B a $p = \frac{\cos x}{1-\sin x} + \frac{1-\sin x}{\cos x} = \frac{\cos^2 x + (1-\sin x)^2}{(1-\sin x)\cos x}$

$= \frac{\cos^2 x + (1 - 2\sin x + \sin^2 x)}{(1-\sin x)\cos x}$

b $p = \frac{2 - 2\sin x}{(1-\sin x)\cos x}$

$= \frac{2(1-\sin x)}{(1-\sin x)\cos x} = \frac{2}{\cos x} = 2\sec x$

$\Rightarrow 2\sec x = p \Rightarrow \sec x = \frac{p}{2}$

S a $\cot^2 x + \operatorname{cosec}^2 x = a \Rightarrow (\operatorname{cosec}^2 x - 1) + \operatorname{cosec}^2 x = a$

$\Rightarrow 2\operatorname{cosec}^2 x - 1 = a \Rightarrow \operatorname{cosec}^2 x = \frac{a+1}{2}$

b $\operatorname{cosec}^2 x = \frac{a+1}{2} \Rightarrow \sin^2 x = \frac{2}{a+1}$

$\Rightarrow 1 - \cos^2 x = \frac{2}{a+1} \Rightarrow \cos^2 x = 1 - \frac{2}{a+1}$

$\Rightarrow \cos^2 x = \frac{a-1}{a+1} \Rightarrow \sec^2 x = \frac{a+1}{a-1}, a \neq 1$

G $z = \frac{1-\tan^2 x}{1+\tan^2 x} = \frac{1-\tan^2 x}{\sec^2 x} = \cos^2 x\left(1 - \frac{\sin^2 x}{\cos^2 x}\right)$

$= \cos^2 x - \sin^2 x = (1 - \sin^2 x) - \sin^2 x$

$= 1 - 2\sin^2 x$

$\Rightarrow \sin^2 x = \frac{1-z}{2} \Rightarrow \operatorname{cosec}^2 x = \frac{2}{1-z}$

Problem solving: Set B

B a i

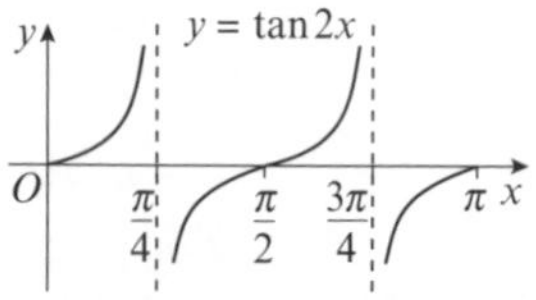

ii $\frac{\pi}{2}$

b i Factorise $\cot^2 2x - 4\cot 2x + 4 = 0$ to give $(\cot 2x - 2)^2 = 0$, $a = 2$

ii $\tan 2x = \frac{1}{2}$, solutions: $x = 0.23, 1.80$

S a $4(\operatorname{cosec}^2 2x - 1) + 12\operatorname{cosec} 2x + 9 = 0$

$4\operatorname{cosec}^2 2x + 12\operatorname{cosec} 2x + 5 = 0$

$(2\operatorname{cosec} 2x + 1)(2\operatorname{cosec} 2x + 5) = 0$

$\operatorname{cosec} 2x = -\frac{1}{2}$ (no solutions) and $\operatorname{cosec} 2x = -\frac{5}{2}$

Therefore $\sin 2x = -\frac{2}{5}$

b $x = 101.8°, 168.2°, 281.8°, 348.2°$

G $x = 0.92, 2.74, 4.06, 5.89$

CHAPTER 7

7.1 Addition formulae

1 a $\sin((90° - A) + B) = \sin(90° - A)\cos B + \cos(90° - A)\sin B$

$\sin(90° - (A - B)) = \sin(90° - A)\cos B + \cos(90° - A)\sin B$

$\sin(90° - A) = \cos A$ and $\cos(90° - A) = \sin A$, therefore

$\cos(A - B) = \cos A\cos B + \sin A\sin B$

b $\cos(A - (-B)) = \cos A\cos(-B) + \sin A\sin(-B)$

$\cos(-B) = \cos B$ and $\sin(-B) = -\sin B$, therefore

$\cos(A + B) = \cos A\cos B - \sin A\sin B$

2 a $\frac{1}{2}\sin x + \frac{\sqrt{3}}{2}\cos x$ b $\frac{\sqrt{3}}{2}\cos x + \frac{1}{2}\sin x$

c $\frac{\tan x + \sqrt{3}}{1 - \sqrt{3}\tan x}$

3 a $\tan 4\theta$ b $\cos 2a$ c $\sin(x - 45°)$

4 $\frac{1 - \tan x\tan y}{\tan x + \tan y}$

5 a $\cos\left(x + \frac{\pi}{3}\right)$ b $\sin\left(x - \frac{\pi}{6}\right)$

6 $\sin\left(x + \frac{\pi}{6}\right) = \cos x \Rightarrow \sin x\cos\frac{\pi}{6} + \cos x\sin\frac{\pi}{6} = \cos x$

$\Rightarrow \sqrt{3}\sin x + \cos x = 2\cos x \Rightarrow \sqrt{3}\sin x = \cos x$

$\Rightarrow \tan x = \frac{1}{\sqrt{3}}$

7 $2\sin\left(x + \frac{5\pi}{6}\right) + 2\sin\left(x + \frac{10\pi}{6}\right)$

$= 2\left(-\frac{\sqrt{3}}{2}\sin x + \frac{1}{2}\cos x\right) + 2\left(\frac{1}{2}\sin x - \frac{\sqrt{3}}{2}\cos x\right)$

$= (1 - \sqrt{3})\sin x + (1 - \sqrt{3})\cos x$

7.2 Using the angle addition formulae

1 a $\frac{\sqrt{3}}{2}$ b $\frac{\sqrt{2}}{2}$ c $\frac{\sqrt{3}}{3}$

2 a $\sin 135° = \sin(90° + 45°)$

$= \sin 90°\cos 45° + \cos 90°\sin 45°$

$= (1)\left(\frac{\sqrt{2}}{2}\right) + 0\left(\frac{\sqrt{2}}{2}\right) = \frac{\sqrt{2}}{2}$

b $\cos 15° = \cos(45° - 30°)$

$= \cos 45°\cos 30° + \sin 45°\sin 30°$

$= \left(\frac{\sqrt{2}}{2}\right)\left(\frac{\sqrt{3}}{2}\right) + \left(\frac{\sqrt{2}}{2}\right)\left(\frac{1}{2}\right) = \frac{\sqrt{6} + \sqrt{2}}{4}$

c $\tan 75° = \tan(45° + 30°)$

$= \frac{\tan 45° + \tan 30°}{1 - \tan 45°\tan 30°}$

$= \frac{\sqrt{3} + 1}{\sqrt{3} - 1}$

$= \frac{(\sqrt{3} + 1)(\sqrt{3} + 1)}{(\sqrt{3} - 1)(\sqrt{3} + 1)}$

$= \frac{4 + 2\sqrt{3}}{2}$

$= 2 + \sqrt{3}$

3 a $\frac{13}{85}$ b $\frac{36}{77}$ c $\frac{85}{84}$

4 a $\frac{\sqrt{3}}{2}$ b $-\sqrt{3}$ c $\frac{1}{2}$

5 a $-\frac{36}{325}$ b $\frac{204}{253}$ c $\frac{325}{323}$

6 a $\dfrac{\tan\frac{\pi}{4} - \tan\frac{\pi}{6}}{1 + \tan\frac{\pi}{4}\tan\frac{\pi}{6}}$

b $\tan\frac{\pi}{12} = \dfrac{1 - \frac{\sqrt{3}}{3}}{1 + \left(1 \times \frac{\sqrt{3}}{3}\right)} = 2 - \sqrt{3}$

7 a $\sin 105° = \sin 60° \cos 45° + \cos 60° \sin 45°$

$= \frac{\sqrt{3}}{2} \times \frac{\sqrt{2}}{2} + \frac{1}{2} \times \frac{\sqrt{2}}{2} = \frac{\sqrt{6} + \sqrt{2}}{4}$

b $\operatorname{cosec} 105° = \frac{4}{\sqrt{6} + \sqrt{2}} = \frac{4}{\sqrt{6} + \sqrt{2}} \times \frac{\sqrt{6} - \sqrt{2}}{\sqrt{6} - \sqrt{2}} = \sqrt{6} - \sqrt{2}$

7.3 Double-angle formulae

1 a $\sin\frac{2\pi}{3}$ b $2\cos 14°$ c $\cot 27°$

2 a $3\sin 10\theta$ b $\sin 2\theta$ c $\cot\theta$

3 a $-\frac{120}{119}$ b $\frac{119}{169}$ c $-\frac{169}{120}$

4 a $y = \frac{4}{5}x^2 - 8$ b $y = \sqrt[4]{\frac{2}{x+1}}$

5 a $\cos^4 x - \sin^4 x \equiv (\cos^2 x + \sin^2 x)(\cos^2 x - \sin^2 x)$

$\equiv \cos 2x$

b $\frac{\sqrt{3}}{2}$

6 a $c = 1 - \frac{a^2}{2}$

b $\sin x = \frac{a}{2}$ and $\cos x = \frac{b}{2}$, so $\tan x = \frac{a}{b}$

$d = \tan 2x = \frac{2\tan x}{1 - \tan^2 x}$

$= \dfrac{2\left(\frac{a}{b}\right)}{1 - \left(\frac{a}{b}\right)^2}$

$= \frac{2ab}{b^2 - a^2}$

7 $\frac{\sqrt{2}}{10}$

7.4 Solving trigonometric equations

1 a $x = 3.0, 6.1$ b $x = 0.5, 3.7$ c $x = 1.2, 5.1$

2 a $\theta = 63.4°, 116.6°$ b $\theta = 0, 180°, 82.8°$

c $\theta = 37.8°, 142.2°$

3 a $\cos\left(x - \frac{\pi}{6}\right) \equiv \cos x \cos\frac{\pi}{6} + \sin x \sin\frac{\pi}{6}$

$\equiv \frac{\sqrt{3}}{2}\cos x + \frac{1}{2}\sin x \equiv \frac{1}{2}(\sqrt{3}\cos x + \sin x)$

b $x = \frac{\pi}{2}, \frac{11\pi}{6}$

4 a $\sin(x - 45°) = \cos x \Rightarrow \frac{\sqrt{2}}{2}\sin x - \frac{\sqrt{2}}{2}\cos x = \cos x$

$\Rightarrow \tan x = 1 + \sqrt{2}$

b $x = 67.5°, 247.5°$

5 a $2\sin\left(x - \frac{\pi}{6}\right) = \sin\left(x + \frac{\pi}{2}\right)$

$\Rightarrow 2\sin x \cos\frac{\pi}{6} - 2\cos x \sin\frac{\pi}{6} = \sin x \cos\frac{\pi}{2} + \cos x \sin\frac{\pi}{2}$

$\Rightarrow \sqrt{3}\sin x - \cos x = \cos x \Rightarrow \sqrt{3}\sin x - 2\cos x = 0$

b $x = -2.28, 0.86$

6 a $\tan 2x - \tan x = 0 \Rightarrow \frac{2\tan x}{1 - \tan^2 x} - \tan x = 0$

$\Rightarrow 2\tan x - \tan x + \tan^3 x = 0 \Rightarrow \tan x + \tan^3 x = 0$

b $x = 0, \pi, 2\pi$

7 a $4\cos^2 x + \cos x - 3 = 0$ b $x = -\pi, -0.72, 0.72, \pi$

8 $x = -\pi, -0.59, 0, 2.55$

7.5 Simplifying $a\cos x \pm b\sin x$

1 a $R = 29$, $\tan\alpha = \frac{21}{20}$

b $R = \sqrt{8} = 2\sqrt{2}$, $\tan\alpha = \frac{\sqrt{5}}{\sqrt{3}}$

c $R = \sqrt{13}$, $\tan\alpha = \frac{3}{2}$

2 a $R = \sqrt{5}$, $\alpha = 63.4°$ b $R = 13$, $\alpha = 22.6°$

c $R = 2\sqrt{5}$, $\alpha = 26.6°$

3 a i $2\sin\left(\theta - \frac{\pi}{6}\right)$

ii
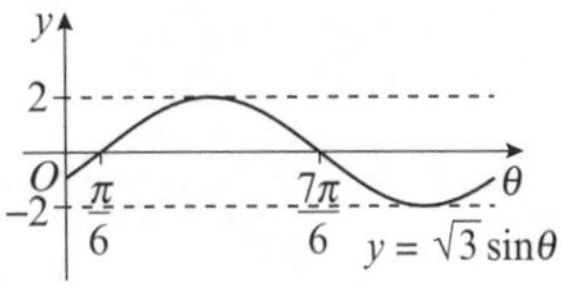

b i $4\cos\left(\theta + \frac{\pi}{3}\right)$

ii
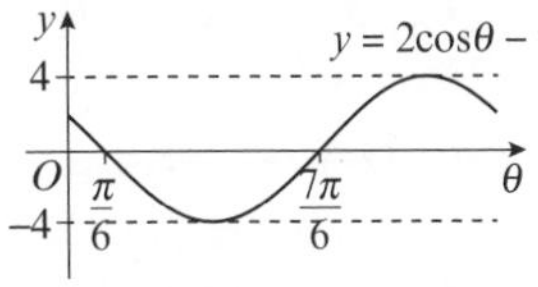

c i $\sqrt{8}\sin\left(\theta + \frac{\pi}{4}\right)$

ii
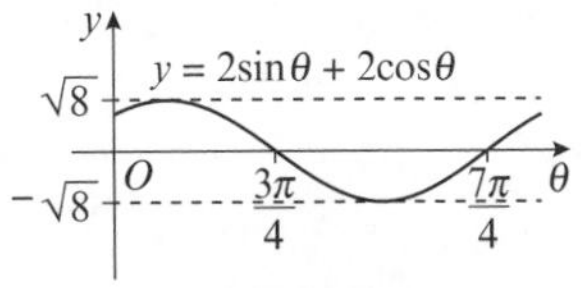

4 a $R = \sqrt{20} = 2\sqrt{5}$, $\alpha = 63.43°$

b $\theta = 74.4°, 338.7°$

5 a $\sqrt{13}\cos(2\theta - 0.588)$

b $\theta = -2.20, -0.35, 0.94, 2.79$

c $k < -\sqrt{13}$, $k > \sqrt{13}$

6 a $17\sin(\theta - 1.08)$

b i $\frac{5}{3}$ ii $\theta = 5.79$

c i $\frac{1}{4}$ ii $\theta = 2.65$

7 a $2\sin\left(x - \frac{\pi}{6}\right) - (\sqrt{3} - 2)\sin x$

$= 2\left(\frac{\sqrt{3}}{2}\sin x - \frac{1}{2}\cos x\right) - \sqrt{3}\sin x + 2\sin x$

$= 2\sin x - \cos x$

b $x = -2.90, 0.69, 3.38$ c 25

7.6 Proving trigonometric identities

1 a $\frac{\sin 2x - \tan x}{\tan x} \equiv \dfrac{2\sin x\cos x}{\frac{\sin x}{\cos x}} - 1 \equiv 2\cos^2 x - 1 \equiv \cos 2x$

b $\frac{\sin 6\theta}{1 - \cos 6\theta} \equiv \frac{2\sin 3\theta\cos 3\theta}{1 - (1 - 2\sin^2 3\theta)}$

$\equiv \frac{2\sin 3\theta\cos 3\theta}{2\sin^2 3\theta} \equiv \frac{\cos 3\theta}{\sin 3\theta} \equiv \cot 3\theta$

c $\frac{1}{4}\sec x \tan 2x \equiv \sec x \frac{2\tan x}{4(1 - \tan^2 x)} \equiv \frac{\sec x \tan x}{2(1 - \tan^2 x)}$

$\equiv \dfrac{\frac{1}{\cos x} \times \frac{\sin x}{\cos x}}{2\left(1 - \frac{\sin^2 x}{\cos^2 x}\right)} \equiv \dfrac{\frac{\sin x}{\cos^2 x}}{2\left(\frac{\cos^2 x - \sin^2 x}{\cos^2 x}\right)}$

$\equiv \frac{\sin x}{2(\cos^2 x - \sin^2 x)} \equiv \frac{1}{2}\sec 2x \sin x$

2 **a** $\cos(x - 30°) - \cos(x + 30°)$

$\equiv (\cos x \cos 30° + \sin x \sin 30°) - (\cos x \cos 30° - \sin x \sin 30°)$

$\equiv \left(\frac{\sqrt{3}}{2}\cos x + \frac{1}{2}\sin x\right) - \left(\frac{\sqrt{3}}{2}\cos x - \frac{1}{2}\sin x\right) \equiv \sin x$

b $\frac{\sin(a+b)}{\sin(a-b)} \equiv \frac{\sin a \cos b + \cos a \sin b}{\sin a \cos b - \cos a \sin b}$

$\equiv \frac{\frac{\sin a \cos b}{\sin a \sin b} + \frac{\cos a \sin b}{\sin a \sin b}}{\frac{\sin a \cos b}{\sin a \sin b} - \frac{\cos a \sin b}{\sin a \sin b}} \equiv \frac{\cot b + \cot a}{\cot b - \cot a}$

c $\cot\left(\frac{\pi}{4} - \theta\right) \equiv \frac{1 + \tan\frac{\pi}{4}\tan\theta}{\tan\frac{\pi}{4} - \tan\theta} \equiv \frac{1 + \tan\theta}{1 - \tan\theta}$

$\equiv \frac{1 + \frac{\sin\theta}{\cos\theta}}{1 - \frac{\sin\theta}{\cos\theta}} \equiv \frac{\frac{\cos\theta + \sin\theta}{\cos\theta}}{\frac{\cos\theta - \sin\theta}{\cos\theta}} \equiv \frac{\cos\theta + \sin\theta}{\cos\theta - \sin\theta}$

3 **a** $2\sin\left(3\theta + \frac{\pi}{3}\right) \equiv 2\sin 3\theta \cos\frac{\pi}{3} + 2\cos 3\theta \sin\frac{\pi}{3}$

$\equiv \left(2 \times \frac{1}{2}\right)\sin 3\theta + \left(2 \times \frac{\sqrt{3}}{2}\right)\cos 3\theta$

$\equiv \sin 3\theta + \sqrt{3}\cos 3\theta$

b $\cos 3A \equiv \cos(2A + A) \equiv \cos 2A \cos A - \sin 2A \sin A$

$\equiv (2\cos^2 A - 1)\cos A - (2\sin A \cos A)\sin A$

$\equiv 2\cos^3 A - \cos A - 2\sin^2 A \cos A$

$\equiv 2\cos^3 A - \cos A - 2(1 - \cos^2 A)\cos A$

$\equiv 2\cos^3 A - \cos A - 2\cos A + 2\cos^3 A$

$\equiv 4\cos^3 A - 3\cos A$

c $\cot 2x + \tan x \equiv \frac{\cos 2x}{\sin 2x} + \frac{\sin x}{\cos x}$

$\equiv \frac{\cos 2x \cos x + \sin x \sin 2x}{\sin 2x \cos x}$

$\equiv \frac{\cos(2x - x)}{\sin 2x \cos x} \equiv \frac{\cos x}{\sin 2x \cos x}$

$\equiv \operatorname{cosec} 2x$

4 $\sqrt{3}\cos x - \sin x \equiv 2\cos 30° \cos x - 2\sin 30° \sin x$

$\equiv 2\cos(x + 30°)$

5 **a** $\frac{\sin 2x}{1 + \cos 2x} \equiv \frac{2\sin x \cos x}{1 + (2\cos^2 x - 1)} \equiv \frac{\sin x}{\cos x} \equiv \tan x$

b $\sqrt{3}$

6 $2\sin\left(2\theta - \frac{\pi}{4}\right) \equiv 2\sin 2\theta \cos\frac{\pi}{4} - 2\cos 2\theta \sin\frac{\pi}{4}$

$\equiv \sqrt{2}\sin 2\theta - \sqrt{2}\cos 2\theta$

$\equiv \sqrt{2}(2\sin\theta\cos\theta) - \sqrt{2}(1 - 2\sin^2\theta)$

$\equiv 2\sqrt{2}\sin\theta\cos\theta - \sqrt{2} + 2\sqrt{2}\sin^2\theta$

7 **a** $\cos^4 x - \sin^4 x \equiv (\cos^2 x + \sin^2 x)(\cos^2 x - \sin^2 x)$

$\equiv 1 \times \cos 2x \equiv \cos 2x$

b $\frac{1}{2}$

7.7 Modelling with trigonometric functions

1 **a** 0.6 m **b** 0.75 seconds **c** 20

d A body moving in the air is better modelled by a parabola.

2 **a** 40.5 cm **b** 43 cm

c 0.5, 2.5, 4.5 seconds

d Minimum depth of water is 38 cm, so pond is not deep enough.

3 **a** 130 mm Hg **b** 80 mm Hg **c** 105 mm Hg

d 0.03, 0.37, 0.83, 1.17, 1.63, 1.97 seconds

4 **a** 9000 in April **b** March, April and May

c 4760 toys **d** This is extrapolation, so he may not be correct.

5 **a** $5\cos(\theta + 45°)$

b **i** −5 **ii** 135°

c 14 m at 04:30 **d** 4 m at 22:30

e **i** 01:30 **ii** 07:30

6 **a** $\frac{\sqrt{65}}{20}\cos(x - 1.1)$ **b** 30.25 °C

c 0.8 °C **d** 0.6 minutes, 3.7 minutes, 6.8 minutes

7 **a** $12\sqrt{157}\sin(x - 0.5)$ **b** 350p in March

c 50p during July **d** June

e £2400 profit

Problem solving: Set A

B **a** $a = 100$, $b = 20$

b $c = 360$; $y = 100 + 20\sin(360x)°$

S **a** $y = 12 + 4\sin(x - 90°)$

b Vertical stretch with scale factor 4, translation by $\begin{pmatrix} 90 \\ 12 \end{pmatrix}$

c 120 days

G **a** $y = 12 + 10\cos(2t - 180°)$

b $y = 12 + 10\cos\left(\frac{5}{2}t - 180°\right)$

c Revathi is correct.

Problem solving: Set B

B **a** $13\sin(2x - 0.395)$

b $12 - 3\operatorname{cosec} 2x = 5\cot 2x \Rightarrow 12 - \frac{3}{\sin 2x} = \frac{5\cos 2x}{\sin 2x}$

$\Rightarrow 12\sin 2x - 5\cos 2x = 3$

c $x = 0.3, 1.7, 3.5, 4.8$

S **a** $5\cos 2x - 4\sin 2x + 2$

b $x = 0.29, 2.18, 3.43, 5.32$

c **i** $10\cos^2 x - 8\sin x \cos x$

$= 10\left(\frac{1 + \cos 2x}{2}\right) - 4(2\sin x \cos x)$

$= 5\cos 2x - 4\sin 2x + 5$

ii $5 + \sqrt{41}$

G **a** $\cos 2x(15\sin 2x - 8\cos 2x - 4)$

b $x = 0.36, 0.79, 1.70, 2.36$ **c** $\frac{1}{9}$

CHAPTER 8

8.1 Parametric equations

1 **a** $y = (x + 3)^2 - 1$, $-6 \leqslant x \leqslant 0$, $-1 \leqslant y \leqslant 8$

b $y = \frac{4}{x^2} + 1$, $x > 0$, $y > 1$

c $y = \frac{12}{(x + 1)^2}$, $x \geqslant 1$, $0 < y \leqslant 3$

2 **a** $y = \frac{1}{e^x + 1}$, $x > 0$, $0 < y < \frac{1}{2}$

b $y = e^{2x} + 2e^x + 1$, $x > 0$, $y > 4$

c $y = x^3 + 2x^2$, $x > 0$, $y > 0$

3 **a** **i** $y = 2x + 5$ **ii** $1 < x \leqslant 5$, $7 < y \leqslant 15$

iii

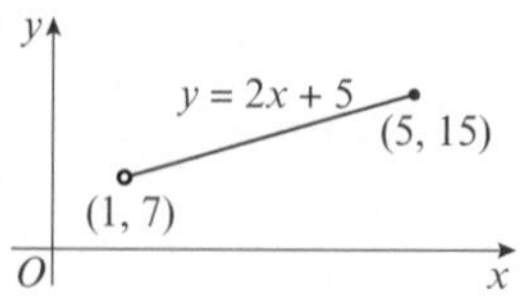

b **i** $y = x^2 + 5x + 6$

ii $-5 \leqslant x \leqslant 1,\ -\frac{1}{4} \leqslant y \leqslant 12$

iii

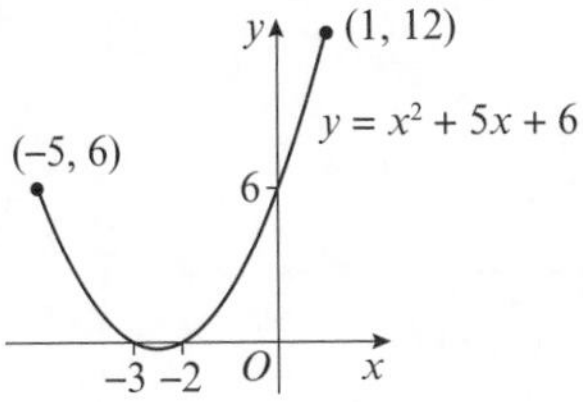

c **i** $y = e^x + 3$ **ii** $x > 0,\ y > 4$

iii

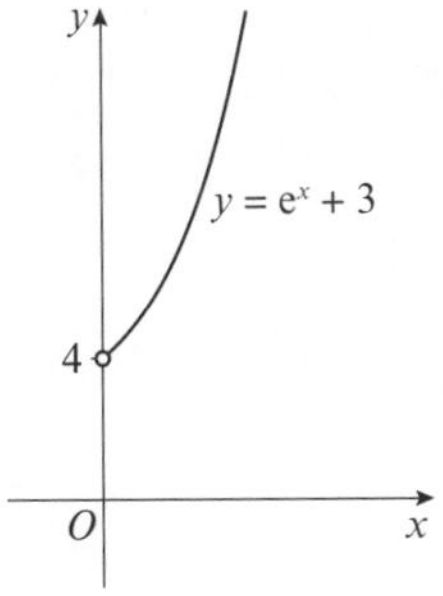

4 **a** $y = 9 - \frac{10}{3}x + \frac{1}{9}x^2,\ 0 \leqslant x \leqslant 24,\ -16 \leqslant y \leqslant 9$

b

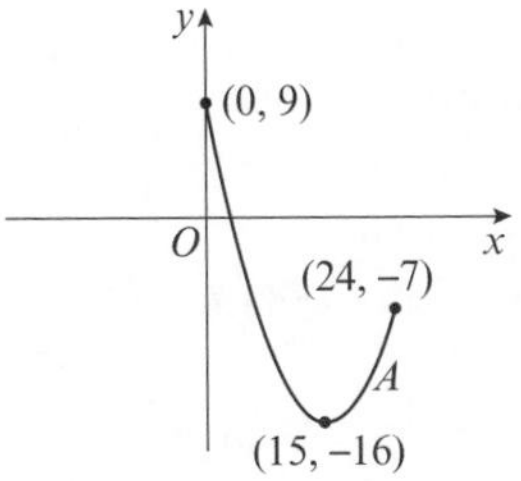

5 **a** $y = 2e^x + 2$ **b** $x = 0,\ y = 4$

6 **a** $y = x^3 - 2x^2 - 5x + 6 = (x + 2)(x - 1)(x - 3)$

b x-axis: $(-2, 0), (1, 0), (3, 0)$, y-axis: $(0, 6)$

7 **a** $C_1: x = 5t^2, y = 3t^2 + 2,$

$\Rightarrow y = 3\left(\frac{x}{5}\right) + 2 \Rightarrow y = \frac{3}{5}x + 2$

C_1 is a straight line, gradient $\frac{3}{5}$

$C_2: x = 3\sqrt{t} - 3, y = 9 - 5\sqrt{t},$

$\Rightarrow y = 9 - 5\left(\frac{x+3}{3}\right) \Rightarrow y = 4 - \frac{5}{3}x$

C_2 is a straight line, gradient $-\frac{5}{3}$

$\frac{3}{5} \times -\frac{5}{3} = -1$, therefore the line segments are perpendicular.

b C_1: $4\sqrt{34}$, C_2: $2\sqrt{34}$

8 $y^2 = x^3$

8.2 Using trigonometric identities

1 **a** $(x + 1)^2 + (y - 3)^2 = 1$ **b** $\frac{x^2}{4} + \frac{y^2}{9} = 1$

c $(x - 2)^2 + (y - 5)^2 = 4$

2 **a** $y = 1 - 2x^2$ **b** $\frac{x^2}{16} - \frac{y^2}{4} = 1$

c $y = 4x^2 - 4x^4$

3 **a** **i** $(x - 3)^2 + (y + 4)^2 = 1$

ii

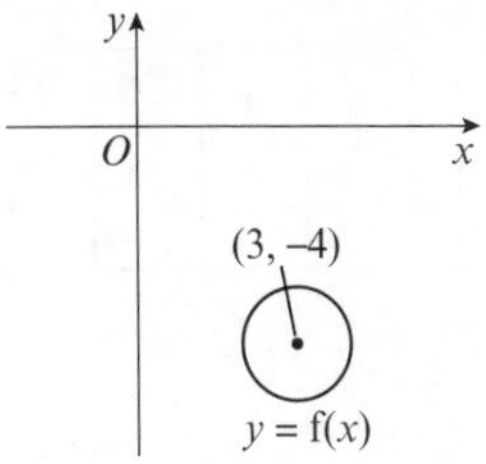

b **i** $y = x^2 - 4$

ii

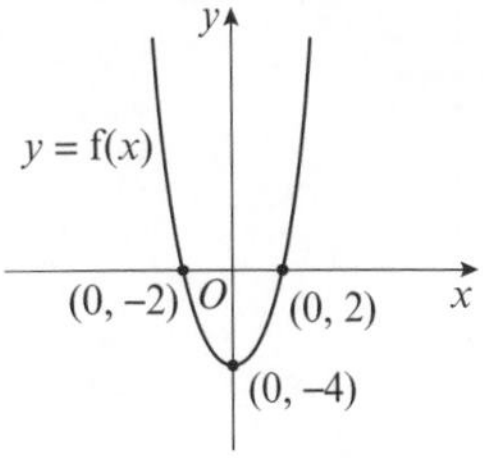

c **i** $y = \frac{20}{x^2}$

ii

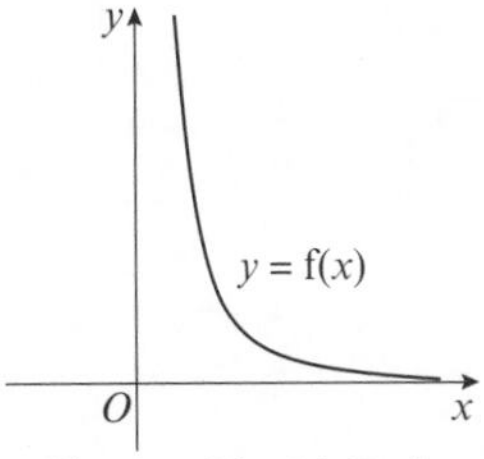

4 **a** $(x - 5)^2 + (y + 2)^2 = 36$. Radius = 6, centre $(5, -2)$

b π

5 **a** $y = \frac{10}{x - 5}$ **b** $x > 0$

6 $x = 2\sin t \Rightarrow \frac{x}{2} = \sin t \Rightarrow \frac{x^2}{4} = \sin^2 t$

$y = \cos\left(t + \frac{\pi}{3}\right) \Rightarrow y = \frac{1}{2}\cos t - \frac{\sqrt{3}}{2}\sin t$

$\Rightarrow y = \frac{1}{2}\sqrt{1 - \sin^2 t} - \frac{\sqrt{3}}{2}\left(\frac{x}{2}\right)$

$\Rightarrow y = \frac{1}{2}\sqrt{1 - \frac{x^2}{4}} - \frac{\sqrt{3}x}{4}$

$\Rightarrow y = \frac{1}{2} \times \frac{\sqrt{4 - x^2}}{2} - \frac{\sqrt{3}x}{4}$

$\Rightarrow y = \frac{1}{4}(\sqrt{4 - x^2} - \sqrt{3}x),\ -2 < x < 2$

7 **a** $y = 3\sqrt{\frac{x-3}{x-2}}$ **b** $x > 3, 0 < y < 3$

8.3 Curve sketching

1

t	−2	−1.5	−1	−0.5	0	0.5	1	1.5	2	2.5	3
$x = 2t + 2$	−2	−1	0	1	2	3	4	5	6	7	8
$y = t^2$	4	2.25	1	0.25	0	0.25	1	2.25	4	6.25	9

$x = 2t + 2,\ y = t^2,\ -2 \leqslant t \leqslant 3$

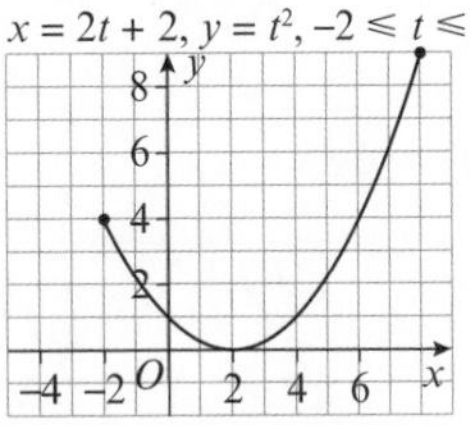

2

t	0	$\frac{\pi}{4}$	$\frac{\pi}{2}$	$\frac{3\pi}{4}$	π	$\frac{5\pi}{4}$	$\frac{3\pi}{2}$	$\frac{7\pi}{4}$	2π
$x = 3\sin t$	0	2.12	3	2.12	0	−2.12	−3	−2.12	0
$y = 5\cos t$	5	3.54	0	−3.54	−5	−3.54	0	3.54	5

$x = 3\sin t,\ y = 5\cos t,\ 0 \leqslant t \leqslant 2\pi$

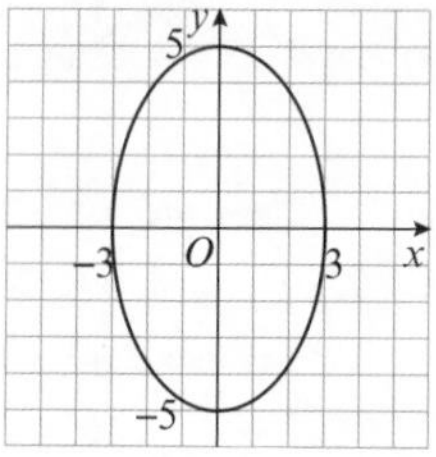

3 a $x = 2t^2,\ y = 4t,\ -2 \leqslant t \leqslant 2$

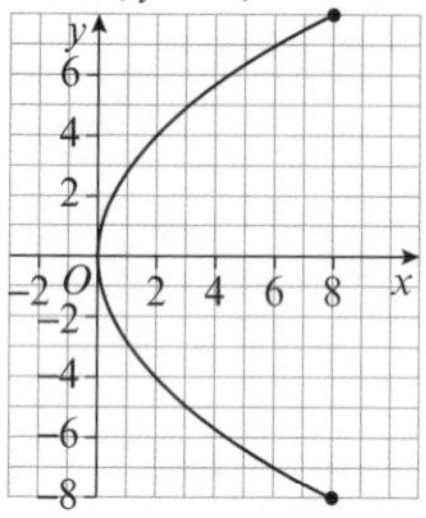

b $x = 3\text{cosec}\ t,\ y = 3\cot t,\ 0 \leqslant t \leqslant 2\pi$

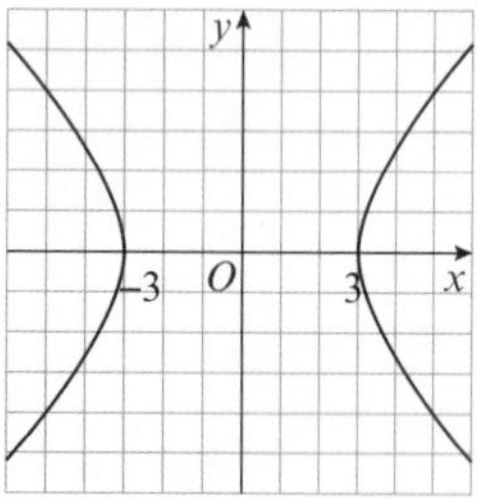

c $x = t + 5,\ y = \frac{1}{t},\ 0 \leqslant t \leqslant 8$

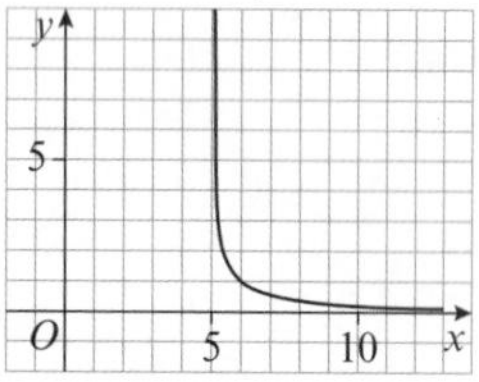

4 a C_1: $y = 2.5 - 0.5x, 1 \leqslant x \leqslant 5$

C_2: $y = 2x, 1 \leqslant x \leqslant 3,$

C_3: $y = 15 - 3x, 3 \leqslant x \leqslant 5$

b

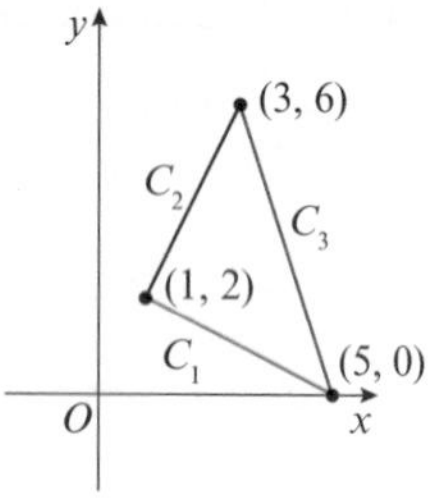

c 10

5 a $y = (2 - x)(x + 3),\ -3 \leqslant x \leqslant 3$

b

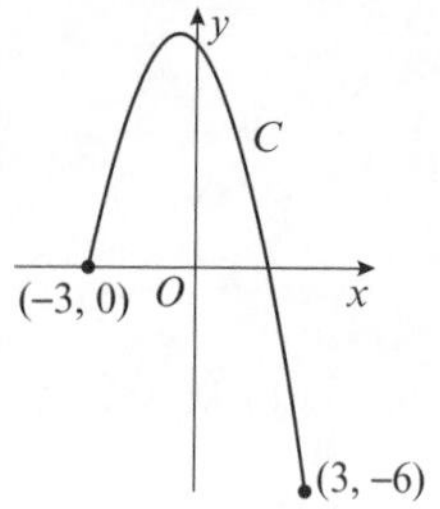

6 a $(x - 3)^2 + (y + 2)^2 = 100$

b

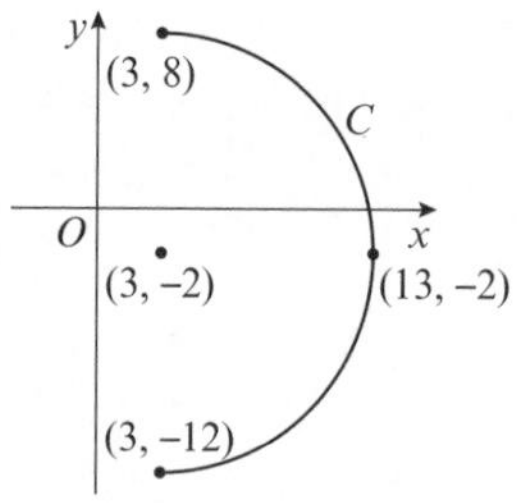

c 10π

8.4 Points of intersection

1 a (−7, 0), (0, 7) b (−6, 0), (3, 0), (0, −6)

c (−2, 0), (30, 0), (0, −3), (0, 5)

2 a (1, 0), (0, 2) b $(-\pi, 0), (\pi, 0), (0, 1)$

c $(\sqrt{2} - 3, 0), (0, 7)$

3 a $t = -1, t = -6$ b (0, 2), (−5, −3)

4 a 3 b $\frac{1}{2}$

5 a $t = 0$ and $t = \ln 3$ b (1, 0), (9, 8)

6 a (0, 1) and (−1, 1)

b Curve will intersect x-axis when $y = 0$

$t = \frac{7\pi}{12}: y = 2\sin\left(2\left(\frac{7\pi}{12}\right)\right) + 1 = 0$

$t = \frac{11\pi}{12}: y = 2\sin\left(2\left(\frac{11\pi}{12}\right)\right) + 1 = 0$

c $\left(-\frac{\sqrt{6} + \sqrt{2}}{4}, 0\right), \left(\frac{\sqrt{2} - \sqrt{6}}{4}, 0\right)$

7 $3y - 2\sqrt{3}x - 8\sqrt{3} = 0$

8 a $y = x - \ln 18$

$\Rightarrow \ln(t - 1) = 2\ln(t + 2) - \ln 18$

$\Rightarrow t - 1 = \frac{(t + 2)^2}{18} \Rightarrow t^2 - 14t + 22 = 0$

$\Rightarrow t = 7 \pm 3\sqrt{3}$

b $(\ln(9 + 3\sqrt{3}), \ln(6 + 3\sqrt{3})), (\ln(9 - 3\sqrt{3}), \ln(6 - 3\sqrt{3}))$

8.5 Modelling with parametric equations

1 a 167 seconds (3 s.f.)

b $y = 2.7 \times \frac{x}{3.6} = 0.75x$ which is a straight line.

c 750 m d $4.5\,\text{m s}^{-1}$

e i The path of the skier is unlikely to follow $y = 0.75x$.

ii The speed of the ski lift is unlikely to be constant.

2 **a** 15 m

b $16 - 7.6 \times \frac{17}{8} - \cos 17 = 0.125 = 12.5$ cm (3 s.f.)

c 17 m

3 **a** 2.59 seconds (3 s.f.) **b** $k = 4.91$ (3 s.f.)

c $x = 9\sqrt{2}\,t \Rightarrow t = \frac{x}{9\sqrt{2}}$

$y = -4.9\left(\frac{x}{9\sqrt{2}}\right)^2 + 9\sqrt{2}\left(\frac{x}{9\sqrt{2}}\right)$

$= -\frac{4.9}{162}x^2 + x$

4 **a** 0.429 seconds (3 s.f.) **b** 2.4 m

c $0.8\text{m} < x < 1.6\text{m}$

5 **a** 7.45 cm (3 s.f.) **b** 17.7 cm (3 s.f.) **c** 8 cm

6 **a** $t = x - 5$, so $y = 5(x - 5) - 2 = 5x - 27$ which is the equation of a straight line.

b $\left(\frac{39}{5}, 12\right)$

c Disagree; particles pass through point at different times.

7 **a** 391 m (3 s.f.) **b** 187 m, 578 m (3 s.f.)

c 31 minutes

8 **a** 20 m **b** $k = \pi$, gradient = 0.615

Problem solving: Set A

B **a** **i** $y = 5\sin 2t = 10\sin t\cos t = x\cos t$

ii $\frac{x}{10} = \sin t, \frac{y}{x} = \cos t \Rightarrow \left(\frac{x}{10}\right)^2 + \left(\frac{y}{x}\right)^2 = 1$

$\Rightarrow 100(y^2 - x^2) + x^4 = 0$

b **i** $(5\sqrt{2}, 5)$

ii $k = 5 - 5\sqrt{2}$

S **a** $y = 4\cos\left(t + \frac{\pi}{3}\right) = 2\cos t - 2\sqrt{3}\sin t$

$= 2\cos t - 2\sqrt{3}\left(\frac{\sqrt{3}}{2}x\right) \Rightarrow y = 2\cos t - 3x$

$\Rightarrow \frac{3x + y}{2} = \cos t$

So $\left(\frac{\sqrt{3}}{2}x\right)^2 + \left(\frac{3x + y}{2}\right)^2 = 1 \Rightarrow (3x + y)^2 + 3x^2 - 4 = 0$

b **i** $t = \frac{\pi}{6} : \left(\frac{\sqrt{3}}{3}, 0\right), t = \frac{\pi}{2} : \left(\frac{2\sqrt{3}}{3}, -2\sqrt{3}\right)$

So gradient of line is $\dfrac{-2\sqrt{3}}{\frac{2\sqrt{3}}{3} - \frac{\sqrt{3}}{3}} = -6$

ii $6x + y - 2\sqrt{3} = 0$

G **a** $y = 2\sin t + \sin 2t = 2\sin t + 2\sin t\cos t$

$= 2\sin t + 2\sin t\left(\frac{x - 2}{2}\right) = x\sin t \Rightarrow \frac{y}{x} = \sin t$

$\Rightarrow \frac{y^2}{x^2} + \frac{(x - 2)^2}{4} = 1 \Rightarrow y^2 = x^3\left(1 - \frac{1}{4}x\right), 2 - \sqrt{2} \leqslant x \leqslant 4$

b $3 + 2\sqrt{2}$ **c** $\{q : 1 \leqslant q \leqslant 3 + 2\sqrt{2}\}$

Problem solving: Set B

B **a** 6.17, 19.1 (3 s.f.)

b $t = \frac{x}{7.6}$

$y = -4.9\left(\frac{x}{7.6}\right)^2 + 16.3\left(\frac{x}{7.6}\right) = -\frac{245}{2888}x^2 + \frac{163}{76}x$

Height = 13.6 m (3 s.f.)

S **a** 32.1 m **b** $(0, -16)$ **c** 1.57 minutes

G **a** $\ln\frac{9765625}{16}$ **b** -0.675

CHAPTER 9

9.1 Differentiating sin x and cos x

1 **a** $6\cos x$ **b** $-\frac{3}{2}\cos\frac{1}{2}x$ **c** $\frac{5}{3}\cos 5x$

d $-4\sin 4x$ **e** $-30\sin 6x$ **f** $\frac{7}{2}\sin 7x$

2 **a** $4\cos x + 3\sin x$ **b** $\cos 2x - 4\sin x - \frac{3}{2}\cos\frac{1}{4}x$

c $\frac{15x^{\frac{1}{2}}}{2} + \frac{8}{x^3} - 2\cos\frac{1}{3}x$ **d** $-\frac{4}{x^{\frac{3}{2}}} - \frac{1}{2}\sin\frac{1}{6}x$

3 $x = -59.0°, 121.0°$

4 $y = 3x - \frac{\pi}{2}$

5 $\left(\frac{\pi}{2}, 9\right), \left(\frac{7\pi}{6}, -\frac{9}{2}\right), \left(\frac{3\pi}{2}, -3\right), \left(\frac{11\pi}{6}, -\frac{9}{2}\right)$

6 $y = -\frac{1}{12}x + \frac{\pi}{12} - 4$

7 $h\left(\frac{\pi}{2}\right) = \frac{24 + \pi^2}{8}$; $h'(x) = 3\cos x + 4\sin x + x$; $h'\left(\frac{\pi}{2}\right) = \frac{8 + \pi}{2}$

Then use the formula $y - h\left(\frac{\pi}{2}\right) = h'\left(\frac{\pi}{2}\right)\left(x - \frac{\pi}{2}\right)$ to find the equation of the tangent.

8 $f'(x) = \lim\limits_{h\to 0}\frac{f(x + h) - f(x)}{h} = \lim\limits_{h\to 0}\frac{\cos(x + h) - \cos x}{h}$

$= \lim\limits_{h\to 0}\frac{\cos x\cos h - \sin x\sin h - \cos x}{h}$

$= \lim\limits_{h\to 0}\left(\left(\frac{\cos h - 1}{h}\right)\cos x - \left(\frac{\sin h}{h}\right)\sin x\right)$

Since $\frac{\cos h - 1}{h} \to 0$ and $\frac{\sin h}{h} \to 1$ the expression inside the limit tends to $(0 \times \cos x - 1 \times \sin x)$

So $\lim\limits_{h\to 0}\frac{\cos(x + h) - \cos x}{h} = -\sin x$

Hence the derivative of $\cos x$ is $-\sin x$.

9.2 Differentiating exponentials and logarithms

1 **a** $-18e^{-3x}$ **b** $10e^{2x} + 7e^{-x}$

c $-\frac{35}{e^{5x}}$ **d** $2e^{2x} - 2e^{-2x}$

2 **a** $\frac{1}{x}$ **b** $\frac{2}{x}$ **c** $-\frac{1}{x}$ **d** $\frac{3}{x}$

3 **a** $3^x\ln 3$ **b** $5^{2x}(2\ln 5)$

c $\left(\frac{2}{5}\right)^{4x}\left(4\ln\frac{2}{5}\right)$ **d** $-\frac{\ln 8}{8^x}$

4 $y = x\ln 2 + \frac{1}{2}(1 + \ln 2)$

5 $-e^{-x} + \frac{6}{x}$

6 $x = 1, y = 3e, \frac{dy}{dx} = 3e - 2$

Rearrange $y - 3e = -\frac{1}{3e - 2}(x - 1)$ to obtain

$x + (3e - 2)y - 9e^2 + 6e - 1 = 0$

7 $x = \frac{1}{2}, y = \frac{5}{2}, \frac{dy}{dx} = \frac{1}{2}\ln\frac{1}{4} + 2\ln 4 = \ln 8$

Rearrange $y - \frac{5}{2} = (\ln 8)\left(x - \frac{1}{2}\right)$ to obtain

$y = (\ln 8)x + \frac{5}{2} - \frac{1}{2}\ln 8$

8 **a** $f(x) = 9^{3x} + 3^{6x} = (3^2)^{3x} + 3^{6x} = 3^{6x} + 3^{6x} = 2(3^{6x})$

b $f'(x) = 2(3^{6x} \times 6 \times \ln 3) = (4\ln 3)(3 \times 3^{6x}) = (4\ln 3)(3^{6x+1})$

9.3 The chain rule

1 **a** $-9(4 - 3x)^2$ **b** $\frac{5}{2}(6 + 5x)^{-\frac{1}{2}}$

c $24x^2(5 + 2x^3)^3$ **d** $-30x(7 + 3x^2)^{-6}$

e $\frac{15}{(4-5x)^{\frac{3}{2}}}$ f $\frac{1}{(6-x)^2}$

g $\frac{8}{3}x^3(3+2x^4)^{-\frac{2}{3}}$ h $\frac{21}{2}x^2(7x^3-4)^{-\frac{1}{2}}$

2 a $3\sin^2 x\cos x$ b $\frac{4}{x}$

c $(-4\sin 4x)e^{\cos 4x}$ d $\frac{2\ln x}{x}$

e $-\tan x$ f $-3e^{-3x}\cos(e^{-3x})$

3 a $-\frac{2}{x}(3-\ln 6x)$ b $-\frac{12}{e^2}$

4 $\frac{1}{20}$

5 $x+10y-12=0$

6 $9x-16y-30=0$

7 $Q\left(-\frac{5\pi}{6}, -\frac{3}{4}\right)$, $\frac{dy}{dx}=10\sin x\cos x$

Simplify $y+\frac{3}{4}=\frac{5\sqrt{3}}{2}\left(x+\frac{5\pi}{6}\right)$ to obtain

$12y-30\sqrt{3}x-25\pi\sqrt{3}+9=0$

8 $A\left(-\sqrt{3}, \frac{2\pi}{3}\right)$, $\frac{dy}{dx}=-\frac{1}{8\cos 4y}$

Simplify $y-\frac{2\pi}{3}=-4(x+\sqrt{3})$ to obtain $4x+y+4\sqrt{3}-\frac{2\pi}{3}=0$

9 $(8\ln 2)x+y+8\ln 2-2=0$

9.4 The product rule

1 a $(4-5x)^3-15x(4-5x)^2$

b $9x^2(2x-1)^6+36x^3(2x-1)^5$

c $\frac{96}{x^2}(6x-7)^3-\frac{8}{x^3}(6x-7)^4$

d $16x(2x^3-4)^{-3}-144x^4(2x^3-4)^{-4}$

2 a $2x\cos 2x-2x^2\sin 2x$

b $3e^{3x}\sin 5x+5e^{3x}\cos 5x$

c $-e^{-x}(2x^2+3)^3+12xe^{-x}(2x^2+3)^2$

d $-6\cos 4x\cos 2x+12\sin 4x\sin 2x$

e $x+2x\ln x$

f $4e^{4x}\ln(\cos 3x)+3e^{4x}\tan 3x$

3 76

4 a $-2xe^{-2x}(x^3-2x^2-3x+3)$

b $12e^{3x}\cos 2x-8e^{3x}\sin 2x-3e^{3x}\sin x-e^{3x}\cos x$

c $2x\ln 4x+x-\frac{5}{x}\cos\frac{1}{2}x+\frac{5}{2}(\ln 4x)\sin\frac{1}{2}x$

5 a $-e^{-x}\cos 3x-3e^{-x}\sin 3x$ b $4x^3\ln(\sin x)+x^4\cot x$

6 a $\frac{dy}{dx}=x^3(2-5x^2)^2(-100x^2+16)$

$n=2$, $a=-100$, $b=0$ and $c=16$

b $x=0, \pm\sqrt{\frac{2}{5}}, \pm\frac{2}{5}$

7 a $f'(x)=e^{4x}(4\sin x+\cos x)=0$

$e^{4x}\neq 0$, so $4\sin x+\cos x=0 \Rightarrow \tan x=-\frac{1}{4}$

b $f\left(\frac{\pi}{2}\right)=e^{2\pi}, f'\left(\frac{\pi}{2}\right)=4e^{2\pi}$

Therefore the gradient of the normal is $-\frac{1}{4e^{2\pi}}$

Simplify $y-e^{2\pi}=-\frac{1}{4e^{2\pi}}\left(x-\frac{\pi}{2}\right)$ to obtain

$x+4e^{2\pi}y-4e^{4\pi}-\frac{\pi}{2}=0$

8 $\frac{dy}{dx}=\sin 2x+2(x-\pi)\cos 2x$

At $x=\frac{3\pi}{4}, y=\frac{\pi}{4}$ and $\frac{dy}{dx}=-1$

Simplify $y-\frac{\pi}{4}=-1\left(x-\frac{3\pi}{4}\right)$ to obtain $x+y=\pi$

9.5 The quotient rule

1 a $-\frac{42}{(2x-9)^2}$ b $\frac{6x(6-5x)}{(3-5x)^2}$

c $\frac{-8(3x^3+2)^2+18x^2(8x-1)(3x^3+2)}{(3x^3+2)^4}$

d $\frac{7x^3+84x-54}{(x^2+6)^{\frac{3}{2}}}$

2 a $\frac{8x(\cos 2x+x\sin 2x)}{\cos^2 2x}$

b $\frac{\ln x+e^{-x}\ln x+\frac{1}{x}e^{-x}-1}{(\ln x)^2}$

c $\frac{e^x(\cos x+2\sin x)}{\cos^3 x}$

d $\frac{e^{-x}\sin 4x-4(5-e^{-x})\cos 4x}{\sin^2 4x}$

3 $-\frac{34}{9}$

4 a $\frac{-2x^2+14x-6}{e^{2x}}$ b $y+\frac{5}{e^2}=-\frac{e^2}{6}(x-1)$

5 $\frac{2\sin x(\cos x-\sin x)}{e^{2x}}$

6 $\frac{e^{4x}(4x^2-22x+5)}{x^2(x-5)^2}$

7 $\sqrt{2}e^{\frac{\pi}{8}}x+3y-1-\frac{3\pi}{8}=0$

8 a $f'(x)=\frac{-2e^x\cos x\sin x-e^x\cos^2 x}{e^{2x}}$

$f'(x)=0 \Rightarrow -2e^x\cos x\sin x-e^x\cos^2 x=0$

Therefore $2\cos x\sin x+\cos^2 x=0$

Solve to obtain $\cos x=0$ or $\tan x=-\frac{1}{2}$

b A: $x=-1.57$; B: $x=-0.46$; C: $x=1.57$; D: $x=2.68$

9.6 Differentiating trigonometric functions

1 a $4\sec^2 4x$ b $-14\operatorname{cosec}^2 2x$

c $-5\cot^4 x\operatorname{cosec}^2 x$ d $-6\tan x\sec^2 x$

2 a $-6\operatorname{cosec} 6x\cot 6x$ b $-20\sec 5x\tan 5x$

c $-\frac{4}{3}(\operatorname{cosec} x)^{\frac{4}{3}}\cot x$ d $-24\sec^3 4x\tan 4x$

3 a $2x\tan 3x+3x^2\sec^2 3x$

b $\frac{(x^2+1)\sec x\tan x e^{\sec x}-2xe^{\sec x}}{(x^2+1)^2}$

c $-2\cot x$

d $-e^{-x}\cot 4x-4e^{-x}\operatorname{cosec}^2 4x$

e $\frac{\sec^2 x(2x\ln x\tan x-1)}{x(\ln x)^2}$

f $\frac{12(4x-1)^2\cot^2 x+2(4x-1)^3\cot x\operatorname{cosec}^2 x}{\cot^4 x}$

4 a $2\cos 2y$ b $\frac{1}{2\sqrt{1-x^2}}$

5 $y=\operatorname{cosec}x=\frac{1}{\sin x}$

$u=1, \frac{du}{dx}=0$; $v=\sin x, \frac{dv}{dx}=\cos x$

$\frac{dy}{dx}=\frac{\sin x\times 0-1\times\cos x}{\sin^2 x}=-\frac{1}{\sin x}\times\frac{\cos x}{\sin x}=-\operatorname{cosec}x\cot x$

6 a Use the chain rule to find $f'(x)=\frac{-2\operatorname{cosec}^2 2x}{\cot 2x}$ and then use trigonometric identities to obtain $f'(x)=-4\operatorname{cosec} 4x$

b $y=\frac{1}{4}x-\frac{\pi}{32}$

7 $\frac{5}{4}$

8 a $4\sec 4y \tan 4y$ b $\frac{1}{4x\sqrt{x^2-1}}$

9.7 Parametric differentiation

1 a $\frac{3t^2}{2}$ b $\frac{t^4}{2}$ c $\frac{e^{4t}+4te^{4t}}{3}$

d $\frac{5}{4}\sec^3 t$ e $\frac{1}{6e^{2t}}$ f $\frac{1}{6t^3}$

2 a $\sin t$ b $y = \frac{\sqrt{2}}{2}x + \frac{\sqrt{2}}{2}$

3 a $-\left(\frac{3t+4}{2}\right)$ b $2x + 5y + 61 = 0$

4 a $4\cot 2\theta$ b $(1, 4)$ and $(1, -4)$

5 a $-4\cos^3\theta$ b $y = 2x - 7$

6 $y = 2x + 28$

7 a $\frac{\operatorname{cosec}^2 t}{2\sec 2t \tan 2t}$

b $m = -\frac{\sqrt{3}}{3}$, simplify $y + 2\sqrt{3} = -\frac{\sqrt{3}}{3}(x+4)$ to obtain $x\sqrt{3} + 3y + 10\sqrt{3} = 0$

8 a $y = -\frac{25}{36}x + \frac{307}{540}$

b Rearrange parametric equation for x to $t = \frac{x}{x+1}$

Then $y = \frac{1}{1+\left(\frac{x}{x+1}\right)^2} = \frac{(x+1)^2}{(x+1)^2+x^2} = \frac{x^2+2x+1}{2x^2+2x+1}$

9.8 Implicit differentiation

1 $u = y^5, \frac{du}{dy} = 5y^4$

$\frac{d}{dx}(y^5) = \frac{du}{dx} = \frac{du}{dy} \times \frac{dy}{dx} = 5y^4\frac{dy}{dx}$

2 $\frac{d}{dx}(x^3y^2) = x^3\frac{d}{dx}(y^2) + \frac{d}{dx}(x^3)y^2$

$= x^3 \times 2y\frac{dy}{dx} + 3x^2y^2$

$= 2x^3y\frac{dy}{dx} + 3x^2y^2$

3 a $\frac{4x^3}{3y^2}$ b $\frac{6x-10xy}{5x^2-8y}$

c $\frac{2xy}{10y+3y^2-x^2}$ d $\frac{4y}{3(x-5)}$

e $\frac{\sin x}{2\sin y \cos y}$ f $\frac{2ye^{2x}+e^{-y}}{xe^{-y}-e^{2x}}$

4 a $\frac{8xy-2x}{2y-4x^2}$ b $\frac{10}{9}$

c $y = \frac{10}{9}x - \frac{29}{9}$

5 $\frac{7}{13}$

6 $\frac{2e^{-2x}-4y}{4x+3e^{-3y}}$

7 a $\frac{\sin 2x}{\cos 2y}$ b $x + 2y = 0$

8 $x + y + \frac{\pi}{12} = 0$

9.9 Using second derivatives

1 a $-e^{-x}\cos 2x - 2e^{-x}\sin 2x$ b $e^{-x}(4\sin 2x - 3\cos 2x)$

2 a $16 + 48e^{4x}$

b $16 \geqslant 0$ and $48e^{4x} \geqslant 0$ for all values of x, hence $f(x)$ is convex for all values of x.

3 a $-4\cos 2x$

b $-\frac{\pi}{2} \leqslant x \leqslant -\frac{\pi}{4}$ and $\frac{\pi}{4} \leqslant x \leqslant \frac{\pi}{2}$

4 a $f'(x) = (2x-1)^5 + 10x(2x-1)^4$

$f''(x) = 20(2x-1)^3(6x-1)$

b $f''\left(\frac{1}{2}\right) = 20 \times 0^3 \times 2 = 0$

$f''\left(\frac{1}{6}\right) = 20 \times \left(-\frac{2}{3}\right)^3 \times 0 = 0$

c $f''(0.1) = 4.096 > 0$ $f''(0.2) = -0.864 < 0$

As there is a sign change, this confirms there is a point of inflection at $x = \frac{1}{6}$

5 $x \geqslant \frac{8}{3}$

6 a $f'(x) = (2x-5)^4 + 8x(2x-5)^3$

$f''(x) = 16(2x-5)^3 + 48x(2x-5)^2$

b $f''(1) = 0$ and $f''(0.95) = -15.376 < 0$ and $f''(1.05) = 13.456 > 0$

So there is a point of inflection at $x = 1$

7 $0.55 \leqslant x \leqslant \frac{\pi}{4}$

8 $x \leqslant -3-\sqrt{3}$ and $-3+\sqrt{3} \leqslant x \leqslant 0$

9.10 Rates of change

1 a $8x$ b 24

2 $\frac{3}{4\sqrt{2}}(5\pi - 4)$

3 $-\frac{3e^8}{64}$

4 a $4\pi r^2$ b $12\pi r^2$

5 a $\frac{dP}{dt} = kP$

b The value of the constant k would be negative, or $\frac{dP}{dt} = -kP$

6 $\frac{dI}{dt} = -k\sqrt{I}$

7 a £4083.69 b Decreasing by £482.25 per year

8 a Substitute $r = \left(\frac{S}{4\pi}\right)^{\frac{1}{2}}$ into $V = \frac{4}{3}\pi r^3$ and simplify.

b $\frac{dV}{dS} = \frac{1}{4}\sqrt{\frac{S}{\pi}}, \frac{dV}{dt} = \frac{dV}{dS} \times \frac{dS}{dt} = \frac{1}{4}\sqrt{\frac{S}{\pi}} \times 4 = \sqrt{\frac{S}{\pi}}$

Problem solving: Set A

B a $\frac{dy}{dx} = 4x^3 - 20x^2 + 28x + 6$

$\frac{d^2y}{dx^2} = 12x^2 - 40x + 28$

b $\frac{d^2y}{dx^2} = 12x^2 - 40x + 28 = 4(x-1)(3x-7)$

For $1 \leqslant x \leqslant \frac{7}{3}$, $x - 1 \geqslant 0$ and $3x - 7 \leqslant 0$

Hence $\frac{d^2y}{dx^2} \leqslant 0$ and the curve is concave.

S $\frac{d^2y}{dx^2} = 24x\ln x^2 + 40x = 8x(3\ln x^2 + 5)$

When $x > 0$, $8x > 0$. So solve $3\ln x^2 + 5 \geqslant 0$,to get $x \geqslant e^{-\frac{5}{6}}$

Hence $\frac{d^2y}{dx^2} \geqslant 0$ when $x \geqslant e^{-\frac{5}{6}}$ and the curve is convex.

G $a \geqslant \frac{1}{2}$

Problem solving: Set B

B a $\frac{2x+y-1}{1-x}$ b $y = -x + 2$

S **a** $(x+1)^2 + (y-3)^2 = 4$; centre $(-1, 3)$ and radius 2

b $2\sin t - 1 = 0 \Rightarrow t = \frac{\pi}{6}, \frac{5\pi}{6}$

$y = 3 + \sqrt{3}$ or $y = 3 - \sqrt{3}$, therefore $y = 3 + \sqrt{3}$ at B

c $3 + 2\sqrt{3}$

G $y = x + \frac{\pi}{6}$ and $y = x - \frac{7\pi}{6}$

CHAPTER 10

10.1 Locating roots

1 **a** The graph crosses the x-axis between $x = -1$ and $x = 0$.

b **i** -0.464 **ii** 0.574

c There is a change of sign between $x = 2.2$ and $x = 2.3$.

2 **a** $f(-1.2) = -0.176 < 0$, $f(-1.1) = 0.733 > 0$

Sign change implies at least one root in interval.

b $f(0.6) = 0.1718... > 0, f(0.7) = -0.2022... < 0$

Sign change implies at least one root in interval.

c $f(-1.11) = 0.0403... > 0$, $f(-1.10) = -0.1265... < 0$

Sign change implies at least one root in interval.

d $f(2.37) = 0.0011... > 0, f(2.38) = -0.0140... < 0$

Sign change implies at least one root in interval.

3 **a** $y = -(x+1)^2 + 6$

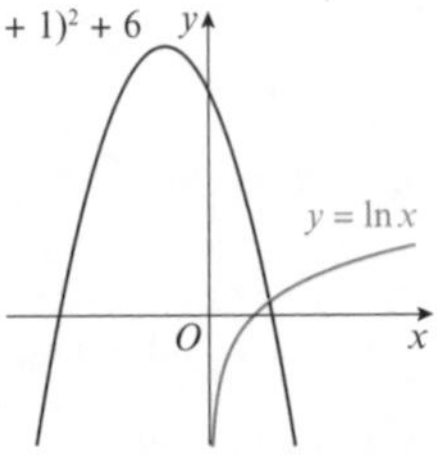

b If $\ln x = -(x+1)^2 + 6$, then $\ln x + (x+1)^2 - 6 = 0$.
As the graphs of $y = \ln x$ and $y = -(x+1)^2 + 6$ only intersect once, $f(x)$ has only one root.

c $f(1.3) = -0.4476... < 0$, $f(1.4) = 0.0964... > 0$

Sign change implies at least one root in interval.

4 **a** $-2\cos x \sin x + 2e^{-2x}$

b $f'(3.1) = 0.0871... > 0$, $f'(3.2) = -0.1132... < 0$

As $f'(x)$ changes sign in the interval [3.1, 3.2], there must be a stationary point in this interval.

c $f'(3.1425) = 0.0019... > 0, f'(3.1435) = -0.00009... < 0$
There is a sign change in the interval (3.1425, 3.1435) so $3.1425 < \alpha < 3.1435$, so $\alpha = 3.143$ to 3 d.p.

5 **a** $g(1.1) = -0.2416... < 0$, $g(1.2) = 0.1392... > 0$

Sign change implies at least one root in interval.

b $g(1.1645) = -0.0008... < 0$, $g(1.1655) = 0.0030... > 0$

There is a sign change in the interval (1.1645, 1.1655) so $1.1645 < \alpha < 1.1655$, so $\alpha = 3.165$ to 3 d.p.

6 **a**

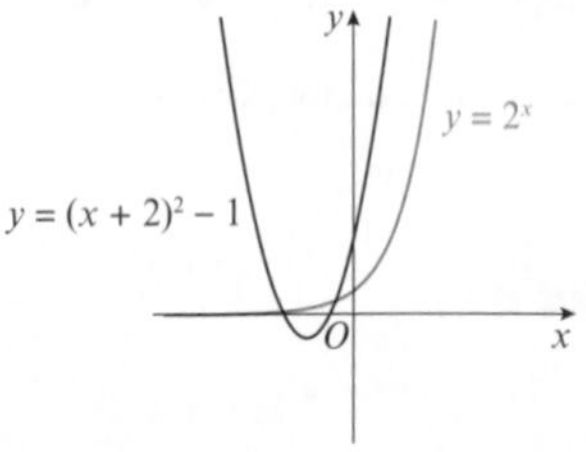

b If $(x+2)^2 - 1 = 2^x$ then $2^x + 1 - (x+2)^2 = 0$
As $y = (x+2)^2 - 1$ and $y = 2^x$ intersect twice, $f(x) = 2^x + 1 - (x+2)^2$ has two roots.

c $f(-0.8) = 0.1343... > 0$, $f(-0.7) = -0.0744... < 0$

Sign change implies at least one root in interval.

7 **a** $f(1.9) = 2.67$ (2 d.p.), $f(2.1) = -10.67$ (2 d.p.)

b $f(2)$ is undefined. **c** $\frac{11}{6}$

8 **a**

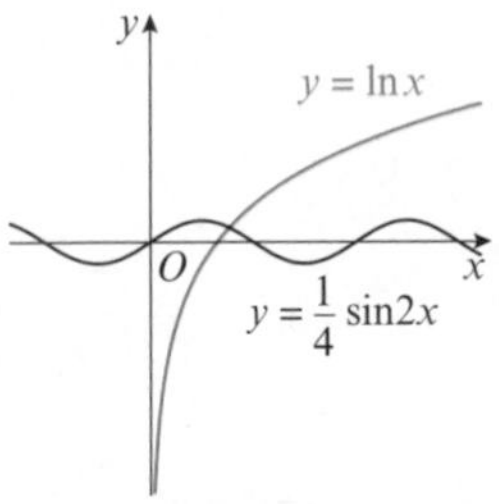

b If $\frac{1}{4}\sin 2x = \ln x$ then $\sin 2x - 4\ln x = 0$. As $y = \frac{1}{4}\sin 2x$ and $y = \ln x$ only intersect once, $h(x) = \sin 2x - 4\ln x$ has only one root.

c $h(1.18) = 0.0423... > 0$, $h(1.19) = -0.0057... < 0$

Sign change implies at least one root in interval.

10.2 Iteration

1 **a** $x^2 = 8x - 3 \Rightarrow x = \sqrt{8x - 3}$

b Divide by x: $x - 8 + \frac{3}{x} = 0 \Rightarrow x = 8 - \frac{3}{x}, x \neq 0$

c $8x = x^2 - 3 \Rightarrow x = \frac{x^2 - 3}{8}$

2 **a** $x^2 = 4x + 2 \Rightarrow x = \sqrt{4x + 2}$

b $x_1 = 4.690$, $x_2 = 4.556$, $x_3 = 4.497$, $x_4 = 4.471$

3 **a** **i** $x^3 = 3x^2 - 1 \Rightarrow x = \sqrt[3]{3x^2 - 1}$

ii $3x^2 = x^3 + 1 \Rightarrow x = \sqrt{\frac{x^3 + 1}{3}}$

b $x_0 = 1.000$, $x_1 = 1.260$, $x_2 = 1.555$, $x_3 = 1.843$, $x_4 = 2.094$

c $x_1 = 0.816$, $x_2 = 0.717$, $x_3 = 0.676$, $x_4 = 0.660$

d The iterations appear to be converging to different numbers.

4 **a** $\frac{1}{2}x^2 = 2\sin x \Rightarrow x = \sqrt{4\sin x}$

b $x_1 = 1.997$, $x_2 = 1.908$, $x_3 = 1.943$

c $f(1.9335) = 0.0006... > 0$, $f(1.9345) = -0.0019... < 0$

Sign change implies at least one root in interval, so $\alpha = 1.934$ to 3 d.p.

5 **a** $A\left(\frac{1-\sqrt{5}}{2}, 0\right), C\left(\frac{1+\sqrt{5}}{2}, 0\right)$

b $5x^2 = x^5 + 2 \Rightarrow x = \sqrt{\frac{x^5 + 2}{5}}$

c $x_1 = 0.637$, $x_2 = 0.649$, $x_3 = 0.650$

d $f(0.6505) = 0.0007... > 0$, $f(0.6515) = -0.0048... < 0$

Sign change implies at least one root in interval, so $\alpha = 0.651$ to 3 d.p.

6 **a** $f(-1.9) = -0.0288... < 0$, $f(-1.8) = 0.6450... > 0$

Sign change implies at least one root in interval.

b $e^{x+4} = 10 - \frac{1}{2}x^2 \Rightarrow x + 4 = \ln\left(10 - \frac{1}{2}x^2\right)$

$\Rightarrow x = \ln\left(10 - \frac{1}{2}x^2\right) - 4$

c $x_1 = -2.295,\ x_2 = -2.003,\ x_3 = -1.921$

d $f(-1.89545) = -0.0002.. < 0,\ f(-1.89535) = 0.0004.. > 0$
Sign change implies at least one root in interval, so $\alpha = -1.8954$ to 4 d.p.

7 a Substitute $x = 0$ and $x = \pi$ into $f(x)$.

b $\sin^2 x + 2x \sin x \cos x$

c $f'(1.8) = 0.1518... > 0,\quad f'(1.9) = -0.2670... < 0$
Sign change implies at least one turning point in interval.

d $\sin^2 x + 2x \sin x \cos x = 0 \Rightarrow 2x \sin x \cos x = -\sin^2 x$
$\Rightarrow \cos x = \frac{-\sin x}{2x} \Rightarrow x = \arccos\left(\frac{-\sin x}{2x}\right)$

e $x_1 = 1.845,\ x_2 = 1.835,\ x_3 = 1.837$

8 a Let $f(x) = \frac{1}{x+1} - x$
$f\left(\frac{1}{2}\right) = 0.1666... > 0,\quad f(1) = -0.5 < 0$
Sign change implies at least one root in interval.

b

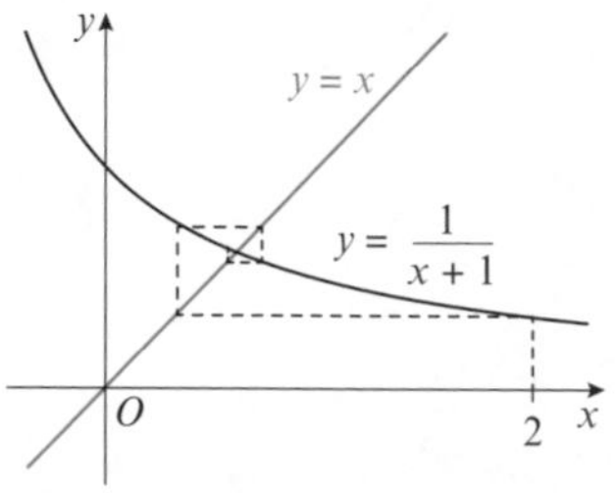

The iteration will converge.

10.3 The Newton–Raphson method

1 a $f(1.5) = 0.25 > 0,\quad f(1.6) = -0.04 < 0$
Sign change implies at least one root in interval.

b -2.8 **c** $1.585\,714$

d $3 - \sqrt{2}, 3 + \sqrt{2}$

e $3 - \sqrt{2} \approx 1.585\,786$, so part **c** answer correct to 3 d.p.

2 a $f(1.2) = -0.0464... < 0,\quad f(1.3) = 0.0861... > 0$
Sign change implies at least one root in interval.

b 1.257

3 B, D, F and H

4 a $f(1.3) = 0.0136... > 0,\quad f(1.4) = -0.1310... < 0$
Sign change implies at least one root in interval.

b $-8 \sin x \cos x + e^{-x}$ **c** 1.308

5 a $f(3.4) = 0.0874... > 0,\quad f(3.5) = -0.0206... < 0$
Sign change implies at least one root in interval.

b 3.481

c $f(3.4805) = 0.0008... > 0,\quad f(3.4815) = -0.0002... < 0$
Sign change implies at least one root in interval, so $\alpha = 3.481$ to 3 d.p.

6 a $f(1.2) = 0.0638... > 0,\quad f(1.3) = -0.0105... < 0$
Sign change implies at least one root in interval.

b $f'(x) = \frac{-2x \sin x \cos x - \cos^2 x}{x^2} - \frac{1}{4x}$

c 1.283

7 a $p = -2$. Gradient at point P is zero, so using Newton–Raphson formula would result in division by zero.

b $f(0.8) = -0.45 < 0,\quad f(0.9) = 0.96 > 0$
Sign change implies at least one root in interval.

c -4.829

10.4 Applications to modelling

1 a $-\frac{2}{25}x^3 + \frac{21}{10}x^2 - 14x + 17$

b $w'(8.3) = -0.273\,96... < 0,\quad w'(8.4) = 0.159\,68... > 0$
There is a change of sign in the interval $8.3 < x < 8.4$, so there is at least one turning point in this interval.

c $-\frac{2}{25}x^3 + \frac{21}{10}x^2 - 14x + 17 = 0$
$\Rightarrow \frac{21}{10}x^2 = \frac{2}{25}x^3 + 14x - 17$
$\Rightarrow x^2 = \frac{10}{21}\left(\frac{2}{25}x^3 + 14x - 17\right)$
$\Rightarrow x = \pm\sqrt{\frac{10}{21}\left(\frac{2}{25}x^3 + 14x - 17\right)}$

d $x_0 = 8.3,\ x_1 = 8.308,\ x_2 = 8.315,\ x_3 = 8.321,\ x_4 = 8.326$

2 a $h(10) = 17.7920... > 0,\quad h(11) = -10.8879... < 0$
Sign change implies at least one root in interval, therefore the boomerang lands between 10 and 11 seconds.

b $\frac{25t}{9}\cos\left(\frac{t^2}{36}\right)$ **c** 10.64 seconds

d $h'(7.515) = 0.0425... > 0,\quad h'(7.525) = -0.0446... < 0$
Sign change implies at least one turning point in interval, so boomerang is at a maximum height at 7.52 seconds, correct to 2 decimal places.

3 a £1.62 **b** $-\frac{1}{9}\sin\left(\frac{x}{3}\right) + \frac{x}{50}$

c $p'(5) = -0.0106... < 0,\quad p'(5.5) = 0.0026... > 0$
Sign change implies at least one turning point in interval.

d $-\frac{1}{9}\sin\left(\frac{x}{3}\right) + \frac{x}{50} = 0 \Rightarrow \frac{x}{50} = \frac{1}{9}\sin\left(\frac{x}{3}\right) \Rightarrow x = \frac{50}{9}\sin\left(\frac{x}{3}\right)$

e $x_1 = 5.449,\ x_2 = 5.389,\ x_3 = 5.415$

4 a $v(5) = 25.592... > 0,\quad v(6) = -16.003... < 0$
Sign change implies at least one root in interval.

b $-225e^{-0.5t} + 40 \sin t$ **c** 5.45 years

d $v(6) \approx -16$, and the value cannot be negative, so this model is not suitable as the phone gets older than 6 years.

5 a $t = 2 \Rightarrow h = 27.0045... > 10$, $t = 3 \Rightarrow h = 2.0799... < 10$.
Therefore at some time between $t = 2$ and $t = 3$ the person is exactly 10 m from the ground.

b At $t = 3$ the person is approximately 2.1 m from the ground, so the jump is not safe.

c $40 \cos t + 50 - 4t^{\frac{2}{3}} = 10 \Rightarrow 40 \cos t = 4t^{\frac{2}{3}} - 40$
$\Rightarrow \cos t = \frac{4t^{\frac{2}{3}} - 40}{40} \Rightarrow t = \arccos\left(\frac{4t^{\frac{2}{3}} - 40}{40}\right)$

d $t_1 = 2.524\,90,\ t_2 = 2.522\,80,\ t_3 = 2.522\,97,\ t_4 = 2.522\,96$

Problem solving: Set A

B a $f(1) = 0.7701... > 0,\quad f(1.5) = -0.0640... < 0$
Sign change implies at least one root in interval.

b $\frac{1}{2}\cos(x^2) = \frac{1}{2}x - 1 \Rightarrow \cos(x^2) = x - 2$
$\Rightarrow x^2 = \arccos(x - 2) \Rightarrow x = \sqrt{\arccos(x - 2)}$

c $x_1 = 1.447,\ x_2 = 1.469,\ x_3 = 1.460$

S a Let $f(x) = x - 3\cos\left(\frac{1}{3}x\right)$
$f(2) = -0.3576... < 0,\quad f(3) = 1.3790... > 0$
Sign change implies at least one root in interval.

b

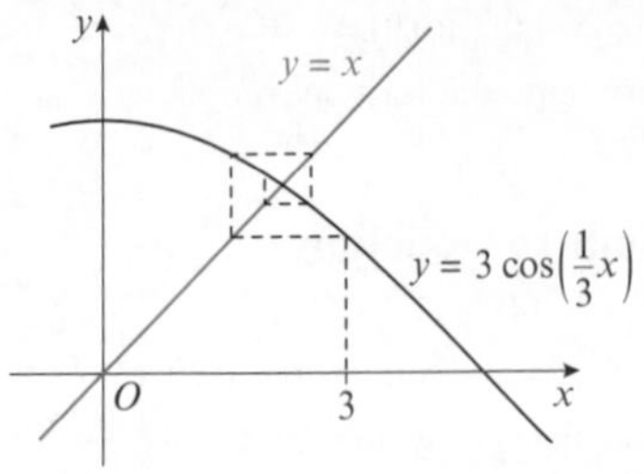

c $x_1 = 1.621$, $x_2 = 2.573$, $x_3 = 1.963$

G **a** Let $f(x) = x - (x - 1)e^x$. $f(1) = 1 > 0$, $f(2) = -5.389... < 0$
Sign change implies at least one root in interval.

b **i** The iteration will converge to the other root, α.

ii The iteration will diverge.

c $f(-0.8065) = -0.000\,04... < 0$, $f(-0.8055) = 0.0013 > 0$
Sign change implies at least one root in interval, so $\alpha = -0.806$ to 3 d.p.

Problem solving: Set B

B **a** $f(1.1) = -0.0601... < 0$, $f(1.2) = 0.2257... > 0$
Sign change implies at least one root in interval.

b 1.123

c $f(1.1225) = -0.003... < 0$, $f(1.1235) = 0.005... > 0$
Sign change implies at least one root interval, so part **b** answer is correct to 3 d.p.

S **a** $f(1.5) = 0.1736... > 0$, $f(2) = -0.1024... < 0$
Sign change implies at least one root in interval.

b 1.772

c $f(1.7715) = 0.0005... > 0$, $f(1.7725) = -0.000\,02... < 0$
Sign change implies at least one root in interval, so part **b** answer is correct to 3 d.p.

G **a** $\left(\frac{1}{2}, \frac{6}{e} - 1\right)$

b $f'(p) = 0$, so would mean dividing by zero in the Newton–Raphson formula, which is not valid.

c 1.41

CHAPTER 11

11.1 Integrating standard functions

1 **a** $e^x - 2\cos x + c$ **b** $4\sin x + \frac{3}{x} + c$
c $5\ln|x| - 2e^x + c$ **d** $\frac{2}{3}x^{\frac{3}{2}} - \frac{3}{4}\cos x + c$
e $\frac{11}{3}x^3 + \frac{1}{2}e^x - 6\ln|x| + c$
f $3\sin x - 2\sqrt{x} + c$

2 **a** $-\cot x + c$ **b** $\sec x + c$
c $-\operatorname{cosec} x + c$ **d** $4\tan x + c$
e $-4\cot x + c$ **f** $8\operatorname{cosec} x + c$

3 **a** $\tan x + \sec x + c$ **b** $\frac{7}{2}x^2 - 5\ln x + c$
c $3e^x + 5\cot x + c$ **d** $\frac{1}{2}x^2 - x + \ln x + c$

4 **a** 15 **b** $\ln\frac{5}{2} - 117$ **c** $4e^{\frac{\pi}{3}} - 3$
d $5 - \sqrt{2}$ **e** 20

5 $5 + \ln\frac{9}{4}$

6 $p = 4$

7 $3e^{\frac{\pi}{6}} - 3e^{\frac{\pi}{3}} = 3(e^{\frac{\pi}{6}} - e^{\frac{\pi}{3}})$

8 $[2x + 3\ln x]_{2a}^{5a} = 6a + 3\ln\frac{5}{2}$
$\Rightarrow 6a + 3\ln\frac{5}{2} = \ln 1000 = 3\ln 10$
$\Rightarrow 6a = 3\ln 4$
$\Rightarrow a = \frac{1}{2}\ln 4 = \ln 2$

11.2 Integrating f(ax+b)

1 **a** **i** $16(4x - 5)^3$ **ii** $-12(3 - 2x)^5$
b **i** $(4x - 5)^4 + c$ **ii** $\frac{1}{16}(4x - 5)^4 + c$
iii $(3 - 2x)^6 + c$ **iv** $-\frac{1}{6}(3 - 2x)^6 + c$

2 **a** $2e^{3x} + c$ **b** $\frac{1}{3}\sin(3x + 2) + c$
c $\frac{1}{24}(4x + 1)^6 + c$ **d** $-\frac{1}{4}\operatorname{cosec}4x + c$
e $\frac{1}{8}\tan(8x - 1) + c$ **f** $\frac{1}{5}\cot(1 - 5x) + c$
g $\frac{5}{2}\ln|2x - 3| + c$ **h** $-11e^{4-x} + c$

3 **a** $-\frac{1}{4(4x - 3)} - \frac{1}{12}(4x - 3)^3 + c$
b $\frac{1}{10}e^{5x} - \frac{2}{3}\tan 3x + c$
c $\frac{1}{4}e^{4x} - 2x - \frac{1}{4}e^{-4x} + c$
d $-\frac{5}{2}\cot 2x + \frac{3}{2}\operatorname{cosec}2x + c$

4 **a** $\ln\frac{7}{3}$ **b** $\sqrt{2} - 1$
c $16\ln 4 - \frac{33}{2}$ **d** $1 - \arctan\left(\frac{\pi}{8}\right)$

5 4

6 $2\frac{\ln 25}{\ln 7}$

7 $54 + \ln 256$

8 $k = -\frac{1}{9}$

11.3 Using trigonometric identities

1 **a** $\frac{1}{2}x - \frac{1}{4}\sin 2x + c$
b $-3\cot x - 3x + c$
c $\frac{3}{2}x + 2\sin x + \frac{1}{4}\sin 2x + c$
d $\tan x - x + c$

2 **a** $\sqrt{3} - 1 - \frac{\pi}{6}$ **b** $\frac{10 - 3\pi}{4}$
c $\frac{4\sqrt{3} - \pi}{3}$ **d** $4 - 2\sqrt{2} - \frac{\pi}{4}$

3 **a** **i** $\cos 5x\cos 2x - \sin 5x\sin 2x$
ii $\cos 5x\cos 2x + \sin 5x\sin 2x$
b L.H.S. $= \cos 7x + \cos 3x$
R.H.S. $= 2\cos 5x\cos 2x$
c $\frac{2}{7}\sin 7x + \frac{2}{3}\sin 3x + c$

4 $$\int_{\frac{\pi}{6}}^{\frac{\pi}{2}} \cos^2 x\,dx = \int_{\frac{\pi}{6}}^{\frac{\pi}{2}} \left(\frac{1}{2}\cos 2x + \frac{1}{2}\right) dx$$
$$= \left[\frac{1}{4}\sin 2x + \frac{1}{2}x\right]_{\frac{\pi}{6}}^{\frac{\pi}{2}}$$
$$= \left(0 - \frac{\pi}{4}\right) - \left(\frac{\sqrt{3}}{2} - \frac{\pi}{12}\right)$$
$$= \frac{\pi}{6} - \frac{\sqrt{3}}{8}$$

5 Use the trigonometric identity $\tan^2 2x + 1 = \sec^2 2x$ to obtain $\int_{\frac{\pi}{12}}^{\frac{\pi}{6}} (\sec^2 2x - 1)\,dx = \left[\frac{1}{2}\tan 2x - x\right]_{\frac{\pi}{12}}^{\frac{\pi}{6}}$

$$= \left(\frac{\sqrt{3}}{2} - \frac{\pi}{6}\right) - \left(\frac{1}{2\sqrt{3}} - \frac{\pi}{12}\right)$$
$$= \frac{\sqrt{3}}{3} - \frac{\pi}{12}$$

6 a $\sin 6x \cos x + \cos 6x \sin x = \sin 7x$ (1)

$\sin 6x \cos x - \cos 6x \sin x = \sin 5x$ (2)

Adding (1) and (2): $2\sin 6x \cos x = \sin 7x + \sin 5x$

b $-\frac{3}{14}\cos 7x - \frac{3}{10}\cos 5x + c$

11.4 Reverse chain rule

1 a i $6x(x^2-4)^2$ ii $8(x+2)(x^2+4x-5)^3$

b i $(x^2-4)^3 + c$ ii $\frac{5}{2}(x^2-4)^3 + c$

iii $-\frac{4}{3}(x^2+4x-5)^3 + c$

2 a $2(x^2-7)^{\frac{3}{2}} + c$ b $-\frac{5}{2}e^{\cos 2x} + c$

c $\frac{1}{5}(4x^3+16x-5)^{\frac{5}{2}} + c$

d $\frac{2}{3}(1+\tan x)^{\frac{3}{2}} + c$

e $-\frac{1}{3}e^{\cot 3x} + c$ f $-\frac{1}{25}\cos^5 5x + c$

3 a $-2\ln|2-x^2| + c$ b $\frac{1}{3}\ln|4-3\cos x| + c$

c $-\frac{1}{2}\ln|14+9x-6x^3| + c$

d $-2\ln|\cos x| + c$

e $\frac{1}{8}\ln|4-\cos 2x| + c$

f $-\frac{1}{3}\ln|1+e^{-3x}| + c$

4 a $\frac{1}{12}$ b $\frac{1}{3}\ln 2$

c $2\ln\frac{28}{9}$ d $\frac{1}{3}(e - e^{\sqrt{2}})$

5 $3 + 4\sqrt{3}$

6 a $\sin^5 x \equiv \sin x(\sin^2 x)(\sin^2 x)$

$\equiv \sin x(1-\cos^2 x)(1-\cos^2 x)$

$\equiv \sin x(1 - 2\cos^2 x + \cos^4 x)$

$\equiv \sin x - 2\sin x\cos^2 x + \sin x\cos^4 x$

b $-\frac{1}{5}\cos^5 x + \frac{2}{3}\cos^3 x - \cos x + c$

7 $32\sqrt{3}$

8 $\frac{1}{4}(e-1)$

9 $\frac{19}{648}$

10 $k = \sqrt{6}$

11.5 Integration by substitution

1 a 1 b $2(u-2)$

c Substitute $2x = 2(u-2)$, $(x+2)^4 = u^4$ and $dx = du$

d $\int 2(u-2)u^4\,du = \int (2u^5 - 4u^4)\,du = \frac{1}{3}u^6 - \frac{4}{5}u^5 + c$

e $\frac{1}{3}(x+2)^6 - \frac{4}{5}(x+2)^5 + c$

2 a $\frac{1}{6}(x-8)^6 + \frac{8}{5}(x-8)^5 + c$

b $-\frac{1}{7}(1+\cos x)^7 + \frac{1}{6}(1+\cos x)^6 + c$

c $-\frac{2}{5}(2+\cot x)^{\frac{5}{2}} + \frac{4}{3}(2+\cot x)^{\frac{3}{2}} + c$

d $\sqrt{x^2+1} + c$

3 a $\frac{16}{15}$ b $8\ln\frac{4}{5}$

c -1 d $2 - \ln 4$

4 $\frac{2}{15} + \frac{10\sqrt{5}}{3}$

5 $\ln\frac{7}{3}$

6 a $x = \tan\theta$, $\frac{dx}{d\theta} = \sec^2\theta$

$$\int \frac{1}{1+x^2}\,dx = \int \frac{1}{1+\tan^2\theta}\sec^2\theta\,d\theta$$
$$= \int \frac{1}{\sec^2\theta}\sec^2\theta\,d\theta$$
$$= \int 1\,d\theta$$
$$= \theta + c$$
$$= \arctan x + c$$

b $\frac{\pi}{12}$

7 $\int_0^4 \frac{5x}{\sqrt{2x+1}}\,dx = \int_1^3 \frac{5}{4}\left(\frac{u^2-1}{2}\right)u\,du = \frac{5}{2}\left[\frac{u^3}{3} - u\right]_1^3 = \frac{50}{3}$

8 $4\sin x - 4\ln|1+\sin x| + c$

11.6 Integration by parts

1 a $x\sin x + \cos x + c$

b $\ln|\cos x| + x\tan x + c$

c $\frac{1}{2}xe^{2x} - \frac{1}{4}e^{2x} + c$

d $\frac{1}{16}\ln|\sin 4x| - \frac{1}{4}x\cot 4x + c$

e $-\frac{1}{4}xe^{-4x} - \frac{1}{16}e^{-4x} + c$

f $-\frac{1}{5}x\cos 5x + \frac{1}{25}\sin 5x + c$

2 a $\frac{1}{2}x^2\ln x - \frac{1}{4}x^2 + c$ b $\frac{1}{4}x^4\ln x - \frac{1}{16}x^4 + c$

c $x\ln x - x + c$

3 a $-\frac{1}{2}x^2\cos 2x + \frac{1}{2}x\sin 2x + \frac{1}{4}\cos 2x + c$

b $-\frac{1}{27}(9x^2+6x+2)e^{-3x} + c$

c $\frac{1}{2}x^2(1+x)^4 - \frac{1}{5}x(1+x)^5 + \frac{1}{30}(1+x)^6 + c$

4 a $\frac{\sqrt{2}}{8}(4-\pi)$ b $\frac{78}{5}$ c π

d $\frac{\pi\sqrt{3}}{12} - \frac{1}{4}\ln 2$ e $-\frac{\pi}{32}$ f $6 - \frac{78}{e^3}$

5 $12\ln 8 - \frac{3}{4}\ln 2 - \frac{45}{8}$

6 $\left[\frac{1}{4}(2x^2-2x+1)e^{2x}\right]_1^2$

$= \frac{1}{4}(5)e^4 - \frac{1}{4}(1)e^2$

$= \frac{e^2}{4}(5e^2 - 1)$

7 a $-\frac{1}{\pi}x\cos\pi x + \frac{1}{\pi^2}\sin\pi x + c$

b $\frac{17\pi^2 - 8}{2\pi^3}$

8 $\frac{\pi}{2} - \frac{\pi^2}{8} + \ln 2$

9 a $\frac{1}{2}x\sin 2x + \frac{1}{4}\cos 2x + c$

b $\frac{1}{4}x^2 - \frac{1}{4}x\sin 2x - \frac{1}{8}\cos 2x + c$

11.7 Partial fractions

1 a $A = \frac{10}{3}$, $B = \frac{14}{3}$

b $\frac{10}{3}\ln|x+2| + \frac{14}{3}\ln|x-4| + c$

2 a $\ln|x+5| + 3\ln|x+2| + c$

b $-4\ln|x-2| - 3\ln|x+3| + c$

c $6\ln|x-1| - 5\ln|x+2| + c$

d $\frac{6}{7}\ln|x-4| - \frac{6}{7}\ln|2x-1| + c$

3 a $(x+4)(2x-1) = 2x^2 + 7x - 4$

$$\begin{array}{r} -1 \\ 2x^2+7x-4\;\overline{)\,-2x^2 \qquad\quad +14} \\ -2x^2-7x+4 \\ \hline 7x+10 \end{array}$$

So $f(x) \equiv \frac{7x+10}{(x+4)(2x-1)} - 1$

b $A = 2$, $B = 3$

c $2\ln|x+4| + \frac{3}{2}\ln|2x-1| - x + c$

4 a Equate coefficients in

$16x^2 - 37x + 17 \equiv A(2x-3)^2 + B(4-x)(2x-3) + C(4-x)$

to get simultaneous equations:

$4A - 2B = 16$

$-12A + 11B - C = -37$

$9A - 12B + 4C = 17$

Then solve to find $A = 5$, $B = 2$ and $C = -1$.

b $-5\ln|4-x| + \ln|2x-3| + \frac{1}{2(2x-3)} + c$

5 a $\frac{6}{x-1} - \frac{3}{x+2}$ b $\ln\frac{4096}{125}$

6 a $A = 1$, $B = -2$, $C = 1$ b $2 + \ln\frac{5}{3}$

7 a $\frac{12}{5(2x+1)} - \frac{6}{5(x+3)}$ b $\frac{6}{5}\ln\frac{4}{3}$

8 a $A = 1$, $B = -\frac{5}{2}$, $C = \frac{5}{2}$ b $2 + \frac{5}{2}\ln\frac{9}{5}$

11.8 Finding areas

1 $\frac{8}{5}$

2 a $x\ln\frac{1}{2}x = 0 \Rightarrow x = 0$ or $\ln\frac{1}{2}x = 0$

So A is where $\ln\frac{1}{2}x = 0$

$\Rightarrow \frac{1}{2}x = 1 \Rightarrow x = 2$

So A has coordinates (2, 0).

b $R_1 = -\int_1^2 x\ln\left(\frac{1}{2}x\right)dx = -\left[\frac{1}{2}x^2\ln\left(\frac{1}{2}x\right) - \frac{1}{4}x^2\right]_1^2 = \frac{3}{4} - \frac{1}{2}\ln 2$

c $R_2 = \int_2^3 x\ln\left(\frac{1}{2}x\right)dx = \left[\frac{1}{2}x^2\ln\left(\frac{1}{2}x\right) - \frac{1}{4}x^2\right]_2^3 = \frac{9}{2}\ln\frac{3}{2} - \frac{5}{4}$

Total area $= R_1 + R_2 = \frac{9}{2}\ln\frac{3}{2} - \frac{1}{2}\ln 2 - \frac{1}{2}$

3 a $f(\pi) = 2\cos\frac{1}{2}\pi + 1 = 1$

$g(\pi) = -\frac{\pi}{\pi} + 2 = 1$

b $4 - \frac{\pi}{2}$

4 a $2t$ b $t = 0$

c $t \neq -2$ because y is positive and $2(-2) + 1 = -3$

d $\frac{44}{3}$

5 a $\frac{1}{2}\left(\frac{\pi}{2}\right)\cos\left(\frac{\pi}{2}\right) = 0$, $\frac{1}{2}\left(\frac{3\pi}{2}\right)\cos\left(\frac{3\pi}{2}\right) = 0$

b $\frac{5\pi}{4} - \frac{1}{2}$

6 a $(\pi^2, 0)$ b 8π

7 a $\sin x = -\cos 2x + 1$

$\Rightarrow \sin x = -(1 - 2\sin^2 x) + 1$

$\Rightarrow 2\sin^2 x - \sin x = 0$

$\Rightarrow \sin x(2\sin x - 1) = 0$

$2\sin x = 1 \Rightarrow x = \frac{\pi}{6}$ or $\frac{5\pi}{6}$

So the x-coordinate of B is $\frac{5\pi}{6}$

b $\frac{2\pi}{3} - \frac{\sqrt{3}}{2}$

8 $15\pi - 30$

11.9 The trapezium rule

1 a

x	0	0.5	1	1.5	2
y	0	0.375	1	1.125	0

b There are 4 trapezia and each has a height of 0.5 as $4 \times 0.5 = 2 = b - a$

c 1.25

d $\frac{4}{3}$

2 a

x	0	0.25	0.5	0.75	1
y	1	0.6116	0.6103	0.7435	0.9183

b 0.731

c $\frac{43}{60} - \frac{1}{4e^4}$

d The graph is convex, so the lines connecting the two endpoints would be above the curve, giving a larger answer than the real answer.

e Decrease the width of each strip by increasing the number of values used.

3 a

x	0	$\frac{\pi}{8}$	$\frac{\pi}{4}$	$\frac{3\pi}{8}$	$\frac{\pi}{2}$
y	0	0.142	0.436	0.531	0

b 0.436 c $\frac{\pi^2}{4} - 2$ d 6.8%

4 a

x	0	0.5	1	1.5	2	2.5	3
y	1.25	1.038	0.933	0.9	0.929	1.041	1.333

b 3.07 c $\ln(12\sqrt{3})$ d 1.2%

5 a

x	0	$\frac{\pi}{8}$	$\frac{\pi}{4}$	$\frac{3\pi}{8}$	$\frac{\pi}{2}$
y	0	0.1155	0.1768	0.0478	0

b 0.1336 c $\frac{2}{15}$

6 a

x	1	1.25	1.5	1.75	2
y	1	1.0872	1.2281	1.4285	1.6931

b 1.273 (3 d.p.)

c $\int\left(\frac{1}{4}x^2\ln x + 1\right)dx = \frac{1}{12}x^3\ln x - \frac{1}{36}x^3 + x + c$

Substitute in the limits and simplify to obtain $\frac{2}{3}\ln 2 + \frac{29}{36}$

11.10 Solving differential equations

1 a $\frac{dy}{dx} = \frac{x}{y} \times (x^2 + 6)^5 \Rightarrow \int y\,dy = \int x(x^2 + 6)^5 dx$

b Using the substitution $u = x^2 + 6$,

$\int y\,dy = \frac{1}{2}\int u^5 du$

$\Rightarrow \frac{1}{2}y^2 = \frac{1}{12}u^6 + c = \frac{1}{12}(x^2 + 6)^6 + c$

2 a $y = \frac{4x}{3} + c$

b $y = \arcsin\left(\frac{1}{2}x - \frac{1}{4}\sin 2x + c\right)$

c $y = Ae^{2x^3+3x^2}$ d $y = -\frac{1}{2}\ln\left|\frac{2}{3}\cos^3 x + c\right|$

3 a $y = \frac{3(x+1)^2}{4(x+2)}$ b $y = \text{arccot}(3 + \ln 2 - e^x - x)$

c $\tan x + \cot y - 2 = 0$

d $x^2 + y^2 = 13^2$

4 a $y = 2x^2 - x + c$

b

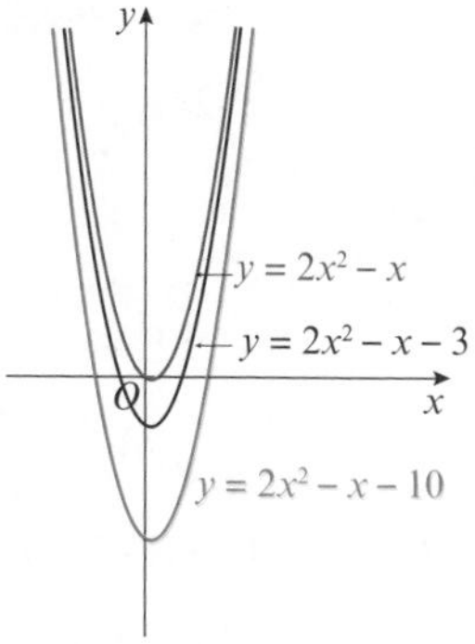

5 $y^2 = 1 - \frac{1}{x^2}e^{-x^2+1}$

6 $\sec y = 2x - \frac{1}{2}\sin 2x + \sqrt{2} + \frac{1}{2} - \frac{\pi}{2}$

7 $\ln|e^{2y} - 4| = 2e^x(x - 1) + c$

8 a $\frac{2}{2x-5} + \frac{3}{x+2}$

b $y = A(2x - 5)(x + 2)^3$

c $y = \frac{1}{5}(2x - 5)(x + 2)^3$

11.11 Modelling with differential equations

1 a Separate the variables: $\int P^{-\frac{1}{3}} dP = \int 3\,dt$ and integrate to obtain $\frac{3}{2}P^{\frac{2}{3}} = 3t + c$.

b $c = 150$

c $\frac{3}{2}P^{\frac{2}{3}} = 3t + 150 \Rightarrow P^{\frac{2}{3}} = 2t + 100 \Rightarrow P = (2t + 100)^{\frac{3}{2}}$

d 42.1 years

2 a i The rate of change of the value of the laptop with respect to time.

ii The value of the laptop is decreasing

iii Proportional to the existing value of the laptop.

b $\int \frac{1}{V} dV = \int -k\,dt \Rightarrow \ln V = -kt + c \Rightarrow V = e^{-kt+c}$

$\Rightarrow V = Ae^{-kt}$

When $t = 0$, $V = V_0 = Ae^{-k \times 0}$, so $A = V_0$ and $V = V_0 e^{-kt}$

c 800

d $k = 0.094$

3 a $\frac{dP}{dt} = kP \Rightarrow \int \frac{1}{P} dP = \int k\,dt$

$\Rightarrow \ln P = kt + c \Rightarrow P = e^{kt+c}$

$\Rightarrow P = Ae^{kt}$

$A = 1600$, $k = \frac{1}{50}\ln\frac{13}{8}$

b 2013

c The model is clearly inaccurate for larger values of t.

4 a $\frac{dT}{dt}$ is the rate of change of the temperature of the soup with respect to time.

$(T - 20)$ is the difference between the temperature of the soup and the room temperature.

$-k$ signifies the soup cooling.

b 15.1 minutes

5 a $\frac{dh}{dt} = \frac{100\pi - 3\pi h}{900\pi}$

$900\frac{dh}{dt} = 100 - 3h$

b $300\ln 4$ seconds

6 a $\frac{dA}{dr} = 2\pi r$

$\frac{dr}{dt} = \frac{dr}{dA} \times \frac{dA}{dt}$

$= \frac{1}{2\pi r} \times \left(-k\sin\left(\frac{t}{4\pi}\right)\right)$

$= -\frac{k}{2\pi r}\sin\left(\frac{t}{4\pi}\right)$

b $r^2 = 75\cos\left(\frac{t}{4\pi}\right) + 25$

c 24.0 minutes

Problem solving: Set A

B $\frac{1}{25}(e^5 - 6)$

S $\frac{86}{5}$

G $16 - \frac{26}{3}\sqrt{3}$

Problem solving: Set B

B a $y = k(x^2 + x + 2)^2$

b $y = \frac{(x^2 + x + 2)^2}{4}$

S $\ln|e^{2y} - 1| = 2e^x(x - 1) + 2 + \ln 3$

G a $T = \frac{80000}{1 + 4e^{-\frac{2}{3}t}}$ b 80000

CHAPTER 12

12.1 3D coordinates

1 a i $\sqrt{61}$ ii $\sqrt{77}$

b $p = 6, q = 5, r = 4$

c $\sqrt{77}$ d They are the same

2 a $5\sqrt{5}$ b $2\sqrt{29}$ c $7\sqrt{5}$

3 a 11 b 15 c $3\sqrt{5}$

4 a $\sqrt{(6-3)^2 + (-1-5)^2 + (3-k)^2} = 7$

$\Rightarrow 9 + 36 + (3 - k)^2 = 49 \Rightarrow (3 - k)^2 = 4$

b $k = 1, k = 5$

5 $k = 2, k = 6$

6 $k = -4, k = 10$

7 $k = 3, k = 13$

8 $k = -1, k = 9$

12.2 Vectors in 3D

1 a $4\mathbf{i} - 3\mathbf{j} + \mathbf{k}$ b $\begin{pmatrix} -2 \\ 6 \\ 5 \end{pmatrix}$

2 a i $-2\mathbf{i} + 5\mathbf{j} - 3\mathbf{k}$

ii $\begin{pmatrix} -2 \\ 5 \\ -3 \end{pmatrix}$

b $\sqrt{38}$ c $\frac{1}{\sqrt{38}}(-2\mathbf{i} + 5\mathbf{j} - 3\mathbf{k})$

3 a i $-6\mathbf{i} - 12\mathbf{j} + 15\mathbf{k}$ ii $2\mathbf{i} + 7\mathbf{j} - 9\mathbf{k}$

b $4\mathbf{m} - \mathbf{n} = 4\begin{pmatrix} 2 \\ -2 \\ 3 \end{pmatrix} - \begin{pmatrix} -4 \\ -5 \\ 6 \end{pmatrix} = \begin{pmatrix} 8+4 \\ -8+5 \\ 12-6 \end{pmatrix} = \begin{pmatrix} 12 \\ -3 \\ 6 \end{pmatrix} = 3\begin{pmatrix} 4 \\ -1 \\ 2 \end{pmatrix}$

4 a $\theta_x = 48.2°$ b $\theta_y = 109.5°$ c $\theta_z = 131.8°$

5 a $\overrightarrow{AB} = -3\mathbf{i} + \mathbf{j} + 7\mathbf{k}$

b $|\overrightarrow{OA}| = \sqrt{38}$, $|\overrightarrow{OB}| = \sqrt{21}$ and $|\overrightarrow{AB}| = \sqrt{59}$.
The lengths of the sides are different, so the triangle is scalene.

6 $\frac{\mathbf{i} - 7\mathbf{j} - 4\mathbf{k}}{\sqrt{66}}$

7 a $\overrightarrow{AB} = \begin{pmatrix} 3 \\ -5 \\ 3 \end{pmatrix}$, $\overrightarrow{AC} = \begin{pmatrix} -5 \\ -3 \\ -3 \end{pmatrix}$ and $\overrightarrow{BC} = \begin{pmatrix} -8 \\ 2 \\ -6 \end{pmatrix}$

b $|\overrightarrow{AB}| = \sqrt{43}$, $|\overrightarrow{AC}| = \sqrt{43}$ and $|\overrightarrow{BC}| = 2\sqrt{26}$.

c Isosceles

8 a $|\overrightarrow{PQ}| = 6$, $|\overrightarrow{QR}| = \sqrt{61}$ and $|\overrightarrow{PR}| = 5$

b $|\overrightarrow{PR}|^2 + |\overrightarrow{PQ}|^2 = |\overrightarrow{QR}|^2$, so $\overrightarrow{QR}$ is the hypotenuse of a right-angled triangle with $\angle RPQ$ as its right angle.

c 50.2°

9 148.1°

12.3 Solving geometric problems

1 a $\mathbf{a} + \mathbf{b} + \mathbf{c}$ b $-\mathbf{a} - \mathbf{b} + \mathbf{c}$

c $-\mathbf{a} + \mathbf{b} + \mathbf{c}$ d $\mathbf{a} + \mathbf{b}$

e $\frac{1}{2}\mathbf{a} + \frac{1}{2}\mathbf{b} + \mathbf{c}$ f $-\frac{1}{2}\mathbf{a} + \frac{1}{2}\mathbf{b} + \mathbf{c}$

g $\frac{1}{2}\mathbf{b} + \frac{1}{2}\mathbf{c}$ h $-\frac{1}{2}\mathbf{a} + \frac{1}{2}\mathbf{c}$

2 a $\overrightarrow{PQ} = -3\mathbf{i} + 4\mathbf{j} - 7\mathbf{k}$, $\overrightarrow{SR} = -3\mathbf{i} + 4\mathbf{j} - 7\mathbf{k}$

b $\overrightarrow{SP} = \mathbf{i} - 5\mathbf{j} + 8\mathbf{k}$, $\overrightarrow{RQ} = \mathbf{i} - 5\mathbf{j} + 8\mathbf{k}$

c $PQRS$ is a parallelogram because there are two pairs of opposite sides that are parallel.

3 $p = -3, q = 2, r = 7$

4 120

5 $a = 4, b = -2, c = 3$

6 86.3

7 13

8 Let $OABCDEFG$ be a cube with side length 5.

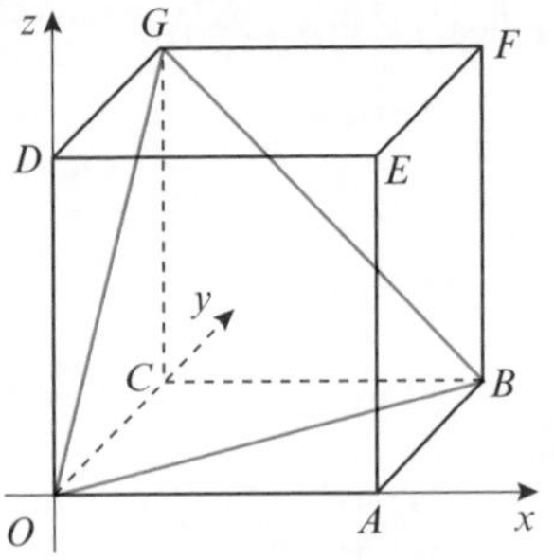

$OB = BG = OG = 5\sqrt{2}$, so triangle is equilateral.
$O(0, 0, 0)$, $B(5, 5, 0)$ and $G(0, 5, 5)$, so triangle OBG is equilateral and has integer coordinates.

12.4 Applications to mechanics

1 a $\mathbf{R} = (-3\mathbf{i} - \mathbf{j} - \mathbf{k})$ N b $\sqrt{11}$ N

2 $a = -2, b = 3$

3 a $6.78\,\text{m s}^{-2}$ (3 s.f.) b $2\sqrt{46}$ m

4 a $(2\mathbf{i} + 6\mathbf{j} + 10\mathbf{k})$ N

b $\left(\frac{1}{2}\mathbf{i} + \frac{3}{2}\mathbf{j} + \frac{5}{2}\mathbf{k}\right)\text{m s}^{-2}$

5 a $20\sqrt{6}\,\text{m s}^{-1}$ b $40\sqrt{6}$ m

6 a $\left(\frac{5}{4}\mathbf{i} - \frac{3}{2}\mathbf{j} + 3\mathbf{k}\right)\text{m s}^{-2}$

b 69.6° (3 s.f.)

7 a $a = 2, b = -7$ b $(2\mathbf{i} + 5\mathbf{j} - 3\mathbf{k})$ N

c $\left(\frac{2}{3}\mathbf{i} + \frac{5}{3}\mathbf{j} - \mathbf{k}\right)\text{m s}^{-2}$ d $\frac{1}{3}\sqrt{38}\,\text{m s}^{-2}$

8 $-\frac{7}{3}$ and -3

Problem solving: Set A

B $k = 18$ or $k = -2$

S $p = \pm 2\sqrt{3}$

G $q = -1, q = \frac{1}{3}$

Problem solving: Set B

B a $\overrightarrow{AB} = 4\mathbf{i} - 6\mathbf{j} + 4\mathbf{k}$ and $\overrightarrow{DC} = 8\mathbf{i} - 12\mathbf{j} + 8\mathbf{k}$

b $\overrightarrow{DC} = 2\overrightarrow{AB}$ c $k = \frac{1}{2}$

d $ABCD$ is a trapezium.

S $(2, 5, -1)$

G Let T_1 be a point on MP. $\overrightarrow{OT_1} = \frac{4}{5}a + \lambda\left(-\frac{3}{5}a + b + c\right)$ for some $\lambda \in \mathbb{R}, 0 \leqslant \lambda \leqslant 1$.
Let T_2 be a point on NQ. $\overrightarrow{OT_2} = a + \frac{4}{5}b + \mu\left(-a - \frac{3}{5}b + c\right)$ for some $\mu \in \mathbb{R}, 0 \leqslant \mu \leqslant 1$.
If T lies on MP and NQ then $\overrightarrow{OT}$ satisfies both equations.
Equating terms gives: $\frac{4}{5} - \frac{3}{5}\lambda = 1 - \mu$, $\lambda = \frac{4}{5} - \frac{3}{5}\mu$ and $\lambda = \mu$.
Solve to obtain $\lambda = \mu = \frac{1}{2}$.
Conclude that MP and NQ intersect at point T which is the midpoint of each line and therefore MP and NQ bisect each other at T.

Exam Question Bank

1 $k = -1, k = 7$

2 **a** $f(2) = -2, f(2.5) = 1$

b $x = \frac{7}{3}$ is an asymptote, and as $2 < \frac{7}{3} < 2.5$, a change of sign in this interval will be caused by the asymptote, so there doesn't have to be a root in this interval.

3 $m = \frac{2}{5n}$

4 **a** $4x + 2 - e^x$ **b** $y = x - 1$

5 $a = 2, b = 0, c = 11, d = -14, e = 9$

6 $x = -150°, -30°, 30°, 150°$

7 **a** $\frac{y^2}{1 - \ln y}$ **b** $\frac{1}{5e^8}$

8 $\pi + 2$

9 $\frac{3}{x+1} - \frac{5}{(x+1)^2} + \frac{4}{x+2}$

10 Cartesian equation of curve is $y = 6x - 2x^2$

$3x + 2 = 6x - 2x^2 \Rightarrow 2x^2 - 3x + 2 = 0$

Using $b^2 - 4ac: (-3)^2 - (4 \times 2 \times 2) = -7 < 0$

So no solutions.

11 **a** $\sin 3x = 3\sin x - 4\sin^3 x$

b $x = 0, \frac{\pi}{4}, \frac{3\pi}{4}, \pi$

12 **a** $\frac{1}{3}x^2 - 3\sin x + 1 = 0 \Rightarrow 3\sin x = \frac{1}{3}x^2 + 1$

$\Rightarrow x = \arcsin\left(\frac{1}{9}x^2 + \frac{1}{3}\right)$

b $x_1 = 0.369, x_2 = 0.356, x_3 = 0.355$ (3 d.p.)

c $d = 0.354$

13 127.1°

14 **a** $\sqrt{9+x} = (9+x)^{\frac{1}{2}} = 9^{\frac{1}{2}}\left(1 + \frac{x}{9}\right)^{\frac{1}{2}}$

$= 3\left(1 + \frac{1}{2} \times \frac{x}{9} + \frac{1}{2} \times \left(-\frac{1}{2}\right) \times \frac{x^2}{81} \times \frac{1}{2!} + \ldots\right)$

$= 3 + \frac{x}{6} - \frac{x^2}{216} + \ldots$ so $k = \frac{1}{216}$

b Expansion is valid for $|x| < 9$, so it is valid for $x = 1$.

15 **a**

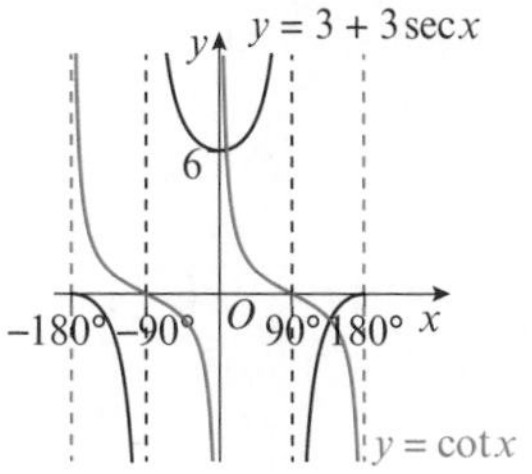

b 2 **c** $\frac{1}{6}$

16 **a** $\left(-\frac{2}{3}\mathbf{i} - \frac{8}{3}\mathbf{j} + \frac{4}{3}\mathbf{k}\right)\text{m s}^{-2}$ **b** 151° (3 s.f.)

17 $\frac{1 + \tan^2 x}{1 - \tan^2 x} \equiv \frac{1 + \frac{\sin^2 x}{\cos^2 x}}{1 - \frac{\sin^2 x}{\cos^2 x}} \equiv \frac{\frac{\cos^2 x + \sin^2 x}{\cos^2 x}}{\frac{\cos^2 x - \sin^2 x}{\cos^2 x}}$

$\equiv \frac{\cos^2 x + \sin^2 x}{\cos^2 x - \sin^2 x} \equiv \frac{1}{\cos 2x} \equiv \sec 2x$

18 **a** Let $f(x) = \frac{4}{5}\sqrt{x+2} - x$

$f(1) = 0.3856... > 0, \quad f(2) = -0.4 < 0$

Sign change implies at least one root in interval.

b Yes, the iteration will converge towards α.

19 $t = \pm 4.5$

20 $\frac{1}{4}x^4\ln(x^2+1) - \frac{1}{4}\ln(x^2+1) - \frac{1}{8}x^2(x^2-2) + c$

21 **a** $\pm\frac{1}{\sqrt{5}}$ **b** $\cos P = \pm\frac{2}{\sqrt{5}} \Rightarrow \sec P = \pm\frac{\sqrt{5}}{2}$

22 **a** $h(9) = 0.7111... > 0, \quad h(10) = -2.7843... < 0$

Sign change implies at least one root in interval, so person reaches bottom of slide between 9 and 10 seconds.

b 9.203

c $h(9.2025) = 0.0007... > 0, \quad h(9.2035) = -0.0028... < 0$

Sign change implies at least one root in interval, so part **b** answer is correct to 3 d.p.

23 $a = 5$ or -7

24 **a** 116

b $S_n = \frac{n}{2}(4 + (n-1) \times 6) = 7450,$

So $n(6n - 2) = 14900$

$\Rightarrow 6n^2 - 2n - 14900 = 0$

which gives $3n^2 - n - 7450 = 0$

So $n = 50$

25 **a** $\frac{1 + \sin 2\theta + \tan 2\theta}{2\cos 2\theta - 1} = \frac{1 + 4\theta}{2\left(1 - \frac{(2\theta)^2}{2}\right) - 1}$

$= \frac{1 + 4\theta}{(1 - 4\theta)^2} = \frac{1 + 4\theta}{(1 + 2\theta)(1 - 2\theta)}$

b 1.124 (3 d.p.) **c** 3.12×10^{-3} %

26 $f(x) = (x-2)(3x-2)(2x+1)$

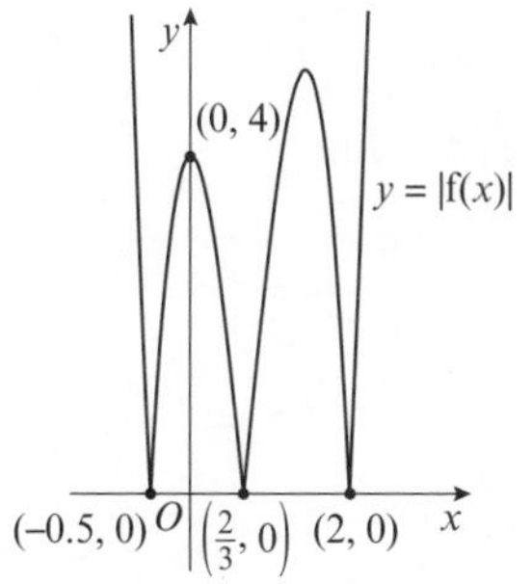

27 **a** $a_2 = 3k - 5$

b $a_3 = 3(3k - 5) - 5 = 9k - 15 - 5 = 9k - 20$

c $k = 1.5$

28 **a** $\frac{dy}{dx} = -2\sin 2x - 4\sin 2x\cos 2x$

$\frac{d^2y}{dx^2} = -4\cos 2x - 8\cos 4x$

b $x = -\pi, -\frac{2\pi}{3}, -\frac{\pi}{2}, -\frac{\pi}{3}, 0$

c At $x = -\frac{\pi}{2}, \frac{dy}{dx} = 0$ and $\frac{d^2y}{dx^2} = -4 \leqslant 0$ which implies a local maximum.

29 **a** $A(0, 0)$ and $B(1, 0)$ **b** $3x^2\ln x + x^2$

c $f'(0.7165) = -0.00006... < 0, f'(0.7175) = 0.0020... > 0$

Sign change implies at least one turning point in interval, so x-coordinate of P is 0.717 to 3 d.p.

d $e^{-\frac{1}{3}}$

30 a $(13\pi - 27.3)$ cm **b** $25.6\,\text{cm}^2$

31 a $(x+4)^2 + (y-1)^2 = 25$

b

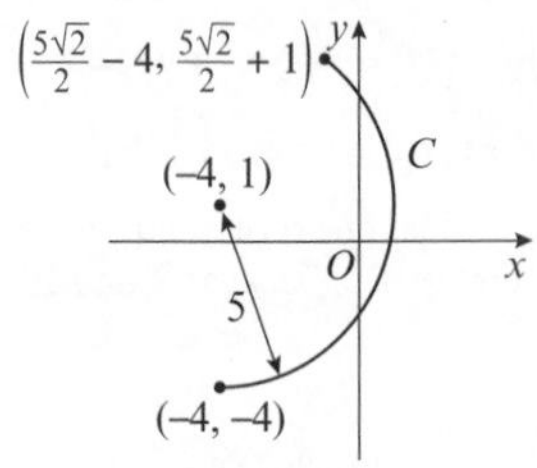

c $\frac{15\pi}{4}$

32 a

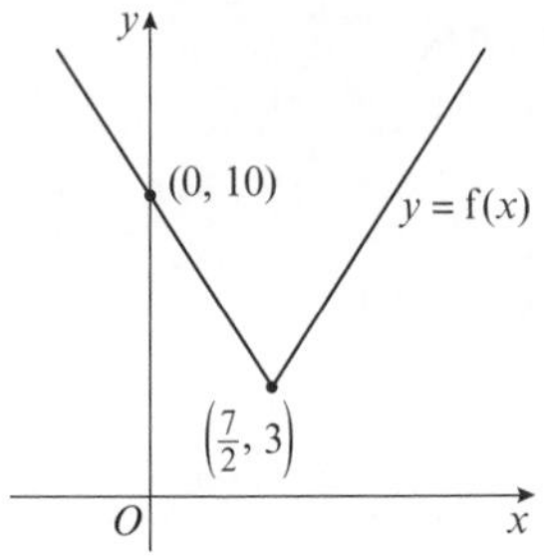

b $f(x) \geqslant 3$ **c** $\left\{x : x < \frac{8}{3}\right\} \cup \{x : x > 6\}$

33 a $\frac{1}{2} + \frac{3x}{16} + \frac{27x^2}{256}$ **b** $4 + 2x + \frac{33x^2}{32}$

34 a 1.9 m **b** $t = 0.66$ seconds **c** 2.51 m

35 a She has used $\frac{\cos\theta}{\sin\theta} = \tan\theta$

She should have used $\frac{\sin\theta}{\cos\theta} = \tan\theta$

b $\sqrt{3}\sin\left(-\frac{\pi}{6}\right) \neq \cos\left(-\frac{\pi}{6}\right)$, so can't be a solution.

Error was caused by squaring.

36 $y = \cos\left(t + \frac{\pi}{3}\right) = \cos t \cos\frac{\pi}{3} - \sin t \sin\frac{\pi}{3}$

$= \frac{1}{2}\cos t - \frac{\sqrt{3}}{2}\sin t$

$= \frac{1}{2}x - \frac{\sqrt{3}}{2}\sqrt{1-x^2},\ -1 < x < 1$

37 a

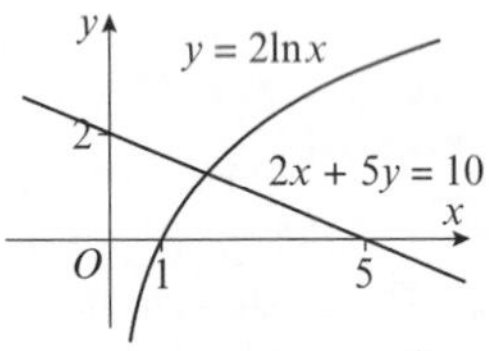

b $2x + 5y = 10 \Rightarrow y = 2 - \frac{2}{5}x$

$2\ln x = 2 - \frac{2}{5}x \Rightarrow 2\ln x + \frac{2}{5}x - 2 = 0$

$\Rightarrow 10\ln x + 2x - 10 = 0$

As the curve $y = 2\ln x$ and the line $2x + 5y = 10$ only intersect once, $f(x)$ has exactly one root.

c $f(1.8) = -0.5221... < 0$, $f(1.9) = 0.2185... > 0$

Sign change implies the root is in this interval.

38 Integral $= \frac{4}{5}\ln\frac{21}{16}$. Answer is independent of k, as k does not appear in the solution.

39 $x = -1, y = \frac{9}{2}, \frac{dy}{dx} = -\frac{15}{2}\ln 2$

Rearrange $y - \frac{9}{2} = \left(-\frac{15}{2}\ln 2\right)(x+1)$ to obtain

$(15\ln 2)x + 2y + 15\ln 2 - 9 = 0$

40 a $\tan(60° + 45°) = \frac{\tan 60° + \tan 45°}{1 - \tan 60° \tan 45°}$

$= \frac{\sqrt{3}+1}{1-(\sqrt{3}\times 1)} = -2 - \sqrt{3}$

b $\cot 105° = \frac{1}{-2-\sqrt{3}} \Rightarrow \frac{1}{-2-\sqrt{3}} \times \frac{-2+\sqrt{3}}{-2+\sqrt{3}} = -2 + \sqrt{3}$

41 a 0.744 **b** $28.4\,\text{m}^2$ **c** 17.6 m

42 a $(\sec^2 x + \tan^2 x)(\sec^2 x - \tan^2 x)$

$= (\sec^2 x + \sec^2 x - 1)(\sec^2 x - \sec^2 x + 1)$

$= (2\sec^2 x - 1)(1) = 2\sec^2 x - 1$

b $x = 73.57°, 106.4°, 253.6°, 286.4°$

43 a $\frac{3x - y}{3y + x}$

b Solve $\frac{12x - 4y}{12y + 4x} = -\frac{3}{5}$ to obtain $9x + 2y = 0$.

44 a $(x-3)(-2x^2 + 2x - 1)$

b $-2y^6 + 8y^4 - 7y^2 + 3 = (y^2 - 3)(-2y^4 + 2y^2 - 1)$

$-2y^4 + 2y^2 - 1 = 0$ has no real solutions

$y^2 - 3 = 0$ has 2 real solutions: $y = \pm\sqrt{3}$

c 3

45 a $y = 2x - 4x^4,\ 0 \leqslant x \leqslant \sqrt{3}$

b $t = \frac{1}{4}$. Range is $2\sqrt{3} - 36 \leqslant f(x) \leqslant \frac{3}{4}$

46 a $2\sqrt{3} = k\sin\left(0 + \frac{\pi}{3}\right) \Rightarrow k = 4$

b $p = \frac{2\pi}{3},\ q = \frac{5\pi}{3}$ **c** 2.40, 4.93

47 $\frac{1}{2}(1 - \ln 2)$

48 a $A\left(-\frac{5}{3}, 0\right), B\left(0, -\frac{5}{2}\right)$ **b** $2y + 3x + 5 = 0$

49 a $A = 6, B = -2, C = 4$ **b** $\ln\frac{784}{9}$

50 a $\sin 2\theta - \tan\theta \equiv 2\sin\theta\cos\theta - \frac{\sin\theta}{\cos\theta}$

$\equiv \frac{2\sin\theta\cos^2\theta - \sin\theta}{\cos\theta}$

$\equiv \frac{\sin\theta(2\cos^2\theta - 1)}{\cos\theta}$

$\equiv \tan\theta\cos 2\theta$

b $x = -\frac{\pi}{4}, 0, \frac{\pi}{4}, 1.107$

51 a $(9 + 7x)^{\frac{1}{2}} = 9^{\frac{1}{2}}\left(1 + \frac{7x}{9}\right)^{\frac{1}{2}}$

$= 3\left(1 + \frac{1}{2} \times \frac{7}{9}x + \frac{1}{2} \times \left(-\frac{1}{2}\right) \times \left(\frac{7x}{9}\right)^2 \times \frac{1}{2!} + ...\right)$

$= 3 + \frac{7}{6}x - \frac{49}{216}x^2$

b i $\sqrt{2} \approx \frac{5651}{4000}$

ii Expansion is valid for $|x| < \frac{9}{7}$ and $\frac{9}{25} < \frac{9}{7}$

52 a $f'(x) = 2x(2 - 5x)^5 - 25x^2(2 - 5x)^4$

$f''(x) = 2(2 - 5x)^5 - 100x(2 - 5x)^4 + 500x^2(2 - 5x)^3$

b 0.04, 0.19, 0.40 (2 d.p.)

c $f''(0.4) = 0$ and $f''(0.35) = 0.82... > 0$ and $f''(0.45) = -1.75... < 0$, so there is a point of inflection at $x = 0.4$.

53 a

x	0	0.5	1	1.5	2	2.5	3
y	0	0.2759	0.4060	0.3361	0.2198	0.1263	0.0669

b 0.699 (3 s.f.)

c $\int_0^3 3x^2e^{-2x}dx = \left[-\frac{3}{4}(2x^2+2x+1)e^{-2x}\right]_0^3$
$= \frac{3}{4} - \frac{75}{4e^6}$

54 **a** $x = \frac{1}{6}\cos t \Rightarrow 6x = \cos t \Rightarrow 216x^3 = \cos^3 t$
$y = \cos 3t = \cos(2t+t) = \cos 2t \cos t - \sin 2t \sin t$
$= (2\cos^2 t - 1)\cos t - (2\sin t \cos t)\sin t$
$= 2\cos^3 t - \cos t - 2(1-\cos^2 t)\cos t = 4\cos^3 t - 3\cos t$
$= 864x^3 - 18x = 18x(48x^2 - 1)$
So $a = 18$, $b = 48$, $c = 1$

b $-\frac{\sqrt{3}}{12} \leqslant x \leqslant \frac{\sqrt{3}}{12}$

c Turning points are $\left(-\frac{1}{12}, 1\right)$ and $\left(\frac{1}{12}, -1\right)$
Range is $-1 \leqslant y \leqslant 1$

55 **a** $x = -\frac{13}{3}, -3$

b **i**

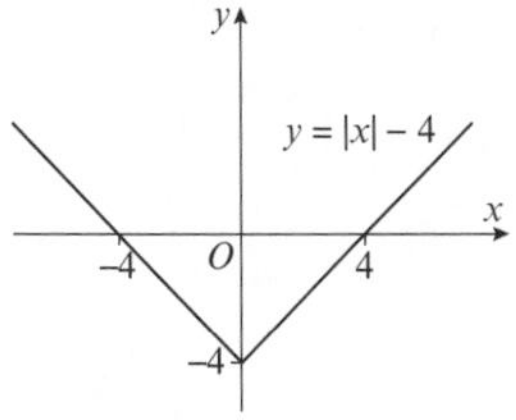

ii For $|x| < 4$, $|x| - 4$ is negative and $|x - 4|$ is always non-negative, so $|x| - 4 < |x - 4|$
For $x \geqslant 4$, $|x| - 4 = |x - 4|$
For $x \leqslant -4$, $|x - 4| = 4 - x$ and $|x| - 4 = -4 - x$
So $|x| - 4 < |x - 4|$

56 **a** $\frac{dV}{dt} = 200 - \frac{1}{5}V$
Multiply by -5 to obtain
$-5\frac{dV}{dt} = V - 1000$

b $V = 1000 + 8000e^{-\frac{1}{5}t}$

c $1000\,m^3$. As $t \to \infty$, $8000e^{-\frac{1}{5}t} \to 0$, therefore $V \to 1000$.

57 **a** $\sqrt{1+6x} \approx 1 + 3x - \frac{9}{2}x^2$ and $(1-x)^{-\frac{1}{2}} \approx 1 + \frac{x}{2} + \frac{3x^2}{8}$
$\left(1 + 3x - \frac{9}{2}x^2\right)\left(1 + \frac{x}{2} + \frac{3x^2}{8}\right) = 1 + \frac{7x}{2} - \frac{21x^2}{8}$

b Expansion is valid for $|x| < \frac{1}{6}$ and $\frac{1}{5} > \frac{1}{6}$

c 3.31562

58 **a** $gh(x) = \arccos\left(\frac{1}{2}x\right)$, $-2 \leqslant x \leqslant 2$

b

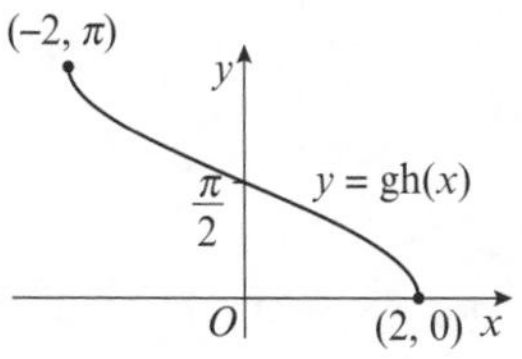

c $(gh)^{-1}(x) = 2\cos x$, $0 \leqslant x \leqslant \pi$

59 **a** $\cos\frac{\theta}{2} = \frac{8^2 + 7^2 - 3^2}{2 \times 8 \times 7} = \frac{13}{14}$ **b** $\frac{239}{4802}$

60 **a** $\frac{1}{9} + \frac{8x}{27} + \frac{16x^2}{27}$ **b** -3 **c** $\frac{8}{27}$

61 **a** $\sum_{r=1}^{12} 2 + \sum_{r=1}^{12} 4r + \sum_{r=1}^{12} 3^r$
$= (2 \times 12) + \frac{12}{2}(8 + 11 \times 4) + \frac{3(3^{12} - 1)}{(3 - 1)}$
$= 797496$

b $u_1 = \frac{3}{4}, u_2 = \frac{-4}{3}, u_3 = \frac{3}{4}, u_5 = \frac{4}{3} \ldots$
$\sum_{r=1}^{200} u_r = 100 \times \left(\frac{3}{4} - \frac{4}{3}\right) = -\frac{175}{3}$

62 **a** Let $p = \sqrt{3}$ and $q = \frac{1}{\sqrt{3}}$, then $pq = \sqrt{3} \times \frac{1}{\sqrt{3}} = 1$
So if p and q are irrational numbers, it does not necessarily follow that pq is also an irrational number.

b Assume that $\sqrt{2}$ is rational. Then $\sqrt{2} = \frac{a}{b}$, where a and b are integers, $b \neq 0$ and the highest common factor of a and b is 1. Then $a = \sqrt{2}b \Rightarrow a^2 = 2b^2$.
So a^2 is divisible by 2 and it must contain a (repeated) factor of 2, and so a is divisible by 2. So $a = 2p$, where p is an integer.
$\Rightarrow (2p)^2 = 2b^2 \Rightarrow b^2 = 2p^2$. So b^2 is divisible by 2 and so b is divisible by 2. As a and b are both divisible by 2, then the highest common factor of a and b is not 1. This contradiction implies that $\sqrt{2}$ is irrational.

63 **a** **i** $(6, -10)$ **ii** $(-3, 5)$

b

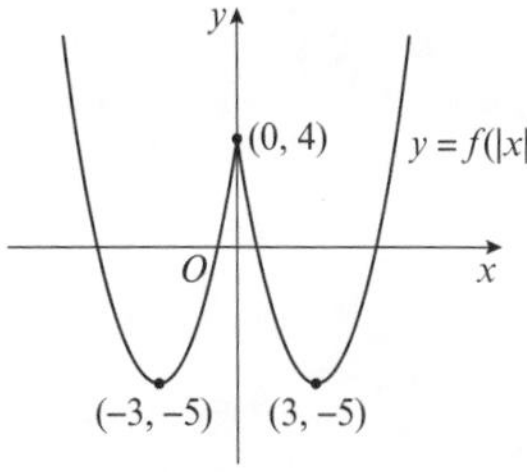

c $f(x) = (x - 3)^2 - 5$

d The function is not one-to-one.

64 **a** 79.9 **b** $N = 11$

65 **a** 44.6 (3 s.f.) **b** 178.4 (3 s.f.)

66 **a** $f(x) = \frac{2x - 5}{x - 2}$, $x > 2$

b $x - 2 \overline{)2x - 5}$ gives quotient 2: $2x - 5 - (2x - 4) = -1$ so $f(x) = 2 - \frac{1}{x - 2}$, $x > 2$

c T_1 is translation by $\begin{pmatrix} 2 \\ 0 \end{pmatrix}$, T_2 is a reflection in the x-axis,
T_3 is translation by $\begin{pmatrix} 0 \\ 2 \end{pmatrix}$

67 **a** $-\frac{1}{16}\operatorname{cosec}\theta$ **b** $32x - 4y - 31 = 0$

c $\frac{961}{256}$

68 **a** 0.000609 **b** 25

c $S_k = \frac{10(1 - 0.6^k)}{(1 - 0.6)} = 25(1 - 0.6^k) > 24.99$
$0.01 > 25 \times 0.6^k$
Dividing both sides by 25 gives $0.0004 > 0.6^k$
So $\log 0.0004 > k \log 0.6$
$\Rightarrow \frac{\log 0.0004}{\log 0.6} < k$
(direction of inequality changed since log 0.6 is negative)
So $k > \frac{\log 0.0004}{\log 0.6}$

d 16

69 **a** $\frac{2(x-1)}{x^2 - 2x - 8} - \frac{1}{x - 4} = \frac{2(x-1)}{(x-4)(x+2)} - \frac{1}{x-4}$
$= \frac{2x - 2 - (x + 2)}{(x-4)(x+2)} = \frac{x - 4}{(x-4)(x+2)} = \frac{1}{x+2}$

b $0 < f(x) < \frac{1}{6}$

c $f^{-1}(x) = \frac{1-2x}{x}$, domain $0 < x < \frac{1}{6}$

d $x = 2\sqrt{5}$

70 **a** $5(3+4x)^{-1} - 3(2-5x)^{-1}$
$= 5\left(\frac{1}{3} - \frac{4x}{9} + \frac{16x^2}{27}\right) - 3\left(\frac{1}{2} - \frac{5x}{4} + \frac{25x^2}{8}\right)$
$= \frac{1}{6} - \frac{215x}{36} - \frac{1385x^2}{216}$

b 0.106 275 3 **c** 0.026%

71 **a** $\frac{\sqrt{34}}{2}\cos(\theta - 1.03)$

b 11.7

c $\theta = -3.03, -2.22, 0.11, 0.92$

72 **a** (1, 4) and (25, 28)

b $5y - 6x - 26 = 0$

73 **a** $60\,000r^{n-1}$

b $60\,000r^{n-1} > 240\,000$, so $r^{n-1} > 4$,
Taking logs: $(n-1)\log r > \log 4$
$n - 1 > \frac{\log 4}{\log r}$
$n > \frac{\log 4}{\log r} + 1$

c Year 20

d £870 000

74 **a** $-\frac{2}{3}$ **b** $2x + 3y = 9\sqrt{3}$ **c** $\frac{5}{4}$

75 **a** $\frac{x-5}{x-3}$ **b** $1 - \frac{2}{x-3}$

c $f(x) = 1 - 2(x-3)^{-1}$
$f'(x) = \frac{2}{(x-3)^2} > 0$ for all real values of x, $x > 3$
Therefore f(x) is an increasing function for all $x > 3$.

76 **a** 1215 **b** 11

77 **a** $x - ey = 4$

b $A(4, 0), B\left(\frac{e^2-3}{e^2}, 0\right)$
Area $= \frac{1}{2} \times \frac{3}{e} \times \left(4 - \frac{e^2-3}{e^2}\right)$
This simplifies to $\frac{9(e^2+1)}{2e^3}$

78 **a** $A = 3, B = -2, C = 4$ **b** $-1 + x - \frac{5x^2}{2}$ **c** $|x| < 1$

79 **a** $f^{-1}(x) = \frac{4x+2}{x+3}$ $x \in \mathbb{R}, x \neq -3$

b $-10 \leqslant g(x) \leqslant 5$ **c** -5 **d** -13

e **i**

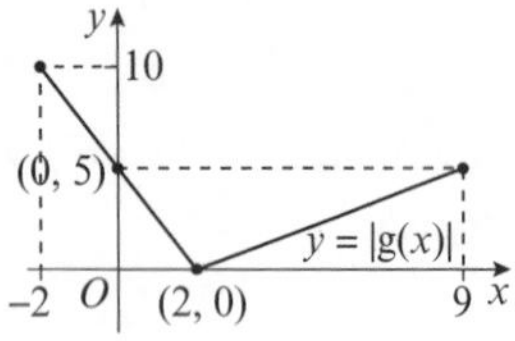

ii

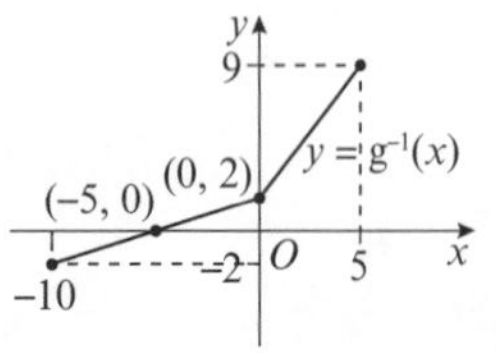

f $-10 \leqslant x \leqslant 5$

80 **a** $(4k-5)^2 = (6k-5)(5-k)$
so $16k^2 - 40k + 25 = 30k - 6k^2 - 25 + 5k$
so $22k^2 - 75k + 50 = 0$
$(11k-10)(2k-5) = 0$ so $k = \frac{5}{2}$ or $\frac{10}{11}$
As $k < 1$, $k = \frac{10}{11}$

b **i** $-\frac{135}{11}$ **ii** -6710

81 **a** $A = 18, B = 9, C = 10$ **b** $-\frac{7}{4} - \frac{17}{4}x - \frac{61}{16}x^2$

c 0.10%

82 **a** $gf(x) = g(3x + \ln 3) = e^{3x + \ln 3} = e^{3x} \times e^{\ln 3} = 3e^{3x}$

b

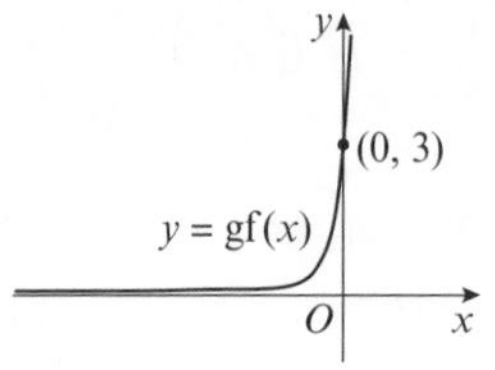

c $gf(x) > 0$ **d** -0.270

83 **a** $\frac{\sqrt{794}}{2}\cos(x - 0.5)$

b **i** 14.1 (3 s.f.) **ii** 0.5

c 30.1 m, 3.5 minutes

d 27.8 m (using original equation) or 28.0 m (using answer from a)

e 1.9 minutes, 5.0 minutes

f 6.0 minutes (2 s.f.)

84 Let P_1 be a point on KR, $\overrightarrow{OP_1} = \frac{1}{3}a + \lambda\left(\frac{1}{3}a + b + c\right)$, for some $\lambda \in \mathbb{R}, 0 \leqslant \lambda \leqslant 1$.
Let P_2 be a point on LS, $\overrightarrow{OP_2} = a + \frac{1}{3}b + \mu\left(-a + \frac{1}{3}b + c\right)$, for some $\mu \in \mathbb{R}, 0 \leqslant \mu \leqslant 1$.
For a point P which lies on KR and LS, $\overrightarrow{OP}$ satisfies both equations.
Solve to obtain $\lambda = \mu = \frac{1}{2}$. Conclude that lines do intersect, as P lies half way along LS and halfway along KR.

85 **a** $f(x) > 5$ **b** $f^{-1}(x) = \ln\left(\frac{1}{x-5}\right), x \in \mathbb{R}, x > 5$

c

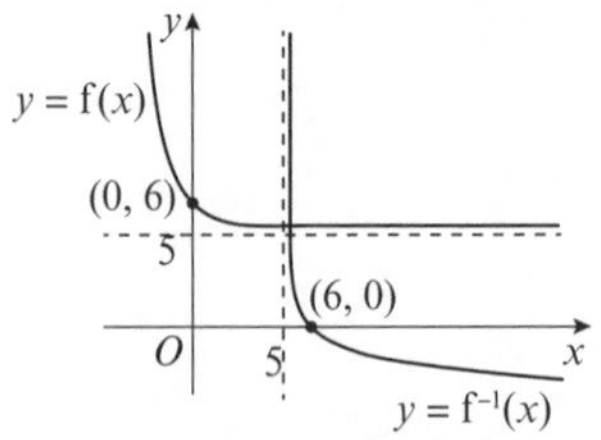

d Graphs meet on the line $y = x$, so at point of intersection
$e^{-x} + 5 = x \Rightarrow \frac{1}{e^x} = x - 5$, so $e^x(x-5) = 1$

86 **a** $T = 4$ **b** 80 m, $t = 2$

c **i** 82.9° (1 d.p.)

ii The model is unlikely to be valid, as the answer to part **i** indicates the rollercoaster would virtually be heading directly into the ground.

d 3410 m² (3 s.f.)